Data Analysis and Related Applications 2

Big Data, Artificial Intelligence and Data Analysis Set

coordinated by
Jacques Janssen

Volume 10

Data Analysis and Related Applications 2

Multivariate, Health and Demographic Data Analysis

Edited by

Konstantinos N. Zafeiris
Christos H. Skiadas
Yiannis Dimotikalis
Alex Karagrigoriou
Christiana Karagrigoriou-Vonta

WILEY

First published 2022 in Great Britain and the United States by ISTE Ltd and John Wiley & Sons, Inc.

ISTE Ltd
27-37 St George's Road
London SW19 4EU
UK

www.iste.co.uk

John Wiley & Sons, Inc.
111 River Street
Hoboken, NJ 07030
USA

www.wiley.com

Library of Congress Control Number: 2022938776

British Library Cataloguing-in-Publication Data
A CIP record for this book is available from the British Library
ISBN 978-1-78630-772-9

Contents

Preface   xv

Konstantinos N. ZAFEIRIS, Yiannis DIMOTIKALIS, Christos H. SKIADAS,
Alex KARAGRIGORIOU and Christiana KARAGRIGORIOU-VONTA

Part 1.   1

Chapter 1. A Topological Clustering of Variables   3

Rafik ABDESSELAM

    1.1. Introduction   3
    1.2. Topological context   5
        1.2.1. Reference adjacency matrices   7
        1.2.2. Quantitative variables.   7
        1.2.3. Qualitative variables   7
        1.2.4. Mixed variables   9
    1.3. Topological clustering of variables – selective review   9
    1.4. Illustration on real data of simple examples   10
        1.4.1. Case of a set of quantitative variables.   10
        1.4.2. Case of a set of qualitative variables   14
        1.4.3. Case of a set of mixed variables   17
    1.5. Conclusion   19
    1.6. Appendix   20
    1.7. References   23

Chapter 2. A New Regression Model for Count Compositions   25

Roberto ASCARI and Sonia MIGLIORATI

    2.1. Introduction   25
        2.1.1. Distributions for count vectors.   26

2.2. Regression models and Bayesian inference   29
2.3. Simulation studies   30
    2.3.1. Fitting study   30
    2.3.2. Excess of zeroes.   32
2.4. Application to real electoral data   34
2.5. References   37

Chapter 3. Intergenerational Class Mobility in Greece with Evidence from EU-SILC 39

Glykeria STAMATOPOULOU, Maria SYMEONAKI and Catherine MICHALOPOULOU

3.1. Introduction   39
3.2. Data and methods   41
3.3. The trends of class mobility between different birth cohorts.   45
3.4. Conclusion   52
3.5. References   52

Chapter 4. Capturing School-to-Work Transitions Using Data from the First European Graduate Survey 55

Maria SYMEONAKI, Glykeria STAMATOPOULOU and Dimitris PARSANOGLOU

4.1. Introduction   55
4.2. Data and methodology   57
4.3. Results   58
4.4. Conclusion   63
4.5. References   64

Chapter 5. A Cluster Analysis Approach for Identifying Precarious Workers 67

Maria SYMEONAKI, Glykeria STAMATOPOULOU and Dimitris PARSANOGLOU

5.1. Introduction   67
5.2. Data and methodology   68
5.3. Results   70
5.4. Conclusion and discussion   74
    5.4.1. Declarations   74
5.5. References   75

Chapter 6. American Option Pricing Under a Varying Economic Situation Using Semi-Markov Decision Process 77

Kouki TAKADA, Marko DIMITROV, Lu JIN and Ying NI

6.1. Introduction   77
6.2. American option pricing   79

6.3. Exercising strategies.   80
   6.3.1. Setting parameter   80
   6.3.2. Relationship between the American option price and
   economic situation i   82
   6.3.3. Relationship between the American option price
   and the asset price s   83
   6.3.4. Relationship between the American option price
   and maturity T   83
   6.3.5. Relationship between the American option price and
   transition probabilities P.   84
   6.3.6. Consideration of the optimal exercise region.   87
6.4. Conclusion   89
6.5. References   89

**Chapter 7. The Implementation of Hierarchical Classifications and
Cochran's Rule in the Analysis of Social Data**   91

Aggeliki YFANTI and Catherine MICHALOPOULOU

7.1. Introduction   91
7.2. Methods   95
7.3. Results   96
7.4. Conclusion   101
7.5. References   102

**Chapter 8. Dynamic Optimization with Tempered Stable Subordinators
for Modeling River Hydraulics**   105

Hidekazu YOSHIOKA and Yumi YOSHIOKA

8.1. Introduction   105
8.2. Mathematical model.   108
8.3. Optimization problem   109
8.4. HJBI equation: formulation and solution   111
8.5. Concluding remarks   115
8.6. Acknowledgments.   116
8.7. References   116

Part 2.   119

**Chapter 9. Predicting Event Counts in Event-Driven Clinical Trials
Accounting for Cure and Ongoing Recruitment.**   121

Vladimir ANISIMOV, Stephen GORMLEY, Rosalind BAVERSTOCK and Cynthia KINEZA

9.1. Introduction   122
9.2. Modeling the process of event occurrence.   123

9.2.1. Estimating parameters of the model.   124

9.3. Predicting event counts for patients at risk   127

    9.3.1. Global prediction   128

9.4. Predicting event counts accounting for ongoing recruitment   129

    9.4.1. Modeling and predicting patient recruitment.   129

    9.4.2. Predicting event counts.   130

    9.4.3. Global forecasting event counts at interim stage   132

9.5. Monte Carlo simulation   133

9.6. Software development.   133

    9.6.1. R package design   134

    9.6.2. R package input data required   136

9.7. R package and implementation in a clinical trial   138

    9.7.1. Introduction   138

    9.7.2. Key predictions   138

    9.7.3. Plots and parameter estimates   138

    9.8. Conclusion.   140

9.9. References   141

Chapter 10. Structural Modeling: An Application to the Evaluation of Ecosystem Practices at the Plot Level.   143

Dominique DESBOIS

10.1. Introduction.   143

10.2. Structural equation modeling using partial least squares   144

    10.2.1. Specification of the internal model.   146

    10.2.2. Specification of the external model   146

    10.2.3. Validation statistics for the external model   147

    10.2.4. Overall validation of structural modeling   148

10.3. Material and method   150

    10.3.1. Agro-ecological context of the study   150

    10.3.2. Data.   152

    10.3.3. The structural model and the estimation.   152

10.4. Results and discussion   154

    10.4.1. Checking the block one-dimensionality   155

    10.4.2. Fitting the external model and assessing the quality of the fit   155

    10.4.3. The structural model after revision.   157

10.5. Conclusion   161

10.6. References   161

Chapter 11. Lean Management as an Improvement Factor in Health Services – The Case of Venizeleio General Hospital of Crete, Greece . . .   163

Eleni GENITSARIDI and George MATALLIOTAKIS

11.1. Introduction.   164
11.2. Theoretical framework.   164
11.3. Purpose of the research   168
11.4. Methodology   168
11.5. Research results   168
11.6. Conclusion   175
11.7. References   176

Chapter 12. Motivation and Professional Satisfaction of Medical and Nursing Staff of Primary Health Care Structures (Urban and Regional Health Centers) of the Prefecture of Heraklion, Under the Responsibility of the 7th Ministry   179

Mihalis KYRIAKAKIS and George MATALLIOTAKIS

12.1. Introduction.   180
12.2. Methodology and material.   180
    12.2.1. Research tools for measuring motivation and professional
    satisfaction for this work   180
    12.2.2. Purpose and objectives of the research   181
    12.2.3. Material and method   181
    12.2.4. Statistical analysis.   182
12.3. Results.   182
12.4. Discussion.   194
12.5. Conclusion   196
12.6. References   197

Chapter 13. Developing a Bibliometric Quality Indicator for Journals Applied to the Field of Dentistry.   199

Pilar VALDERRAMA, Ana M. AGUILERA and Mariano J. VALDERRAMA

13.1. Introduction.   199
13.2. Methodology   200
13.3. Discussion and conclusion.   206
13.4. Acknowledgments   207
13.5. Appendix   208
13.6. References   210

Chapter 14. Statistical Process Monitoring Techniques for Covid-19   211

Emmanouil-Nektarios KALLIGERIS and Andreas MAKRIDES

14.1. Introduction.   211
14.2. Materials and methods   212
14.3. Behavior of Covid-19 disease in the Mediterranean region   214
14.4. Conclusion   218
14.5. Acknowledgments   221
14.6. References   221

Part 3.   223

Chapter 15. Increase of Retirement Age and Health State of Population in Czechia   225

Tomáš FIALA, Jitka LANGHAMROVÁ and Jana VRABCOVÁ

15.1. Introduction.   225
15.2. Data and methodological remarks   227
15.3. Statutory retirement age   228
15.4. Development of the state of health of population   230
15.5. Development of the state of health of population in productive and post-productive ages   232
15.6. Conclusion   234
15.7. Acknowledgment.   235
15.8. References   235

Chapter 16. A Generalized Mean Under a Non-Regular Framework and Extreme Value Index Estimation.   237

M. IVETTE GOMES, Lígia HENRIQUES-RODRIGUES and Dinis PESTANA

16.1. Introduction.   237
16.2. Preliminary results in the area of EVT for heavy tails and asymptotic behavior of MO_p functionals.   239
  16.2.1. A brief review of first- and second-order conditions   239
  16.2.2. Asymptotic behavior of the Hill EVI-estimators   240
  16.2.3. Asymptotic behavior of MO_p EVI-estimators under a regular framework   241
  16.2.4. A brief reference to additive stable laws.   241
  16.2.5. Asymptotic behavior of EVI-estimators under a non-regular framework   242
16.3. Finite-sample behavior of MO_p functionals   243

16.4. A non-regular adaptive choice of p and k 247
16.5. Concluding remarks 248
16.6. References 248

Chapter 17. Demography and Policies in V4 Countries 251

Michaela KADLECOVÁ, Filip HON and Jitka LANGHAMROVÁ

17.1. Introduction 251
17.2. Demographic development in the V4 countries 252
17.3. Development of fertility and family policy 255
17.4. Pension systems of the Visegrad Four countries. 258
17.5. Prediction of future development of V4 populations 261
17.6. Conclusion 265
17.7. Acknowledgments 266
17.8. References 267

Chapter 18. Decomposing Differences in Life Expectancy with and without Disability: The Case of Czechia 271

David MORÁVEK, Tomáš BĚLOCH and Jitka LANGHAMROVÁ

18.1. Introduction 271
18.2. Methodology and data 273
18.3. Main results 276
    18.3.1. Effect of mortality 278
    18.3.2. Effects of mortality and health 279
18.4. Conclusion 281
18.5. Acknowledgments 282
18.6. References 283

Chapter 19. Assessing the Predictive Ability of Subjective Survival Probabilities 285

Apostolos PAPACHRISTOS and Georgia VERROPOULOU

19.1. Introduction 285
    19.1.1. Actual mortality patterns 286
    19.1.2. Objectives of the study 286
19.2. Methods 286
    19.2.1. Data 286
    19.2.2. Force of subjective mortality 287
    19.2.3. Variables 291
    19.2.4. Statistical modeling 291

19.3. Results.   292
    19.3.1. Sample   292
    19.3.2. Multivariable analyses   294
19.4. Discussion.   297
19.5. Conclusion   298
19.6. Acknowledgments   298
19.7. References   299

Chapter 20. Exploring Excess Mortality During the Covid-19 Pandemic with Seasonal ARIMA Models 303

Karl-Heinz JÖCKEL and Peter PFLAUMER

20.1. Introduction.   304
20.2. Binomial mortality model and the empirical distribution of daily
deaths in Germany   305
20.3. Non-seasonal ARIMA model for weekly data in Germany.   307
20.4. Seasonal ARIMA models of weekly deaths for Spain,
Germany and Sweden   311
20.5. Measuring excess mortality, especially in Spain, Germany and Sweden . . .   322
20.6. Forecasting daily deaths in Germany   324
20.7. Conclusion   330
20.8. Appendix   331
    20.8.1. Estimation results of the other age classes   331
    20.8.2. Time series decomposition   332
20.9. References   334

Chapter 21. The Impact of Cesarean Section on Neonatal Mortality in Rural–Urban Divisions in a Region of Brazil 337

Carlos SANTOS and Neir PAES

21.1. Introduction.   338
21.2. Materials and methods   339
    21.2.1. Multilevel logistic model   340
21.3. Results and discussion   341
21.4. Conclusion   345
21.5. References   346

Chapter 22. Analysis of Alcohol Policy in Czechia: Estimation of Alcohol Policy Scale Compared to EU Countries. 349

Kornélia SVAČINOVÁ, Markéta Majerová PECHHOLDOVÁ and Jana VRABCOVÁ

22.1. Introduction.   350
22.2. Literature review   351
22.3. Methods   352

22.4. Results.   354
22.5. Discussion.   359
22.6. Conclusion   360
22.7. Acknowledgment.   360
22.8. References   360

Chapter 23. Alcohol-Related Mortality and Its Cause-Elimination in Life Tables in Selected European Countries and USA: An International Comparison.   363

Jana VRABCOVÁ, Markéta Majerová PECHHOLDOVÁ and Kornélia SVAČINOVÁ

23.1. Introduction.   364
23.2. Data and methods   365
23.3. Alcohol consumption in European countries by the OECD   367
23.4. Czechia   369
23.5. Poland.   369
23.6. Belarus   371
23.7. Russia   371
23.8. France   371
23.9. USA   371
23.10. Conclusion.   374
23.11. Acknowledgment   375
23.12. References.   375

Chapter 24. Labor Force Aging in the Czech Republic: The Role of Education and Economic Industry   377

Martina SIMKOVA and Jaroslav SIXTA

24.1. Introduction.   377
24.2. The setting of the statutory retirement age   378
24.3. The economic status of elderly workers   379
24.4. The structure of working people by factors   380
24.5. The change in the number of workers   382
24.6. Conclusion   385
24.7. Acknowledgment.   385
24.8. References   386

List of Authors   387

Index.   393

Summary of Volume 1   395

Preface

This book is a collective work with contributions by leading experts on "*Data Analysis and Related Applications: Theory and Practice*".

The field of data analysis has grown enormously over recent decades due to the rapid growth of the computer industry, the continuous development of innovative algorithmic techniques and recent advances in statistical tools and methods. Due to the wide applicability of data analysis, a collective work is always needed to bring all recent developments in the field, from all areas of science and engineering, under a single umbrella.

The contributions to this collective work are by a number of leading scientists, analysts, engineers, demographers, health experts, mathematicians and statisticians who have been working on the front end of data analysis. The chapters included in this collective volume represent a cross-section of current concerns and research interests in the scientific areas mentioned. The material is divided into three parts and 24 chapters in a form that will provide the reader with both methodological and practical information on data analytic methods, models and techniques, together with a wide range of appropriate applications.

Part 1 focuses mainly on multivariate data analysis and related fields, with eight chapters covering clustering techniques, regression modeling, contingency tables, stochastic and financial analysis, classification methods, employment patterns and job insecurity, and dynamic optimization.

Part 2 focuses mainly on health data analysis and related fields, with six chapters covering service quality, statistical quality control, bibliometric quality, lean management, prediction methods and ecosystem-based practices.

Part 3 focuses mainly on demographic data analysis and related fields, with 10 chapters covering retirement age, population aging, pension reform, force of mortality, demographic policies, excess mortality, neonatal mortality, alcohol-related mortality, prediction and forecasting methods, statistics of extremes and life expectancy.

Konstantinos N. ZAFEIRIS
Yiannis DIMOTIKALIS
Christos H. SKIADAS
Alex KARAGRIGORIOU
Christiana KARAGRIGORIOU-VONTA

April 2022

PART 1

A Topological Clustering of Variables

The clustering of objects (individuals or variables) is one of the most used approaches to exploring multivariate data. The two most common unsupervised clustering strategies are hierarchical ascending clustering (HAC) and k-means partitioning used to identify groups of similar objects in a dataset to divide it into homogeneous groups.

The proposed topological clustering of variables, called TCV, studies a homogeneous set of variables defined on the same set of individuals, based on the notion of neighborhood graphs, some of these variables being more-or-less correlated or linked according to the type quantitative or qualitative of the variables. This topological data analysis approach can then be useful for dimension reduction and variable selection. It is a topological hierarchical clustering analysis of a set of variables which can be quantitative, qualitative or a mixture of both. It arranges variables into homogeneous groups according to their correlations or associations studied in a topological context of principal component analysis (PCA) or multiple correspondence analysis (MCA). The proposed TCV is adapted to the type of data considered; its principle is presented and illustrated using simple real datasets with quantitative, qualitative and mixed variables. The results of these illustrative examples are compared to those of other variables clustering approaches.

1.1. Introduction

The objective of this chapter is to propose a new approach for classifying variables. This is a topological approach that is different from those that already exist and with which it is compared.

Chapter written by Rafik ABDESSELAM.
For a color version of all the figures in this chapter, see www.iste.co.uk/zafeiris/data2.zip.

Besides the classical and well-known methods devoted to the clustering of objects, there are some approaches specifically devoted to the clustering of variables, the Varclus classification procedure (SAS Institute Inc. 2011) implemented in the SAS software, the ClustOfVar approach (Chavent et al. 2012), the CVLC approach (Vigneau and Qannari 2003; Vigneau et al. 2006) for clustering variables around latent components and the Clustatis approach (Llobell and Qannari 2019), but as far as we know, no approach is proposed in a topological context.

A clustering of variables can also be considered as a dimension reduction approach, like a factor analysis. The purpose of the classification of variables is to group together the variables strongly related to each other, i.e. to separate the variables into classes of variables. It will be possible to summarize each class of variables by a single quantitative synthetic variable.

The interest here is to understand the structures underlying the data, to constitute a summary of the information carried by the data or to detect redundancies, for example with a view to reducing the number of variables in another process.

The objective of the clustering of variables is to obtain linked and redundant classes of variables. Specific algorithms have thus been developed for the clustering of variables. To create profiles from variables grouped in a questionnaire, we can achieve this using two main types of methods: non-hierarchical clustering such as k-means or dynamic clusters, and hierarchical clustering of the ascending or descending type.

Similarity measures play an important role in many areas of data analysis. The results of any operation involving structuring, clustering or classifying objects are strongly dependent on the proximity measure chosen.

Generally, the variables are homogeneous in the sense that they revolve around a particular theme. Unlike the clustering of individuals, which is generally done from a single set of homogeneous variables relating to a single theme, the clustering of variables can process several sets of homogeneous variables from several different themes. The clusters of variables of the chosen partition can be considered as a selection of variables; each cluster of variables can then be synthesized separately using a factor analysis, for example.

The TCV can be considered as a method of reduction of dimensions where each class of correlated variables of the partition can be represented by the synthesis variable of the variables of the class, or again, as a method of selection of variables where each class can be represented by the significant variables of the class.

This study proposes a topological hierarchical clustering of variables, with no restriction on the type, quantitative, qualitative or a mixture of both.

Several topological studies have been proposed in the factorial analysis context, discrimination analysis (Abdesselam 2019b), simple and multiple correspondence analyses (Abdesselam 2020) and principal component analysis (Abdesselam 2021) but none on the clustering of variables.

Therefore, this chapter focuses on unsupervised clustering of a set of variables of any type, quantitative, qualitative or a mixture of both. The eventual associations or correlations between the variables partly depend on the database being used and the results of the topological clustering of these variables can change according to the selected proximity measure. A proximity measure is a function that measures the similarity or dissimilarity between two objects or variables within a set.

This chapter is organized as follows. In section 1.2, we briefly recall the basic notion of neighborhood graphs, and define and show how to construct an adjacency matrix associated with a proximity measure within the framework of the analysis of the correlation or association structure of a set of variables. Section 1.3 presents the principles of the TCV according to the three types of variables. It is illustrated in section 1.4 using simple examples on real data. The TCV results are compared according to the type of variables, with those of different known clustering of variables approaches. Finally, section 1.5 gives concluding remarks on this work.

1.2. Topological context

Topological data analysis is an approach based on the concept of the neighborhood graph. The basic idea is actually quite simple, for a given proximity measure for continuous or binary data and for a chosen topological structure, we can match a topological graph induced on the set of objects.

Consider a set $E = \{x^1, \cdots, x^j, \cdots x^p, y^{11}, \cdots, y^{1m_1}, \ldots, y^{q1}, \cdots, y^{qm_q}\}$ of a mixture of variables, p the quantitative variables $\{x^1, \cdots, x^j, \cdots x^p\}$ and q the qualitative variables $\{y^1, \cdots, y^k, \cdots y^q\}$, where $m = \sum_{k=1}^{q} m_k$ is the total number of modalities and m_k denotes the number of modalities of the variable y^k.

We can, by means of a proximity measure u, define a neighborhood relationship V_u to be a binary relationship on $E \times E$. There are many possibilities for building this neighborhood binary relationship.

Thus, for a given proximity measure u, we can build a neighborhood graph on E, where the vertices are the variables and the edges are defined by a property of the neighborhood relationship.

Many definitions are possible to build this binary neighborhood relationship. We can choose the minimal spanning tree (MST) (Kim and Lee 2003), the Gabriel graph (GG) (Park et al. 2006) or, as is the case here, the relative neighborhood graph (RNG) (Toussaint 1980).

For any proximity measure u listed in Table 1.9 given in the appendix, we construct the associated adjacency binary symmetric matrix V_u of order $p + m$, where all pairs of neighboring variables in E satisfy the following RNG property:

$$V_u(x^k, x^l) = \begin{cases} 1 \text{ if } u(x^k, x^l) \leq \max[u(x^k, x^t), u(x^t, x^l)]; \\ \qquad \forall x^k, \ x^l, \ x^t \in E, \ x^t \neq x^k \ and \ x^t \neq x^l \\ 0 \text{ otherwise.} \end{cases}$$

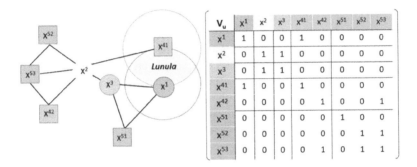

V_u	x^1	x^2	x^3	x^{41}	x^{42}	x^{51}	x^{52}	x^{53}
x^1	1	0	0	1	0	0	0	0
x^2	0	1	1	0	0	0	0	0
x^3	0	1	1	0	0	0	0	0
x^{41}	1	0	0	1	0	0	0	0
x^{42}	0	0	0	0	1	0	0	1
x^{51}	0	0	0	0	0	1	0	0
x^{52}	0	0	0	0	0	0	1	1
x^{53}	0	0	0	0	1	0	1	1

Figure 1.1. *RNG structure, Euclidean proximity measure and associated adjacency matrix*

This means that if two variables x^k and x^l that verify the RNG property are connected by an edge, the vertices x^k and x^l are neighbors.

Figure 1.1 shows an example in $\mathbb{R}^2$ of a set of eight objects, three quantitative variables $\{x^1, x^2, x^3\}$ and five dummy variables $\{x^{41}, x^{42}, x^{51}, x^{52}, x^{53}\}$ of two qualitative variables $\{x^4, x^5\}$, which verify the RNG graph structure with the chosen proximity measure u, the Euclidean distance.

For example, for the first quantitative variable x^1 and the first modality of the first qualitative variable x^{41}, $V_u(x^1, x^{41}) = 1$, it means that on the geometrical plane, the hyper-Lunula (intersection between the two hyperspheres centered on the two variables x^1 and x^{41}) is empty.

For a given neighborhood property (MST, GG or RNG), each measure u generates a topological structure on the objects in E which are totally described by the adjacency binary matrix V_u.

1.2.1. *Reference adjacency matrices*

Three topological approaches are described according to the type of variables considered, quantitative or qualitative or a mixture of both.

1.2.2. *Quantitative variables*

We assume that we have at our disposal a set $\{x^j; j = 1, \cdots, p\}$ of p quantitative variables and n individuals-objects. The interest lies in whether there is a topological correlation between all the considered variables (Abdesselam 2021).

We construct the adjacency matrix denoted by $V_{u_\star}$, which corresponds to the correlation matrix. Thus, to examine the correlation structure between the variables, we look at the significance of their linear correlation coefficient. This adjacency matrix can be written as follows using the t-test or Student's t-test of the linear correlation coefficient ρ of Bravais–Pearson:

DEFINITION 1.1.– *The reference adjacency matrix $V_{u_\star}$ associated with reference measure $u_\star$ is defined as:*

$$V_{u_\star}(x^k, x^l) = \begin{cases} 1 \text{ if } p - value = P[\,|\,T_{n-2}\,|\, > \, t - value\,] \leq \alpha \; ; \; \forall k, l = 1, p \\ 0 \text{ otherwise.} \end{cases}$$

where p-value is the significance test of the correlation coefficient for the two-sided test of the null and alternative hypotheses, $H_0 : \rho(x^k, x^l) = 0$ vs. $H_1 : \rho(x^k, x^l) \neq 0$.

Let T_{n-2} be a t-distributed random variable of Student with $\nu = n - 2$ degrees of freedom. In this case, the null hypothesis is rejected with a p-value less than or equal to a chosen α significance level, for example $\alpha = 5\%$. Using the linear correlation test, if the p-value is very small, it means that there is a very small opportunity that the null hypothesis is correct, and therefore we can reject it. Statistical significance in statistics is achieved when a p-value is less than a chosen significance level of α. The p-value is the probability of obtaining results which acknowledge that the null hypothesis is true.

1.2.3. *Qualitative variables*

We assume that we have at our disposal $\{y^k; k = 1, .., q\}$, a set of $q \geq 2$ qualitative variables and partitions of $n = \sum_{k=1}^{q} n_k$ individuals-objects into m_k modalities-subgroups. The interest lies in whether there is a topological association between all these variables (Abdesselam 2019b).

$-Y_k = Y_{(n, m_k)}$ the disjunctive matrix, data matrix associated with the m_k dummy variables of the qualitative variable y^k with n rows-objects and m_k columns-modalities, we check that $\forall_{i=1,n}, \Sigma_{k=1}^{m_k} y_i^k = 1$ and $\Sigma_{i=1}^{n} y_i^k = n_k$.

– $Y_{(n,m)} = [Y_1|Y_2| \cdots |Y_q]$ the indicator matrix, juxtaposition of the q binary tables Y_k, with n rows-objects and $m = \sum_{k=1}^{q} m_k$ columns-modalities, we check that $\sum_{k=1}^{m_k} y_i^k = q$, $\forall_i$ and $\sum_{i=1}^{n} \sum_{k=1}^{m_k} y_i^k = nq$.

– $\mathcal{B}_{(m,m)} = {}^t Y\, Y$ the symmetric Burt matrix of the two-way cross-tabulations of the q variables.

The dissimilarity matrix associated with a proximity measure is computed from data given by the Burt table $\mathcal{B}$. The attributes of any two points' modalities' y^k and y^l in $\{0,1\}^n$ of the proximity measures can easily be written and calculated from the Burt matrix.

A contingency table is one of the most common ways to summarize categorical data. Generally, the interest lies in whether there is an association between the row variable and the column variable that produce the table; sometimes there is further interest in describing the strength of that association. The data can arise from several different sampling frameworks, and the interpretation of the hypothesis of no association depends on the framework. The question of interest is whether there is an association between the two variables.

In this case, we build the adjacency matrix V_{u_*}, which corresponds best to the Burt table. Thus, to examine similarities between the modalities, we examine the gap between each profile-modality and its average profile, i.e. the gap to independence. This best adjacency matrix can be written as follows:

DEFINITION 1.2.– *The reference adjacency matrix V_{u_*} associated with the reference measure u_* is defined as:*

$$V_{u_*}(y^{kr}, y^{ls}) = \begin{cases} 1 \ if\ \frac{\mathcal{B}_{kr\,ls}}{\mathcal{B}_{kr\,..}} \geq \frac{\mathcal{B}_{kr\,..}}{nq^2}; \ \ \forall k, l = 1, q\ ;\ r = 1, m_k\ and\ s = 1, m_l \\ 0\ otherwise. \end{cases}$$

$\mathcal{B}_{kr\,ls} = \sum_{i=1}^{n} y_i^{kr} y_i^{ls}$, *element of the Burt matrix that corresponds to the number of individuals who have the modality r of the variable k and the modality s of the variable l;*

$\mathcal{B}_{kr\,..} = \sum_{l=1}^{q} \sum_{s=1}^{m_s} b_{kr\,ls}$ *is the row margin of the modality r of the variable k;*

$\frac{\mathcal{B}_{kr\,ls}}{\mathcal{B}_{kr\,..}}$ *is the row profile of the modality r of the variable k;*

$\frac{\mathcal{B}_{kr\,..}}{nq^2}$ *is the average profile of the modality r of the variable k, nq^2 being the total number.*

1.2.4. *Mixed variables*

In this case, the variables for clustering can be a mixture of both quantitative and qualitative variables.

Let $\{x^j; j = 1, \cdots, p\}$ and $\{y^k; k = 1, \cdots, q\}$ be the two sets with p quantitative variables and q qualitative variables, respectively, with partitions of $n = \sum_{k=1}^{q} n_k$ individuals-objects into m_k modalities-subgroups which total $m = \sum_{k=1}^{q} m_k$ modalities. The interest lies in whether there is a topological dependency between all the mixed variables.

Simultaneous treatment of mixed data (quantitative and qualitative) cannot be achieved directly by conventional methods of data analysis. Therefore, first, we transform qualitative data into quantitative data (Abdesselam 2008). This transformation is based on multivariate analysis of variance (MANOVA) and on the maximization of the mixed criterion, proposed in terms of correlation squares by (Saporta 1990) and geometrically in terms of square cosines of angles by (Escofier 1979). Then, second, we build the adjacency matrix V_{u_*}, associated with reference proximity measure u_*, from the correlation matrix of all variables, quantitative and transformed qualitative variables, according to Definition 1.1.

1.3. Topological clustering of variables – selective review

Whatever the type of the set of variables considered, the binary and symmetric adjacency matrix build V_{u_*} is associated with an unknown reference proximity measure u_*.

The robustness according to the α error risk chosen for the null hypothesis: no linear correlation in the case of quantitative variables, or the positive deviation from independence in the case of qualitative variables, can be studied by setting a minimum threshold in order to analyze the sensitivity of the results. Certainly, the numerical results will change, but probably not their interpretation.

In order to describe the similarities between variables and to group them into homogeneous groups, we apply the notion of the thémascope or structural analysis of survey data (Lebart 1989), which is a methodological sequence of a clustering method on the principal components of a factorial analysis method. In this case here, it is a topological factorial analysis followed by a Hierarchical Ascendant Classification (HAC). For the topological factorial analysis method, we carry out the classical Multidimensional Scaling (MDS), namely factorial analysis on the similarity table (Caillez 1976), the reference adjacency matrix V_{u_*} associated with the proximity measure $u*$, the most appropriate measure for the considered data.

DEFINITION 1.3.– *The topological clustering of variables (TCV) consist of performing an HAC algorithm based on the Ward criterion[1] (Ward 1963), on the significant components, of the topological multiple correspondence analysis (TMCA) if the variables are qualitative or of the topological principal component analysis (TPCA) if the variables are quantitative or a mixture of quantitative and qualitative variables.*

The TCV hierarchical approach and its dendrogram are easily programmable from the PCA and HAC procedures of the SPAD, SAS or R software.

As for classical methods devoted to the clustering of observations, there are many methods devoted specifically to the clustering of variables, particularly quantitative ones. One of the most used is the Varclus procedure (SAS Institute Inc. 2011) of the SAS software, but we can also apply the ClustOfVar procedure (Chavent et al. 2012) implemented in R, the CVLC procedure (Vigneau et al. 2006), clustering around latent variables or the Clustatis procedure (Llobell and Qannari 2019).

In the case of the TCV of quantitative variables, it is considered that two positively correlated variables are related and that two negatively correlated variables are related, but remote. We will therefore take into account the sign of the correlation between variables. It should be noted that the Varclus procedure implemented in the SAS software, dedicated to the classification of variables, also includes this option. The Varclus procedure is more precisely a hierarchical descending classification (HDC).

1.4. Illustration on real data of simple examples

We illustrate the TCV approach in each of the three types of variables: quantitative, qualitative and mixed variables.

1.4.1. *Case of a set of quantitative variables*

The illustrative data table from (Govaert 2009) includes 38 French brands of bottled water described by eight variables relating to the ion composition (mg/liter). The data comes from the information provided on the bottle labels. The objective is to group together these variables that form a homogeneous set of the ion contents of French brands of bottled water. Simple statistics of these variables are displayed in Table 1.1.

---

1 Aggregation based on the criterion of the loss of minimal inertia. Ward's method is a criterion applied in hierarchical cluster analysis; it is a general agglomerative hierarchical clustering procedure. With the square of the Euclidean distance, this criterion allows us to minimize the total within-cluster variance or, equivalently, maximize the between-cluster variance.

Variable	Frequency	Mean	Standard Deviation (N)	Coefficient of variation (%)	Min	Max
CA – Calcium	38	104.184	114.40	109.81	1.00	528.00
MG – Magnesium	38	28.105	29.50	104.95	0.00	95.00
NA – Sodium	38	115.658	210.43	181.94	0.00	968.00
K – Potassium	38	15.079	28.18	186.89	0.00	130.00
SULP – Sulphates	38	119.237	289.83	243.07	1.00	1342.00
NO3 – Nitrates	38	1.842	2.64	143.06	0.00	12.00
HC03 – Carbonates	38	561.368	696.23	124.02	4.00	3380.00
CL – Chlorides	38	40.868	75.35	184.37	0.00	387.00

Table 1.1. *Summary statistics of ion content of French brands of bottled water*

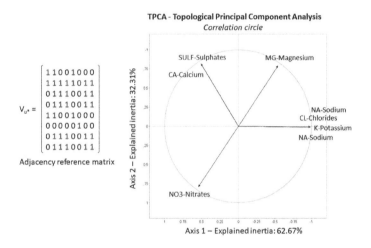

Figure 1.2. *Representation of the ion composition of French brands of bottled water*

Figure 1.2 presents the adjacency matrix $V_{u_\star}$ associated with the proximity measure $u_\star$ adapted to the data considered, which is built from the correlation matrix Table 1.6 given in the appendix, according to Definition 1.1.

The correlation circle of the two first TPCA factors gives an overview of groups of correlated and uncorrelated variables; an HAC according to Ward's criterion is then applied on the TPCA components.

The dendrogram cluster given in Figure 1.3 makes it possible to visualize and identify the topological structure of the variables. The aggregation indices of TCV suggest a partition of the eight variables into three clusters.

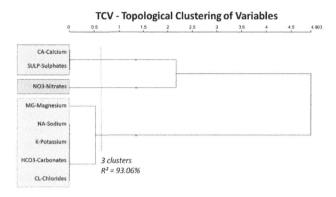

Figure 1.3. *TCV dendrogram of the ion composition
of French brands of bottled water*

The characterization of the classes by the variables, Table 1.2, shows with a risk of error less than or equal to 5%, that the first cluster composed of two variables, calcium and sulfates, are positively correlated and negatively correlated with the variables sodium, potassium, carbonates and chlorides. The nitrates variable alone constitutes the second cluster; it is negatively correlated with the magnesium variable. As for the third cluster, composed of five variables, only four variables, sodium, potassium, carbonates and chlorides, are positively correlated with each other, and the magnesium variable does not significantly characterize this class.

Cluster	Cluster 1	Cluster 2	Cluster 3
Frequency (%)	2 (25.00%)	1 (12.50%)	5 (62.50%)
Profile	CA – Calcium	NO3 – Nitrates	NA – Sodium
	SULF – Sulphates		K – Potassium
			HCO3 – Carbonates
			CL – Chlorides
Anti – profile	NA – Sodium	MG – Magnesium	
	K – Potassium		
	HCO3 – Carbonates		
	CL – Chlorides		

Table 1.2. *Characterization of clusters*

From a dimension reduction or variable selection point of view, we can perform in each of the three clusters, a PCA of the variables that characterize it significantly (see Table 1.2). We can then keep only the first principal component of each of the three PCAs. We thus end up with three synthetic variables of the clusters.

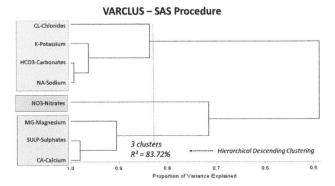

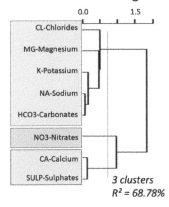

Figure 1.4. *Varclus and ClustOfVar dendrograms*

For comparison, Figures 1.4 and 1.5 show dendrograms of other variables clustering approaches. Note that for a three-cluster partition, the constitution of the clusters is the same except for the Varclus approach.

Table 1.3 presents the percentages of the total variance explained by the three-cluster partition of the different approaches. The percentage of the TCV approach is much higher than the percentages of the other four approaches, so the TCV clusters are more homogeneous.

Clustering approach	TCV	Varclus	CVLC	Clustatis	ClustOfVar
R^2 : variance explained (%)	**93.06**	83.72	73.43	73.43	68.78

Table 1.3. *Comparison criteria*

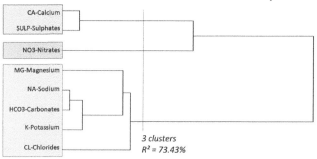

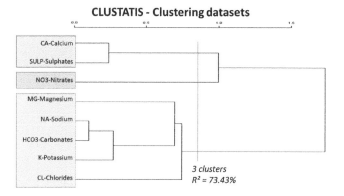

Figure 1.5. *CVLC and Clustatis dendrograms*

1.4.2. *Case of a set of qualitative variables*

To illustrate our approach from a set of qualitative variables, we consider a study on female entrepreneurship conducted in Dakar, Senegal in 2014. The data displayed in Table 1.4 were collected from 153 women from the Dakar region. The objective here is to provide a topological clustering of the demographic characteristics of the female entrepreneurs.

In Figure 1.6, we can see the adjacency matrix $V_{u_\star}$ associated with the best adapted proximity measure $u_\star$ to the considered data established from the profile Table 1.6 given in the appendix, according to Definition 1.2.

Modality Variable	Age			Marital status				Number of children			Level of study		
Under 25	22	0	0	18	2	1	1	13	3	6	3	1	18
25–50 years	0	80	0	16	9	21	34	14	11	55	58	5	17
Over 50	0	0	51	3	8	24	16	8	35	8	30	10	11
Single	18	16	3	37	0	0	0	20	3	14	9	1	27
Divorcee	2	9	8	0	19	0	0	3	10	6	13	5	1
Monogamous bride	1	21	24	0	0	46	0	7	21	18	26	5	15
Polygamous bride	1	34	16	0	0	0	51	5	15	31	43	5	3
No children	13	14	8	20	3	7	5	35	0	0	11	5	19
From one to three children	3	11	35	3	10	21	15	0	49	0	27	9	13
More than three children	6	55	8	14	6	18	31	0	0	69	53	2	14
Illiterate – Primary	3	58	30	9	13	26	43	11	27	53	91	0	0
Secondary	1	5	10	1	5	5	5	5	9	2	0	16	0
Higher	18	17	11	27	1	15	3	19	13	14	0	0	46

Table 1.4. *Burt's table: female entrepreneurship in Dakar, Senegal*

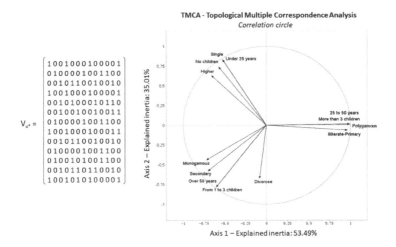

Figure 1.6. *TCV: the demographic characteristics of women entrepreneurs*

The representation on the first principal plane of TMCA gives a first view of the linked groups of modalities, then, a Ward's HAC was performed on the TMCA principal components.

Figure 1.7 shows the dendrogram of the 13 demographic characteristics of the female entrepreneurs. We choose according to the dendrogram to cut this hierarchical tree into three clusters.

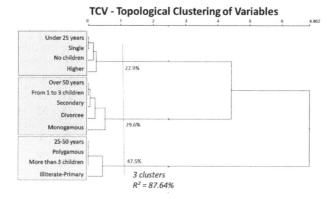

Figure 1.7. *TCV: dendrogram of the demographic characteristics of women entrepreneurs*

Figure 1.8 shows the hierarchical dendrogram obtained by the Corresp and Cluster procedures of SAS software; its percentage of total explained inertia (32.90%) is much lower than that of the TCV approach (87.64%) for a partition into three clusters.

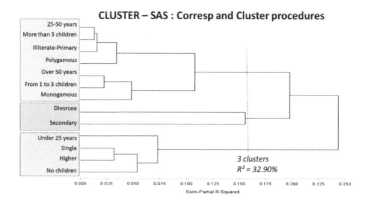

Figure 1.8. *CLUSTER: tree diagram of the demographic characteristics of women entrepreneurs*

Figure 1.9 is given as an indication and not for comparison; the ClusOfVar approach partitions the qualitative variables and not the modalities of the variables as is the case with the TCV and Cluster approaches.

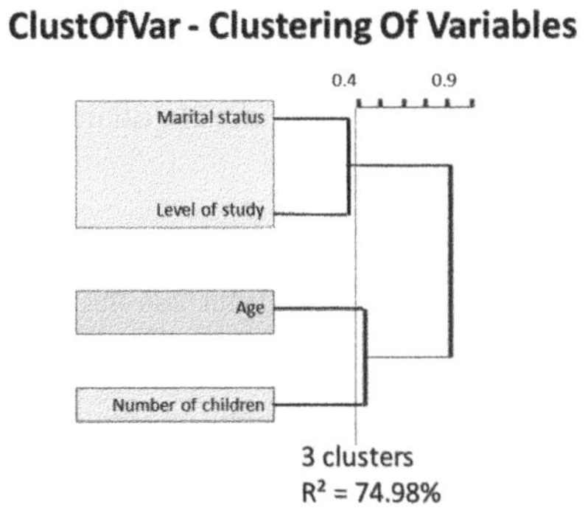

ClustOfVar - Clustering Of Variables

3 clusters
$R^2 = 74.98\%$

Figure 1.9. *ClusOfVar: tree diagram of the demographic characteristics of women entrepreneurs*

1.4.3. *Case of a set of mixed variables*

In some real data situations, variables of a thematic are measured on different scales with a mixture of quantitative and qualitative variables.

Quantitative variable	Frequency	Mean	Std dev (N)	Minimum	Maximum
Urban consumption	27	7.14	1.12	5.60	9.30
Cubic capacity	27	1,165.63	204.17	903.00	1,597.00
Maximum speed	27	154.26	21.94	115.000	200.00
Boot volume	27	901.41	301.67	202.00	1,200.00
Weight/power	27	18.65	5.42	10.20	33.10
Length	27	3.62	0.07	3.40	3.70

Qualitative variable	Modality	Frequency	Percent	Cumulative frequency	Cumulative percent
Horsepower	HP4	13	48.15	13	48.15
	HP5	5	18.52	18	66.67
	HP6	9	33.33	27	100.00
Brand country manufacturer	French	10	37.04	10	37.04
	Foreign	17	62.96	27	100.00
Price	Price 1	10	37.04	10	37.04
	Price 2	5	18.52	15	55.56
	Price 3	8	29.63	23	85.19
	Price 4	4	14.81	27	100.00

Table 1.5. *Summary statistics and frequency distributions*

To illustrate this approach, we take the data published in Lambin (1990); they cover a sample of 27 small cars on the Belgian market. We have a homogeneous theme of nine mixed variables of which there are six quantitative and three qualitative characteristics totaling nine modalities.

The objective here is to synthesize simultaneously in the sense of correlations all of these mixed characteristics. Table 1.5 summarizes the elementary statistics of the mixed variables.

Figure 1.10 gives the adjacency matrix V_{u_*} associated with the adapted proximity measure u_* for the considered data, which is built from the correlation matrix (see Table 1.8 given in the appendix), according to Definition 1.1. The correlation circle of the two first TPCA factors gives an overview of groups of correlated and uncorrelated quantitative and modalities of qualitative variables. An HAC according to Ward's criterion is then applied on the TPCA components represented by the dendrogram of the characteristics of small cars on the Belgian market presented in Figure 1.11.

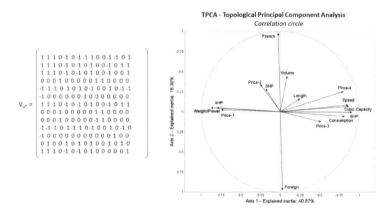

Figure 1.10. *Representation of the car characteristics*

The TCV percentage of total explained inertia is equal to 78.94% for the partition into four classes.

Figure 1.12 presents, as an indication and not for comparison, the tree diagram of hierarchical clusters of the ClustOfVar approach; the latter considers the qualitative variables and not their modalities.

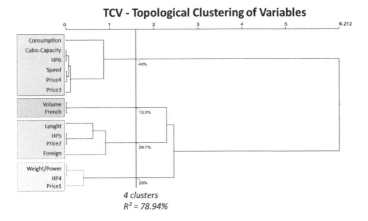

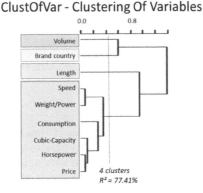

Figure 1.11. *TCV: car characteristics dendrogram*

Figure 1.12. *ClusOfVar – car characteristics dendrogram*

1.5. Conclusion

This chapter proposes a new topological method of clustering of variables which enriches the methods of data analysis within the framework of the clustering of a set of quantitative or qualitative variables or a mixture of both. The results of the proposed topological approach of classifying variables, based on the notion of neighborhood graph, are as well as good, or even better, according to the R square as those of the existing methods. This approach is easily implemented on SAS, SPAD or R software. Future work consists of extending this topological approach to other methods of data analysis, in particular in the context of evolutionary data analysis, both in the concept of a factorial analysis and that of a clustering as well individuals and variables.

1.6. Appendix

Variable	CA	MG	NA	K	SULF	NO3	HCO3	CL
CA	1.0000							
MG	0.6672 (< .0001)	1.0000						
NA	0.0042 (0.9757)	0.5649 (< .0001)	1.0000					
K	0.1072 (0.4358)	0.6703 (< .0001)	0.8817 (< .0001)	1.0000				
SULF	0.8997 (< .0001)	0.5629 (< .0001)	-0.0957 0.4872	-0.0546 0.6923	1.0000			
NO3	-0.0473 (0.7317)	-0.1756 (0.1998)	-0.0830 0.5469	-0.1529 0.2650	-0.1288 0.3486	1.0000		
HCO3	0.1491 0.2774	0.6583 (< .0001)	0.9474 (< .0001)	0.8866 (< .0001)	-0.0573 0.6776	-0.0541 0.6947	1.0000	
CL	0.0578 0.6749	0.52094 (< .0001)	0.5646 (< .0001)	0.7187 (< .0001)	-0.0276 0.8406	-0.1053 0.4443	0.4794 (0.0002)	1.0000

Table 1.6. *Pearson's correlation matrix (p-values). For a color version of the table, see www.iste.co.uk/zafeiris/data2.zip*

Row-Profiles	Age			Marital status				Number of children			Level of study		
Under 25 years	0.25	0	0	0.205	0.023	0.011	0.011	0.148	0.034	0.068	0.034	0.011	0.205
25–50 years	0	0.25	0	0.050	0.028	0.066	0.106	0.044	0.034	0.172	0.181	0.016	0.053
Over 50 years	0	0	0.25	0.015	0.039	0.118	0.078	0.039	0.172	0.039	0.147	0.049	0.054
Single	0.122	0.108	0.020	0.25	0	0	0	0.135	0.020	0.095	0.061	0.007	0.182
Divorcee	0.026	0.118	0.105	0	0.25	0	0	0.040	0.132	0.079	0.171	0.066	0.013
Monogamous	0.005	0.114	0.130	0	0	0.25	0	0.038	0.114	0.098	0.141	0.027	0.082
Polygamous	0.005	0.167	0.078	0	0	0	0.25	0.025	0.074	0.152	0.211	0.025	0.015
No children	0.093	0.100	0.057	0.143	0.021	0.050	0.036	0.25	0	0	0.079	0.036	0.136
From one to three children	0.015	0.056	0.179	0.015	0.051	0.107	0.077	0	0.25	0	0.138	0.046	0.066
More than three children	0.022	0.199	0.029	0.051	0.022	0.065	0.112	0	0	0.25	0.192	0.007	0.051
Illiterate – Primary	0.008	0.159	0.082	0.025	0.036	0.071	0.118	0.030	0.074	0.146	0.25	0	0
Secondary	0.016	0.078	0.156	0.016	0.078	0.078	0.078	0.078	0.141	0.031	0	0.25	0
Superior	0.098	0.092	0.060	0.147	0.005	0.082	0.016	0.103	0.071	0.076	0	0	0.25
Average profile	0.036	0.131	0.083	0.061	0.031	0.075	0.083	0.057	0.080	0.113	0.149	0.026	0.075

Table 1.7. *Row and average profiles. For a color version of the table, see www.iste.co.uk/zafeiris/data2.zip*

Variable	Consumption	Cubic capacity	Speed	Volume	Weight/Power	Length	HP4	HP5	HP6	French	Foreign	Price1	Price2	Price3	Price4
Consumption	1.0000														
Cubic Capacity	0.7966 (<.0001)	1.0000													
Speed	0.78044 (<.0001)	0.83222 (<.0001)	1.0000												
Volume	0.2946 (0.1358)	0.1125 (0.5766)	0.0220 (0.9134)	1.0000											
Weight/Power	-0.6825 (<.0001)	-0.7788 (<.0001)	-0.9376 (<.0001)	0.1020 (0.6127)	1.0000										
Length	0.1966 (0.3258)	0.2897 (0.1427)	0.1552 (0.4396)	-0.0734 (0.7161)	-0.0977 (0.6280)	1.0000									
HP4	-0.5481 (0.0031)	-0.8376 (<.0001)	-0.6602 (0.0002)	-0.1048 (0.6031)	0.6091 (0.0007)	-0.3058 (0.1208)	1.0000								
HP5	-0.3819 (0.0494)	0.0611 (0.7621)	-0.1447 (0.4714)	-0.2655 (0.1807)	0.1083 (0.5909)	0.1650 (0.4109)	-0.4594 (0.0159)	1.0000							
HP6	0.8957 (<.0001)	0.8375 (<.0001)	0.8190 (<.0001)	0.3298 (0.0930)	-0.7348 (<.0001)	0.1882 (0.3472)	-0.6814 (<.0001)	-0.3371 (0.0855)	1.0000						
French	-0.0939 (0.6415)	0.0431 (0.8310)	-0.0100 (0.6198)	0.4093 (0.0340)	0.2039 (0.3077)	0.1488 (0.4589)	-0.1251 (0.5342)	0.2267 (0.2555)	-0.0542 (0.7882)	1.0000					
Foreign	0.0939 (0.6415)	-0.0431 (0.8310)	0.0100 (0.6198)	-0.4093 (0.0340)	-0.2039 (0.3077)	-0.1488 (0.4589)	0.1251 (0.5342)	-0.2267 (0.2555)	0.0542 (0.7882)	-1.0000 (<.0001)	1.0000				
Price1	-0.4020 (0.0376)	-0.6767 (0.0001)	-0.6035 (0.0009)	-0.0110 (0.9568)	0.5475 (0.0031)	-0.4024 (0.0374)	0.7959 (<.0001)	-0.3656 (.0607)	-0.5423 (0.0035)	-0.1118 (0.5789)	0.1118 (0.5789)	1.0000			
Price2	-0.3904 (0.0441)	-0.2901 (0.1422)	-0.2969 (0.1327)	-0.1015 (0.6145)	0.3086 (0.1173)	0.1254 (0.5330)	0.1131 (0.5744)	0.2636 (0.1839)	-0.3371 (0.0855)	0.2267 (0.2555)	-0.2267 (0.2555)	-0.3656 (0.0607)	1.0000		
Price3	0.2465 (0.2151)	0.4807 (0.0112)	0.3251 (0.0980)	-0.0232 (0.9086)	-0.3901 (0.0443)	0.2313 (0.2458)	-0.6253 (0.0005)	0.3171 (0.1071)	0.4015 (0.0379)	-0.3297 (0.0931)	0.3297 (0.0931)	-0.4977 (0.0083)	-0.3093 (0.1164)	1.0000	
Price4	0.6565 (0.0002)	0.6191 (0.0006)	0.7270 (<.0001)	0.1557 (0.4382)	-0.5803 (0.0015)	0.1126 (0.5760)	-0.4019 (0.0377)	-0.1988 (0.3202)	0.5898 (0.0012)	0.3278 (0.0950)	-0.3278 (0.0950)	-0.3199 (0.1039)	-0.1988 (0.3202)	-0.2706 (0.1722)	1.0000

Table 1.8. *Pearson's correlation matrix (p-values)*

Measure	Distance and Dissimilarity for continuous data
Euclidean	$u_{Euc}(x,y) = \sqrt{\sum_{j=1}^{P}(x_j - y_j)^2}$
Manhattan	$u_{Man}(x,y) = \sum_{j=1}^{P}|x_j - y_j|$
Minkowski	$u_{Min_\gamma}(x,y) = (\sum_{j=1}^{P}|x_j - y_j|^\gamma)^{\frac{1}{\gamma}}$
Tchebychev	$u_{Tch}(x,y) = max_{1 \leq j \leq p}|x_j - y_j|$
Normalized Euclidean	$u_{NE}(x,y) = \sqrt{\sum_{j=1}^{P}\frac{1}{\sigma_j^2}[(x_j - \overline{x}) - (y_j - \overline{y})]^2}$
Cosine dissimilarity	$u_{Cos}(x,y) = 1 - \frac{\sum_{j=1}^{P}x_j y_j}{\sqrt{\sum_{j=1}^{P}x_j^2}\sqrt{\sum_{j=1}^{P}y_j^2}} = 1 - \frac{<x,y>}{\|x\|\|y\|}$
Canberra	$u_{Can}(x,y) = \sum_{j=1}^{P}\frac{|x_j - y_j|}{|x_j|+|y_j|}$
Pearson's correlation	$u_{Cor}(x,y) = 1 - \frac{(\sum_{j=1}^{P}(x_j - \overline{x})(y_j - \overline{y}))^2}{\sum_{j=1}^{P}(x_j - \overline{x})^2 \sum_{j=1}^{P}(y_j - \overline{y})^2} = 1 - \frac{(<x-\overline{x}, y-\overline{y}>)^2}{\|x-\overline{x}\|^2 \|y-\overline{y}\|^2}$
Squared chord	$u_{Cho}(x,y) = \sum_{j=1}^{P}(\sqrt{x_j} - \sqrt{y_j})^2$
Overlap measure	$u_{Dev}(x,y) = max(\sum_{j=1}^{P}x_j, \sum_{j=1}^{P}y_j) - \sum_{j=1}^{P}min(x_j, y_j)$
Weighted Euclidean	$u_{WEu}(x,y) = \sqrt{\sum_{j=1}^{P}\alpha_j(x_j - y_j)^2}$
Gowers dissimilarity	$u_{Gow}(x,y) = \frac{1}{p}\sum_{j=1}^{P}|x_j - y_j|$
Shape distance	$u_{Sha}(x,y) = \sqrt{\sum_{j=1}^{P}[(x_j - \overline{x}_j) - (y_j - \overline{y}_j)]^2}$
Size distance	$u_{Siz}(x,y) = |\sum_{j=1}^{P}(x_j - y_j)|$
Lpower	$u_{Lpo_\gamma}(x,y) = \sum_{j=1}^{P}|x_j - y_j|^\gamma$

where p is the dimension of space, $x = (x_j)_{j=1,\ldots,p}$ and $y = (y_j)_{j=1,\ldots,p}$ two points in R^P, $\overline{x}_j$ is the mean, σ_j is the standard deviation, $\alpha_j = \frac{1}{\sigma_j^2}$ and $\gamma > 0$.

Measure	Similarity and Dissimilarity for binary data		
Jaccard	$s_1 = \frac{a}{a+b+c}$	;	$u_1 = 1 - s_1$
Dice, Czekanowski	$s_2 = \frac{2a}{2a+b+c}$	;	$u_2 = 1 - s_2$
Kulczynski	$s_3 = \frac{1}{2}(\frac{a}{a+b} + \frac{a}{a+c})$	;	$u_3 = 1 - s_3$
Driver, Kroeber and Ochiai	$s_4 = \frac{a}{\sqrt{(a+b)(a+c)}}$	;	$u_4 = 1 - s_4$
Sokal and Sneath 2	$s_5 = \frac{a}{a+2(b+c)}$	;	$u_5 = 1 - s_5$
Braun-Blanquet	$s_6 = \frac{a}{max(a+b,a+c)}$	;	$u_6 = 1 - s_6$
Simpson	$s_7 = \frac{a}{min(a+b,a+c)}$	;	$u_7 = 1 - s_7$
Kendall, Sokal-Michener	$s_8 = \frac{a+d}{a+b+c+d}$	;	$u_8 = 1 - s_8$
Russell and Rao	$s_9 = \frac{a}{a+b+c+d}$	;	$u_9 = 1 - s_9$
Rogers and Tanimoto	$s_{10} = \frac{a+d}{a+2(b+c)+d}$	;	$u_{10} = 1 - s_{10}$
Pearson's ϕ	$s_{11} = \frac{ad-bc}{\sqrt{(a+b)(a+c)(d+b)(d+c)}}$	;	$u_{11} = \frac{1-s_{11}}{2}$
Hamann	$s_{12} = \frac{a+d-b-c}{a+b+c+d}$	;	$u_{12} = \frac{1-s_{12}}{2}$
Sokal and Sneath 5	$s_{14} = \frac{ad}{\sqrt{(a+b)(a+c)(d+b)(d+c)}}$	;	$u_{14} = 1 - s_{14}$
Michael	$s_{15} = \frac{4(ad-bc)}{(a+d)^2+(b+c)^2}$	;	$u_{15} = \frac{1-s_{15}}{2}$
Baroni, Urbani and Buser	$s_{16} = \frac{a+\sqrt{ad}}{a+b+c+\sqrt{ad}}$	;	$u_{16} = 1 - s_{16}$
Yule Q	$s_{17} = \frac{ad-bc}{ad+bc}$	;	$u_{17} = \frac{1-s_{17}}{2}$
Yule Y	$s_{18} = \frac{\sqrt{ad}-\sqrt{bc}}{\sqrt{ad}+\sqrt{bc}}$	;	$u_{18} = \frac{1-s_{18}}{2}$
Sokal and Sneath 4	$s_{19} = \frac{1}{4}(\frac{a}{a+b} + \frac{a}{a+c} + \frac{d}{d+b} + \frac{d}{d+c})$	;	$u_{19} = 1 - s_{19}$
Gower and Legendre	$s_{21} = \frac{a+d}{a+\frac{(b+c)}{2}+d}$	;	$u_{21} = 1 - s_{21}$
Sokal and Sneath 1	$s_{22} = \frac{2(a+d)}{2(a+d)+b+c}$	;	$u_{22} = 1 - s_{22}$

where $a = |X \cap Y|$ is the number of attributes common to both points x and y, $b = |X - Y|$ is the number of attributes present in x but not in y, $c = |Y - X|$ is the number of attributes present in y but not in x, and $d = |\overline{X} \cap \overline{Y}|$ is the number of attributes in neither x nor y and $|.|$ is the cardinality of a set.

Table 1.9. *Some proximity measures for continuous and binary data*

1.7. References

Abdesselam, R. (2008). Analyse en composantes principales mixte. Classification : points de vue croisés, RNTI-C-2. *Revue des nouvelles technologies de l'information*, Cépaduès Editions, 31–41.

Abdesselam, R. (2019a). A topological multiple correspondence analysis. *Journal of Mathematics and Statistical Science*, 5(8), 175–192.

Abdesselam, R. (2019b). A topological discriminant analysis. In *Data Analysis and Applications 2: Utilization of Results in Europe and Other Topics*. Skiadas, C.H. and Bozeman, J.R. (eds). ISTE, London, and John Wiley & Sons, New York.

Abdesselam, R. (2020). Selection of proximity measures for a topological correspondence analysis. In *Data Analysis and Applications 3: Computational, Classification, Financial, Statistical and Stochastic Methods*. Makrides, A., Karagrigoriou. A., Skiadas, C.H. (eds). ISTE, London, and John Wiley & Sons, New York.

Abdesselam, R. (2021). A topological principal component analysis. *International Journal of Data Science and Analysis*, 7(2), 20–31.

Batagelj, V. and Bren, M. (1995). Comparing resemblance measures. *Journal of Classification*, 12, 73–90.

Benzécri, J.P. (1976a). *L'Analyse des Données. Tome 1 : La Taxinomie*, 2nd edition. Dunod, Paris.

Benzécri, J.P. (1976b). *L'Analyse des Données. Tome 2 : L'analyse des correspondances*, 2nd edition. Dunod, Paris.

Caillez, F. and Pagès, J.P. (1976). *Introduction à l'analyse des données*. SMASH, Paris.

Chavent, M., Kuentz, V., Liquet, B., Saracco, J. (2012). ClustOfVar: An R package for the clustering of variables. *Journal of Statistical Software*, 50, 1–16.

Cohen, J. (1960). A coefficient of agreement for nominal scales. *Educational and Psychological Measurement*, 20, 27–46.

Demsar, J. (2006). Statistical comparisons of classifiers over multiple data sets. *The Journal of Machine Learning Research*, 7, 1–30.

Escofier, B. (1979). Traitement simultané de variables qualitatives et quantitatives en analyse factorielle. *Cahier de l'analyse des données*, 4(2), 137–146.

Govaert, G. (2009). *Data Analysis*. ISTE Ltd and John Wiley & Sons, New York.

Hubert, L. and Arabie, P. (1985). Comparing partitions. *Journal of Classification*, 193–218.

Kim, J.H. and Lee, S. (2003). Tail bound for the minimal spanning tree of a complete graph. *Statistics & Probability Letters*, 4(64), 425–430.

Lambin, J.J. (1990). *La recherche marketing. Analyser – Mesurer – Prévoir*. McGraw-Hill, New York.

Lebart, L. (1989). Stratégies du traitement des données d'enquêtes. *La Revue de MODULAD*, 3, 21–29.

Lesot, M.J., Rifqi, M., Benhadda, H. (2009). Similarity measures for binary and numerical data: A survey. *IJKESDP*, 1(1), 63–84.

Llobell, F. and Qannari, E.M. (2019). Clustering datasets by means of Clustatis with identification of atypical datasets. Application to sensometrics. *Food Quality and Preference*, 75, 97–104.

Mantel, N. (1967). A technique of disease clustering and a generalized regression approach. *Cancer Research*, 27, 209–220.

Park, J.C., Shin, H., Choi, B.K. (2006). Elliptic Gabriel graph for finding neighbors in a point set and its application to normal vector estimation. *Computer-Aided Design*, 38(6), 619–626.

Rifqi, M., Detyniecki, M., Bouchon-Meunier, B. (2003). Discrimination power of measures of resemblance. Paper, IFSA'03 Citeseer.

Saporta, G. (1990). Simultaneous treatment of quantitative and qualitative data. *Attidela XXXV Riunone scientifica; Società Italiana di Statistica*, 63–72.

SAS Institute Inc. (2011). SAS/STAT®9.3 User's Guide The VARCLUS Procedure (Chapter) [Online]. Available at: http://support.sas.com/documentation/onlinedoc/stat/930/varclus.pdf.

Schneider, J.W. and Borlund, P. (2007a). Matrix comparison, Part 1: Motivation and important issues for measuring the resemblance between proximity measures or ordination results. *Journal of the American Society for Information Science and Technology*, 58(11), 1586–1595.

Schneider, J.W. and Borlund, P. (2007b). Matrix comparison, Part 2: Measuring the resemblance between proximity measures or ordination results by use of the Mantel and Procrustes statistics. *Journal of the American Society for Information Science and Technology*, 11(58), 1596–1609.

Toussaint, G.T. (1980). The relative neighbourhood graph of a finite planar set. *Pattern Recognition*, 12(4), 261–268.

Vigneau, E. and Qannari, E.M. (2003). Classification of variables around latent components. *Communications in Statistics – Simulation and Computation*, 32(4), 1131–1150.

Vigneau, E., Qannari, E.M., Sahmer. K., Ladiray, D. (2006). Classification de variables autour de composantes latentes *Revue de statistique appliquée*, 54(1), 27–45.

Ward, J.R. (1963). Hierarchical grouping to optimize an objective function. *Journal of the American Statistical Association JSTOR*, 58(301), 236–244.

Warrens, M.J. (2008). Bounds of resemblance measures for binary (presence/absence) variables. *Journal of Classification*, 25(2), 195–208.

Zighed, D., Abdesselam, R., Hadgu, A. (2012). Topological comparisons of proximity measures. In *16th PAKDD 2012 Conference*, Tan, P.-N., Chawla, S., Ho, C.K., Bailey, J. (eds). Springer-Verlag, Berlin Heidelberg.

A New Regression Model
for Count Compositions

Count compositions are vectors of non-negative integers summing to a fixed constant. The most popular distribution for this kind of data is the multinomial one, which has many advantages, but it is poorly parameterized in terms of the covariance matrix. An interesting approach to overcome this issue is to compound the multinomial distribution with a distribution defined on the simplex. For example, compounding the multinomial distribution with the Dirichlet leads to the well-known Dirichlet-multinomial (DM). With an additional parameter, the DM distribution fits real data better than the multinomial one, but its covariance structure may still be too rigid. The aim of this work is to propose a new distribution for count compositions and to develop a regression model based on it. The new distribution is obtained by compounding the multinomial with the flexible Dirichlet, and it can be expressed as a structured finite mixture with particular DM components. Thanks to this mixture structure and the additional parameters introduced, the new distribution can provide a better fit and an interesting interpretation in terms of latent groups. We compare the regression models based on these distributions through a simulation study and an application to a real dataset. Inferential issues are dealt with by a Bayesian approach through the Hamiltonian Monte Carlo algorithm.

2.1. Introduction

In this section, we briefly recall the main results regarding two of the most popular distributions for count vectors, namely the multinomial and the Dirichlet-multinomial

Chapter written by Roberto ASCARI and Sonia MIGLIORATI.

For a color version of all the figures in this chapter, see www.iste.co.uk/zafeiris/data2.zip.

(DM). Moreover, we highlight some drawbacks of using these distributions to model real datasets and propose a new model based on a compound approach: the flexible Dirichlet-multinomial (FDM). In section 2.2, we define regression models based on the illustrated distributions, while in section 2.3, we present the results of two simulation studies. Finally, in section 2.4, we present an application based on a real dataset concerning the results of the Italian general elections held in 2018.

2.1.1. *Distributions for count vectors*

Let us suppose we have a random experiment with D mutually exclusive outcomes, and that we are going to repeat it n times. We can count the number of occurrences of each outcome among the n trials, summarizing the counts by a vector $\mathbf{Y} = (Y_1, \ldots, Y_D)^\mathsf{T}$, subject to the constraint $\sum_{r=1}^{D} Y_r = n$. A classical probability distribution for the discrete random vector (rv) $\mathbf{Y}$ is the multinomial one, which is characterized by the following probability mass function (pmf):

$$f_M(\mathbf{y}; \boldsymbol{\pi}) = \frac{n!}{\prod_{r=1}^{D}(y_r!)} \prod_{r=1}^{D} \pi_r^{y_r},$$

where the parameter $\boldsymbol{\pi} = (\pi_1, \ldots, \pi_D)^\mathsf{T}$ is a D-dimensional vector of probabilities. Thus, $\boldsymbol{\pi}$ lies in the D-part simplex $\mathcal{S}^D = \{\mathbf{q} \in \mathbb{R}^D : q_r > 0, \sum_{r=1}^{D} q_r = 1\}$. The parameterization of the multinomial distribution could be insufficient to model real data. Indeed, it is possible to show that its first two order moments can be expressed as

$$\mathbb{E}[\mathbf{Y}] = n\boldsymbol{\pi},$$
$$\mathbb{V}(\mathbf{Y}) = n\left(\mathrm{Diag}(\boldsymbol{\pi}) - \boldsymbol{\pi}\boldsymbol{\pi}^\mathsf{T}\right). \tag{2.1}$$

From the above formulas, it is easy to see that once the mean vector has been fixed, there are no parameters left to model the covariance matrix. This strict connection among the barycenter and the covariance matrix can lead to a very bad fit of the model to real datasets. For this reason, some alternatives have been proposed in the statistical literature, one of the most powerful and general being the use of a compound distribution. Let $\mathbf{Y}|\boldsymbol{\Pi} = \boldsymbol{\pi}$ be a multinomial distributed rv with probability vector $\boldsymbol{\pi}$, and let us assume that $\boldsymbol{\Pi}$ follows a distribution defined on $\mathcal{S}^D$, let us say $\mathcal{F}$. Then, a compound distribution for $\mathbf{Y}$ can be defined by marginalizing over $\mathcal{F}$ the joint distribution of $\mathbf{Y}$ and $\boldsymbol{\Pi}$.

This approach is so interesting because, thanks to the total expectation, total variance and total covariance laws, it is possible to write the moments of $\mathbf{Y}$ in terms of moments of $\boldsymbol{\Pi}$, namely:

$$\mathbb{E}\left[\mathbf{Y}\right] = \mathbb{E}\left[\mathbb{E}\left[\mathbf{Y}|\boldsymbol{\Pi}\right]\right] = n\mathbb{E}\left[\boldsymbol{\Pi}\right]$$

$$\mathrm{Var}\left(Y_r\right) = \mathbb{E}\left[\mathrm{Var}\left(Y_r|\boldsymbol{\Pi}\right)\right] + \mathrm{Var}\left(\mathbb{E}\left[Y_r|\boldsymbol{\Pi}\right]\right)$$
$$= n\left((n-1)\mathrm{Var}\left(\Pi_r\right) + \mathbb{E}\left[\Pi_r\right]\left(1 - \mathbb{E}\left[\Pi_r\right]\right)\right)$$

$$\mathrm{Cov}\left(Y_r, Y_h\right) = \mathbb{E}\left[\mathrm{Cov}\left(Y_r, Y_h|\boldsymbol{\Pi}\right)\right] + \mathrm{Cov}\left(\mathbb{E}\left[Y_r|\boldsymbol{\Pi}\right], \mathbb{E}\left[Y_h|\boldsymbol{\Pi}\right]\right)$$
$$= n\left((n-1)\mathrm{Cov}\left(\Pi_r, \Pi_h\right) - \mathbb{E}\left[\Pi_r\right]\cdot\mathbb{E}\left[\Pi_h\right]\right)$$

Thus, choosing a rich enough distribution $\mathcal{F}$ for $\boldsymbol{\Pi}$, we can obtain a distribution for $\mathbf{Y}$ with additional parameters which could be used to model the covariance matrix. One of the most popular distributions defined on the simplex is the Dirichlet. This distribution is characterized by the following probability density function (pdf):

$$f_{\mathrm{Dir}}(\boldsymbol{\pi};\boldsymbol{\mu},\alpha^+) = \frac{\Gamma(\alpha^+)}{\prod_{r=1}^{D}\Gamma(\alpha^+\mu_r)}\prod_{r=1}^{D}\pi_r^{(\alpha^+\mu_r)-1}, \qquad [2.2]$$

where $\boldsymbol{\mu} \in \mathcal{S}^D$ and $\alpha^+ > 0$. The parameterization used in [2.2] is known as "mean-precision" parameterization, since if $\boldsymbol{\Pi} \sim \mathrm{Dir}(\boldsymbol{\mu},\alpha^+)$, then $\mathbb{E}\left[\boldsymbol{\Pi}\right] = \boldsymbol{\mu}$ and α^+ represents a precision parameter, as the variance of each element of $\boldsymbol{\Pi}$ can be expressed as a decreasing function of α^+. Compounding the multinomial distribution with the Dirichlet one leads to the DM, a discrete multivariate distribution which is frequently used as an alternative to the multinomial. Its pmf results to be

$$f_{\mathrm{DM}}(\mathbf{y};\boldsymbol{\mu},\alpha^+) = \frac{n!}{\prod_{r=1}^{D}(y_r!)}\int_{\mathcal{S}^D}\prod_{r=1}^{D}\pi_r^{y_r}\cdot\frac{\Gamma(\alpha^+)}{\prod_{r=1}^{D}\Gamma(\alpha^+\mu_r)}\prod_{r=1}^{D}\pi_r^{(\alpha^+\mu_r)-1}d\boldsymbol{\pi}$$
$$= \frac{n!\,\Gamma(\alpha^+)}{\Gamma(n+\alpha^+)}\prod_{r=1}^{D}\frac{\Gamma(y_r+(\alpha^+\mu_r))}{(y_r!)\,\Gamma(\alpha^+\mu_r)}.$$
$$[2.3]$$

The DM possesses an additional parameter with respect to the multinomial model. It helps in modeling the covariance structure of the count vector since we can express the mean vector and the covariance matrix of the DM as

$$\mathbb{E}\left[\mathbf{Y}\right] = n\boldsymbol{\mu},$$

$$\mathbb{V}\left(\mathbf{Y}\right) = n\mathbf{M}\left[1 + \frac{n-1}{\alpha^+ + 1}\right], \qquad [2.4]$$

where $\mathbf{M} = (\mathrm{Diag}(\boldsymbol{\mu}) - \boldsymbol{\mu}\boldsymbol{\mu}^{\mathsf{T}})$. Now, even if the expected value of $\mathbf{Y}$ (which is proportional to $\boldsymbol{\mu}$) is fixed, there is a parameter to model $\mathbb{V}\left(\mathbf{Y}\right)$. Although this additional parameter greatly improves the fit of the model, the DM deserves just a single parameter to model the entire $D(D+1)/2$ elements in the covariance matrix, which can be insufficient to deal with complex datasets. We propose to take advantage of another distribution defined on $\mathcal{S}^D$, namely the flexible Dirichlet (FD) (Ongaro and Migliorati 2013; Migliorati et al. 2017). The latter is a structured finite mixture with Dirichlet components, which entails some constraints among the components' parameters to ensure identifiability of the mixture.

More specifically, its pdf can be expressed as

$$f_{\text{FD}}(\boldsymbol{\pi}; \boldsymbol{\mu}, \alpha^+, w, \mathbf{p}) = \sum_{j=1}^{D} p_j f_{\text{Dir}}\left(\boldsymbol{\pi}; \boldsymbol{\lambda}_j, \frac{\alpha^+}{1-w}\right), \qquad [2.5]$$

where

$$\boldsymbol{\lambda}_j = \boldsymbol{\mu} - w\mathbf{p} + w\mathbf{e}_j, \qquad [2.6]$$

is the component-specific mean vector, $\boldsymbol{\mu} = \mathbb{E}\left[\boldsymbol{\Pi}\right] \in \mathcal{S}^D$, $\alpha^+ > 0$, $\mathbf{p} \in \mathcal{S}^D$, $0 < w < \min\left\{1, \min_r\left\{\frac{\mu_r}{p_r}\right\}\right\}$, and $\mathbf{e}_j$ is a vector with all elements equal to zero except for the j-th which is equal to one. Equation [2.5] points out that the Dirichlet components have different mean vectors and a common precision parameter, the latter being determined by a α^+ and w. By examining equation [2.6], it is possible to observe that any two component means $\boldsymbol{\lambda}_r$ and $\boldsymbol{\lambda}_l$, $r \neq l$ coincide for all the elements except for the r-th and the l-th. Generally speaking, it is easy to show that $\boldsymbol{\lambda}_r$ is characterized by a value of the r-th element higher than the r-th element of all the other component means.

Compounding the multinomial distribution with the FD leads to the definition of a new distribution for count vectors, which we will call flexible Dirichlet-multinomial (FDM). We can write the pmf of the FDM as

$$f_{\text{FDM}}(\mathbf{y}; \boldsymbol{\mu}, \alpha^+, \mathbf{p}, w) = \sum_{r=1}^{D} p_j f_{\text{DM}}\left(\mathbf{y}; \boldsymbol{\lambda}_j, \frac{\alpha^+}{1-w}\right) \qquad [2.7]$$

$$= \sum_{j=1}^{D} p_j \frac{n! \Gamma(\frac{\alpha^+}{1-w})}{\Gamma(\frac{\alpha^+}{1-w} + n)} \prod_{r=1}^{D} \frac{\Gamma(y_r + \frac{\alpha^+}{1-w}\lambda_{jr})}{(y_r!)\Gamma(\frac{\alpha^+}{1-w}\lambda_{jr})}.$$

The FDM distribution is the multivariate case of the flexible beta-binomial distribution, which is a generalization of the binomial model, successful in dealing with overdispersion (Ascari and Migliorati 2021).

By examining equation [2.7], it is possible to note that the FDM can be expressed as a finite mixture, with DM components showing a common precision parameter and different probability vectors $\boldsymbol{\lambda}_j$, $j = 1, \ldots, D$. Denoting by $\phi = \alpha^+/(1-w)$ the common precision parameter of the DM components, the first two order moments of the FDM are

$$\mathbb{E}\left[\mathbf{Y}\right] = n\boldsymbol{\mu},$$

$$\mathbb{V}\left(\mathbf{Y}\right) = n\mathbf{M}\left[1 + \frac{n-1}{\phi+1}\right] + n\frac{(n-1)\phi w^2}{\phi+1}\mathbf{P}, \qquad [2.8]$$

where $\mathbf{P} = (\text{Diag}(\mathbf{p}) - \mathbf{p}\mathbf{p}^{\mathsf{T}})$. The covariance matrix of the FDM distribution expressed in [2.8] can be seen as composed of two terms. The first one coincides with the covariance matrix of the DM in [2.4], whereas the second one depends on the mixture structure of the FDM model. This new covariance matrix has D additional parameters with respect to the DM, so that it could model a wider range of scenarios.

2.2. Regression models and Bayesian inference

Since it is possible to show that $w \in \left(0, \min\left\{1, \min_r \left\{\frac{\mu_r}{p_r}\right\}\right\}\right)$, we can define a normalized version of w, namely $\tilde{w}$, which varies between 0 and 1:

$$\tilde{w} = \frac{w}{\min\left\{1, \min_r \left\{\frac{\mu_r}{p_r}\right\}\right\}} \in (0, 1). \qquad [2.9]$$

It is noteworthy that, due to the link between $\boldsymbol{\mu}$ and the component-specific means expressed in equation [2.6], when we model $\boldsymbol{\mu}$ we are also (indirectly) modeling all the λ's.

The parameterization of the FDM proposed in the previous section highlights the parameter $\boldsymbol{\mu} = \mathbb{E}\left[\mathbf{Y}/n\right]$. This parameter represents the probability of each of the D possible outcomes we are interested in and, thus, it is a reasonable parameter to be linked to subject-specific covariates. More precisely, let $\mathbf{Y} = (\mathbf{Y}_1, \ldots, \mathbf{Y}_N)^{\mathsf{T}}$ be a set of independent multivariate responses collected on a sample of N subjects/units. For the i-th subject, $\mathbf{Y}_i$ counts the number that each of D possible outcomes occurred among n_i trials and $\mathbf{x}_i$ is a $(K+1)$-dimensional vector of covariates. We can define the multinomial regression (MultReg), the DM regression (DMReg) and the FDM regression (FDMReg) models assuming that $\mathbf{Y}_i$ follows a Mult$(\boldsymbol{\mu}_i)$, DM$(\boldsymbol{\mu}_i, \phi)$ or FDM$(\boldsymbol{\mu}_i, \alpha^+, \mathbf{p}, \tilde{w})$ distribution, respectively. Following a GLM-type approach (McCullagh and Nelder 1989), we can link the parameter $\boldsymbol{\mu}_i$ to the linear predictor through a proper link function. Since $\boldsymbol{\mu}_i \in \mathcal{S}^D$, we can take advantage of the multinomial logit link function, i.e.

$$g(\mu_{ir}) = \log\left(\frac{\mu_{ir}}{\mu_{iD}}\right) = \mathbf{x}_i^{\mathsf{T}}\boldsymbol{\beta}_r, \qquad r = 1, \ldots, D-1, \qquad [2.10]$$

where $\boldsymbol{\beta}_r = (\beta_{r0}, \beta_{r1}, \ldots, \beta_{rK})^{\mathsf{T}}$ is a vector of regression coefficients for the r-th element of $\boldsymbol{\mu}_i$. Please note that the last category has been chosen as a baseline category; thus, $\boldsymbol{\beta}_D = \mathbf{0}$.

The parameterization of the FDMReg based on $\boldsymbol{\mu}$, $\mathbf{p}$, α^+ and $\tilde{w}$ defines a variation independent parameter space, meaning that no constraints exist among parameters. In a Bayesian framework, this greatly simplifies the specification of the joint prior distribution, since it allows us to assume prior independence. Thus, we can specify a prior distribution for each parameter separately. In order to use non- or weakly informative priors to induce minimum impact on the posterior distribution, we select the following priors:

1) $\boldsymbol{\beta}_r \sim N_{K+1}(\mathbf{0}, \Sigma)$, where $\mathbf{0}$ is the $(K+1)$-vector with zero elements, and Σ is a diagonal matrix with "large" variance values;

2) $\alpha^+ \sim Gamma(g_1, g_2)$ for small values of g_1 and g_2;

3) $\tilde{w} \sim Unif(0,1)$;

4) $\mathbf{p} \sim Dirichlet(\mathbf{1})$.

Note that a subset of these priors can be adopted for the MultReg (namely prior 1.) and for the DMReg (priors 1. and 2.) models. Inferential issues are dealt with by a Bayesian approach through a Hamiltonian Monte Carlo (HMC) algorithm (Neal 1994), which is a generalization of the Metropolis–Hastings combining classical Markov Chain Monte Carlo (MCMC) and deterministic simulation methods. The Stan modeling language (Stan Development Team 2017) allows for implementing a HMC method to obtain a simulated sample from the posterior distribution.

To compare the fit of the models, we use the Watanabe-Akaike information criterion (WAIC) (Watanabe 2013; Vehtari et al. 2017), a fully Bayesian criterion that balances between goodness-of-fit and complexity of a model: lower values of WAIC indicate a better fit.

2.3. Simulation studies

In this section, we show the results of two simulation studies. The first one aims at comparing the fitting abilities of the considered models under two data-generating mechanisms, whereas the second one deals with a higher percentage of zeroes than the one assumed by the model.

2.3.1. Fitting study

In the first scenario (i), we consider $B = 500$ replications of a sample of size $N=150$ generated under the FDMReg model with $D = 3$ and considering a continuous covariate x uniformly distributed on the (-0.5, 0.5) interval. The number of trials for each unit has been drawn from a Poisson distribution with mean 50. The goal of this simulation study is twofold. Indeed, even if the FDMReg model is naturally favored in a fitting comparison, we can draw some conclusions both on the reliability of the estimation procedure and on the performance of simpler models when the true data-generating mechanism is a non-standard one (i.e. the FDMReg model). In Table 2.1, we can see the true value for all the parameters, the Monte Carlo (MC) approximation for the expectation of the Bayesian estimators (chosen as the posterior mean) and the coverage levels of the simulated 95% credible sets (CSs) for the three considered regression models. It is easy to see that, even if the DMReg leads to a coverage level for β_{11} and β_{12} (i.e. the two regression coefficients associated with the covariate) close to the nominal level, it slightly overestimates these important parameters. More interestingly, it completely underestimates the precision parameter α^+. Conversely, the FDMReg model is able to provide good estimates for all the parameters, and the coverage level of the CSs is very close to the 95% nominal one. The mean of the WAIC over 500 replications confirms that the DMReg model fits the simulated data better than the MultReg, thanks to its additional parameter. Nonetheless, the FDMReg is (not surprisingly) the best model.

	MultReg	DMReg	FDMReg
$\beta_{01}=-1$	-1.015 (0.382)	-1.144 (0.784)	-1.003 (0.948)
$\beta_{11}=1.5$	1.549 (0.498)	1.756 (0.940)	1.520 (0.942)
$\beta_{02}=0.5$	0.498 (0.532)	0.314 (0.362)	0.501 (0.962)
$\beta_{12}=-3$	-3.035 (0.480)	-2.733 (0.910)	-3.023 (0.958)
$\alpha^+=50$	(—)	3.838 (0.000)	63.771 (0.936)
$\tilde{w}=0.8$	(—)	(—)	0.799 (0.962)
$p_1=0.25$	(—)	(—)	0.248 (0.940)
$p_2=0.4$	(—)	(—)	0.405 (0.968)
$p_3=0.35$	(—)	(—)	0.347 (0.970)
WAIC	4484.931	1869.356	1614.353

Table 2.1. *Scenario (i): MC approximation of the expectation of the estimators (posterior mean) and coverage level of the simulated 95% CSs (in parentheses)*

The second scenario we considered (scenario (ii)) generates data according to a DMReg model, considering the same covariate x as in scenario (i). In this scenario, the FDMReg model has a number of parameters that may be excessive compared to the data generation mechanism. From Table 2.2, we can see that the FDMReg is a valid competitor of the DMReg, as it produces reliable estimates and CSs, leading to a WAIC that is almost identical.

Lastly, we can look at the regression curves under the three considered models (Figure 2.1). Even if the three black curves, referring to the μ parameter under different models, are close to each other, the FDMReg allows for three component-specific regression curves associated with the λ's to better grasp all the points. Please note that in each panel, all the λ's are overlapped except one, which is the highest in that particular panel. This is due to the relationship between the generic λ_j and μ expressed in equation [2.6].

	MultReg	DMReg	FDMReg
β_{01}=-1	-1.005 (0.596)	-1.006 (0.950)	-1.000 (0.948)
β_{11}= 1.5	1.502 (0.636)	1.500 (0.958)	1.488 (0.954)
β_{02}=0.5	0.503 (0.586)	0.503 (0.946)	0.505 (0.944)
β_{12}=-3	-3.023 (0.596)	-3.023 (0.950)	-3.024 (0.948)
α^+=10	(—)	10.178 (0.936)	10.489 (0.954)
$\tilde{w}$	(—)	(—)	0.243 (—)
p_1	(—)	(—)	0.362 (—)
p_2	(—)	(—)	0.313 (—)
p_3	(—)	(—)	0.325 (—)
WAIC	2634.853	1809.927	1810.370

Table 2.2. *Scenario (ii): MC approximation of the expectation of the estimators (posterior mean) and coverage level of the simulated 95% CSs (in parentheses)*

2.3.2. *Excess of zeroes*

In the second simulation study, we consider an important problem that often affects discrete data: excess of zeroes (Tang and Chen 2019). In particular, we generate $B = 500$ datasets from a MultReg model with $D = 3$, considering the same β_1 and β_2 as in the first simulation study and a precision parameter $\alpha^+ = 10$. Then, we randomly selected 5% (scenario (a)) or 10% (scenario (b)) of the data points and artificially modified them to obtain a vector with two out of three null elements. More formally, let us say that we must modify the i-th response vector $\mathbf{y}_i = (y_{i1}, y_{i2}, y_{i3})^\mathsf{T}$. Then, $\mathbf{y}_i^{\text{New}} = (0, 0, n_i)^\mathsf{T}$, where $n_i = y_{i1} + y_{i2} + y_{i3}$ is the number of trials for observation i.

Looking at the mean of the WAICs in Figure 2.2, we can see that increasing the percentage of responses affected by the excess of zero problem, both the MultReg and the DMReg perform worse. Interestingly, and contrarily to its competitors, the FDMReg shows a better fit when the proportion of zeroes increases. This is explained by the fact that λ_3 is devoted to modeling the group of modified observations (the mean of the estimates of p_3 over 500 replications resulting in 0.066 and 0.102 in scenarios (a) and (b), respectively).

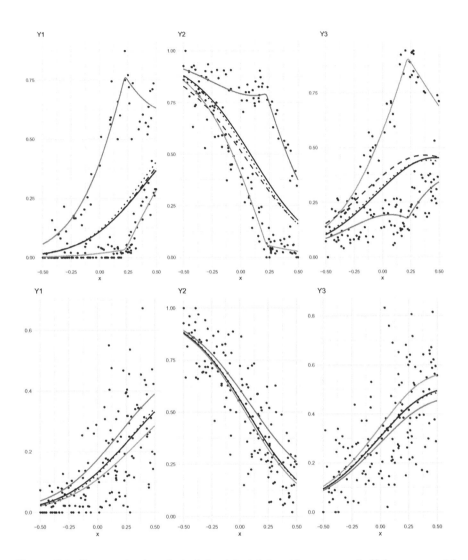

Figure 2.1. *One randomly selected simulated dataset from scenario (i) (upper panels) and scenario (ii) (lower panels). Additional curves represent the overall regression μ under the MultReg (black dotted), the DMReg (black dashed) and the FDMReg (black solid) models and the component-specific regression curves λ₁ (green), λ₂ (orange) and λ₃ (blue)*

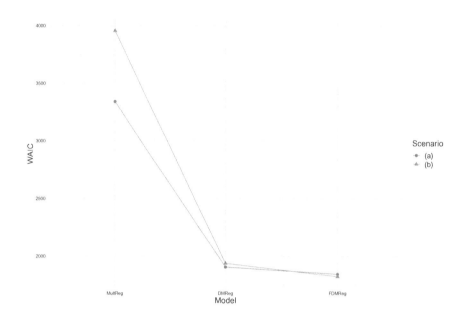

Figure 2.2. *Mean of the WAIC by model and scenario*

2.4. Application to real electoral data

On March 4, 2018, elections took place in Italy for the two Chambers of the Parliament. Approximately 73% of the Italian adult citizens entitled to vote took part in these elections, in which they were summoned to vote for the preferred candidate among more than 17 parties. The dataset summarizing the electoral results can be found in the `FlexReg` package (Di Brisco et al. 2022) available in the R environment. We collected the distribution of votes for 231 Italian electoral districts and computed a four-part composition regarding the number of votes received by the "Partito Democratico" (PD, Democratic Party), "Lega" (League), "Movimento 5 Stelle" (M5S, 5 Stars Movement) and by any other party (including blank votes). Thus, our response is

$$\mathbf{Y}_i = (\text{PD, Lega, M5S, Other parties})_i^\mathsf{T}, \qquad i = 1, \dots, 231,$$

where each marginal represents the number of votes received by that party. To better illustrate the results of the analysis, we considered just a single continuous covariate, the age index (AI), which is defined as

$$\text{AI} = \frac{\text{Number of} > 64 \text{ y.o. people}}{\text{Number of} < 14 \text{ y.o. people}}.$$

	MultReg	DMReg	FDMReg
β_{01}	-1.262 (-1.266, -1.258)	-1.243 (-1.532, -0.953)	-1.267 (-1.478, -1.051)
β_{11}	0.480 (0.478, 0.483)	0.469 (0.294, 0.651)	0.472 (0.344, 0.599)
β_{02}	-1.074 (-1.078, -1.069)	-1.654 (-1.952, -1.351)	-1.676 (-1.926, -1.426)
β_{12}	0.313 (0.310, 0.315)	0.578 (0.391, 0.762)	0.574 (0.428, 0.717)
β_{03}	0.622 (0.618, 0.625)	0.488 (0.234, 0.748)	0.746 (0.560, 0.926)
β_{13}	-0.382 (-0.385, -0.380)	-0.320 (-0.487, -0.154)	-0.443 (-0.560, -0.321)
α^{+}	—	25.316 (22.841, 28.039)	47.691 (41.864, 54.107)
$\tilde{w}$	—	—	0.397 (0.362, 0.433)
p_1	—	—	0.022 (0.001, 0.058)
p_2	—	—	0.186 (0.157, 0.218)
p_3	—	—	0.763 (0.717, 0.805)
p_4	—	—	0.029 (0.009, 0.059)
WAIC	3712955.4	14739.0	14473.8

Table 2.3. *Election data. Posterior mean and 95% CS for the parameters of the three regression models*

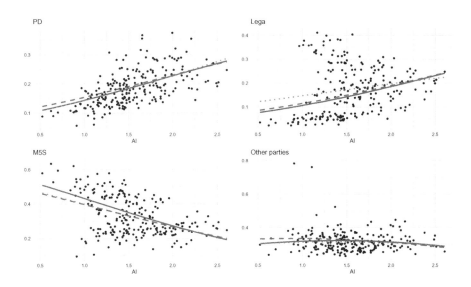

Figure 2.3. *Election data. Additional curves represent the overall regression μ under the MultReg (blue dotted), the DMReg (green dashed) and the FDMReg (orange solid) models*

From Table 2.3, it is possible to observe that the regression coefficients are all significantly different from 0 (i.e. the CSs do not contain the value 0) and their estimates are similar across models. Consequently, the regression curves are also similar to each other (Figure 2.3). The FDMReg model captures four latent groups, the first and the fourth being very small (mixing weights equal to 0.022 and 0.029, respectively). These groups are devoted to modeling a small group of electoral districts characterized by a high proportion of votes received by the PD (top-left panel of Figure 2.4) and the electoral districts that prefer other parties (bottom-right panel). More specifically, these districts belong to the "*Provincia autonoma di Bolzano*", which is a very special part of the north of Italy in terms of the political/governmental point of view. The WAIC points to the FDMReg model as the best one. It is interesting to note that the MultReg model results in a WAIC which is much greater than its competitor. This is due to several aspects such as: (i) the poor parameterization of the covariance matrix adopted by this model; (ii) the high number of statistical units; and (iii) the multivariate discrete nature of the response vectors.

If we color each electoral district in the scatterplots according to its location (i.e. a categorical variable "Zone" assuming categories "North", "Center", "South" or "Islands"), we can also characterize the second and third groups. Indeed, λ_2 models the northern districts, whereas λ_3 is devoted to modeling the districts in the south and the islands of Italy. Please note that this interesting and noteworthy result has been obtained without considering the "Zone" variable in the analysis.

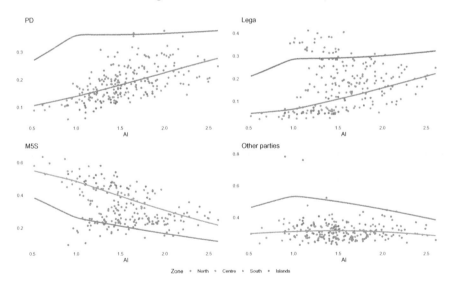

Figure 2.4. *Election data. Each district has been colored according to its geographical location in Italy. Additional curves represent the component-specific regression curves λ_1 (green), λ_2 (orange), λ_3 (blue) and λ_4 (purple)*

2.5. References

Ascari, R. and Migliorati, S. (2021). A new regression model for overdispersed binomial data accounting for outliers and an excess of zeros. *Statistics in Medicine*, 1–20.

Di Brisco, A.M., Ascari, R., Migliorati, S., Ongaro, A. (2022). Package Flexreg: Regression models for bounded responses [Online]. Available at: https://cran.r-project. org/web/packages/FlexReg/FlexReg.pdf.

McCullagh, P. and Nelder, J.A. (1989). *Generalized Linear Models*. Chapman & Hall, London.

Migliorati, S., Ongaro, A., Monti, G.S. (2017). A structured Dirichlet mixture model for compositional data: Inferential and applicative issues. *Statistics and Computing*, 27, 963–983.

Neal, R.M. (1994). An improved acceptance procedure for the hybrid Monte Carlo algorithm. *Journal of Computational Physics*, 111(1), 194–203.

Ongaro, A. and Migliorati, S. (2013). A generalization of the Dirichlet distribution. *Journal of Multivariate Analysis*, 114, 412–426.

Stan Development Team (2017). Stan modeling language users guide and reference manual [Online]. Available at: https://mc-stan.org/users/documentation/.

Tang, Z.-Z. and Chen, G. (2019). Zero-inflated generalized Dirichlet multinomial regression model for microbiome compositional data analysis. *Biostatistics*, 20(4), 698–713.

Vehtari, A., Gelman, A., Gabry, J. (2017). Practical Bayesian model evaluation using leave-one-out cross-validation and WAIC. *Statistics and Computing*, 27(5), 1413–1432.

Watanabe, S. (2013). A widely applicable Bayesian information criterion. *Journal of Machine Learning Research*, 14(1), 867–897.

Intergenerational Class Mobility in Greece with Evidence from EU-SILC

In the present chapter, the degrees of intergenerational social mobility in Greece are investigated, in order to provide up-to-date evidence on the changes in the mobility patterns for both men and women aged between 30 and 60 years. The main purpose is to examine the relationship between the socio-economic status of parents and their children and the evolution of the mobility patterns between different birth cohorts. For the analysis, we use data drawn from the EU-SILC, and the European Socio-economic Classification (ESeC) to measure the mobility between the social class of origin and destination. Applying the Markov system theory, and a wide range of measures and models, this work focuses on the magnitude and the direction of the movements that are taking place in the Greek labor market, as well as the level of social fluidity. Three-way Markov mobility matrices are presented, where the transition probabilities between the classes of origins and destination are calculated for different cohorts. A wide range of absolute and relative mobility rates, as well as distance measures are also estimated.

3.1. Introduction

Intergenerational mobility concerns the transitions that take place in a social system from one generation to another. It has traditionally been used as a proxy for the measurement of social inequalities and social justice and also as an indicator for the "openness" of the society. The weaker the linkage between parents and their children in their social outcome, the more mobile and "open" the society is (Breen 2004). From that point of view, the international research has focused on the study of intergenerational mobility in recent decades, intending to answer if there is

Chapter written by Glykeria STAMATOPOULOU, Maria SYMEONAKI and Catherine MICHALOPOULOU.

a convergence or divergence in the distributions of origins and destination and how mobility patterns have changed over time.

The interest in a systematic theoretical and empirical study of intergenerational mobility emerged mainly after World War II, when the antifascist governments of the Western world turned to a restructure of capitalism under the threat of social revolution and economic instability. The Keynesian model set the well-being of all citizens as one of the primary goals and governments committed to promoting full employment, increased wages, better living conditions and social security. The policymakers focused on the social inequalities that are inherited from one generation to another and tried to eliminate them through fiscal, monetary and redistributed policies (Themelis 2013). In this context, the first postwar empirical studies show that although the rates of social mobility have increased in the Western countries and upward movements predominate over the downward mobility as a result of the industrialism and the economic growth (Blau and Duncan 1967), the patterns of relative mobility and social fluidity have not changed and inequalities between social classes have remained stable over time (Lipset and Zetterberg 1959; Erikson and Goldthorpe 1992). Thus, individuals from disadvantaged backgrounds continue to have more chances of "getting stuck" in lower occupational positions, attaining lower levels of education and having lower incomes.

The most recent comparative research has come to the same conclusion, as in most OECD countries upward movements are detected, in absolute terms, but the relative rates remain the same (OECD 2018). In Europe, cross-country variations in the absolute rates capture different structural changes between countries, while the levels of relative class mobility seem to converge across the European continent (Bukodi et al. 2017; Eurofound 2017). Recent developments in the area have indicated the formation of new mobility indices, as is the case of the positive labor market mobility index suggested in Symeonaki and Stamatopoulou (2020). As far as Greece is concerned, systematic research on intergenerational social mobility is quite limited (Lambiri-Dimaki 1983; Kasimati 1990/1998; Papatheodorou and Piachaud 1998; Daouli et al. 2010; Themelis 2013; Symeonaki and Stamatopoulou 2014a, 2014b; Maloutas 2016; Symeonaki et al. 2016; Papanastasiou 2018).

The present chapter examines the trends in social mobility in Greece, providing updated evidence on the association between parental and individuals' social class, defined here in terms of occupation. The main purpose is to examine how similar or dissimilar the distributions of classes of origins and destination are and to what extent social status passes from parents to children. Moreover, we are interested in how the mobility trends have changed over time. Therefore, three birth cohorts (1959–1969, 1970–1979 and 1980–1989) are distinguished and a synchronic cohort analysis is applied.

3.2. Data and methods

In the present analysis, data is drawn from the 2019 European Survey on Income and Living Conditions (EU-SILC). It is a set of cross-national sample surveys that has replaced the European Community Household Panel (ECHP) since 2003. In Greece, the survey is implemented on an annual basis by the Hellenic Statistical Authority (EL.STAT.), providing detailed data on living conditions, income, occupation and the labor market and aims to compile structural indicators of social cohesion, such as at-risk-poverty rates, social exclusion rates or inequality of income distributions. The EU-SILC 2019 is the latest dataset that includes adequate information on both parental and individuals' social characteristics in Greece in its ad-hoc module on "Intergenerational Transmission of Poverty", even if they do not share the same household. The final sample size of the database was 22,739 households, i.e. 34,836 individuals, aged above 16 years old.

The social class scheme that we use in the analysis is defined by the occupational status and the employment relations. Because of the amount of missing values for the maternal occupational characteristics, we focus only on the father's social class. The variables of the occupation, the employment status, the supervision status and the size of the enterprise are used for the construction of the class scheme. Thus, both fathers and respondents are allocated into nine categories according to the European Socioeconomic Categories (ESeC) schema, as follows[1]:

Class 1	Large employers, higher-grade professional, administrative and managerial occupations: "the higher salariat"
Class 2	Lower-grade professional, administrative and managerial occupations: higher-grade technician and supervisory occupations: "the lower salariat"
Class 3	Intermediate occupations: "higher-grade white collar workers"
Classes 4 and 5	Small employers and self-employed in non-professional occupations: "petit-bourgeoisie or independents" in non-agriculture and in agriculture sector
Class 6	Lower supervisory and lower technician occupations: "higher-grade blue collar workers"
Class 7	Lower services, sales and clerical occupations: "lower-grade white collar workers"

1 The SPSS script of Rose and Harisson (see https://www.iser.essex.ac.uk/archives/esec/matrices-and-syntax) is used for the construction of ESeC and the script of Ganzeboom and Treiman (Harry and Treiman) for the conversion of ISCO-08 into ISCO-88, as it is required for the class schema.

Class 8   Lower technical occupations: "skilled workers"

Class 9   Routine occupations: "semi- and unskilled workers"

Because of an inadequate sample size, we combined classes 3 and 6 under the label "intermediate employee". Respondents that have never worked in the past are not included in the analysis, while those who declare that they were not working at the time of the survey (such as unemployed, pensioners, etc.) are classified according to their last occupation. People aged under 30 years are excluded from the analysis, as it is assumed that they have not yet acquired occupational maturity (Bukodi et al. 2017). As the EU-SILC provides only the major occupational groups of ISCO (1-digit ISCO-08) for the parents, we code the parental occupation into three-digit ISCO-08, as it is required for the construction of the ESeC classification.

Using Markov system theory, three-way mobility matrices of origin×destination×cohort are constructed that includes the outflow percentages for each cohort, defined as f_{ij}/f_{i+} and give the conditional distribution of destination (j) for each origin (i) (Erikson and Goldthorpe 1992). The elements off the main diagonal of the matrices represent the transition probabilities, p_{ij}, that relate to the probability of moving to state j at time t under the condition that the individual was at state i at time $t\text{-}1$. In the case under study, i and j belong to the set of social classes, $S = \{1, 2, \ldots, n\}$, while the probabilities of individuals being immobile, p_{ii}, are located on the main diagonal.

A range of measures are computed, shedding light on different aspects of the relationship between classes of origins and destination (see also Symeonaki and Stamatopoulou 2014a, 2014b; Stamatopoulou et al. 2016; Symeonaki et al. 2016; Symeonaki and Filopoulou 2017). In this regard, the distance measures (Cowell 1985; Fields and Ok 1999) can be used as an indicator of the degree of the structural mobility, as their values show differences in the marginal distributions between classes of origin and destination, reflecting the changes in the structure of a society from one generation to another. More specifically, the most widely known distance, the Euclidean distance between the vectors p_i and p_j is the length of the line segment that connects the two points, and it is given by equation [3.1]:

$$d_{Euc} = \sqrt{\sum_{i=1}^{d} |p_i - p_j|^2} \qquad \text{Euclidean distance} \qquad [3.1]$$

The Manhattan distance, in equation [3.2], is calculated as the sum of the absolute difference between the two distributions, in order to show the total variation of classes of origins and destination.

$$d_{Man} = \sum_{i=1}^{d} |p_i - p_j| \qquad \text{Manhattan distance} \qquad [3.2]$$

The Sorensen index, or Sorensen's similarity coefficient, also measures the distance between the two distributions and is equal to the Manhattan distance divided by 2, which is given in equation [3.3].

$$d_{Sor} = \frac{\sum_{i=1}^{d} |p_i - p_j|}{\sum_{i=1}^{d} |p_i + p_j|} = \frac{\sum_{i=1}^{d} |p_i - p_j|}{2} \qquad \text{Sorensen distance} \qquad [3.3]$$

Finally, the Chebyshev distance is given by equation [3.4], and it represents the maximum proportional variation of the occupational distribution between parents and individuals.

$$d_{Cheb} = \max_{i} |p_i - p_j| \qquad \text{Chebyshev distance} \qquad [3.4]$$

In general, higher values of these measures indicate greater distances between classes of origins and destination, and thus greater levels of structural mobility.

In addition, absolute mobility indices are estimated to provide the degrees of the observed mobility, as well as the direction of the movements (Bibby 1975; Papadakis 1993; Goldthorpe and Jackson 2007). In particular, the total mobility rate (equation [3.5]) is a measure of the observed transitions in the society and represents the sum of the elements that are located off the main diagonal of a mobility table N ($tr\mathbf{N}$). The index takes values between 0 and 1, with higher rates indicating greater mobility.

$$TM = \frac{1}{N} \sum_{i \neq j} n_{ij} = 1 - \frac{1}{N} tr\mathbf{N} \qquad \text{Total Mobility} \qquad [3.5]$$

Focus on the direction of the flows, the upward and downward mobility indices are calculated as the sum of the elements n_{ij} below (equation [3.6]) or above (equation [3.7]) the main diagonal ($tr\mathbf{N}$). Both indices refer to hierarchical systems where a change in the social position can be advantageous or disadvantageous. Since the class schema is not fully hierarchical in our case, the transitions that represent no change in the social hierarchy are not taken into consideration for the computation of these indices. The sum of the values of both upward and downward mobility thus implies the total vertical mobility in the social system.

$$UM = \frac{1}{N} \sum_{j>i} n_{ij}, \ \forall i \notin \{3,4,5,6\} \ AND \ \forall j$$
$$\notin \{3,4,5,6\}$$

Upward Mobility   [3.6]

$$DM = \frac{1}{N} \sum_{j<i} n_{ij}, \forall i \notin \{3,4,5,6\} \ AND \ \forall j$$
$$\notin \{3,4,5,6\}$$

Downward Mobility   [3.7]

In the same context, the horizontal mobility index refers to the sum of those elements that represent transitions between social classes that are in the same level in the hierarchical scale and it is defined by equation [3.8].

$$HM = \frac{1}{N} \sum_{i \neq j} n_{ij}, \ \forall i \in \{3, 4,5,6\} \ AND \ \forall j \in \{3,4,5,6\}$$ Horizontal Mobility   [3.8]

Except for the direction of the movements, mobility can be distinguished between the structural and the pure/exchange mobility (Boudon 1973). In this context, the Yasuda index (1964) gives the total observed structural mobility, focusing on the marginal distributions of classes of origins and destination. It is obvious (equation [3.9]) that the index is the ratio of the sum of the "pure real mobility" to the sum of "pure perfect mobility" (Naoi and Slomczynski 1986). The index is equal to zero when there is no pure mobility in the social system and therefore any observed mobility is entirely due to structural factors. On the other hand, its maximum value indicates that classes of origins and destination are independent and therefore there is perfect pure mobility.

$$M_Y = \frac{\min(n_{i.}, n_{.i}) - n_{ii}}{\min(n_{i.}, n_{.i}) - n_{i.}n_{.i}/N}$$ Yasuda Index   [3.9]

The relative mobility rates are also delivered, which quantify social fluidity, i.e. the chances of individuals to move to a different social position than that of their parents (Eurofound 2017; Harry and Treiman). In particular, we calculate three relative mobility indices. The Bartholomew index (1982) is given by equation [3.10] and refers to the transitions that take place in the social system, by weighting the distance that the individuals cover to move from the state of their parents i to their own state j. In other words, the index summarizes how far the individuals move from the main diagonal of a transition probability matrix P. Thus, the long-range distances between classes of origins and destination give greater weight to the movements and result in higher values of the index, while zero indicates that no movement is observed in the system.

$$M(\mathbf{B}) = \frac{1}{k}(\sum_{j=1}\sum_{j=1} p_{ij}|i - j|)$$ Bartholomew Index   [3.10]

The Prais–Shorrocks index (Shorrocks 1978; Prais 1955) is defined by equation [3.11], where $tr(\mathbf{P})$ is again the sum of the main diagonal of the matrix P and n is the number of states, which is equal to 8 in our case. The index takes values in the interval [0,1]. By M(**PS**) = 0, it is implied that every member in the system remains in the same state as their parents (perfect immobility), and M(**PS**) = 1 implies a system where everybody moves upwards or downwards (perfect mobility). Additionally, the immobility index (equation [3.12]) is also calculated and reveals the rate of the persistence of individuals in the social state of their parents.

$$M(\mathbf{PS}) = \left(\frac{1}{n-1}\right)(n - tr(\mathbf{P}))$$ Prais–Shorrocks Index   [3.11]

$$IM = \left(\frac{tr(\mathbf{P})}{n}\right)$$ Immobility index   [3.12]

Finally, the odds ratios are provided giving estimates for the level of social fluidity in Greece, without them being affected by the marginal distributions and structural effects. This is true as they focus on the relative chances of individuals of different class origins moving to a given class destination, avoiding another destination. If all odds ratios in a matrix are equal to 1, then the system is perfectly mobile. Equation [3.13] is used to estimate the necessary odds ratios (Cowell 1985; Breen 2004):

$$\theta_{ij} = \frac{f_{ij}/f_{i(j+1)}}{f_{(i+1)j}/f_{(i+1)(j+1)}}$$ [3.13]

3.3. The trends of class mobility between different birth cohorts

In Figure 3.1, the marginal distributions of the social class of the respondents are outlined, given the upgrading of the occupations through birth cohorts. In general, differences are detected in the social structure of Greece. More specifically, a constant decline in the proportion of the farmers (ESeC 5) is obvious, as the farming sector seems to decline by 6% from the oldest (1959–1969) to the youngest birth cohort (1980–1989). Similarly, the downward trend is also notable in class 4 of ESeC and the percentages of small employers and self-employed decrease from 14.2% to 8.7%. This depopulation of the "petit-bourgeoisie" is counterbalanced by a gradual increase in "the higher salariat" (ESeC 1). At the same time, a significant raise is also evident for the non-manual working class (ESeC 7) and also for the unskilled manual workers (ESeC 9) for those born between the years 1980 and 1989.

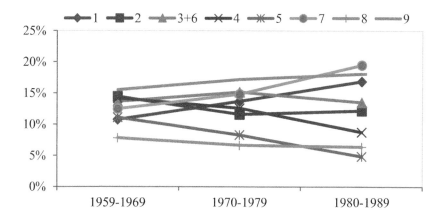

Figure 3.1. *Occupational upgrading in Greece by cohorts. For a color version of this figure, see www.iste.co.uk/zafeiris/data2.zip*

The next step in the analysis is to examine the relationship between class of origins and destination, in order to shed light on whether or not the social class is "transferred" across generations. First, the computed distance measures are presented in Table 3.1, given the percentage differences between class of origins and destination for all birth cohorts. It can easily be observed that greater distances are displayed in the distributions of fathers and individuals from the older birth cohort, while a downward trend of all indices is detected. In particular, the values of the Chebyshev index, which takes into account only the highest distance, also decrease for the case of "independents" in the farming sector (ESeC 5), meaning that the distributions of respondents and their parents present a smaller distance for younger cohorts.

	1959–1969	**1970–1979**	**1980–1989**
d_{EUC}	0.345	0.301	0.283
d_{MAN}	0.791	0.717	0.648
d_{SOR}	0.396	0.358	0.324
d_{CHEB}	0.268	0.187	0.184

Table 3.1. *Distance measures between class of origins and class of destination, by birth cohorts. Source: EU-SILC 2019, weighted data for Greece*

In Figure 3.2, the proportional dissimilarities between the distributions of origins and destination are presented for each social class separately. The index takes positive values, when the participation rates are higher in the case of the respondents (D), while the negative values indicate that the parents show higher proportions. The index equals zero, when the distributions are similar. At first glance, fathers are outnumbered only in classes 5 and 7. The larger percentage difference is detected in the oldest cohort of the farming sector (EseC 5), and it is equal to 26.8%, with 13.2% of the people of this cohort being farmers, compared to 41.9% of their fathers, while the distance between the two distributions seems to decrease significantly, reaching 13.9% for the cohort 1980–1989. The self-employed and own account workers (ESeC 4) and the "lower-grade salariat" (EseC 1) also contribute to the declining trends of the distance measures. On the contrary, the relationship of origin and destination in the manual skilled occupations (ESeC 8) and the lower services, sales and clerical occupations (ESeC 7) seems to become stronger in the two younger cohorts.

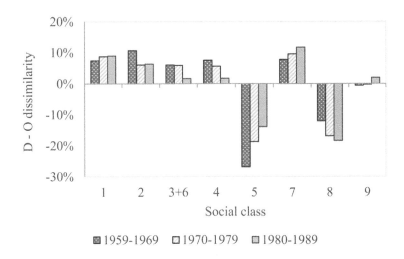

Figure 3.2. *Proportional dissimilarities between classes of origins (O) and destination (D), by birth cohorts. For a color version of this figure, see www.iste.co.uk/zafeiris/data2.zip*

The differences in the fathers' and respondents' distributions are also reflected in the outflow percentages of Table 3.3, which reflect the transition probabilities of the cohort 1959–1969 (upper cells) and the cohort 1980–1989 (lower cells). Concerning the main diagonal of the transition matrix, it is obvious that the "lower-grade salariat" (ESeC 2) exhibits the greater decrease in the immobility percentages, with 23.4% of younger respondents having higher probabilities of following their fathers' footsteps, against 29.1% of those who belong to the older cohort. A significant increase in the probabilities of the younger cohort remaining in their fathers' class is also notable for "independent" farmers (ESeC 5), which seems to reflect differences in the horizontal marginal distributions of Table 3.3. Indeed, it is evident that 40% (2032 in absolute number) of those who belong to the older cohort are occupied in the farming sector, in contrast to one-fifth of the 1980–1989 cohort (529 in absolute number). Nonetheless, from those who do move, the older respondents are more likely to make horizontal movements towards the class of small employers and self-employed ($p_{54} = 0.153$), while the younger cohort has a 0.111 probability of moving upward to the higher-grade "salariat". Finally, the differences between cohorts observed in those who come from manual households are also noteworthy. Along with the greater immobility rates of the younger cohort in the manual occupations, it seems that this cohort shows close movements towards the class of lower-grade "white collar working class" ($p_{97} = 0.225$, $p_{87} = 0.227$).

Origins	Destination								Total
	1	2	3+6	4	5	7	8	9	N
1	**45.2**	21.5	11.0	5.7	0.5	8.0	1.1	6.9	146
	46.5	18.2	13.8	0.7	0.4	11.3	2.0	7.1	171
2	19.5	**36.0**	15.3	4.8	0.2	13.9	2.7	7.7	183
	24.0	**23.4**	28.2	4.9	0.3	13.9	1.6	3.8	144
3+6	21.2	22.5	**18.3**	10.2	2.2	15.0	4.2	6.2	372
	28.5	17.0	**19.1**	4.6	0.9	16.3	2.6	11.1	328
4	14.9	16.4	16.5	**24.7**	0.8	15.7	5.7	5.2	337
	15.8	13.2	13.1	**20.3**	1.7	18.0	4.1	13.8	185
5	4.8	9.8	9.1	15.3	**27.2**	9.6	7.1	17.0	2,032
	11.1	6.4	9.7	8.0	**21.6**	17.2	6.7	19.4	529
7	16.6	17.3	16.9	10.2	4.7	**21.4**	5.6	7.3	246
	23.4	13.4	16.5	7.8	0.6	**21.1**	4.7	12.6	186
8	10.8	14.8	14.1	15.6	3.6	13.1	**11.9**	16.0	918
	8.2	10.9	13.1	10.7	2.9	22.7	**10.7**	20.7	709
9	7.5	11.9	16.7	13.4	4.5	12.6	10.0	**23.4**	723
	9.8	7.6	8.9	10.4	2.9	22.5	8.8	**29.1**	429
N	492	708	600	773	693	563	357	771	4957
	391	303	356	260	179	503	178	511	2,681

Table 3.2. *Transition mobility rates: outflow percentages and marginal distributions by cohort (1959–1969: upper cells; 1980–1989: lower cells). Source: EU-SILC 2019, weighted data for Greece*

In order to have a complete picture of the changes in the mobility patterns between individuals of different birth cohorts, we now proceed with the presentation of the absolute and relative mobility indices. In Table 3.3, the total mobility rate takes high values, indicating that over 75% of the respondents are differentiated from their fathers' class, regardless of the birth cohort they belong to. At the same time, the Yasuda index (Naoi and Slomczynski 1986) is also high and seems to increase significantly from the older to the younger birth cohort, capturing differences in the marginal distributions and reflecting the impact of the structural changes on the absolute mobility.

The same pattern is also prominent in the vertical rates, as the younger cohort shows 4% higher upward and downward movements, when compared to the older one. Concerning horizontal mobility, there is a gradual decrease of 6.5% across cohorts and younger individuals record only 4.7% who stay in same level as their family environment. Unlike the absolute rates, the relative mobility seems to remain almost constant across cohorts, as it is assumed by the theory of social reproduction, with the Prais–Shorrocks index slightly increasing only by two percentage points. The values of Bartholomew index show no particular change (Figure 3.3).

	1959–1969 (a)	1980–1989 (b)	Difference (b-a)
Total mobility (*TM*)	76.6	78.2	+1.6
Yasuda index (M_Y)	77.1	82	+4.9
Upward mobility (*UM*)	41.6	45.7	+4.1
Downward mobility (*DM*)	23.9	27.8	+3.9
Horizontal mobility (*HM*)	11.2	4.7	-6.5
Upward/downward (UM/DM)	1.7	1.6	-0.1
Immobility	26.0	24.0	-2
M(PS)	84.6	86.9	+2.3
M(B)	2.06	2.06	.

Table 3.3. *Absolute and relative mobility rates between the oldest and the youngest cohort. Source: EU-SILC 2019, weighted data for Greece*

The symmetrical odds ratios are also reported in Table 3.4 for the older and younger birth cohorts. It is worth noting that the higher values in odds ratios are detected in classes 1 and 2, i.e. the "salariat", where discrepancies are present between individuals from different origins. In particular, the odds of being in class 1 or 2 are significantly greater for the individuals coming from the same class than for those whose origins are farmers (ESeC 5). At the same time, individuals coming from the manual working class have fewer chances of ending up in the upper classes than those from most advantaged families. On the other hand, the odds ratios tend to be close to 1 between individuals in the upper classes (ESeC 1–3) or between those who come from the working class (ESeC 7–9), reflecting the immobility or short-range mobility in these classes as observed in the mobility matrices. Finally, in general, a downward trend of the odds ratios is apparent from the older to the younger birth cohort, even though there are some exceptions. Most noteworthy, the odds ratios increase from 13.1 to 80.7 between cohorts for those who originate in Class 4 (self-employed workers) and move to Class 1 of the "salariat", while a significant increase is also clear in the odds ratios for those coming from the working class and moving to Class 2

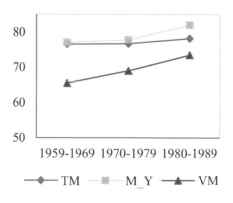

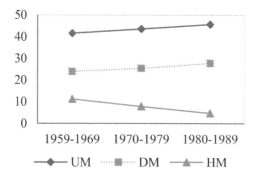

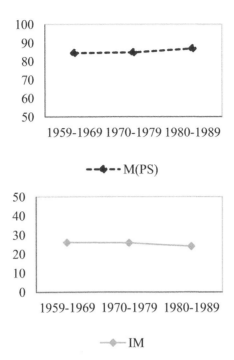

Figure 3.3. *Evolution of absolute and relative mobility indices through birth cohorts. For a color version of this figure, see www.iste.co.uk/zafeiris/data2.zip*

Class	2	3+6	4	5	7	8	9
1	3.9	3.6	13.1	493.5	7.2	46.5	20.3
	2.5	2.3	80.7	215.5	3.7	30.8	19.3
2			1.9	11.3	568.0	3.2	10.9	9.2
			0.9	7.4	299.1	2.7	14.8	24.0
3+6			2.7	24.4	1.9	3.7	4.1
			6.5	47.7	1.6	6.1	5.6
4				55.2	3.3	3.3	8.3
				33.4	3.1	5.0	4.1
5					12.8	12.6	8.3
					46.2	12.0	11.1
7						3.5	5.5
						2.1	2.2
8							1.7
							1.7

Table 3.4. *Symmetrical odds ratios by cohort (1959–1969: upper cells; 1980–1989: lower cells). Source: EU-SILC 2019, weighted data for Greece*

3.4. Conclusion

In this work, the latest data of 2019 EU-SILC and its ad hoc module of "Intergenerational Transmission of Poverty" are used, and a range of well-established mobility rates are calculated, in order to give an up-to-date picture of the transitions that have occurred in Greek society over recent decades. The concept of distance is also used to shed light on how dissimilar the distributions of origins and destination are between different birth cohorts. The results show that a downward trend of all distance measures is detected between cohorts, meaning that the distributions of respondents and their parents exhibit smaller dissimilarities between the parents and the younger cohorts (1980–1989). This trend mainly reflects the changes that occur in the social and occupational morphology of Greece during the period 1960–1980. In particular, the significant reduction of the employment rates in the agricultural sector, as well as the higher participation rates in the sectors of industry, tourism and trade are captured in the distributions of the older birth cohorts, compared to their parents.

On the contrary, the absolute mobility rates show variation in mobility patterns between cohorts, with those born between 1959 and 1969 being the most immobile, with less upward, downward or horizontal movements. Indeed, it has already been proved empirically that the changes in the structure of the division of labor, as well as the democratization of education have resulted in the expansion of the higher education and the upgrading of the occupations. In this regard, an increase of the movements into higher employment status and social classes makes sense. However, both the Bartholomew and Prais–Shorrocks indices show no change, meaning that the relative chances of individuals changing their social status compared with their parents remain stable over time.

Finally, the outcomes from the odds ratios reveal that discrepancies can be found for the salariat between individuals from different origins, while the odds ratios tend to be close to 1 between individuals inside the upper classes or between those from the working class. The social reproduction in the classes of large employers, professionals and administrative and managerial occupations on the one hand, and the working class on the other hand is also evident in other national studies, such as in Kasimati (1990/1998). Between cohorts, a downward trend of odds ratios is apparent in general from the older to the younger birth cohort, although exceptions are notable.

3.5. References

Bartholomew, D.J. (1982). *Stochastic Models for Social Processes*. Wiley, London.

Bibby, J. (1975). Methods of measuring mobility. *Quality & Quantity: International Journal of Methodology*, 9(2), 107–136.

Blau, P.M. and Duncan, O.D. (1967). *The American Occupational Structure*. John Wiley & Sons Inc, Hoboken.

Boudon, R. (1973). *Mathematical Structures of Social Mobility*. Elsevier, Amsterdam.

Breen, R. (2004). *Social Mobility in Europe*. Oxford University Press, Oxford.

Bukodi, E., Paskov, M., Nolan, B. (2017). Intergenerational class mobility in Europe: A new account and an old story. INET Oxford Working Paper, 03.

Cowell, F.A. (1985). Measures of distributional change: An axiomatic approach. *Review of Economic Studies*, 52, 135–151.

Daouli, J., Demoussis, M., Giannokopoulos, N. (2010). Mothers fathers and daughters: Intergenerational transmission of education in Greece. *Economics of Education Review*, 29(1), 83–93.

Erikson, R. and Goldthorpe, J. (1992). *The Constant Flux: A Study of Class Mobility in Industrial Societies*. Clarendon Press, Oxford.

Eurofound (2017). *Social Mobility in the EU*. Publications Office of the European Union, Luxembourg.

Fields, G.S. and Ok, E. (1999). Measurement movement of incomes. *Economica*, 66, 455–471.

Goldthorpe, J.H. and Jackson, M. (2007). Intergenerational class mobility in contemporary Britain: Political concerns and empirical findings. *The British Journal of Sociology*, 58, 525–546 [Online]. https://doi.org/10.1111/j.1468-4446.2007.00165.x.

Harry, H.G. and Treiman, D. (1996). International stratification and mobility file: Conversion tools. Department of Social Research Methodology, Amsterdam [Online]. Available at: http://www.harryganzeboom.nl/ismf/index.htm.

Kasimati, K. (1990/1998). *Research on the Social Characteristics of Employment Study*. EKKE, Athens.

Lambiri-Dimaki, J. (1983). *Social Stratification in Greece 1962–1982: Eleven Essays*. Ant. N. Sakkoulas, Athens.

Lipset, S.M. and Zetterberg, H. (1959). *Social Mobility in Industrial Societies*. University of California Press, Berkley.

Luijkx, R. (2017). Intergenerational mobility: Methods of analysis. In *The Blackwell Encyclopedia of Sociology*, Ritzer, G. (ed.). John Wiley & Sons, Hoboken.

Maloutas, T. (2016). Intergenerational social mobility: Social inequality in the access of young people to education and occupation during the 2000s. Athens Social Atlas [Online]. Available at: https://www.athenssocialatlas.gr/en/article/intergenerational-mobility/.

Naoi, A. and Slomczynski, M. (1986). The Yasuda index of social mobility: A proposal for its modification. *Sociological Theory and Methods*, 1(1), 87–99.

OECD (2018). *A Broken Social Elevator? How to Promote Social Mobility*. OECD Publishing, Paris [Online]. https://doi.org/10.1787/9789264301085-en.

Papadakis, M. (1993). *Techniques for the Analysis of Social Mobility*. Vita, Athens (in Greek).

Papanastasiou, S. (2018). *Intergenerational Social Mobility and Types of Welfare State in Europe*, Athens, Gutenberg (in Greek).

Papatheodorou, C. and Piachaud, D. (1998). Family background, education and poverty in Greece. In *Poverty and Social Exclusion in the Mediterranean Area*, Korayem, K. and Petmesidou, M. (eds). CROP, Bergen.

Prais, S. (1955). Measuring social mobility. *Journal of the Royal Statistical Society, Series A*, 118, 56–66.

Shorrocks, A. (1978). The measurement of social mobility. *Econometrica*, 46, 1013–1024.

Stamatopoulou, G., Symeonaki, M., Michalopoulou, C. (2016). Occupational and educational gender segregation in southern Europe. In *Stochastic and Data Analysis Methods and Applications in Statistics and Demography*, Bozeman, J.R., Oliveira, T., Skiadas, C.H. (eds). ISAST.

Symeonaki, M. and Filopoulou, C. (2017). Quantifying gender distances in education, occupation and unemployment. *Equality, Diversity and Inclusion: An International Journal*, 36(4), 1–25. DOI: 10.10.1108/EDI-11-2016-0106.

Symeonaki, M. and Stamatopoulou, G. (2014a). Exploring the transition to Higher Education in Greece: Issues of intergenerational educational mobility. *Policy Futures in Education*, 12(5), 681–694. DOI: 10.2304/pfie.2014.12.5.681.

Symeonaki, M. and Stamatopoulou, G. (2014b). Intergenerational mobility as a distance measure between probability distribution functions. In *Theoretical and Applied Issues in Statistics and Demography*, Skiadas, C.H. (ed.). ISAST, Oakland.

Symeonaki, M. and Stamatopoulou, G. (2020). On the measurement of positive labour market mobility. *SAGE Open*, 10(3), 1–13. DOI: 10.1177/2158244020934489.

Symeonaki, M., Stamatopoulou, G., Michalopoulou, C. (2016). Intergenerational educational mobility in Greece: Transitions and social distances. *Communication in Statistics – Theory and Methods*, 45, 6.

Themelis, S. (2013). *Social Change and Education in Greece: A Study in Class Struggle Dynamics*. Palgrave Macmillan, New York.

Yasuda, S. (1964). A methodological inquiry into social mobility. *American Sociological Review*, 29, 16–23.

4

Capturing School-to-Work Transitions Using Data from the First European Graduate Survey

The transition from education to work represents a critical stage in the lives of young individuals. Over the past decades, the transition into the working life has increasingly come to be seen as more varied and less standardized. The reasons for more varied transition patterns are certainly multi-faceted. This chapter serves both descriptive and analytic aims. From a descriptive perspective, we focus primarily on addressing the question of whether, how and to what extent transitions differ between European countries. Alongside, attempts to identify and explain the mechanisms behind different transition patterns are explored. The analysis is cross-national with data drawn from the EUROGRADUATE Pilot Survey, a one-off pilot survey of recent graduates in eight European countries.

4.1. Introduction

One of the most significant current discussions in labor sociology is the successful entrance of young individuals into the labor market. When we specifically examine university-to-work transitions, the term *successful* refers to finding a job that meets a number of necessary criteria: the type of employment contract matches the employee's desire (in the sense that the graduate is not part-time or has a fixed contract against their will), the earnings can cover their basic needs and it is satisfactory (in the sense that it is relevant to the subject studied and the level of educational attainment). It is also becoming increasingly difficult to

Chapter written by Maria SYMEONAKI, Glykeria STAMATOPOULOU and Dimitris PARSANOGLOU.

For a color version of all the figures in this chapter, see www.iste.co.uk/zafeiris/data2.zip.

ignore the fact that young people are the ones who face a more difficult and more uncertain entrance to the labor market, and that higher rates of unemployment, long-term unemployment and longer spells of unemployment, and part-time and temporary employment are more customary for younger ages. In addition, relevant studies prove that graduates of lower-secondary educational attainment and women in general are more vulnerable to being inactive or out of the educational system (OECD 2016). Recent developments in labor sociology have indicated that the variation of national institutional and structural configurations may account for the variance in transition patterns amongst European countries, and also may explain the discrepancies in the impact of the economic crisis (Scherer 2004; Brzinsky-Fay 2007; De Lange et al. 2013; Hora et al. 2016; Riphahn and Zibrowius 2016; Caroleo et al. 2017; Pastore 2018). However, additional risk factors may form the transition probabilities from education to the labor market, i.e. gender, educational attainment, parental education and social background (Gangl 2003; Scherer 2004; Garrouste and Loi 2011; Plantenga et al. 2013; Eurofound 2014; Brzinsky-Fay 2015; Karamessini et al. 2019; Mathys 2019, among others). *Early job insecurity* which is a rather new term used in the area of labor sociology and labor statistics emerged recently in an effort to explain the degrees of insecurity which are present in the first steps of moving from education to the labor market and is closely linked with the notion of flexibility and precarity. The latter can be used alternatively to quantify early job insecurity, since for instance fixed-term employment, temporary and atypical jobs or low quality contracts are all linked to early job insecurity to a lesser or greater extent (Dingeldey et al. 2015). Recent developments in the field of early job insecurity have led to renewed interest in the quantification of early job insecurity and the development of composite indicators for its measurement. Two indicators, well-established in the literature, are the KOF Youth Labour Market Index (KOF YLMI) (Renold et al. 2014) and the Early Job Insecurity Indicator (EJI) (Symeonaki et al. 2017a, 2017b, 2019a, 2019b, 2019c; Karamessini et al. 2019) and the EJSec indicator (Symeonaki et al. (submitted)). Thus, several studies have produced indicators measuring school-to-work transition indicators, but there is still insufficient data for cross-national comparisons with a focus on university graduates and a common questionnaire.

This chapter uses raw data drawn from the EUROGRADUATE pilot survey, a one-off pilot survey of recent graduates in eight European countries, which aimed to lay the foundations for a sustainable European-wide graduate survey. This was initiated by the need to map the lived experiences of European graduates as students and their later professional lives as European citizens.

This chapter first gives a brief overview of the data and methodology used in the analysis. It then goes on to the next section which presents the results for the participating countries. Finally, section 4.4 lays out the theoretical and practical implications of our research.

4.2. Data and methodology

The research questions of the EUROGRADUATE pilot survey were to test how satisfied the graduates were with their studies, how they sustained themselves during their studies, how mobile they were, how long it took them to find a job after leaving education and, in general, how prepared they feel for the "adult" world of work and active citizenship. The eight EUROGRADUATE pilot countries were Austria, Croatia, Czechia, Germany, Greece, Lithuania, Malta and Norway, which were involved in the planning, design and implementation of the EUROGRADUATE pilot survey for this purpose. This survey was carried out in the eight pilot countries between October 2018 and February 2019. More specifically, the EUROGRADUATE pilot study includes graduates of ISCED levels 6 (Bachelor) and 7 (Master, Diploma) and, as far as it exists in higher education, ISCED level 5 (short courses for Malta). These are the degrees on the basis of which graduates were asked to take part in the survey (reference degree). Nevertheless, the graduates of these programs may have carried on with their studies and meanwhile attained further degrees. Therefore, there are also Bachelor's graduates with a Master's or PhD degree in the dataset. In the survey, two cohorts are distinguished, graduates who completed their studies in the academic year 2012–2013 and those belonging to the second cohort who completed their studies in the academic year 2016–2017. The survey used a common e-questionnaire disseminated to the graduates along with individualized links that the graduates used for answering the questionnaire. Around 140,000 graduates in eight countries were contacted and the response rate was approximately equal to 12%.

The principal limitation is that the initial circumstances and restraints in the eight pilot countries varied significantly. In some countries, the population data was not optimal, the contact information for graduates was diverse, occasionally did not cover the entire graduate population, or was outdated (email addresses affiliated to the universities were not valid), while readiness of higher education institutions to support the data collection process varied strongly across and within countries (Mühleck et al. 2020, p. 10). The sampling process was also challenging in some countries, for example, Greece, especially if the institution/university had to contact the graduates itself. The data was centrally cleaned, tested on plausibility, labeled and weighted. The process of central data management improved comparability and the quality of the data produced. Despite problems encountered and a relatively adequate response rate, the data quality is satisfactory (Mühleck et al. 2020). The results generated with the data, the country and group differences perceived, resemble disparities recognized in national graduate surveys or general population data, a fact that supports the sufficiency of the quality of the data produced.

4.3. Results

One of the first aspects we examine is the percentage of graduates who were employed, unemployed or inactive at the time of the survey. More specifically, we are interested in the labor market situation of the graduates who were not enrolled at the time of the survey, i.e. those who have left education and moved to the labor market. In what follows, outcomes are presented for the two cohorts separately and by educational attainment (Bachelor's and Master's degree). The percentage of employed graduates who are not enrolled per surveyed country, ISCED level and cohort are presented in Figure 4.1. The lower percentages of employment can be found in the 2016–2017 cohort for Bachelor's graduates, with Germany, Greece and Croatia exhibiting the lowest values. On the contrary, the higher values can be found in the 2012–2013 cohort of Master's graduates in Malta and Norway.

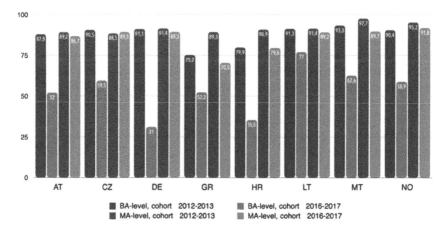

Figure 4.1. *Percentage of employed graduates who are not enrolled per surveyed country, ISCED level and cohort*

It is also apparent from Figure 4.2 that the unemployment rates of the graduates are generally low, except for Greece, Croatia and Lithuania where higher percentages of unemployment are found. The highest percentage of unemployment corresponds to the most recent BA-level graduates (cohort 2016–2017) in Greece (15.5%).

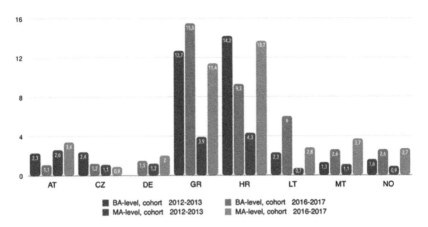

Figure 4.2. *Percentage of unemployed graduates who are
not enrolled per surveyed country, ISCED level and cohort*

It is also notable that most recent BA-level graduates (cohort 2016–2017) exhibit higher degrees of inactivity (not being a part of the labor market), i.e. they have much higher inactivity rates than all other groups (Figure 4.3). The fact that these percentages correspond to the percentages of graduates who are neither employed nor currently enrolled implies a relatively high NEET rate for this category and cohort.

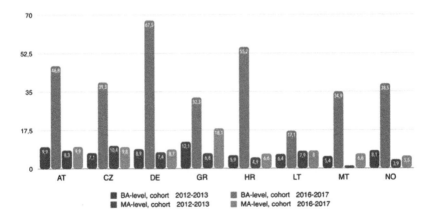

Figure 4.3. *Percentage of inactive graduates who are not
enrolled per surveyed country, ISCED level and cohort*

We next examine quality of jobs whereby full-time and part-time employment is distinguished. The results are presented in Figure 4.4. Again, the values differ between cohorts and ISCED levels with Greece exhibiting the lowest full-time employment percentage of MA-level graduates (62%) for 2012–2013 and Austria for BA-level 2016–2017. Again, Malta exhibits the highest scores of almost 99% of full-time employment for BA-level, 2012–2013 cohort and MA-level, 2016–2017 cohort. The percentages are reasonably high in general.

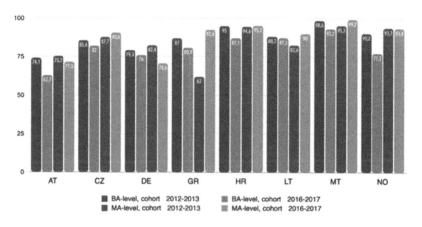

Figure 4.4. *Percentage of graduates who are full-time employed per surveyed country, ISCED level and cohort*

The discrepancies between countries are also evident in relation to another fundamental issue linked to the evaluation of job quality, which is the length of contact. Figure 4.5 depicts the results relating to the percentage of graduates employed under an unlimited term contract. Apparently, MA-level graduates, five years after graduation in Greece show the highest value for permanent employment, while the percentages are also high for BA-level graduates in Lithuania for the cohort 2012–2013.

The earnings declared by the respondents differ significantly between the surveying countries. Figure 4.6 presents the mean gross monthly income from main job per county, ISCED level and cohort. Graduates who are employed in Norway, for example, earn far more than any other category of graduates, as is apparent from Figure 4.6. In general, in all countries, graduates who have completed ISCED level 7 (MA-level) earn more than BA-level graduates, when comparing the same cohorts. It is also apparent that in some countries, such as Croatia, Lithuania, Greece and the Czech Republic, the estimated mean gross earnings from main job are low or very low.

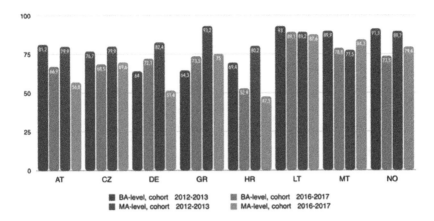

Figure 4.5. *Percentage of graduates who are employed under an unlimited term contract per surveyed country, ISCED level and cohort*

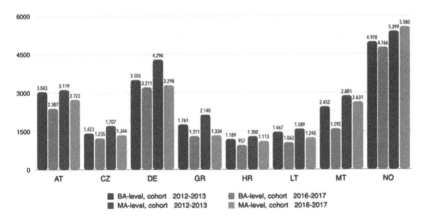

Figure 4.6. *Mean gross monthly income of graduates per surveyed country, ISCED level and cohort*

Another element that is worth examining is the mean number of months that the graduates have spent being unemployed since graduation (Figure 4.7). Again, Greece is found to possess the worse score for the BA-level graduates who had left education five years before the survey. These graduates claim that the mean value of the number of months that they have been unemployed is equal to 18.29, followed by the MA-level graduates of the same cohort and country. Relatively low are the scores for graduates in the Czech Republic, Norway, Lithuania and Austria.

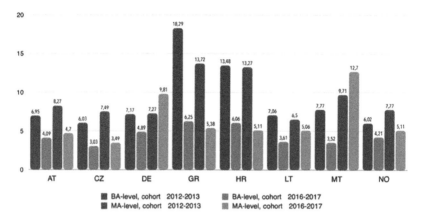

Figure 4.7. *Mean number of months being unemployed
per surveyed country, ISCED level and cohort*

It is also very important to examine whether the job/work that the graduates perform matches their qualifications and field of study. This is examined through measurement of the subjective opinion of the graduates in relation to their job/work mismatch, where they have to choose from a predefined set of answers: graduate's ISCED level matches what they assume is appropriate, graduate's ISCED level is lower than what they assume is appropriate, graduate's ISCED level is higher than what they assume is appropriate. Figure 4.8 presents the percentages of those that have selected the first choice, meaning that they assume that their ISCED level matches the qualifications needed for their current job/work. The lower value is found for BA-level graduates, cohort 2016–2017 in the Czech Republic, with only 41.9% believing their qualifications match their job/work. The highest percentage is found among Norwegian MA-level graduates of the 2012–2013 cohort. Relatively low percentages are also detected in Greece for all categories and Austria for BA-level graduates of the 2016–2017 cohort.

Another key element of integrating university graduates into the labor market is related to the percentage of graduates who have moved abroad and are employed per surveyed country and cohort. By far the highest percentages are identified in Greece with the 2012–2013 cohort exhibiting the highest values. On the contrary, low values can be found in Germany and Norway with values ranging between 3.3 and 7.4. Apparently, the lowest values correspond to Lithuania for the Bachelor's graduates of the 2012–1013 cohort.

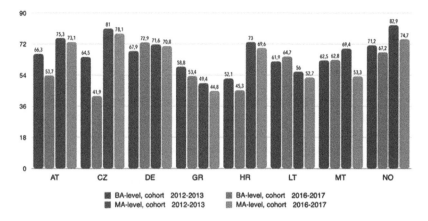

Figure 4.8. *Graduate's ISCED level matches what they assume appropriate per surveyed country, ISCED level and cohort*

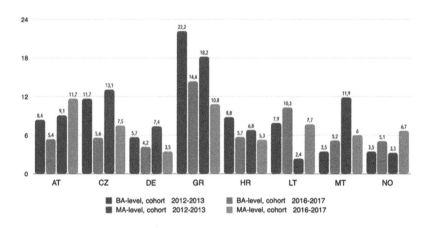

Figure 4.9. *Percentage of graduates moving abroad per surveyed country and cohort*

4.4. Conclusion

In this chapter, the results from the first European Graduate Survey, EUROGRADUATE, have been presented for the eight participating European countries and the differences between the two cohorts under survey (2012–2013 and 2016–2017) have been identified. The analysis shows that the employment status of the respondents differs by educational attainment, with the most recent BA-level graduates (2016–2017) exhibiting the lowest employment rates in their transition to the labor market, and also the highest risk of staying out of the labor market. On the contrary, variations between countries are observed in unemployment rates of the graduates, with Greece and Croatia comprising by far the highest percentages of unemployed individuals, and also the longer period of unemployment for both cohorts. Concerning the security perceived from their job, it seems that the majority of the graduates are full time employed with permanent contracts. However, certain exceptions are notable, the most noteworthy of which is the case of Croatia, where almost 50% of the 2016–2017 cohort are employed in temporary jobs, regardless of their educational degree. Concerning the earnings from the main job, in all countries, the most educated graduates seem to have a higher mean gross monthly income. Finally, relatively low skill mismatch rates are observed in Greece compared to the other countries, while a significant number of the Greek graduates moved abroad, searching for a better job.

4.5. References

Brzinsky-Fay, C. (2007). Lost in transition? Labour market entry sequences of school leavers in Europe. *European Sociological Review*, 23, 409–422.

Brzinsky-Fay, C. (2015). Gendered school-to-work transitions? A sequence approach to how women and men enter the labor market in Europe. In *Gender, Education and Employment: An International Comparison of School-to-Work Transitions*, Blossfeld, H.P., Skopek, J., Triventi, M., Buchholz, S. (eds). Edward Elgar, Northampton.

Caroleo, F.E., Ciociano, E., Destefanis, S. (2017). The role of the education systems and the labour market institutions in enhancing youth employment: A cross-country analysis. Working Paper. CRISEI, Italy.

De Lange, M., Gesthuizen M., Wolbers, M. (2013). Youth labour market integration across Europe: The impact of cyclical, structural, and institutional characteristics. *European Societies*, 16(2), 194–212 [Online]. Available at: https://doi.org/10.1080/14616696.2013.821621.

Dingeldey, I., Hvinden, B., Hyggen, C., O'Reilly, J., Schøyen, M. (2015). Understanding the consequences of early job insecurity and labour market exclusion: The interaction of structural conditions, institutions, active agency and capability. Working Paper, NEGOTIATE HiOA, Oslo, Norway.

Eurofound (2014). Mapping youth transitions in Europe. Publications Office of the European Union, Luxembourg.

Gangl, M. (2003). The structure of labour market entry in Europe: A typological analysis. In *Transitions from Education to Work in Europe*, Muller, W. and Gangl, M. (eds). Oxford University Press, New York.

Garrouste, C. and Loi, M. (2011). School-to-work transitions in Europe: Paths towards a permanent contract, MPRA Paper 37167, University Library of Munich, Germany.

Hora, O., Horáková, M., Sirovátka, T. (2016). Institutional determinants of early job insecurity in nine European countries. Working Paper [Online]. Available at: https://negotiate-research.eu/files/2015/04/NEGOTIATE-working-paper-D3.4.pdf.

Karamessini, M., Symeonaki, M., Parsanoglou, D., Stamatopoulou, G. (2019). Mapping early job insecurity impacts of the crisis in Europe. In *Youth Unemployment and Early Job Insecurity in Europe: Concepts, Consequences and Policy Approaches*, Hvinden, B., Sirovátka, T. and O'Reilly, J. (eds). Edward Elgar, Northampton.

Mathys, Q. (2019). From school to work: An analysis of youth labour market transitions [Online]. Available at: https://ilo.org/wcmsp5/groups/public/---dgreports/---stat/documents/publication/wcms_732422.pdf.

Mühleck, K., Meng, C., Oelker, S., Unger, M., Lizzi, R., Maurer, S., Rimac, I., Rutjes, H., Wessling, K. (2020). *Eurograduate Pilot Study: Technical Assessment of the Pilot Survey and Feasibility of a Full Rollout*. European Commission, Brussels.

OECD (2016). *Society at a Glance 2016: OECD Social Indicators*. OECD Publishing, Paris.

Pastore, F. (2018). Why so slow? The school-to-work transition in Italy. *Studies in Higher Education*, 44(8), 1358–1371.

Plantenga, J., Remery, C., Lodovici, M.S. (2013). *Starting Fragile: Gender Differences in the Youth Labour Market*. European Commission, Luxembourg.

Renold, U., Bolli, T., Egg, M.E., Pusterla, F. (2014). *On the Multiple Dimensions of Youth Labour Markets – A Guide to the KOF Youth Labour Market Index*. KOF Swiss Economic Institute, Zurich.

Riphahn, R. and Zibrowius, M. (2016). Apprenticeship, vocational training, and early labor market outcomes – Evidence from East and West Germany. *Education Economics*, 24(1), 33–57.

Scherer, S. (2004). Patterns of labour market entry – Long wait or career instability? An empirical comparison of Italy, Great Britain and West Germany. *European Sociological Review*, 21, 427–440.

Symeonaki, M., Karamessini, M., Stamatopoulou, G. (2017a). Introducing an index of early job insecurity: A comparative analysis among European countries with evidence from the EU-LFS. *Proceedings of the 5th European User Conference, Microdata from Eurostat SILC, LFS, AES, SES, CIS, CSIS, EHIS, HBS and TUS*, Mannheim, Germany.

Symeonaki, M., Karamessini, M., Stamatopoulou, G. (2017b). Introducing an index of labour mobility for youth. *Proceedings of the 13th Conference of the European Sociological Association, (Un)Making Europe: Capitalism, Solidarities, Subjectivities*, Athens, Greece.

Symeonaki, M., Karamessini, M., Stamatopoulou, G. (2019a). Gender-based differences in the impact of the economic crisis on labor market flows in Southern Europe. In *Data Analysis and Applications: New and Classical Approaches*, Bozeman, J. and Skiadas, C. (eds). ISTE Ltd, London, and John Wiley & Sons, New York.

Symeonaki, M., Karamessini, M., Stamatopoulou, G. (2019b). Measuring school-to-work transition probabilities in Europe with evidence from the EU-SILC. In *Data Analysis and Applications: New and Classical Approaches*, Bozeman, J., Oliveira, T., Skiadas, C., Silvestrov, S. (eds). ISTE Ltd, London, and John Wiley & Sons, New York.

Symeonaki, M., Karamessini, M., Stamatopoulou, G. (2019c). *The Evolution of Early Job Insecurity in Europe* [Online]. Available at: https://doi.org/10.1177/2158244019845187.

Symeonaki, M., Stamatopoulou, G., Parsanoglou, D. (2022) (submitted). Measuring the unmeasurable: Defining and rating precarity with the aid of EU-LFS data. *Quality and Quantity* (under review).

A Cluster Analysis Approach for Identifying Precarious Workers

A number of efforts have been made in the past to capture the multifaced phenomenon of employment precarity. However, only a very short body of literature provides quantitative methods that measure the degree and forms of precarity and a way to perform cross-national comparisons. In this chapter, we apply an unsupervised clustering algorithm in order to capture the degree of precarity employment with raw data drawn from the European Labour Force Survey (EU-LFS). The approach engages indicators such as unemployment, part-time employment, temporary contracts, existence of social and health security, among others and is implemented for the case of Greece, with the latest data available at the time, i.e. for the year 2018. However, the methodology could be adopted for other EU member states with no amendments, due to the use of a common questionnaire in the survey for all participating countries. The proposed approach identifies three clusters of workers that exhibit different degrees of precarity. The socio-demographic characteristics of each group are discovered via the cluster centers.

5.1. Introduction

This chapter provides a comprehensive methodology of measuring and defining levels of precarity using raw data drawn from the European Labour Force Survey (EU-LFS). The methodology is implemented using data for the case of Greece, and three levels of precarious workers are identified based on several characteristics that are used in the literature to conceptualize precarity. In the literature, precarious labor is highly related to the discussion on flexibility of labor and labor markets, which first appeared in the 80's (Klau and Mittelstadt 1985; Atkinson and Meager 1986;

Chapter written by Maria SYMEONAKI, Glykeria STAMATOPOULOU and Dimitris PARSANOGLOU.

Reilly 2001; Rodgers 2007). Over the years, this discussion has been taken further to incorporate all possible new forms of unsure, insecure, not guaranteed, flexible types of employment. If we wished to describe the theoretical basis of precarity discussions, we would have to include the post-Marxist theory of the Italian autonomy tradition combined with Foucault's convention of biopolitics (Gill and Pratt 2008) and the interpretations of the regulation school (Aglietta 1979; Bonefeld and Holloway 1991; Lipietz 1992). However, what makes precarious labor a paradigmatic form of labor is not only its flexible character, nor its allegedly cognitive content and requirements. Contemporary sociological research and critical political thought have defined precarious labor as the multiplication of non-standard and irregular forms of labor (Mezzadra and Neilson 2013), and precarious workers as bearing common characteristics, such as a short-term work/job, and/or a part-time contract and an organisation around the product of work (subcontracting, project-specific or freelance work and unsupportive entitlements). They moreover vary significantly, forming groupings of unequally remunerated workers, from working poor to highly paid temporary skilled workers. In addition, they lack unionism, despite irregular struggles to join traditional unions. Olsthoorn (2014) perceives precarious employment as a feature of the employment relation, i.e. as insecure jobs employed by vulnerable employees, who can presume insufficient entitlements to income support when unemployed. Precarity is also linked with job insecurity, as a subset of the wider insecure set (Karamessini et al. 2019; Symeonaki et al. 2019). Symeonaki et al. (2022) provided a set theory solution to defining precarity. This chapter incorporates the theoretical discussion on precarity and tries to quantify precarious employment using a number of variables linked to the above characteristics, which can be measured using raw data from the EU-LFS survey and cluster analysis to provide levels of precarity and their features. A similar approach to a similar end can be found in Symeonaki (2015) and Michalopoulou and Symeonaki (2017).

This chapter is outlined in the following way: section 5.2 provides a description of the data being used in the analysis and the methodology behind it, followed by section 5.3, which provides the results of the proposed method. Section 5.4 discusses the results and their theoretical and practical implications, and proposes steps for further development of the research.

5.2. Data and methodology

The EU-LFS is a European cross-sectional household sample survey, which provides monthly, quarterly and annual data on the participation of Europeans and non-EU nationals that live in Europe in the labor market, their working conditions and job characteristics, providing the necessary indicators to quantify them. Consequently, it provides the estimations of unemployment rates and other structural indicators, such as labor market participation, NEET rates, part-time and temporary employment, participation in life-long learning, among others. Thus, the EU-LFS database offers a means of quantifying significant characteristics, using common definitions (e.g. ILO's definition of unemployment) and classifications (e.g. ISCED-11 classification for educational attainment) to ensure comparability between the outcomes and performance of EU member countries, and the EFTA countries Norway, Switzerland and Iceland.

Several variables that are linked to precarity in the relevant discussion in the literature are examined and estimated using raw data drawn from the EU-LFS, for the case of Greece. More specifically, the values of the following precarity indicators are estimated:

– temporary employment, defined as the share of employed people that have a contract with a limited duration;

– involuntary temporary employees, i.e. the temporary employees who could not find a permanent job;

– part-time employment as perceived by the respondents' own view about their main job;

– involuntary part-time employment, defined as the share of the self-defined part-time workers who declare that they could not find a full-time job;

– short-term contract, that is, contracts that last less than three months;

– absence of health insurance;

– absence of social security;

– low-paid workers, that is, individuals whose monthly income does not surpass the two-thirds of the median of incomes of the respondents according to ILO definition. For the case of Greece, the cutting point is equal to 560 euros;

– sources of income apart from the main job, in the sense that lower percentages of using supplementary sources mean greater employment precarity.

These variables are then used in order to cluster workers together and for this reason, a K-means clustering algorithm is proposed. In general, clustering involves the process of allocating data points into clusters, so that cases (in our case workers) allocated in the same cluster are as similar as possible and items in different classes are as dissimilar as possible (Symeonaki and Michalopoulou 2011). Clustering techniques are used to convert a large number of cases into a small number of distinct clusters, using the cluster centers as prototypes (Aldenderfer and Blashfield 1984; Everitt 1993). Specifically, K-means is an unsupervised learning algorithm that classifies a given data set into a fixed number of clusters. Hierarchical clustering was also used in the present analysis to detect the optimal number of clusters that best group the respondents in the survey. Based on the visual information from the dendrogram, three and four cluster solutions were implemented using K-means cluster analysis using IBM Statistics, v.20. The evaluation of the two different K-means solutions revealed that the three-cluster solution was more consistent with the current theoretical discussion of precarity. Within-cluster R^2 was calculated for each cluster as a measure of cluster similarity and the ANOVA outcomes were examined providing information on the hypothesis of cluster means equality.

In our case, the specific characteristics of the individuals that would lead to their classification as precarious workers (or not) were formed by their answers to the questions-variables described above. Three clusters are detected, and their cluster centers are used to define each cluster, involving different levels of precarity.

5.3. Results

The present section delivers the results of the proposed method. Before we proceed to the analysis, the cases are weighted as required by theory and several indicators all linked to precarious employment and its conceptualization are estimated. The values for these variables are presented in Table 5.1, for individuals who were aged above 18 and were not unemployed or inactive at the time of the survey.

Indicators	Percent (%)
Temporary employment	11.3
Part-time employment	9.2
Involuntary part-time employment	67.2
Without social insurance	2.4
Without other sources apart from work	9.6
Low paid (<2/3 median=560)	18.3
Without medical insurance	2.3
Involuntary temporary employment	5.9

Table 5.1. *Precarity variables, Greece, EU-LFS, 2018.*
Source: EU-LFS 2018, weighted data for Greece

After implementing an agglomerative hierarchical clustering method and producing the respective dendrogram, the optimal number of clusters is decided upon. The number of clusters chosen is also validated through a thorough investigation of the iteration history of the K-means algorithm and the ANOVA table. In what follows, the results of an unsupervised K-means clustering algorithm are presented with a fixed number of clusters equal to three. Therefore, the algorithm leads to a division of workers into three clusters, enabling a comparison among the formed groups.

The final cluster centers (centroids) that were identified by the executed algorithm are the following:

$$C(1) = (1\ 1\ 1\ 0\ 0\ 0), \qquad\qquad [5.1]$$

$$C(2) = (1\ 2\ 1\ 1\ 0\ 0), \qquad\qquad [5.2]$$

$$C(3) = (2\ 1\ 1\ 1\ 1\ 1). \qquad\qquad [5.3]$$

To get a clearer picture on the defining features of each cluster and what the membership in each cluster means, the characteristics of each cluster are examined with the use of the variable *cluster membership* produced during the clustering process. More specifically, the characteristics studied are the demographics (gender, marital status, age and nationality) and other important variables such as occupation, employment permanency, gross monthly income and sector of economic activity, among others. The descriptives of these characteristics and those belonging to the first, second and third cluster are exhibited in Tables 5.2 and 5.3 and in Figure 5.1.

More specifically, in Table 5.2, the employment characteristics of the three clusters are presented. Apparently, the first cluster corresponds to a more "privileged" group of workers compared to the other two, as its members are permanently employed (99%) and mainly full-time (92.1%). Individuals who are grouped in this category who declared that they never work in the evenings or at night are also the majority (53.2% and 79.5%, respectively), while their mean monthly income is the highest among clusters (995.87 euros). As we move to the next cluster, precarity becomes more evident. Individuals in Cluster 2 are also permanently employed to a lesser extent (79.9%) and part-time workers outnumber the ones who work full-time. Most of the members in this cluster usually work in the evening (44.5%), but not at night (88.7%), and earn half of the income compared to the previous cluster. In the same line, Cluster 3 is formed by individuals on a temporary or fixed-term contract (57.1), while the percentage of those working part-time is also noteworthy (66.9%). Their total monthly earnings are relatively low (491.43 euros).

A more illustrative representation of the above results is given in Figure 5.1, where the precarious form of employment is exhibited for each cluster separately. It is obvious that Cluster 1 has the most advantageous position in the labor market, except for the fact that it has a higher percentage of night work.

Forms of employment	Cluster 1	Cluster 2	Cluster 3
Permanency of Job			
Permanent job/work contract of unlimited duration	**99.0**	**79.9**	42.9
Temporary job/work contract of unlimited duration	1.0	21.1	**57.1**
Full-time/part-time distinction			
Full-time	**92.1**	48.1	**66.9**
Part-time	7.9	**51.9**	33.1
Evening work			
Usually	28.6	**44.5**	38.4
Sometimes	18.2	14.7	22.3
Never	**53.2**	40.7	**39.3**
Night work			
Usually	6.6	6.1	8.3
Sometimes	14.0	5.2	9.7
Never	**79.5**	**88.7**	**82.0**
Mean monthly income	995.87 €	415.44 €	491.43 €

Table 5.2. *The employment characteristics of clusters.*
Source: EU-LFS 2018, data for Greece

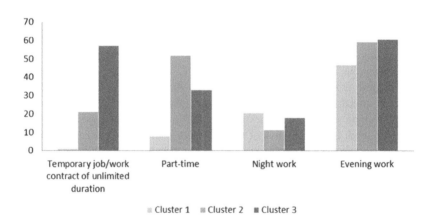

Figure 5.1. *The precarious forms of employment by cluster. For a*
color version of this figure, see www.iste.co.uk/zafeiris/data2.zip

	Cluster 1	Cluster 2	Cluster 3
Gender			
Male	**57.8**	40.5	**50.6**
Female	42.2	**59.5**	49.4
Marital status			
Single	28.2	**48.6**	**51.9**
Married	**65.5**	45.1	36.2
Other	6.4	6.3	11.9
Nationality			
Greek	**94.8**	**87.2**	**60.3**
EU	0.8	2.0	11.3
Other	4.4	10.8	28.5
Occupation (main job, 1-digit), ISCO-08			
1 – Managers	1.9	0.1	0.5
2 – Professionals	**24.9**	9.5	6.4
3 – Technicians and associate professionals	11.4	6.2	2.7
4 – Clerical support workers	15.6	12.7	6.9
5 - Service and sales workers	20.9	**38.5**	25.2
6 – Skilled agricultural, forestry, fishery workers	0.4	0.8	2.6
7 – Craft and related trades workers	8.9	8.1	12.2
8 – Plant, machine operators and assemblers	8.6	5.3	2.6
9 – Elementary occupations	7.4	18.8	**40.8**
Mean age	42.47	36.17	37.34
Sector (mode)	Trade, accommodation and food service activities		

Table 5.3. *Socio-demographic characteristics of the workers by cluster. Source: EU-LFS 2018, data for Greece*

After we examined the employment characteristics of workers in each cluster, we proceeded with the presentation of their socio-demographic characteristics, to explore which groups of people in Greece are more vulnerable to precarious forms of employment. As we can see from Table 5.3, the first cluster, i.e. the cluster with the most privileged workers, mainly consists of men (57.8%) who are married (65.5%) and Greek (94.8%). They are mostly *professionals*, for example, teaching, health, social and cultural professionals, and their mean age, equal to 42.47, is higher than the mean age of individuals in the other two categories. Most individuals can be found within the sector *Trade, accommodation and food service activities*. Moving to the second cluster, the mean age drops substantially to 36.17, while it is worth noting that 10.8% of the members in this group are non-EU nationals. Moreover, Cluster 2 mainly consists of women (almost 60%), who are single (48.6%) and Greek (87.2%). The broad category of occupation also changes, and in this case, *Service and sales workers* are the majority; however, the same sector is also over-present in this group: *Trade, accommodation and food service activities*. Cluster 3 is formed by males and females in approximately the same percentage, which are mostly single (51.9%) and Greek (60.3%), but with a significantly higher percentage of EU nationals (11.3%) and non-EU nationals (28.5%) than the other two categories. *Elementary occupations* are mostly linked to this category, such as helpers and cleaners and their mean age is 37.34. Interestingly, the same sector is detected as the one with the highest percentage (*Trade, accommodation and food service activities*).

5.4. Conclusion and discussion

The results of the unsupervised clustering algorithm that was used produced an optimal solution of three clusters of workers with different levels of precarity and uncovered the groups of people who are more at risk for job insecurity and precarity. From the analysis, it emerged that the most privileged group of workers, namely, those with lower levels of precarity are men, married and Greek people, whose mean age is around 42 years old. Concerning the occupational sectors, it is evident that those occupied in professional and technical occupations have better prospects for higher income and employment security. Consequently, the most vulnerable groups of people are women, single, young people and non-EU nationals, who occupied elementary or service and sales occupations. To go beyond the typical clustering algorithms and as a direction for future work, a fuzzy K-means algorithm can be applied, since the borders between clusters are not distinct, but fuzzy.

5.4.1. *Declarations*

Funding: this research was co-financed by Greece and the European Union (European Social Fund – ESF) through the Operational Program "Human Resources Development, Education and Lifelong Learning 2014–2020" in the context of the project "Investigating patterns of job insecurity and precarity in Greece" (MIS 5049097 – ID: 50854(2020/1).

Conflicts of interest/competing interests: no conflicts of interest to declare.

Availability of data and material: data can be accessed through an application to the Hellenic Statistical Authority of Greece and/or EUROSTAT (access to micro data service).

Ethics approval: this research was approved by the Research Committee of Panteion University of Social and Political Sciences.

5.5. References

Aglietta, M. (1979). *A Theory of Capitalist Regulation: The US Experience*. New Left Books, London.

Aldenderfer, M. and Blashfield, R. (1984). *Cluster Analysis*. Sage, London.

Atkinson, J. and Meager, N. (1986). *Changing Working Patterns: How Companies Achieve Flexibility to Meet New Needs*. Institute of Manpower Studies, National Economic Development Office, London.

Bonefeld, W. and Holloway, J. (1991). *Post-Fordism and Social Form: A Marxist Debate on the Post-fordist State*. Macmillan (The Conference of Socialist Economists), London.

Everitt, B. (1993). *Cluster Analysis*. Arnold, New York.

Gill, R. and Pratt, A. (2008). In the social factory? Immaterial labour, precariousness and cultural work . *Theory, Culture & Society*, 25(7–8), 1–30.

Karamessini, M., Symeonaki, M., Parsanoglou, D., Stamatopoulou, G. (2019). Mapping early job insecurity impacts of the crisis in Europe. In *Youth Unemployment and Early Job Insecurity in Europe: Concepts, Consequences and Policy Approaches*, Hvinden, B., Sirovátka, T., O'Reilly, J. (eds). Edward Elgar, Chelternham.

Klau, F. and Mittelstadt, A. (1985). Labour market flexibility. Economics and Statistics Department, OECD [Online]. Available at: http://www.oecd.org/eco/growth/3555 8438.pdf.

Lipietz, A. (1992). *Towards a New Economic Order: Post-Fordism, Ecology and Democracy*. Polity Press, Cambridge.

Mezzadra, S. and Neilson, B. (2013). *Border as Method, or the Multiplication of Labour*. Duke University Press, Durham and London.

Michalopoulou, C. and Symeonaki, M. (2017). Improving Likert scales raw scores with K-means clustering. *Bulletin de Methodologie Sociologigue*, 135, 101–109. DOI: 10.1177/0759106317710863.

Olsthoorn, M. (2014). Measuring precarious employment: A proposal for two indicators of precarious employment based on set-theory and tested with Dutch labor market-data. *Social Indicators Research*, 119, 421–441 [Online]. Available at: https://doi.org/10.1007/s11205-013-0480-y.

Reilly, P. (2001). *Flexibility at Work: Balancing the Interests of Employers and Employee.* Gower Publishing, Hampshire.

Rodgers, G. (2007). Labour market flexibility and decent work. DESA Working Paper No. 47, United Nations, Department of Economic and Social Affairs, New York [Online]. Available at: http://www.un.org/esa/desa/papers/2007/wp47_2007.pdf.

Symeonaki, M. (2015). Identifying quality of life patterns in the third age: A cluster analysis approach with evidence from SHARE. In *Statistical, Stochastic and Data Analysis Methods and Applications*, Karagrigoriou, A., Oliveira, T., Skiadas, C.H. (eds). ISAST.

Symeonaki, M. and Michalopoulou, C. (2011). Measuring xenophobia in Greece: A cluster analysis approach. *14th Conference of the Applied Stochastic Models and Data Analysis International Society (ASMDA)*, Rome, Italy, 7–10 June.

Symeonaki, M., Parsanoglou, D., Stamatopoulou, G. (2019). The evolution of early job insecurity in Europe. *SAGE Open*, 1–23. DOI: 10.1177/2158244019845187.

Symeonaki, M., Stamatopoulou, G., Parsanoglou, D. (2022). Measuring the unmeasurable: Defining and rating precarity with the aid of EU-LFS data. *Quality and Quantity* (under review).

American Option Pricing Under a Varying Economic Situation Using Semi-Markov Decision Process

In this chapter, we consider the problem of American option pricing when the asset price dynamics follow a binomial model dominated by a varying economic situation. We assume that the economic situation transits based on a semi-Markov chain. The pricing procedure is formulated using a semi-Markov decision process, as the decision-maker decides whether to exercise early or hold the option. Some properties on the optimal exercise regions and the monotonicity of option prices are discussed based on simulation results when each parameter is changed, and the optimal strategies are investigated.

6.1. Introduction

A financial option is a derivative traded in a market that gives its holder a right, but not the obligation, to buy or sell an underlying asset at a predetermined strike price K. If the holder has the right to buy, it is called the call option, and if the holder has the right to sell, it is a put option. Options have a maturity that enables the exercising of rights. Typically, they are divided into European options that can only be exercised on their maturity and American options that can be exercised at any time before their maturity.

Option prices mainly fluctuate depending on asset prices, and the volatilities of asset prices differ depending on the economic situation. Therefore, when pricing

Chapter written by Kouki TAKADA, Marko DIMITROV, Lu JIN and Ying NI.

For a color version of all the figures in this chapter, see www.iste.co.uk/zafeiris/data2.zip.

American options, a binomial model can express changes in asset prices during changes in the economic situations with relative ease. In addition, a method that involves a Markov chain and pricing options can describe changes in the economic situation using a Markov decision process.

There are several models suitable for option pricing. Kim and Byun (2004) defined a simple binomial model with constant volatility, and Broadie and Detemple (1999) considered the properties of the optimal exercise region of the option assuming that asset prices follow the geometric Brownian motion. Guo and Zhang (2004) studied an optimal stopping time problem for pricing of an American put option in a regime switching model, and described the value function in a closed form. Carriere (1996) focused on the valuing of American options using simulations of stochastic processes and showed how to value the optimal stopping time for any Markovian process in finite discrete time. Kijima and Yoshida (1993) used the Black–Scholes model to price options when asset price changes followed the binomial model. However, when using the Black–Scholes model, we cannot consider a fat tail for the asset return distribution or create a volatility smile (Shi et al. 2016). Therefore, Nasir et al. (2020) proposed a Markov decision process for option pricing as a model that incorporates uncertainties and features that affect option pricing. Also, Nasir et al. (2020) stated that the literature about this proposal shows that the options trading problem can be formulated as an optimal stopping problem using a Markov decision process (Bertsekas 2000). In addition, Bertsekas and Tsitsiklis (1995) showed that the optimal policy could be determined using a dynamic decision-making method of a Markov decision process.

The following is a list of previous studies on pricing options that use a Markov decision process. Sato and Sawaki (2012) assumed that the economic situation could be directly observed and transitions follow a Markov chain; they priced options using a discrete-time Markov decision process and examined the properties of the optimal exercise region. After that, Sato and Sawaki (2018) made the economic situations unobservable, priced options using a partially observable Markov decision process and considered the optimal strategy. Based on Sato and Sawaki's work (2018), Ishidomaru (2020) examined the conditions for changes in asset prices and the economic situation in order to show optimal strategies. Jin et al. (2019) followed the framework in Sato and Sawaki's work (2018) and considered valuation and optimal strategies using a partially observable Markov decision process. Dimitrov et al. (2021) represented the transitions of asset prices using a binomial model that uses risk-neutral distribution, and numerically considered the properties of the threshold of the optimal exercise region using the partially observable Markov decision process of three states. In these studies, time intervals between changes in the economic situation are assumed to be discrete and equal. Option prices should be considered, in which transitions may randomly change along with random changes in a real economy. D'Amico et al. (2009) priced the options using a semi-Markov process when the economic situation was steady and numerically examined the changes in the option prices for each remaining period.

In this study, we price an American option when transitions in economic situations are represented by semi-Markov chains, in which the amount of time in each economic situation before a transition occurs is randomized, and asset price changes follow a binomial model that uses risk-neutral distribution. In addition, we numerically examine changes in option prices, the optimal exercise region and its threshold.

The rest of this chapter is organized as follows. In section 6.2, American options are formulated using a semi-Markov decision process. In section 6.3, changes in option prices and optimal exercise regions are numerically considered. In section 6.4, our work is summarized, and future research is discussed.

6.2. American option pricing

Consider an American option with a strike price K, an asset price s and a maturity T in a changing economic situation.

Let Z_0 be the initial economic situation at the start of options trading. For $n \geq 1$, let Z_n denote the economic situation immediately after the n-th transition occurs, and let S_n be the asset price at the n-th transition. The dynamic in asset price is given by

$$S_n = S_{n-1} X_n^{Z_n},$$

where the price relative to X_n depends on the economic situation Z_n.

Next, suppose that the economic situation Z_n takes a value from a finite state space $\mathbb{Z} = \{1, 2, 3\}$. The economic situations are ordered in ascending order, with 1 being the worst economic situation and 3 being the best. Assume that the transition of economic situation Z follows a known transition probability law given by $\mathbf{P} = [p_{ij}]_{i,j \in \mathbb{Z}}$, where p_{ij} is the probability that the economic situation transitions from level i to level j. Let

$$F_{ij}(m) = P(t \leq m | Z_n = i, Z_{n+1} = j),$$

represent the distribution function that an economic situation's transition will take place within an amount of time m, given that the process has just entered i and will enter j next.

Let $r > 0$ be the continuously compounded risk-free interest rate, and let δ be the continuously compounded dividend yield. Assume that changes in asset prices are distributed as the well-known risk-neutral distribution in a binomial tree,

$$P(X_j(m) = x_j(m)) = \begin{cases} q_j(m) & x_j(m) = u_j(m) \\ 1 - q_j(m) & x_j(m) = d_j(m) = 1/u_j(m) \end{cases}, \quad j \in \mathbb{Z}$$

where

$$q_j(m) = \frac{e^{(r-\delta)m} - d_j(m)}{u_j(m) - d_j(m)}, \quad u_j(m) = e^{\sigma_j \sqrt{m}}, \quad j \in \mathbb{Z}.$$

The arbitrage opportunities are excluded when

$$d_j(m) < e^{(r-\delta)m} < u_j(m), \quad j \in \mathbb{Z}.$$

The economic situations are ordered based on volatility σ_j. The larger the σ_j value, the worse the economy, and the smaller the σ_j value, the better the economy.

At each transition between economic situations, the current information determines whether rights are either exercised or held until the next economic situation. The payoff function for put (call) is given by $v^e(s) = \max\{K - s, 0\}(v^e(s) = \max\{s - K, 0\})$ with domain $s \in [0, \infty)$.

Consider the American option when a set of the current asset price, economic situation and time is (s, i, t). The option price $v_n(s, i, t)$ is given by the following equation:

$$v_n(s, i, t) = \max \begin{cases} v^e(s) = \max\{K - s, 0\} \quad \text{or} \quad \max\{s - K, 0\} \\ v_n^h(s, i, t) \end{cases}$$

where

$$v_n^h(s, i, t) = \sum_{j=1}^{3} p_{ij} \sum_{k=1}^{2} \int_0^{T-t} e^{-rm} v_{n+1}(sx_j^k(m), j, t + m) P(x_j^k(m)) f_{ij}(m) dm.$$

Here, $x_j^1(m) = u_j(m)$, $x_j^2(m) = d_j(m)$ and $f_{ij}(m)$ is the probability density function of $F_{ij}(m)$.

Recall that $v^e(s)$ is the payoff function which gives the exercise value of the option. On the other hand, notation $v_n^h(s, i, t)$ in the above equation stands for the hold value of the option. Since the hold value at maturity is zero, $v_n(s, i, T) = \max\{v^e(s), v_n^h(s, i, T)\} = v^e(s)$.

6.3. Exercising strategies

Section 6.3 provides some numerical calculations after setting the parameters.

6.3.1. *Setting parameter*

The transitions and properties of option prices are examined numerically. The parameters are set as shown in Table 6.1, which is partially based on the work of Dimitrov et al. (2021).

Name	Notation	Parameter
Maturity time	T	$80/252$
Time duration of a step	τ	$8/252$
Volatility vector	σ	$(0.25, 0.15, 0.05)$
Strike price	K	100
Interest rate	r	0.02
Dividend yield (American call)	δ	0.1
Transition probability matrix	P	$[p_{ij}]_{i,j=1,2,3}$

Table 6.1. *Each parameter used in this study*

In the simulation, equidistant time intervals $\tau = \frac{8}{252}$ were prepared, and the expected value of option price can be calculated as follows:

$$v_n^h(s,i,t) = \sum_{j=1}^{3} p_{ij} \sum_{k=1}^{2} \sum_{m=1}^{\frac{T-t}{\tau}} e^{-rm\tau} v_{n+1}(sx_j^k(m\tau), j, t+m\tau) P(x_j^k(m\tau)) f_{ij}(m\tau)$$

The following asset price dataset was used in the simulation:

$$S_p^* = \left\{ \left(0.4 + \frac{1.31}{10000} \times i \right) \times K : i \in \{0, 1, ..., 10000\} \right\}$$

$$S_c^* = \left\{ \left(0.58 + \frac{1.64}{10000} \times i \right) \times K : i \in \{0, 1, ..., 10000\} \right\}$$

The range of asset prices used in the simulation is $40 \leq s \leq 171$ for the American put option and $58 \leq s \leq 222$ for the American call option. Note that the final asset price range used for analysis is $70 \leq s \leq 100$ for the American put option and $100 \leq s \leq 130$ for the American call option. However, in the above dataset, the asset price value is not exactly 70 or 100 for the American put option. Therefore, we extract and analyze the range from $s = 69.999$ when $i = 2290$ to $s = 99.998$ when $i = 4580$.

We assume that the distribution function $F_{ij}(m)$ follows a gamma distribution with shape parameter $\alpha = 2$ and scale parameter $\theta = 238$.

$$f_{ij}(m) = P(t \leq m | Z_n = i, Z_{n+1} = j) = \frac{1}{\Gamma(\alpha)\theta^\alpha} m^{\alpha-1} e^{-\frac{m}{\theta}}$$

Also, P is given as follows:

$$P = \begin{bmatrix} 0.70 & 0.20 & 0.10 \\ 0.10 & 0.40 & 0.50 \\ 0.05 & 0.25 & 0.70 \end{bmatrix}$$

6.3.2. *Relationship between the American option price and economic situation* i

Numerical calculations of American put and call options were performed using a basic dataset given in section 6.3.1.

Figure 6.1 shows graphs of the expected option price when exercising was selected for s, $v^e(s)$ and the expected option price when holding was selected for current information (s, i, t), $v_n^h(s, i, t)$, during changes in economic situations. Here, $s = 94.889$ for the American put option and $s = 104.920$ for the American call option. Table 6.2 shows the option prices used when creating the graph in Figure 6.1.

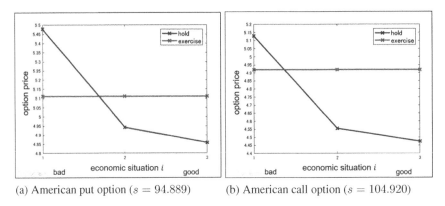

(a) American put option ($s = 94.889$)   (b) American call option ($s = 104.920$)

Figure 6.1. *Changes in option prices due to economic situations* i

(a) American put option

	economic situation i		
	1	2	3
hold	5.4875	4.9428	4.8588
exercise	5.1110	5.1110	5.1110

(b) American call option

	economic situation i		
	1	2	3
hold	5.1289	4.5551	4.4754
exercise	4.9204	4.9204	4.9204

Table 6.2. *Details of option prices used in Figure 6.1*

Figure 6.1 shows that the holding value of the option $v_n^h(s, i, t)$ decreased as the economic situation improved for the American put and call options. This happens because the volatility of asset price will increase if the economic situation is bad, and there is a greater chance of exercising at a better price in the future, so the holding value of the option will increase. Conversely, the volatility of asset price will decrease if the economic situation is good, and there is less chance of exercising at a better price in the future, so the holding value of the option will increase.

The value calculated here and the graph are used as the basis. In the following, we calculate the option price when each parameter is changed, and consider how the option price changes using the value and the graph.

6.3.3. *Relationship between the American option price and the asset price* s

Using the parameters in Table 6.1, the American put and call options are considered when only the initial asset price changes, holding all other variables fixed.

Figure 6.2 shows a graph of the exercise value of the option $v^e(s)$ and holding value of the option $v_n^h(s, i, t)$ due to changes in the initial asset price s for American put and call options. The economic situation here is $i = 2$.

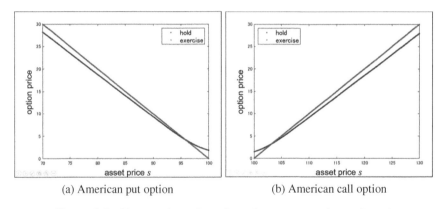

(a) American put option   (b) American call option

Figure 6.2. *Changes in option prices due to asset prices* s ($i = 2$)

As Figure 6.2 shows, the holding value of the option $v_n^h(s, i, t)$ decreased for the American put option as the asset price increased, and increased for the American call option as the asset price increased. This occurs because the value of the asset price approaches the strike price for the American put option as the asset price increases, and the future payoff decreases, so $v_n^h(s, i, t)$ is considered to be smaller. Also, the value of the asset price moves away from the strike price for the American call option as the asset price increases, and the future payoff increases, so $v_n^h(s, i, t)$ is considered to be greater.

6.3.4. *Relationship between the American option price and maturity* T

Using the parameters in Table 6.1, the American put and call options are considered when only the maturity is changed.

Figure 6.3 shows graphs of the holding value of the option $v_n^h(s, i, t)$ when the maturity is $T = \frac{64}{252}, \frac{80}{252}, \frac{96}{252}$. $s = 94.889$ for the American put option and $s = 104.920$ for the American call option. Table 6.3 shows the option prices used when creating the graph in Figure 6.3.

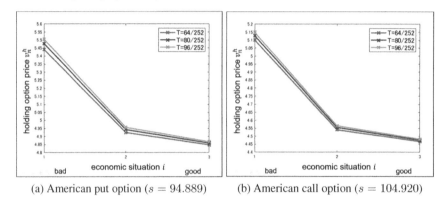

(a) American put option ($s = 94.889$)   (b) American call option ($s = 104.920$)

Figure 6.3. *Changes in option prices due to maturity* M

(a) American put option	economic situation i		
	1	2	3
$T = \frac{64}{252}$	5.4416	4.9245	4.8479
$T = \frac{80}{252}$	5.4780	4.9428	4.8588
$T = \frac{96}{252}$	5.5051	4.9566	4.8670

(b) American call option	economic situation i		
	1	2	3
$T = \frac{64}{252}$	5.1015	4.5406	4.4667
$T = \frac{80}{252}$	5.1289	4.5551	4.4754
$T = \frac{96}{252}$	5.1494	4.5654	4.4815

Table 6.3. *Details of option prices used in Figure 6.3*

As Figure 6.3 shows, the holding value of the option $v_n^h(s, i, t)$ increased as the maturity increased for the American put and call options. If the maturity is long, asset prices are more likely to fluctuate, and there is a greater chance of exercising at a better price in the future, so the holding value of the option will increase. Conversely, if the maturity is short, asset prices are less likely to fluctuate, and there is a smaller chance of exercising at a better price in the future, so the holding value of the option will decrease.

6.3.5. *Relationship between the American option price and transition probabilities* P

We note that the relationship between the American option price and economic situation, asset price and maturity, addressed in sections 6.3.2–6.3.4, is consistent with the general properties of the American options. However, the relationship between

American option price and transition probabilities P is not easy to speculate. This will be investigated carefully in this section.

Using the parameters in Table 6.1, American put and call options are considered when only the transition probabilities change.

Let P given in section 6.3.1 represents the "normal" economy. We newly set a "stable" economy in which economic situations were difficult to change and an "unstable" economy in which economic situations were easy to change.

Matrices P_s and P_u that represent the "stable" and "unstable" economies are given as follows:

$$P_s = \begin{bmatrix} 0.85 & 0.10 & 0.05 \\ 0.10 & 0.75 & 0.15 \\ 0.05 & 0.15 & 0.80 \end{bmatrix} \qquad P_u = \begin{bmatrix} 0.40 & 0.30 & 0.30 \\ 0.25 & 0.35 & 0.40 \\ 0.20 & 0.30 & 0.50 \end{bmatrix}$$

Figure 6.4 shows graphs of the holding value of the option $v_n^h(s, i, t)$ for changes in each economy. $s = 94.889$ for the American put option and $s = 104.920$ for the American call option. Table 6.4 shows the option prices used when creating the graph in Figure 6.4.

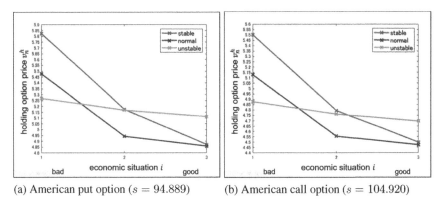

(a) American put option ($s = 94.889$)   (b) American call option ($s = 104.920$)

Figure 6.4. *Changes in holding values of the option due to P*

As Figure 6.4 shows, the "stable" economy had higher holding values of the option than the "normal" economy for the American put and call options when the economic situation was $i = 1, 2$. A "stable" economy is less likely to transition into other economic situations than a "normal" economy, and the volatility of the asset price of $i = 1, 2$ is larger than that of $i = 3$. Therefore, when the economic situation is $i = 1, 2$, there will be an even greater chance of exercising at a better price in the future, so the holding value of the option will increase.

	economic situation i		
	1	2	3
stable	5.8235	5.1751	4.8724
normal	5.4780	4.9428	4.8588
unstable	5.2683	5.1676	5.1122

(a) American put option

	economic situation i		
	1	2	3
stable	5.5019	4.7948	4.4985
normal	5.1289	4.5551	4.4754
unstable	4.8765	4.7609	4.6960

(b) American call option

Table 6.4. *Details of option prices used in Figure 6.4*

Also, the holding value of the option did not change much in an "unstable" economy, even if the economic situation changed because it is difficult to predict the future of an "unstable" economy. Therefore, the holding value of the option will be the same regardless of the current economic situation.

Matrix P_u has partial ordering, totally positive of order 2 (TP$_2$) and stochastic increasing (SI). The partial ordering, TP$_2$ and SI are defined below.

– **Totally positive of order 2 (TP$_2$)** (Karlin 1968)
Let $P = [p_{ij}]$ be an $n \times m$ matrix for which

$$\begin{vmatrix} p_{ij} & p_{ij'} \\ p_{i'j} & p_{i'j'} \end{vmatrix} \geq 0$$

for any $1 \leq i < i' \leq n$ and $1 \leq j < j' \leq m$, then matrix P has a property of TP$_2$.

– **Stochastic increasing (SI)** (Marshall et al. 1979)
Let $P = [p_{ij}]$ be an $n \times m$ matrix for which

$$\sum_{j=k}^{m} x_{ij} \leq \sum_{j=k}^{m} y_{i'j}$$

for any $1 \leq i < i' \leq n$ and $1 \leq k \leq m$, then matrix P has a property of SI.

Jin et al. (2019) showed that the TP$_2$ property of the transition probability matrix for the economic situation was important for having a monotonically decreasing option price as the economic situation improves. For the following two matrices, $P_{u,\text{SI}}$ and $P_{u,\text{None}}$, it is true that $P_{u,\text{SI}}$ does not have the TP$_2$ property, and has the SI property, while matrix $P_{u,\text{None}}$ has neither the properties of TP$_2$ nor of SI.

$$P_{u,\text{SI}} = \begin{bmatrix} 0.50 & 0.20 & 0.30 \\ 0.30 & 0.30 & 0.40 \\ 0.20 & 0.30 & 0.50 \end{bmatrix}, \qquad P_{u,\text{None}} = \begin{bmatrix} 0.20 & 0.40 & 0.40 \\ 0.40 & 0.20 & 0.40 \\ 0.40 & 0.40 & 0.20 \end{bmatrix}$$

Figure 6.5 shows graphs of the holding value of the option $v_n^h(s, i, t)$ for $\boldsymbol{P}_{u,\mathrm{SI}}$ and $\boldsymbol{P}_{u,\mathrm{None}}$. The initial asset prices are $s = 94.889$ for the American put option and $s = 104.920$ for the American call option. Table 6.5 shows the option prices used when creating the graph in Figure 6.5.

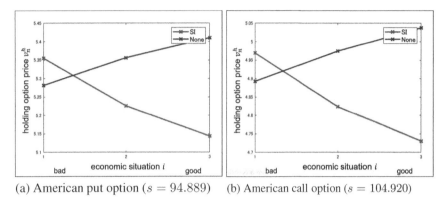

(a) American put option ($s = 94.889$)   (b) American call option ($s = 104.920$)

Figure 6.5. *Changes in holding values of the option due to partial ordering*

(a) American put option

	economic situation i		
	1	2	3
SI	5.3548	5.2258	5.1437
None	5.2813	5.3561	5.4107

(b) American call option

	economic situation i		
	1	2	3
SI	4.9693	4.8240	4.7306
None	4.8926	4.9745	5.0377

Table 6.5. *Details of option prices used in Figure 6.5*

Figure 6.5 shows that for the American put and call options, the holding value of the option $v_n^h(s, i, t)$ decreased as the economic situation improved when using $\boldsymbol{P}_{u,\mathrm{SI}}$, and $v_n^h(s, i, t)$ increased when using $\boldsymbol{P}_{u,\mathrm{None}}$. Even when a transition probability matrix had SI (a looser condition than TP$_2$), the option price decreased monotonically. However, when a transition probability matrix had neither the TP$_2$ nor the SI property, the monotonicity of the option price was not established. This result implies that the TP$_2$ property may be sufficient but not necessary for the establishment of monotone investment strategies. However, some milder condition, such as the SI property, is necessary to ensure the monotonicity of option price.

6.3.6. *Consideration of the optimal exercise region*

We created diagrams of the optimal exercise region for the American put and call options and considered the properties of holding and exercising thresholds (switching points).

Figure 6.7 shows the optimal exercise region for the American put and call options when applying the parameters in Table 6.1. Figures 6.6 and 6.8 show the optimal exercise regions for the American put and call options when the maturity is $T = \frac{64}{252}$ and $T = \frac{96}{252}$, respectively.

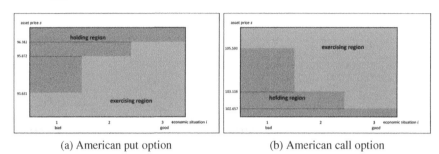

(a) American put option   (b) American call option

Figure 6.6. *Optimal exercise region with maturity* $T = \frac{64}{252}$

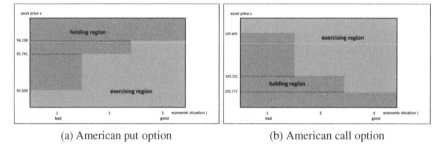

(a) American put option   (b) American call option

Figure 6.7. *Optimal exercise region with maturity* $T = \frac{80}{252}$

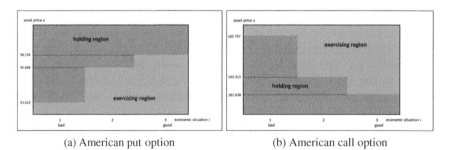

(a) American put option   (b) American call option

Figure 6.8. *Optimal exercise region with maturity* $T = \frac{96}{252}$

As Figure 6.7 shows, the critical value of the asset prices (the threshold for holding and exercising) increased for the American put option. It decreased for the American call option as the economic situation improved. Also, the holding region in the American put and call options decreased, and the exercising region increased as the economic situation improved. As explained in section 6.3.2, this occurs because the worse the economic situation, the greater the chance of exercising at a better price in the future, so the holding region increases. Conversely, the better the economic situation, the less the possibility of exercising at a better price in the future, so the holding region decreases.

Comparing Figures 6.6–6.8, the longer the maturity in the American put and call options, the greater the holding region and the smaller the exercising region. As explained in section 6.3.4, the holding region grows larger because the longer the maturity, the greater the chance of exercising at a better price in the future. However, the shorter the maturity, the smaller the chance of exercising at a better price in the future, so the holding region will decrease.

6.4. Conclusion

We used a semi-Markov decision process to price American options when asset price dynamics followed a binomial model, with the volatility parameter governed by a varying economic situation. The transitions of the economic situation is based on a semi-Markov chain. We found that the American option price has a monotone property with respect to the economic situation, the initial asset price and the maturity time. Moreover, we investigated the relationship between the option price and the transition probabilities for the semi-Markov chain. Our experiments have shown that the monotonicity of the option price is not established if the transition probability matrix has neither a TP_2 property nor an SI property. Our numerical results have also suggested that the TP_2 property may be sufficient but not necessary for the establishment of the monotonicity. A milder condition like the SI property may be necessary.

In this study, we assumed that an economic situation could be observed directly. However, an economic situation in a spot market sometimes cannot be observed directly. Only observations such as economic indicators can provide partial information related to a real economic situation. In future work, we will extend the model of the changing economic situation to a directly unobservable one and investigate the properties of the option price and exercise region.

6.5. References

Bertsekas, D. (2000). *Dynamic Programming and Optimal Control, Volume 1*, 4th edition. Athena Scientific, Belmont, MA.

Bertsekas, D. and Tsitsiklis, J.N. (1995). Neuro-dynamic programming: An overview. *Proceedings of 1995 34th IEEE Conference on Decision & Control*, New Orleans, LA.

Broadie, M. and Detemple, J. (1999). American options on dividend-paying assets. *Fields Institute Communications*, 22, 22–97.

Carriere, J.F. (1996). Valuation of the early-exercise price for options using simulations and nonparametric regression. *Mathematics and Economics*, 19(1996), 19–30.

D'Amico, G., Janssen, J., Manca, R. (2009). European and American options: The semi-Markov case. *Physica A*, 388, 3181–3194.

Dimitrov, M., Jin, L., Ni, Y. (2021). Properties of American options under a Markovian Regime Switching Model. *Communications in Statistics: Case Studies, Data Analysis and Applications*, 1–7, July 30.

Guo, X. and Zhang, Q. (2004). Closed-form solutions for perpetual American put options with regime switching. *SIAM Journal on Applied Mathematics*, 64(6), 2034–2049.

Ishidomaru, Y. (2020). Study about pricing American option using regime switching model and optimal strategy. Bachelor's Thesis, University of Electro-Communication, Tokyo (in Japanese).

Jin, L., Dimitrov, M., Ni, Y. (2019). Valuation and optimal strategies for American options under a Markovian regime-switching model. *Stochastic Processes and Algebraic Structures, Volume 1. Stochastic Processes, Statistical Methods, and Engineering Mathematics 1*, Malyarenko, A., Ni, Y., Rancić, M. (eds). Springer International Publishing, Cham (forthcoming).

Karlin, S. (1968). *Total Positivity*. Stanford University Press, Palo Alto, CA.

Kijima, M. and Yoshida, T. (1993). A simple option pricing model with Markovian volatilities. *Journal of the Operations Research Society of Japan*, 36, 3.

Kim, I.J. and Byun, S.J. (2004). Optimal exercise boundary in a binomial option pricing model. *Journal of Financial Engineering*, 3(2), 137–158.

Marshall, A.W., Olkin, I., Arnold, B.C. (1979). *Inequalities: Theory of Majorization and Its Applications*. Academic Press, Inc., Orlando, FL.

Nasir, A., Khursheed, A., Ali, K., Mustafa, F. (2020). A Markov decision process model for optimal trade of options using statistical data. *Computational Economics*, 58(2), 327–346.

Sato, K. and Sawaki, K. (2012). The valuation of callable financial options with regime switches: A discrete-time model (financial modeling and analysis). *RIMS Kokyuroku*, 1818, 22–46.

Sato, K. and Sawaki, K. (2018). The dynamics valuation of callable contingent claims with a partially observable regime switch. Available at SSRN: 3284489.

Shi, X., Zhang, L., Kim, Y.S.A. (2016). A Markov chain approximation for American option pricing in the tempered stable GARCH models. *Frontiers in Applied Mathematics and Statistics*, 1(13), 1–12.

The Implementation of Hierarchical Classifications and Cochran's Rule in the Analysis of Social Data

In social sample survey research and the census, international organizations have developed classifications for the measurement of background variables such as the level of educational attainment (ISCED), economic activities (ISIC) and occupations (ISCO) to ensure the cross-national and overtime comparability of measurement. In this context, Eurostat developed the *Nomenclature des Unités territoriales statistiques* – Nomenclature of Territorial Units for Statistics (NUTS) and the European socio-economic classification (ESeC). All of these classifications – with the exception of ISCED – are categorical schemas, defined hierarchically to allow for different levels of detail in the analyses. However, when performing bivariate analyses with these classifications, Cochran's well-known rule of thumb of expected values larger than five in order to use the chi-square test should also be taken into account in presenting the results. In this chapter, we investigate the implementation of ESeC to regions (NUTS) to demonstrate how to statistically decide on the appropriate level of classification to be used in the analysis of social data. The analysis is based on the 2016 European Social Survey (ESS) datasets for five European countries: Austria, Belgium, France, Ireland and Italy.

7.1. Introduction

In social sample survey research and the census, as mentioned in previous work (Yfanti and Michalopoulou 2020; Yfanti et al. 2020), international organizations have developed classifications to provide the standardized measurement of certain

Chapter written by Aggeliki Yfanti and Catherine Michalopoulou.

background variables so as to ensure their cross-national and overtime comparability (Kish 1994; Hoffmann and Chamie 1999; d'Errico et al. 2017; Yfanti et al. 2019). The most commonly used classifications such as this are the International Standard Classification of Education (ISCED) based on the level of educational attainment that was developed by UNESCO, the International Standard Industrial Classification (ISIC) of all economic activities developed by the United Nations Statistics Division and the International Standard Classification of Occupations (ISCO) developed by the International Labour Organization. In this context, Eurostat developed the *Nomenclature des unités territoriales statistique* (NUTS) for the socio-economic analyses of the European Union (EU) regions (Eurostat n.d.a) and the European socio-economic classification (ESeC) for the study of "differences in social structures and socio-economic inequalities across the European Union" (Cochran 1952; Rose et al. 2010; see also Harrison and Rose 2006; Eurostat 2007; Lambert and Bihagen 2007, 2014; Rose and Harrison 2010; Penissat and Rowell 2015; Yfanti and Michalopoulou 2020; Yfanti et al. 2020). All of these classifications are categorical schemas with the exception of ISCED which is ordinal categorical. They are "hierarchically structured, such that all categories at lower levels are sub-categories of a category at the next level up" (Hancock 2013; d'Errico et al. 2017) so as to allow for different levels of detail in the analyses (Eurostat n.d.b; Gordon 1981, 1987; Hancock 2017).

The Eurostat (n.d.a) NUTS classification (Figure 7.1) is a "geographical nomenclature subdividing the economic territory of the European Union (EU) into regions at three different levels, NUTS 1, 2 and 3, respectively, moving from larger to smaller territorial units. Above NUTS 1, there is the 'national' level of the Member States". Eurostat (n.d.a) defines the three NUTS levels as follows: "major socio-economic regions (NUTS 1); basic regions for the application of regional policies (NUTS 2); small regions for specific diagnoses (NUTS 3)".

The Eurostat (n.d.c) NUTS classification ensures the stability of definitions so "that data refers to the same regional unit for a certain period of time", i.e. the period of stability.

> However, sometimes national interests require changing the regional breakdown of a country. When this happens the country concerned informs the European Commission about the changes. The Commission in turn amends the classification at the end of the period of stability according to the rules of the NUTS Regulation.

(Eurostat n.d.c) So far, six amendments have been regulated and the last was applied from January 1, 2021, listing 104, 283 and 1,345 regions at NUTS levels 1, 2 and 3, respectively (for the territorial typologies manual see Eurostat (2019)).

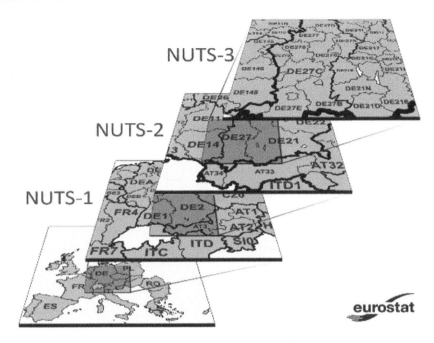

Figure 7.1. *A graphical representation of the three NUTS levels (source: Eurostat n.d.a.). Available at: https://ec.europa.eu/eurostat/web/nuts/background. For a color version of this figure, see www.iste.co.uk/zafeiris/data2.zip*

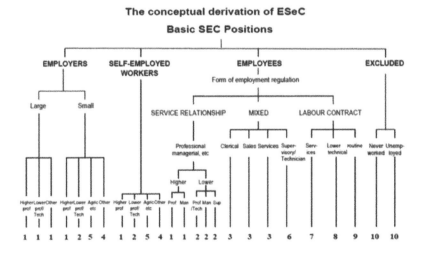

Figure 7.2. *Conceptual derivation of ESeC (source: Harrison and Rose (2006))*

The ESeC is considered to be a "useful diagnostic tool [to assess] the impact of social and economic policy on different social groups [...] to describe but also to understand how socio-economic position relates to relevant key social indicators, variables and social domains" (Rose et al. 2010; Eurostat n.d.a). In Figure 7.2, the conceptual derivation of ESeC is presented.

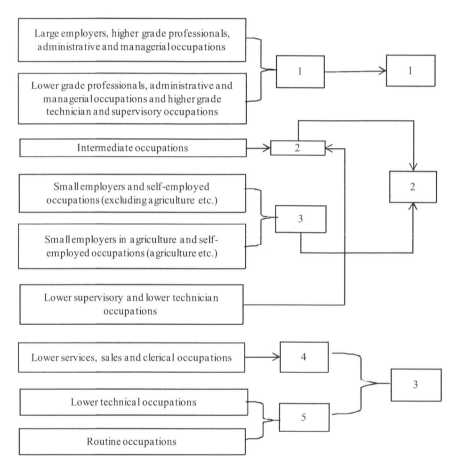

Figure 7.3. *definition of the 9 ESeC classes and the derivation of the 5- and 3- class levels (source: Rose et al. (2010))*

As shown, the ESeC classification distinguishes between employers (large and small, professional and non-professional), the self-employed (professional and non-professional), employees according to their employment relations and the two categories (10) of the unemployed and those that have never worked, which are excluded. Therefore, the ESeC classification is defined by 9 classes which may be collapsed to 5 and 3 classes, as presented in Figure 7.3 (Rose et al. 2010; Penissat and Rowell 2015).

Although these classifications have been widely used in social research, when performing bivariate analyses with them – or for that matter with any other hierarchical classification – Cochran's well-known rule of thumb of expected values larger than five, in order to use the chi-square test (Cochran 1954; Blalock 1979; Agresti 2013; d'Errico et al. 2017; Kroonenberg and Verbeek 2018), should also be taken into account in presenting the results.

In this chapter, we investigate the implementation of ESeC to regions (NUTS) to demonstrate how to statistically decide on the appropriate level of classifications to be used in the analysis of social data. The analysis is based on the 2016 European Social Survey (ESS) datasets for five European countries.

7.2. Methods

The analysis was based on the European Social Survey Round 8 Data (European Social Survey 2016) for the following European countries: Austria, Belgium, France, Ireland and Italy. In Table 7.1, the number of cells in the bivariate analyses of regions, defined at NUTS levels 1, 2 and 3 by the ESeC 9-, 5- and 3-class levels is presented for each country. As expected, as the number of cells increases, the more detail is required for the analysis. It should be noted that ESS data at the NUTS 3 level is provided only for Ireland.

For each country, bivariate analyses of regions, defined at the three NUTS levels by the ESeC 9-, 5- and 3-class levels were performed. Only statistically significant ($p < .001$) results were to be considered.

Cochran's rule of thumb is formulated as follows: "*Contingency tables with more than 1 d.f.* If relatively few expectations are less than 5 (say in 1 cell out of 5 or more, or 2 cells out of 10 or more), a minimum expectation of 1 is allowable in computing χ^2" (Cochran 1954, 420; see also Blalock 1976; Agresti 2013). As Kroonenberg and Verbeek (2018, p. 178) pointed out, "Cochran indicated what he meant by 'allowable': A disturbance [i.e. a difference between the exact and tabulated P] is regarded as unimportant if when the P is 0.05 in the χ^2 table, the exact P lies between 0.04 and 0.06, and if when the tabular P is 0.01, the exact P lies between 0.007 and 0.015 (Cochran 1952, p. 328 and p. 329)".

NUTS by	Country				
ESeC	Austria	Belgium	France	Ireland	Italy
3x9	35x9=315	40x9=360	101x9=909	8x9=64	110x9=990
3x5	35x5=175	40x5=200	101x5=505	8x5=40	110x5=550
3x3	35x3=105	40x3=120	101x3=303	8x3=24	110x3=330
2x9	9x9=81	11x9=99	21x9=189	3x9=27	21x9=189
2x5	9x5=45	11x5=55	21x5=105	3x5=15	21x5=105
2x3	9x3=27	11x3=33	21x3=63	3x3=9	21x3=63
1x9	3x9=27	3x9=27	12x9=108	1x9=9	5x9=45
1x5	3x5=15	3x5=15	12x5=60	1x5=5	5x5=25
1x3	3x3=9	3x3=9	12x3=36	1x3=3	5x3=15

Table 7.1. *Number of cells in the bivariate analysis of regions defined at the three levels of the Nomenclature of Territorial Units for Statistics (NUTS 1, 2 and 3) by the ESeC 9-, 5- and 3-class levels for each country*

Therefore, to assess the bivariate analyses results, apart from presenting the value of the χ^2-test, the relevant degrees of freedom (*d.f.*) and the *p*-value, Cochran's rule of thumb also requires information on the number of cells with an expected value of less than 5 and the minimum expected values. In SPSS, this information is to be found in the footnote of the χ^2-test output (Figure 7.4).

Chi-Square Tests

	Value	df	Asymp. Sig. (2-sided)
Pearson Chi-Square	251.861[a]	160	.000
Likelihood Ratio	263.429	160	.000
N of Valid Cases	1,330		

a. 105 cells (55.6%) have expected count less than 5. The minimum expected count is 0.11.

Figure 7.4. *The SPSS χ^2-test results of the bivariate analysis of the 9-class version of ESeC by the 21 French NUTS 2 regions (source: European Social Survey (2016))*

7.3. Results

In Table 7.2, the frequency count of the ESeC 3-class level is presented.

Country/	ESeC frequency count									
ESeC level	1	2	3	4	5	6	7	8	9	NA
Austria: N= 2,010										
9-class	117	131	99	128	30	231	184	176	131	782
5-class	247	331	158	184	307					
3-class	247	488	492							
Belgium: N= 1,766										
9-class	144	176	52	151	9	298	143	64	109	620
5-class	320	350	160	143	173					
3-class	320	510	316							
France: N= 2,070										
9-class	148	203	47	176	11	459	106	88	93	739
5-class	351	506	187	106	181					
3-class	351	693	287							
Ireland: N= 2,757										
9-class	312	194	89	209	68	357	146	86	227	1,067
5-class	506	447	277	146	313					
3-class	506	724	459							
Italy: N= 2,626										
9-class	120	138	74	303	31	194	160	112	219	1,275
5-class	258	268	334	160	331					
3-class	258	602	491							

Data weighted by the design weight (dweight).

Table 7.2. *Frequency distribution of the three European socio-economic classification (ESeC) levels by country (source: European Social Survey (2016))*

As shown, in all datasets, certain values of the full 9-class version of the ESeC have a relatively small number of cases implying that when performing bivariate analyses there would be cells with expected values less than five. The most indicative in such a case is value 5 for Belgium and France with 9 and 11 cases, respectively.

In Table 7.3, the bivariate analysis χ^2-test results that are available in the ESS dataset NUTS levels, by the three ESeC levels of 9, 5 and 3 classes for each country, are presented.

Country/NUTS / ESeC level	χ^2	df	No of cells with Exp. value < 5	Min. exp. Value	p-value
Austria					
NUTS 2 (9)					
9-class	131.126	64	13 cells (16.0%)	1.11	.000
5-class	75.653	32	0 cells (0.0%)	5.55	.000
3-class	46.947	16	0 cells (0.0%)	8.61	.000
NUTS 1 (3)					
9-class	32.225	16	0 cells (0.0%)	7.11	.009
5-class	23.664	8	0 cells (0.0%)	35.93	.003
3-class	14.791	4	0 cells (0.0%)	56.75	.005
Belgium					
NUTS 2 (11)					
9-class	158.498	89	32 cells (32.3%)	0.25	.000
5-class	76.282	40	6 cells (10.9%)	3.99	.000
3-class	41.341	20	0 cells (0.0%)	8.82	.003
NUTS 1 (3)					
9-class	47.046	16	3 cells (11.1%)	0.86	.000
5-class	26.382	8	0 cells (0.0%)	13.73	.001
3-class	16.048	4	0 cells (0.0%)	30.33	.003
France					
NUTS 2 (21)					
9-class	251.861	160	105 cells (55.6%)	0.11	.000
5-class	139.456	80	27 cells (25.7%)	0.95	.000
3-class	53.513	40	6 cells (3.2%)	2.59	.075
NUTS 1 (12)					
9-class	143.368	88	30 cells (27.8%)	0.47	.000
5-class	93.187	44	2 cells (3.2%)	4.59	.000
3-class	26.615	22	0 cells (0.0%)	12.22	.226
Ireland					
NUTS 3 (8)					
9-class	123.704	56	1 cells (1.4%)	5.00	.000
5-class	59.691	28	0 cells (0.0%)	10.62	.000
3-class	30.744	14	0 cells (0.0%)	33.45	.006

Country/NUTS / ESeC level	χ^2	df	No of cells with Exp. value < 5	Min. exp. Value	p-value
NUTS 2 (3)					
9-class	47.949	16	0 cells (0.0%)	17.96	.000
5-class	16.787	8	0 cells (0.0%)	38.10	.032
3-class	8.207	4	0 cells (0.0%)	120.24	.084
Italy					
NUTS 2 (21)					
9-class	244.846	152	94 cells (52.2%)	0.14	.000
5-class	123.357	76	27 cells (27.0%)	0.71	.000
3-class	70.251	38	10 cells (16.7%)	1.14	.001
NUTS 1 (5)					
9-class	58.008	32	1 cells (2.2%)	2.68	.003
5-class	36.715	16	0 cells (0.0%)	13.87	.002
3-class	17.199	8	0 cells (0.0%)	22.34	.028

exp. = expected. In parentheses, the number of regions is presented for each NUTS level. Data weighted by the design weight (dweight).

Table 7.3. *Bivariate analysis χ²-test results of the Nomenclature of Territorial Units for Statistics (NUTS) levels by the three European socio-economic classification (ESeC) levels for each country (source: European Social Survey (2016))*

As shown, the χ^2-test results for Austria were statistically significant ($p < .001$) at the NUTS 2 level defined by nine regions for all three ESeC levels of 9, 5 and 3 classes with 13 (81 in total), 0 (45 in total) and 0 (27 in total) cells, with an expected value of less than 5, respectively, and minimum expected values larger than 1.11 (9-class).

In the case of Belgium, statistically significant results were obtained at the NUTS 1 level of three regions for both the ESeC 9- and 5-class levels with 3 (27 in total) and 0 (15 in total) cells with an expected value of less than 5, respectively, and minimum expected values larger than 0.86 (9-class). The same results were obtained at the NUTS 2 level of 11 regions, for the ESeC 9- and 5-class levels, with 32 (99 in total) and 6 (55 in total) cells with an expected value of less than 5, respectively, and minimum expected values larger than 0.25 (9-class).

In the case of France, statistically significant results were obtained at the NUTS 1 level of 12 regions for the ESeC 9- and 5-class levels with 30 (108 in total) and 2 (60 in total) cells with an expected value of less than 5, respectively, and minimum expected values larger than 0.47 (9-class). The same results were obtained at the NUTS 2 level of 21 regions, for the two ESeC levels of 9 and 5 classes with 105 (189 in total) and 27 (105 in total) cells with an expected value of less than 5, respectively, and minimum expected values larger than 0.11 (9-class).

In the case of Ireland, statistically significant results were obtained at the NUTS 2 level of three regions only for the ESeC 9-class level with 0 (27 in total) cells with an expected value of less than 5, respectively, and minimum expected values larger than 17.96 (9-class). The same results were obtained at the NUTS 3 level of eight regions, for both the ESeC 9- and 5-class levels with 1 (64 in total) and 0 (40 in total) cells with an expected value of less than 5, respectively, and minimum expected values larger than 5.00 (9-class).

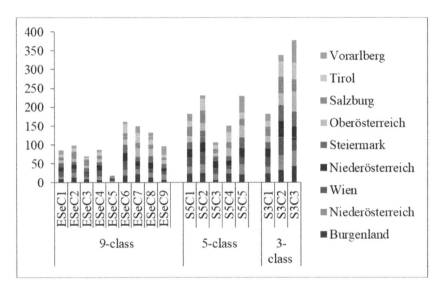

Figure 7.5. *Statistically significant results (p < .001) of the NUTS 2 regional distribution of the three European socio-economic classification (ESeC) levels of 9, 5 and 3 classes for Austria (source: European Social Survey (2016))*

In the case of Italy, statistically significant results were obtained only at the NUTS 2 level of 21 regions for all three ESeC levels of 9, 5 and 3 classes with 94 (189 in total), 27 (105 in total) and 10 (63 in total) cells with an expected value of less than 5, respectively, and minimum expected values larger than 0.14 (9-class).

In Figure 7.5, the results of the nine NUTS 2 regions by the three ESeC levels of 9, 5 and 3 classes are presented for Austria to demonstrate how these findings may be used in social research.

As shown, in designing social policy (NUTS 2), different details in the analysis of ESeC are provided for each region. As all findings are statistically significant, the decision of which ESeC level is more appropriate to use depends on the purposes of the social researchers' questions and analyses.

7.4. Conclusion

In this chapter, we considered Cochran's rule of thumb in statistically deciding on the appropriate level of two hierarchical classifications, NUTS and ESeC, to be used in the analysis of social data. Both of these classifications are defined at three levels: NUTS 1, 2 and 3 and ESeC 9-, 5- and 3-classes. The analysis was based on the 2016 European Social Survey (ESS) datasets for five European countries: Austria, Belgium, France, Ireland and Italy.

The χ^2-test findings showed that statistically significant results ($p < .001$) were obtained in the cases of Austria and Italy for all three ESeC levels at NUTS 2. In the cases of Belgium and France, such results were obtained for the ESeC 9- and 5-class levels at both NUTS 1 and NUTS 2. In the case of Ireland, such results were provided for the ESeC 9-class level at NUTS 2 and the ESeC 9- and 5-class levels at NUTS 3. Based on these results, the choice of which level of the classifications should be used in the analyses depends on the formulation of the research hypotheses (Yfanti and Michalopoulou 2020).

In assessing the performance of the two classifications between countries, the analysis showed that statistically significant results for the ESeC 9-class level were obtained at NUTS 1 level for Belgium and France; at NUTS 2 level for all five countries; and at NUTS 3 level for Ireland. Relevant results for the ESeC 5-class level were obtained at NUTS 1 level for Belgium and France; at NUTS 2 level for all countries except Ireland; and at NUTS 3 level for Ireland. Statistically significant results for the ESeC 3-class level were obtained at NUTS 2 level for Austria and Italy.

It is well known that the application of the χ^2-test requires a large total number of cases N "because of the fact that the sampling distribution of the test statistic approximates the sampling distribution given in the chi-square table only when N is large" (Blalock 1979, p. 290). In the case of large-scale sample surveys such as the ESS we have considered, the total number of cases is large enough for most variables. However, in the case of 2x2 tables where N is small, Fisher's exact test is more appropriate (Agresti 2013; Blalock 1979).

Although we considered three ESeC levels of 9, 5 and 3 classes, Rose et al. (2010, p. 20 and p. 21 also proposed a 6-class version. Since its four values are identical to the 5-class version with separate values for the lower technical and routine occupations that are collapsed in the 5-class version, we decided to present only the analysis based on the latter version. However, the same tests should be carried out before deciding on the level of ESeC to be used in further analysis.

This study demonstrates that hierarchical classifications defined at various levels allow for deciding between them, not only in terms of analytical purposes but also under statistical considerations.

7.5. References

Agresti, A. (2013). *Categorical Data Analysis*, 3rd edition. John Wiley & Sons, New York.

Blalock Jr., H. (1979). *Social Statistics*. McGraw-Hill Kogakusha, Tokyo.

Cochran, W.G. (1952). The χ^2 test of goodness of fit. *Annals of Mathematical Statistics*, 23(3), 315–345.

Cochran, W.G. (1954). Some methods for strengthening the common χ^2 tests. *Biometrics*, 10(4), 417–451.

d'Errico, A., Ricceri, F., Stringhini, S., Carmeli, C., Kivimaki, M., Bartley, M., Bartley, M., McCrory, C., Bochud, M., Vollenweider, P. et al. (2017). Socioeconomic indicators in epidemiologic research: A practical example from the LIFEPATH study. *PLoS ONE*, 12(5), 1–32.

European Social Survey (2016). Round 8 Data [Online]. Available at: https://www. europeansocialsurvey.org/download.html?file=ESS8e02_2&y=2016.

Eurostat (2007). Task force on core social variables: Final report (Theme: Population and social conditions; Collection: Methodologies and working papers). Office for Official Publications of the European Communities, Luxembourg.

Eurostat (2019). Methodological manual on territorial typologies – 2018 edition. Publications Office of the European Union, Luxembourg.

Eurostat (n.d.a). NUTS – Nomenclature territorial units for statistics: Background [Online]. Available at: https://ec.europa.eu/eurostat/web/nuts/background.

Eurostat (n.d.b). Your guide to international statistical classifications. Integrated system of statistical classifications of economic activities and products: General introduction. [Online]. Available at: https://ec.europa/eurostat/miscellaneous/index.cfm?TargetUrl=DS P_INTRO_STAT_CLASS.

Eurostat (n.d.c). NUTS – Nomenclature territorial units for statistics: History of NUTS [Online]. Available at: https://ec.europa.eu/eurostat/web/nuts/history.

Gordon, A.D. (1981). *Classification*. Chapman & Hall, London.

Gordon, A.D. (1987). A review of hierarchical classifications. *Journal of the Royal Statistical Society, Series A (General)*, 150(2), 119–137.

Hancock, A. (2013). Best practice guidelines for developing international statistical classifications [Online]. Available at: https://unstats.un.org/unsd/classifications/bestpractices/Best_practice_Nov_2013.pdf.

Hancock, D. (2017). The modernisation of statistical classifications in knowledge and information management systems. *The Electronic Journal of Knowledge Management*, 15(2), 126–144.

Harrison, E. and Rose, D. (2006). The European socio-economic classification (ESeC) user guide. Institute for Economic and Social Research, University of Essex, Colchester.

Hoffmann, E. and Chamie, M. (1999). Standard statistical classifications: Basic principles. International Labour Office, United Nations Statistics Division, Geneva.

Kish, L. (1994). Multi-population survey designs: Five types with seven shared aspects. *International Statistical Review*, 62(2), 167–186.

Kroonenberg, P.M. and Verbeek, A. (2018). The tale of Cochran's rule: My contingency table has so many expected values smaller than 5, what am I to do? *The American Statistician*, 72(2), 175–183.

Lambert, P.S. and Bihagen, E. (2014). Using occupation-based social classifications. *Work, Employment & Society*, 28(3), 481–494.

Lambert, P.S. and Bihagen, E. (2017). Concepts and measures: Empirical evidence on the interpretation of ESeC and other occupation-based social classifications. Paper, Research Committee 28 (RC28) on Social Stratification and Mobility Summer Meeting, Montreal, 14–17 August.

Penissat, E. and Rowell, J. (2015). The creation of a European socio-economic classification: Limits of expert-driven statistical integration. *Journal of European Integration*, 37(2), 281–297.

Rose, D. and Harrison, E. (eds) (2010). *Social Class in Europe: An Introduction to the European Socio-economic Classification*. Routledge, New York.

Rose, D., Harrison, E., Pevalin, D. (2010). The European socio-economic classification: A prolegomenon. In *Social Class in Europe: An Introduction to the European Socio-economic Classification*, Rose, D. and Harrison, E. (eds). Routledge, New York.

Yfanti, A. and Michalopoulou, C. (2020). The regional distribution of the European socio-economic classification (ESeC) and Cochran's rule: Evidence from the 2018 European Social Survey for five European countries. Paper, European Sociological Association (ESA) RN21 (Quantitative Methods) Midterm Conference "Quantitative Approaches to Analyzing Social Change", Lucerne, October, 9–10.

Yfanti, A., Michalopoulou, C., Zachariou, S. (2019). The impact of definitions in classifying the employed, unemployed and inactive when comparing measurements from different sources. *Communications in Statistics: Case Studies, Data Analysis and Applications*, 5(1), 46–45.

Yfanti, A. Charalampi, A., Michalopoulou, C. (2020). Assessing the performance of the European socio-economic classification (ESeC) in eight European countries for 2018. In *Proceedings of the 6th Stochastic Modeling Techniques and Data Analysis (SMTDA) International Conference*, Skiadas, C.H. (ed.). International Society for the Advancement of Science and Technology (ISAST), Athens.

Dynamic Optimization with Tempered Stable Subordinators for Modeling River Hydraulics

We apply a tempered stable subordinator to modeling and control of river hydraulics, such as streamflow and water quality dynamics. The streamflow dynamics follow a stochastic differential equation driven by a tempered stable subordinator with self-excitation. An entropic dynamic risk measure is employed to evaluate a flood risk under model uncertainty. The problem is solved via a Hamilton–Jacobi–Bellman–Isaacs (HJBI) equation. From the HJBI equation, we explicitly derive an optimal flood mitigation policy of a hydraulic structure, along with the worst-case probability measure of streamflow. An interesting point is that it has a bifurcation point around which the value function diverges or not. A related backward stochastic differential equation for water quality dynamics is also briefly discussed.

8.1. Introduction

Lévy processes are additive and time-homogeneous jump–diffusion processes that have independent increments (Kyprianou 2014). Lévy processes that have infinite activities serve as building blocks for modern mathematical modeling and analysis of stochastic dynamical systems, such as finance and insurance (Molina-Muñoz et al. 2020), and machine learning (Li et al. 2021). Tempered stable subordinators have recently been found to be the right candidates for describing hydraulic processes occurring in river environments (Yoshioka and Yoshioka 2021a; Yoshioka and Yoshioka 2021c). A Lévy process is completely characterized by its

Chapter written by Hidekazu YOSHIOKA and Yumi YOSHIOKA.

Lévy measure, which is an integral kernel as a map from a space of jumps to a positive value (Kyprianou 2014).

A subordinator is a pure jump process having only positive jumps. The Lévy measure v as an integral kernel of a tempered stable subordinator is given by

$$v(dz) = \frac{a \exp(-bz)}{z^{1+\alpha}} dz \, , z > 0. \qquad [8.1]$$

Here, z is an independent variable representing the jump size, $a > 0$ is a parameter modulating the jump frequency, $b > 0$ is a parameter tilting large jumps and $\alpha \in [0,1)$ is the intermittency parameter characterizing the intermittent nature of jumps. The extreme case $\alpha = 0$ corresponds to the Gamma subordinator generating probably the sparsest jump events among all the tempered stable subordinators. We have the divergence behavior of the integral

$$\int_0^\infty v(dz) = +\infty \, , \qquad [8.2]$$

while the boundedness of the moment

$$\int_0^\infty zv(dz) = ab^{\alpha-1}\Gamma(1-\alpha) \, , \qquad [8.3]$$

implying that there are infinitely many jumps in each bounded time interval and their first-order moment is bounded.

The infinite-activities nature combined with the moment boundedness allows us to consider stochastic differential equations (SDEs) driven by tempered stable subordinators. Especially, previous studies (Yoshioka and Yoshioka 2021a; Yoshioka and Yoshioka 2021c) showed that the following tempered stable Ornstein–Uhlenbeck model is a candidate for a continuous-time streamflow time series model:

$$dY_t = -\rho Y_t dt + dZ_{\rho t} \, , \, t > 0 \qquad [8.4]$$

with

$$Q_t = \underline{Q} + Y_t \, , \qquad [8.5]$$

where $\rho > 0$ is the recession rate, $\underline{Q} > 0$ is the minimum flow discharge, $\left(Z_t\right)_{t \geq 0}$ is a Lévy process of the tempered stable type, $\left(Q_t\right)_{t \geq 0}$ is the flow discharge and $\left(Y_t\right)_{t \geq 0}$ is the discharge fluctuation as a non-negative variable.

Later, the authors extended the model to a self-exciting model that can reproduce clustered jumps representing massive flood events, such as floods induced by rainy storms and snowmelts (Yoshioka and Yoshioka 2021b). Set a space-time Poisson random measure $N = N\left(\mathrm{d}z, \mathrm{d}u, \mathrm{d}t\right)$ on $\left(0, +\infty\right)^3$ having the compensator $\rho v\left(\mathrm{d}z\right)\mathrm{d}u\mathrm{d}t$ (Theorem 9.5 from Li (2011)). The compensated measure $\tilde{N} = \tilde{N}\left(\mathrm{d}z, \mathrm{d}u, \mathrm{d}t\right)$ on $\left(0, +\infty\right)^3$ is $N\left(\mathrm{d}z, \mathrm{d}u, \mathrm{d}t\right) - \rho \mathrm{d}u v\left(\mathrm{d}z\right)\mathrm{d}t$. Then, the self-exciting counterpart of the SDE [8.4] is set as

$$\mathrm{d}Y_t = -\rho Y_t \mathrm{d}t + \int_0^{Y_{t-} + \underline{Q}} \int_0^\infty z N\left(\mathrm{d}z, \mathrm{d}u, \mathrm{d}t\right), t > 0. \qquad [8.6]$$

The streamflow discharge is again calculated using the relationship [8.5]. The main difference between the SDEs [8.4] and [8.6] is the noise term; the former is exogenous, while the latter is endogenous. In particular, the noise term of the self-exciting SDE [8.6] is formally seen as a Lévy process that has the state-dependent Lévy(-like) measure

$$v_{Y_{t-}}\left(\mathrm{d}z\right) = \frac{a\left(Y_{t-} + \underline{Q}\right)\exp\left(-bz\right)}{z^{1+\alpha}}\mathrm{d}z, z > 0. \qquad [8.7]$$

A measure transform of the self-exciting SDE [8.6] is presented in Proposition 4.1 from Jiao et al. (2019). The similarity between the integral kernels [8.1] and [8.7] is effectively used in constructing a numerical scheme for simulating sample paths of the self-exciting SDE [8.7]. We assume

$$ab^{\alpha-1}\Gamma\left(1-\alpha\right) < 1, \qquad [8.8]$$

so that [8.6] allows a non-trivial probability measure in a long run ($t \to +\infty$); otherwise, the flow discharge becomes arbitrarily large with probability 1 as $t \to +\infty$, which is clearly an unphysical situation.

The main objective of this chapter is to present an exactly-solvable risk-minimizing stochastic differential game for flood management in rivers. The streamflow dynamics follow stochastic differential equations driven by a tempered stable subordinator. An entropic dynamic risk measure is employed to evaluate a flood risk under model uncertainty. The problem is solved via a

Hamilton–Jacobi–Bellman–Isaacs (HJBI) equation. We explicitly derive an optimal flood mitigation policy of a hydraulic structure along with the worst-case probability measure of river flows. A related backward stochastic differential equation for water quality dynamics is also briefly discussed with demonstrative application using data collected at a river.

8.2. Mathematical model

We use the convention $0 \ln 0 = 0$. We extend the approach of the robust control from Anderson et al. (2003) to the self-exciting SDE [8.4]. We firstly define the Radon–Nikodým derivative between the benchmark and distorted models. Let $\mathbb{P}$ denote the probability measure of the benchmark model, which is the model [8.4] in our case. Following Jiao et al. (2019), set for each real-valued process $(\theta_t)_{t \geq 0}$ that is progressively measurable with respect to the natural filtration generated by the space-time Poisson random measure N, set the continuous-time process $(W_t)_{t \geq 0}$ by

$$W_t = \int_0^t \int_0^{Y_{s-}+Q} \int_0^\infty \left(e^{\theta_{s-}z} - 1 \right) \tilde{N}(\mathrm{d}z, \mathrm{d}u, \mathrm{d}s), \, t \geq 0. \tag{8.9}$$

We should restrict the range of the variable θ_t so that the right-hand side of equation [8.9] is bounded almost surely (a.s.). Considering the specific form of the measure [8.1], to see boundedness of the integral [8.9] we should at least have

$$\theta_t < b. \tag{8.10}$$

Then, set the Radon–Nikodým derivative as the unique non-negative and square-integrable solution (unique non-negative strong solution) $(Z_t)_{t \geq 0}$ of the Itô's SDE

$$\mathrm{d}Z_t = W_t Z_t \mathrm{d}t, \, t > 0 \text{ with } Z_0 = 1. \tag{8.11}$$

Its solution is expressed as

$$\ln Z_t = \int_0^t \int_0^{Y_{s-}+Q} \int_0^\infty \left\{ \theta_{s-} z \cdot N(\mathrm{d}z, \mathrm{d}u, \mathrm{d}s) - \rho \left(e^{\theta_{s-}z} - 1 \right) v(\mathrm{d}z) \mathrm{d}u \mathrm{d}s \right\}. \tag{8.12}$$

To ensure the square integrability, because equation [8.11] is a linear SDE driven by a continuous-time process $(W_t)_{t \geq 0}$, we should have

$$\mathbb{E}\left[W_t^2 \right] = \rho \mathbb{E}\left[\int_0^t \left(Y_{s-} + Q \right) \left(\int_0^\infty \left(e^{\theta_{s-}z} - 1 \right)^2 v(\mathrm{d}z) \right) \mathrm{d}s \right] < +\infty, \, t \geq 0. \tag{8.13}$$

This is satisfied if we always have

$$\theta_t < b / 2 \qquad\qquad\qquad\qquad [8.14]$$

which will be sufficient to guarantee [8.10], although the discussion here can be made more rigorous in the future. Hereafter, we assume equation [8.14], with which the SDE [8.11] allows a unique non-negative strong solution that is known as the Radon–Nikodým derivative.

The expectation evaluated on the probability measure $\mathbb{P}$ ($\mathbb{Q}$) is denoted as $\mathbb{E}_{\mathbb{P}}[\cdot]$ ($\mathbb{E}_{\mathbb{Q}}[\cdot]$). The relative entropy evaluated at some time instance T conditioned on the information up to the time $t(\leq T)$ is then set as

$$\mathbb{E}_{\mathbb{Q}}^{t}[\ln Z_T] = \mathbb{E}_{\mathbb{P}}^{t}[Z_T \ln Z_T]. \qquad\qquad\qquad [8.15]$$

The superscript t stands for the time at which the expectation is conditioned.

8.3. Optimization problem

As an application of the self-exciting SDE [8.6] to streamflow management, we consider a problem of diverting streamflow into a main channel and auxiliary channel. A motivating example of this problem is the optimization of a flood diversion facility that diverts flood water into a main channel and an auxiliary channel. We assume that a city area to be protected from floods is placed downstream of the main channel. This hydraulic problem was originally considered in Yoshioka and Yoshioka (2021a) with the linear SDE [8.4]. We therefore revisit the problem from the viewpoint of the nonlinear SDE [8.6]. Figure 8.1 gives the conceptual image of this problem.

The variables appearing in Figure 8.1 are explained as follows. At each time t, the diversion ratio g_t, which is a progressively measurable process with respect to the natural filtration, is defined in a way that the discharge $g_t Q_t$ is diverted into the main channel, while $(1 - g_t) Q_t$ is diverted into the auxiliary channel. The effort required to divert the streamflow with the diversion ratio g_t is evaluated as $n^{-1} g_t^n (Y_t + \underline{Q})$ with a constant $n > 1$. Considering the definitions of the diverted discharges, the cumulative water volume $(X_t)_{t \geq 0}$ flowing into the main channel satisfies the SDE

$$\mathrm{d}X_t = (1 - g_t)(Y_t + \underline{Q})\mathrm{d}t, \ t > 0, \ X_0 = 0. \qquad\qquad [8.16]$$

In addition, the SDE of the cumulative diversion effort $(U_t)_{t \geq 0}$ is set as another SDE

$$dU_t = n^{-1} g_t^n \left(Y_t + \underline{Q} \right) dt , \quad t > 0 , \quad U_0 = 0. \tag{8.17}$$

The other SDEs to be coupled with equations [8.16] and [8.17] are the self-exciting SDE [8.4] governing the discharge fluctuation and the SDE [8.11] of the Radon–Nikodým derivative. Consequently, we have a 4-D SDE to be optimized.

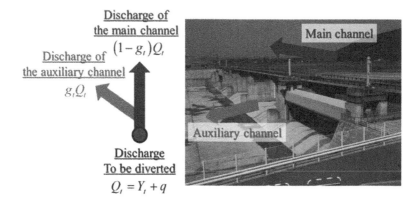

Figure 8.1. *A conceptual image of the flood diversion problem. Left: diversion scheme. Right: a flood diversion facility of the H River, Japan. For a color version of this figure, see www.iste.co.uk/zafeiris/data2.zip*

The control variables of our optimization problem are the diversion ratio g and the ambiguity factor θ; the former is dynamically optimized by the decision-maker, the operator of the flood diversion facility, while the latter is dynamically optimized by the opponent called nature, who acts as the worst-case model uncertainty. Set the admissible sets of the controls g and θ, both of which are progressively measurable with respect to the natural filtration generated by N:

$$\mathcal{G} = \left\{ (g_t)_{t \geq 0} \middle| g_t \text{ is valued in } [0,1] \text{ for each } t \geq 0 \right\} \tag{8.18}$$

and

$$\mathcal{T} = \left\{ (\theta_t)_{t \geq 0} \middle| \theta_t \text{ is valued in } \mathbb{R} \text{ for each } t \geq 0 \right\}. \tag{8.19}$$

The condition [8.14] of θ is checked a posteriori.

Set the fixed terminal time $T > 0$. The performance functional is a map $\psi : [0,T] \times \mathbb{R}_+^4 \times \mathcal{G} \times \mathcal{T} \to \mathbb{R}$, which is a dynamic risk measure considering the multiple factors under ambiguity:

$$
\begin{aligned}
&\psi\left(t, x, y, u, m; g, \theta\right) \\
&= \mathbb{E}_{\mathbb{Q}}^t\left[wX_T + w'U_T - \ln Z_T \big| \left(X_t, Y_t, U_t, Z_t\right) = \left(x, y, u, m\right)\right] \\
&= \mathbb{E}_{\mathbb{P}}^t\left[Z_T\left(wX_T + w'U_T - \ln Z_T\right) \big| \left(X_t, Y_t, U_t, Z_t\right) = \left(x, y, u, m\right)\right]
\end{aligned}
\qquad [8.20]
$$

The first to third terms of equation [8.20] represent the cumulative downstream flood damage that is assumed to be proportional to the cumulative water volume flowing into the main channel (first term), the cumulative diversion effort (second term) and a penalty between the benchmark and distorted models (third term). Here, w, $w' > 0$ are the weighting parameters of the first and second terms. We may consider a weighting factor of the third term, but it can be set to be 1 without any loss of generality. Larger $\min\{w, w'\}$ implies larger uncertainty-aversion of the decision-maker.

The value function is then set as the saddle point

$$
\Phi\left(t, x, y, u, m\right) = \inf_{g \in G} \sup_{\theta \in T} \psi\left(t, x, y, u, m; g, \theta\right). \qquad [8.21]
$$

In this way, the optimization problem is a zero-sum differential game between the decision-maker as a minimizing player and the nature as a maximizing player. Controls that give the value function are called optimal controls and are denoted as $\left(g, \theta\right) = \left(g^*, \theta^*\right)$.

8.4. HJBI equation: formulation and solution

For the sake of simplicity, let us forget the constraint [8.14] for a while. Instead, later, we explore the existence of value functions and associated optimal controls complying with it. Applying a dynamic programming to equation [8.21] considering the system dynamics yields the degenerate parabolic integro-PDE, called the HJBI equation:

$$
\inf_{g \in [0,1]} \sup_{\theta \in \mathbb{R}} L^{g,\theta} \Phi\left(t, x, y, u, m\right) = 0 \text{ for } t \in [0,T) \text{ and } x, y, u, m > 0 \qquad [8.22]
$$

with the terminal condition

$$\Phi(T,x,y,u,m) = m(wx + w'u - \ln m) \quad \text{for } x,y,u,m > 0 \tag{8.23}$$

and the integro-PDE part

$$L^{g,\theta}\Phi = \frac{\partial\Phi}{\partial t} + (1-g)(y+\underline{Q})\frac{\partial\Phi}{\partial x} + \frac{g^n}{n}(y+\underline{Q})\frac{\partial\Phi}{\partial u} - \rho y\frac{\partial\Phi}{\partial y}$$
$$+ \rho(y+\underline{Q})\int_0^\infty \left(\begin{array}{c} \Phi(t,x,y+z,u,me^{\theta z}) - \Phi(t,x,y,u,m) \\ -(e^{\theta z}-1)m\dfrac{\partial\Phi}{\partial m} \end{array}\right) v(\mathrm{d}z). \tag{8.24}$$

We can exchange the order of maximization and minimization in equation [8.22] since these operations are decoupled. With an abuse of notations, the optimal controls are found through the HJBI equation as

$$g_t^* = \arg\min_{g\in[0,1]}\left\{(1-g)(y+\underline{Q})\frac{\partial\Phi}{\partial x} + \frac{g^n}{n}(y+\underline{Q})\frac{\partial\Phi}{\partial u}\right\}, \tag{8.25}$$

$$\theta^*(t,z) = \arg\max_{\theta\in\mathbb{R}} \int_0^\infty \left(\begin{array}{c} \Phi(t,x,y+z,u,me^{\theta z}) - \Phi(t,x,y,u,m) \\ -(e^{\theta z}-1)m\dfrac{\partial\Phi}{\partial m} \end{array}\right) v(\mathrm{d}z). \tag{8.26}$$

Here, the right-hand sides of equations [8.25] and [8.26] are evaluated at the state $(t,x,y,u,m) = (t, X_t, Y_t, U_t, Z_t)$.

Following the strategy from Yoshioka and Yoshioka (2021a), the HJBI equations [8.22]–[8.24] allow a smooth solution of the form:

$$\Phi(t,x,y,u,m) = wxm + w'um - m\ln m + A_t my + B_t m \in C^1\left([0,T]\times\mathbb{R}_+^4\right) \tag{8.27}$$

The time-dependent coefficients A_t, B_t solve the system

$$\frac{\mathrm{d}A_t}{\mathrm{d}t} + \hat{w} - \rho A_t + \rho\int_0^\infty \left(e^{A_t z} - 1\right) v(\mathrm{d}z) = 0 \tag{8.28}$$

And

$$\frac{dB_t}{dt} + \underline{Q}\hat{w} - \rho\underline{Q}\int_0^\infty \left(e^{Az} - 1\right)v(dz) = 0 \qquad [8.29]$$

subject to the terminal condition $A_T, B_T = 0$ and the constants $\hat{w} = (1 - \overline{g})w + n^{-1}\overline{g}''w'$ and $\overline{g} = \arg\min_{g\in[0,1]}\left\{(1-g)w + n^{-1}g''w'\right\}$. Their solutions are not obtained analytically because of the nonlinearity. We should assume that $\left(e^{Az} - 1\right)v(dz)$ is integrable over $(0,\infty)$ for all $t \in [0,T]$ to guarantee the existence of the solution [8.27]; otherwise, it is essentially unbounded because the last terms of equations [8.28] and [8.29] diverge.

We consider a long-term flood mitigation problem $T \to +\infty$, where for the coefficients for such a problem to be meaningful, we should have a non-trivial positive solution $A = A_\infty$ to the nonlinear equation:

$$A - \frac{\hat{w}}{\rho} = \int_0^\infty \left(e^{Az} - 1\right)v(dz). \qquad [8.30]$$

The left side of equation [8.30] is a linear function, while the right side is a convex function diverging towards $+\infty$ as $A \to b-0$.

How many positive solutions are there in equation [8.30]? The total number of positive solutions should be 0, 1 or 2 because of the linear and convex properties of the left and right sides. If $\hat{w}$ is large (if the decision-maker is highly uncertainty-averse), then there exists no positive solution to equation [8.30] and the value function diverges. By contrast, if $\hat{w}$ is small (if the decision-maker is close to be uncertainty-neutral), then by equation [8.8], there exist two positive solutions ($\underline{A}, \overline{A}$ with $0 < \underline{A} < \overline{A} < b$), the former is not larger than the latter and both of them coincide at exactly one value of $\hat{w} > 0$. The smaller solution $A = \underline{A}$ is the stable equilibrium corresponding to A_∞, while the larger solution $A = \overline{A}$ is a saddle equilibrium not corresponding to A_∞. The smaller solution $A = \underline{A}$ is decreasing with respect to $\hat{w}$, while the larger solution $A = \overline{A}$ is increasing with respect to $\hat{w}$. The smaller solution $A = \underline{A}$ approaches towards 0 as $\hat{w}$ decreases. We can therefore conclude that the decision-maker should be sufficiently close to be uncertainty-neutral, or equivalently, the model uncertainty should be sufficiently small to obtain meaningful optimal controls. Of course, $(\theta_\infty =)\underline{A}$ should comply with equation [8.14], which is satisfied for small $\hat{w}$.

The solution [8.27], if it exists, is the value function because it is a smooth and hence a classical solution to the HJBI equation. The existence is guaranteed for small $\hat{w}$, as discussed above. The associated optimal controls are derived as

$$
g_t^* = \begin{cases} 1 & (w \geq w') \\ \left(\dfrac{w}{w'}\right)^{\frac{1}{n-1}} & (w < w') \end{cases} \quad \text{and } \theta_t^* = A_t z , \tag{8.31}
$$

implying that the diversion ratio can be controlled in an open-loop manner and the model uncertainty has an exponential impact on the measure change with the exponent A_t. The integral kernel of the tempered stable subordinator [8.1] under the worst-case should be understood as the exponentially modulated one

$$
v'(\mathrm{d}z) = \frac{a \exp\left(-(b - A_t)z\right)}{z^{1+\alpha}} \mathrm{d}z , z > 0. \tag{8.32}
$$

This integral inherits the properties [8.2] and [8.3] with a different constant in the latter.

We finally present a brief application of the HJBI equation and its solution, focusing on the relationship in a long run [8.30]. We focus on the flood diversion system of the H River, Japan, presented in Figure 8.1. There is the M city in the downstream of the main channel, which is a core city in the watershed of this river. Hourly time series data of flow discharge is available at an observation station located 4 km upstream of this flood diversion facility.

We identified the parameters of the self-exciting SDE [8.1] using the data from January 1, 2016 to December 31, 2018. The parameters $a, b, \alpha, \underline{Q}$ of the model are identified in a least-squares manner so that the sum of the relative errors of average, standard deviation, skewness and kurtosis between the empirical and analytical flow discharges is minimized. These statistics using the time series data are 3.640×10^1 $(\mathrm{m}^3/\mathrm{s})$, 3.972×10^1 $(\mathrm{m}^3/\mathrm{s})$, 4.358×10^0 (-) and 2.832×10^1 (-). As a result, we obtain the parameter values as follows: $\alpha = 0.000$ (-), $a = 9.285 \times 10^{-3}$ $(\mathrm{m}^3/\mathrm{s})$, $b = 1.599 \times 10^{-2}$ $(\mathrm{s}/\mathrm{m}^3)$ and $\underline{Q} = 1.526 \times 10$ $(\mathrm{m}^3/\mathrm{s})$, suggesting that the Gamma type subordinator is as an appropriate model in this case. We obtain $ab^{\alpha-1}\Gamma(1-\alpha) = a/b = 0.58 < 1$ and therefore the assumption [8.8] is satisfied. The average, standard deviation, skewness and kurtosis using the model are 3.640×10^1 $(\mathrm{m}^3/\mathrm{s})$, 3.972×10^1 $(\mathrm{m}^3/\mathrm{s})$, 4.282×10^0 (-) and 2.833×10^1 (-), implying a good agreement between the data and model. The recession rate ρ is then estimated by comparing the empirical and analytical autocorrelations as 2.474×10^{-2} (1/h) or equivalently 6.872×10^{-6} (1/s). Thus, the maximum value of $\hat{w}$ that the algebraic equation [8.30] allows at least one positive solution is

$$\rho \left(b - a - \int_0^\infty \left(e^{(b-a)z} - 1 \right) v(dz) \right) = \rho \left(b - a - a \int_0^\infty \left(e^{(b-a)z} - 1 \right) \frac{e^{-bz}}{z} dz \right) \ (1/m^3) \qquad [8.33]$$

$$= 1.137 \times 10^{-8}$$

This is the threshold value of $\hat{w}$ above which the HJBI equation does not allow the analytical solution [8.27].

8.5. Concluding remarks

We presented a self-exciting SDE describing streamflow time series in a simple manner. The SDE is nonlinear because it has a state-dependent and hence non-standard jump kernel. In addition, we considered a tractable flood diversion problem using the self-exciting SDE. The problem has a bifurcation point around which the value function exists or not.

We finally give a remark on an application of the self-exciting SDE of streamflow time series to dynamic water quality analysis. Conventionally, loading $l = (l_t)_{t \geq 0}$ of a water quality index is approximated as a power function of the discharge: $l_t = C_1 \left(Y_t + \underline{Q} + C_3 \right)^{C_2}$ with positive constants C_1, C_2, C_3. Dissolved silica loading, which can be an important water quality index for assessing eutrophication, has been found to satisfy [10] $C_1 = 0.00382$ (kg/m^3), $C_2 = 1$ and $C_3 = 1.84$ (m^3/s) in an unspam river of a dam–reservoir system in Japan. In this way, we can simply couple streamflow and water quality dynamics parsimoniously. For example, if we are interested in evaluating the expected cumulative water quality loading $\Psi_t^T = \mathbb{E} \left[\int_t^T l_s ds \middle| Y_t \right]$ during some fixed interval $(0, T)$, $T > 0$, conditioned on the state observation (t, Y_t), $0 < t < T$, then we should solve the following backward stochastic differential equation:

$$d\Psi_t^T = -l_t dt + \int_0^{Y_{t-} + \underline{Q}} \int_0^\infty M(z, t-) \tilde{N}(dz, du, dt), \ 0 < t < T \qquad [8.34]$$

with the terminal condition $\Psi_T^T = 0$ and an appropriate space-time map $M(z,t)$ coupled with the formula $l_t = C_1 \left(Y_t + \underline{Q} + C_3 \right)^{C_2}$.

Mathematical modeling and control using the tempered stable subordinators and related SDEs including the presented self-exciting ones will be continued in the future for a deeper understanding of river hydraulics from a stochastic viewpoint.

8.6. Acknowledgments

This research was supported by a Grant for Environmental Research Projects from the Sumitomo Foundation (no. 203160).

8.7. References

Anderson, E.W., Hansen, L.P., Sargent, T.J. (2003). A quartet of semigroups for model specification, robustness, prices of risk, and model detection. *Journal of the European Economic Association*, 1(1), 68–123.

Jiao, Y., Ma, C., Scotti, S., Sgarra, C. (2019). A branching process approach to power markets. *Energy Economics*, 79, 144–156.

Kyprianou, A.E. (2014). *Fluctuations of Lévy Processes with Applications: Introductory Lectures*. Springer, Heidelberg. New York, Dordrecht, London.

Li, Z. (2011). *Measure-Valued Branching Markov Processes*. Springer, Berlin.

Li, Y., Duan, J., Liu, X. (2021). Machine learning framework for computing the most probable paths of stochastic dynamical systems. *Physical Review E*, 103(1), 012124.

Molina-Muñoz, J., Mora-Valencia, A., Perote, J. (2020). Market-crash forecasting based on the dynamics of the alpha-stable distribution. *Physica A: Statistical Mechanics and its Applications*, 557, 124876.

Yoshioka, H. and Yoshioka, Y. (2020). Tempered stable Ornstein–Uhlenbeck model for river discharge time series with its application to dissolved silicon load analysis. *Proceedings of CEESD 2020 in Conjunction with WPCE 2020 & WSM 2020*, 4 December (forthcoming).

Yoshioka, H. and Yoshioka, Y. (2021a). A simple model on streamflow management with a dynamic risk measure. *7th International Conference on Mathematics and Computing (ICMC 2021)*, 2–5 March (forthcoming for Springer Proceedings) [Online]. Available at: https://arxiv.org/abs/2010.15290.

Yoshioka, H. and Yoshioka, Y. (2021b). Streamflow modeling and optimal control based on polynomial jump processes. (forthcoming for *Proceedings of Computational Engineering Conference in 2021*) (in Japanese with English Abstract).

Yoshioka H. and Yoshioka Y. (2021c) Designing cost-efficient inspection schemes for stochastic streamflow environment using an effective Hamiltonian approach. *Optimization and Engineering* [Online]. Available at: https://doi.org/10.1007/s11081-021-09655-7.

Predicting Event Counts in Event-Driven Clinical Trials Accounting for Cure and Ongoing Recruitment

We consider event-driven clinical trials, where analysis is performed when a pre-determined number of clinical events has occurred, for example, progression in oncology and a stroke in cardiovascular trials. We refer to this number of events as the "sample size". At the interim stage, one of the main tasks is predicting the number of events over time and the time to reach specific milestones, accounting for events that may occur in patients yet to be recruited. Therefore, in such trials, we need to model patient recruitment and event counts together.

In this chapter, we develop a new analytic approach which accounts for the opportunity of patients to be cured and also for them to dropout and be unavailable for a follow-up.

Recruitment is modeled using a Poisson–gamma model developed in previous publications. For the process of event occurrence, we assume that the time to the main event and the time to dropout are independent random variables and we have developed a few models using exponential, Weibull and log-normal distributions. This technique is supported by well-developed, tested and documented software. The results are illustrated using simulation and a real dataset with reference to the developed software.

Chapter written by Vladimir ANISIMOV, Stephen GORMLEY, Rosalind BAVERSTOCK and Cynthia KINEZA.
For a color version of all the figures in this chapter, see www.iste.co.uk/zafeiris/data2.zip.

9.1. Introduction

An important aspect of event-driven trials is the operational design at the initial and interim stages, i.e. predicting the event counts over time and the time to reach specific milestones, accounting for events that may occur in patients yet to be recruited. Therefore, in event-driven trials, we need to model patient recruitment and event counts together.

There are different techniques for recruitment modeling described in the literature, and one of the main directions is using mixed Poisson models. This direction has a long history, with several papers devoted to the use of Poisson processes with fixed recruitment rates to describe the recruitment process (Senn 1997, 1998; Carter et al. 2005). However, in real clinical trials, the recruitment rates in different centers vary. Therefore, to model this variation, Anisimov and Fedorov (2007) introduced a Poisson–gamma (PG) model, where the variation in rates in different centers is modeled using a gamma distribution (see also (Anisimov 2008)). Some applications to real trials are considered in Anisimov et al. (2007). This technique was developed further in several publications to predict and re-forecast the interim recruitment process under various conditions (see (Anisimov 2011a, 2020)). Other approaches to recruitment modeling primarily deal with global recruitment. These approaches use different techniques, and we refer the interested readers to the survey papers by Barnard et al. (2010), Heitjan et al. (2015) and Gkioni et al. (2019), and also to a discussion paper by Anisimov (2016b) on using Poisson models with random parameters, with other references therein.

A larger number of clinical trials are event-driven, where the number of clinical events is required to be large enough to allow for reliable statistical conclusions to be made about the parameters of patient responses. For such trials, one of the main tasks is predicting not only the required number of recruited patients, but also the number of events that may occur and the time to reach particular milestones. A useful review of different approaches for event-driven trials is provided in Heitjan et al. (2015). However, for predicting the number of events over time and the time to stop the trial, the authors of papers cited primarily use a Monte Carlo simulation technique, for example, Bagiella and Heitjan (2001). Therefore, Anisimov (2011b) developed an analytic methodology for predictive modeling of the event counts together with patient recruitment in ongoing event-driven trials, also accounting for patient dropout. This methodology is developed further to forecast multiple events at start-up and interim stages under exponential assumptions (Anisimov 2020) and predict some operational characteristics during follow-up times (Anisimov 2016a).

Also of interest in event-driven trials is that a number of patients under treatment will not experience the event within the time of exposure (i.e. time from randomization to a particular milestone), as the therapy for different diseases is improving. Therefore, an interesting direction is to investigate the opportunity to be cured. Here, we note the paper by Chen (2016), but he also uses a simulation technique for predicting event timing and does not consider the case of patient dropout.

Therefore, in this chapter, we developed a new analytic approach to this problem which accounts for ongoing recruitment, patient dropout and also for the opportunity for patients to be cured with some probability.

We assume that the patient recruitment is modeled using a PG model developed in Anisimov and Fedorov (2007) and Anisimov (2011a). We consider non-repeated events and assume that the times to the main event and dropout are independent random variables and there is an opportunity to be cured. Several new models have been developed using exponential, Weibull and log-normal distributions with cure. The focus is on the interim stage, where the parameters of different models are estimated using maximum likelihood technique. The predictive distributions of the number of future events for all considered models are derived in the closed forms; thus, a Monte Carlo simulation is not required.

The developed technique and R-tools allow forecasting the event counts over time and the time to stop the trial with mean and predictive bounds. The results are illustrated using a Monte Carlo simulation and the real dataset.

This chapter is organized as follows: section 9.2 presents the basic models for the process of event occurrence; section 9.3 describes predicting event counts for patients at risk; section 9.4 describes predicting event counts accounting for ongoing recruitment; section 9.5 presents the testing of the Weibull model with cure using a Monte Carlo simulation; section 9.6 deals with software development and an R-package; and section 9.7 illustrates the implementation of a real clinical trial.

9.2. Modeling the process of event occurrence

Consider a trial at some interim time t_1 and assume that there is one type of non-repeated event: the main event of interest A, and the patients also can be lost to follow-up (call it dropout).

Then, all patients that were recruited in the trial until a given interim time can be divided into three groups:

1) group A: a patient experiences event A. Denote by n_A the total number of patients and by $\{x_k, k = 1, .., n_A\}$ the lengths of follow-up periods from randomization date until the event;

2) group O: each patient is censored at interim time; thus, the event and dropout do not occur. Denote by n_O the total number of patients, and by $\{z_i, i = 1, .., n_O\}$ the lengths of follow-up periods from randomization date until interim time;

3) group L: patients are lost to follow-up before interim time. Denote by n_L the total number of patients, and by $\{y_j, j = 1, .., n_L\}$ the lengths of follow-up periods until censoring by dropout.

Consider the following cure model describing the process of event occurrence for every patient.

Assume that after randomization, the patient can either be cured with some probability r, or with probability $1 - r$ can experience event A after some random time τ_A. If a patient is cured, then event A cannot occur.

There is also time to dropout τ_L, and if event A does not occur before τ_L, the patient experiences dropout with no regard for if this patient is cured or not (in this case, event A cannot occur).

Assume that the events for different patients occur independently and the times τ_A and τ_L are also independent random variables with cumulative distribution functions (CDF) $F_A(x)$ and $F_L(x)$, respectively. Suppose that $F_A(x)$, $F_L(x)$ and the probability of being cured r are the same for all patients, though potentially we can consider different treatment groups with different parameters. Assume also that these functions are continuously differentiable and denote by $f_A(x)$ and $f_L(x)$ the corresponding probability density functions (pdf).

9.2.1. *Estimating parameters of the model*

Consider the maximum likelihood method. Denote for convenience, $S_A(x) = 1 - F_A(x)$ and $S_L(x) = 1 - F_L(x)$.

For a patient in group O with exposure time z_i, the probability that event A and dropout will not occur is $S_L(z_i)\left(r + (1 - r)S_A(z_i)\right)$.

For a patient in group A with exposure time x_k, the probability that event A occurs in a small interval $(x_k, x_k + \mathrm{d}x)$ before dropout is $(1 - r)f_A(x_k)\,S_L(x_k)\mathrm{d}x$.

For a patient in group L with exposure time y_j, the probability that dropout occurs in a small interval $(y_j, y_j + \mathrm{d}y)$ before event A is $f_L(y_j)\left(r + (1 - r)S_A(y_j)\right)\mathrm{d}y$.

Given data, the maximum likelihood function has the form

$$P(F_A, F_L, r) = \prod_{i=1}^{n_O} S_L(z_i)\Big(r + (1-r)S_A(z_i)\Big)$$

$$\times \prod_{k=1}^{n_A} (1-r)f_A(x_k)S_L(x_k)$$

$$\times \prod_{j=1}^{n_L} f_L(y_j)\Big(r + (1-r)S_A(y_j)\Big)$$

Correspondingly, the log-likelihood function is

$$\mathcal{L}(F_A, F_L, r) = \sum_{i=1}^{n_O} \log(S_L(z_i)) + \sum_{i=1}^{n_O} \log\Big(r + (1-r)S_A(z_i)\Big)$$

$$+ n_A \log(1-r) + \sum_{k=1}^{n_A} \log(f_A(x_k)) + \sum_{k=1}^{n_A} \log(S_L(x_k))$$

$$+ \sum_{j=1}^{n_L} \log(f_L(y_j)) + \sum_{j=1}^{n_L} \log\Big(r + (1-r)S_A(y_j)\Big)$$

For different types of distributions, this expression will have a different form.

9.2.1.1. *Exponential with the cure model*

This model assumes that the variables τ_A and τ_L are exponentially distributed with rates μ_A and μ_L, respectively. This is a three-parameter model: (μ_A, μ_L, r).

By equating the derivatives of the log-likelihood functions to zero, the relationship $\mu_L = n_L/\Sigma_1$ can be established, resulting in a simplified two-parameter log-likelihood function:

$$\mathcal{L}(\mu_A, r) = -\mu_A \Sigma_A + n_A \log(1-r) + n_A \log(\mu_A)$$

$$+ \sum_{i=1}^{n_O} \log\Big(r + (1-r)\exp(-\mu_A z_i)\Big)$$

$$+ \sum_{j=1}^{n_L} \log\Big(r + (1-r)\exp(-\mu_A y_j)\Big)$$

$$+ n_L\Big(\log(n_L) - \log(\Sigma_1) - 1\Big)$$

where $\Sigma_A = \sum_{k=1}^{n_A} x_k$ and $\Sigma_1 = \sum_{k=1}^{n_A} x_k + \sum_{j=1}^{n_L} y_j + \sum_{i=1}^{n_O} z_i$.

To find the estimators, optimization is carried out by maximizing the log-likelihood function. The initial values are set as $\mu_A(0) = n_A/\Sigma_1$ and $r(0)$ taken to be some range of values in $(0, 1)$. In optimization, new variables (θ_1, θ_2) are considered:

$$\mu_A = \exp(\theta_1); \qquad r = \frac{\exp(\theta_2)}{1 + \exp(\theta_2)}$$

After optimization, the variables are transformed back to the original parameters.

9.2.1.2. *Weibull with the cure model*

By definition, the pdf and CDF of a Weibull distribution are

$$f_W(x, \alpha, b) = \frac{\alpha}{b^\alpha} x^{\alpha-1} e^{-(x/b)^\alpha}, \; F_W(x, \alpha, b) = 1 - e^{-(x/b)^\alpha}, \; x > 0$$

where (α, b) are shape and scale parameters. For ease of notation, we use the parameterization $g = 1/b^\alpha$. Then, pdf and CDF have the form

$$\widetilde{f}_W(x, \alpha, g) = \alpha g x^{\alpha-1} e^{-gx^\alpha}, \; \widetilde{F}_W(x, \alpha, g) = 1 - e^{-gx^\alpha}, \; x > 0$$

Weibull with the cure model assumes that the variables τ_A and τ_L have Weibull distribution with parameters (α_A, g_A) and (α_L, g_L), respectively. This is a five-parameter model: $(\alpha_A, g_A, \alpha_L, g_L, r)$. The log-likelihood function:

$$\mathcal{L}(\alpha_A, g_A, \alpha_L, g_L, r) = -g_L \sum_{i=1}^{n_O} z_i^{\alpha_L} + \sum_{i=1}^{n_O} \log\left(r + (1-r)\exp(-g_A z_i^{\alpha_A})\right)$$

$$+ n_A \left(\log(1-r) + \log(\alpha_A) + \log(g_A)\right)$$

$$+ (\alpha_A - 1) \sum_{k=1}^{n_A} \log(x_k) - g_A \sum_{k=1}^{n_A} x_k^{\alpha_A} - g_L \sum_{k=1}^{n_A} x_k^{\alpha_L}$$

$$+ n_L \left(\log(\alpha_L) + \log(g_L)\right) + (\alpha_L - 1) \sum_{j=1}^{n_L} \log(y_j)$$

$$- g_L \sum_{j=1}^{n_L} y_j^{\alpha_L} + \sum_{j=1}^{n_L} \log\left(r + (1-r)\exp(-g_A y_j^{\alpha_A})\right)$$

Optimization is carried out in the same way as for the exponential model, with initial values: $\alpha_A(0) = 1; g_A(0) = n_A/\Sigma_1; \alpha_L(0) = 1; g_L(0) = n_L/\Sigma_1; r(0)$ taken to be some range of values in $(0, 1)$. The new variables $(\theta_1, \theta_2, \theta_3, \theta_4, \theta_5)$ are:

$$\alpha_A = e^{\theta_1}; g_A = e^{\theta_2}; \alpha_L = e^{\theta_3}; g_L = e^{\theta_4}; r = \frac{e^{\theta_5}}{1 + e^{\theta_5}}$$

Similarly, the log-likelihood function can also be derived for a log-normal with the cure model.

9.3. Predicting event counts for patients at risk

For convenience, let us introduce the time of the occurrence of event A, ν_A, so $\mathbf{P}(\nu_A \leq z) = (1 - r)F_A(z)$. Note that if $r > 0$, then ν_A is an improper random variable as $\mathbf{P}(\nu_A < +\infty) = 1 - r$.

Consider a conditional probability for a patient in group O to experience an event in the future time interval $[t_1, t_1 + x]$, given that the follow-up period until the interim time t_1 is z:

$$
\begin{aligned}
p_A(x, z) &= \mathbf{P}(\nu_A \leq z + x, \tau_L > \nu_A \mid \nu_A > z, \tau_L > z) \\[6pt]
&= \frac{\mathbf{P}(z < \nu_A \leq z + x, \tau_L > \nu_A)}{\mathbf{P}(\nu_A > z, \tau_L > z)} \\[10pt]
&= \frac{(1 - r) \int_z^{z+x} f_A(u) S_L(u)\,du}{S_L(z)\big(r + (1 - r)S_A(z)\big)}
\end{aligned}
\tag{9.1}
$$

For the exponential model, $p_A(x, z)$ can be calculated in a closed form:

$$
p_A(x, z) = \frac{\mu_A}{\mu} \frac{(1 - r)e^{-\mu_A z}(1 - e^{-\mu x})}{r + (1 - r)e^{-\mu_A z}}
\tag{9.2}
$$

where $\mu = \mu_A + \mu_L$.

Note that for the exponential model, if $r = 0$, $p_A(x, 0) = \frac{\mu_A}{\mu}(1 - e^{-\mu x})$, so this expression does not depend on z and we have a memoryless property. However, for $r > 0$, the memoryless property is lost.

For the Weibull with the cure model, $p_A(x, z)$ has the following form:

$$
p_A(x, z) = \frac{(1 - r)W_2(x, z, \alpha_A, g_A, \alpha_L, g_L)}{\exp(-g_L z^{\alpha_L})\big(r + (1 - r)\exp(-g_A z^{\alpha_A})\big)}
\tag{9.3}
$$

where

$$
W_2(x, z, \alpha_A, g_A, \alpha_L, g_L) = \alpha_A g_A \int_z^{z+x} u^{\alpha_A - 1} \exp(-g_A u^{\alpha_A} - g_L u^{\alpha_L})\,du
\tag{9.4}
$$

To compute this function in applications, we can use a numerical integration.

9.3.1. *Global prediction*

Assume that the recruitment of new patients is already completed; thus, the events in the future may occur only in patients at risk in group O. Denote by $R_O(t_1, t, \{z_k\})$ the total predictive number of events A that may occur in future time interval $[t_1, t_1+t]$ for patients in group O, where $\{z_k, k = 1, .., n_O\}$ are the times of exposure. Let $\mathrm{Br}(p)$ be a Bernoulli random variable, $\mathbf{P}(\mathrm{Br}(p) = 1) = 1 - \mathbf{P}(\mathrm{Br}(p) = 0) = p$.

LEMMA 9.1.– *The process $R_O(t_1, t, \{z_k\})$ can be represented in the form:*

$$R_O(t_1, t, (z_k)) = \sum_{k \in O} \mathrm{Br}(p_A(t, z_k)) \qquad [9.5]$$

where the variables $\mathrm{Br}(p_A(t, z_k))$ are independent and the probability $p_A(t, z)$ is defined above in section 9.3 and depends on the type of distribution.

For a rather large number of patients in group O, (> 20), we can apply a normal approximation for the process $R_O(t_1, t, \{z_k\})$ using simple formulae for the mean and the variance:

$$M(t_1, t) = \sum_{k \in O} p_A(t, z_k), \ V^2(t_1, t) = \sum_{k \in O} p_A(t, z_k)(1 - p_A(t, z_k)) \qquad [9.6]$$

Then, $\mathbf{E}[R_O(t_1, t, \{z_k\}] = M(t_1, t)$ and $(1 - \delta)$-predictive interval at time $t_1 + t$ is $\left(M(t_1, t) - z_{1-\delta/2} V(t_1, t), M(t_1, t) + z_{1-\delta/2} V(t_1, t) \right)$, where z_a is an a-quantile of a standard normal distribution.

For a not so large number of patients, a distribution of $R_O(t_1, t, \{z_k\})$ can be calculated numerically as a convolution of the sum of Bernoulli variables.

Let us evaluate the predictive distribution for the time to reach a given target K for the total planned number of events in the study.

Recall that in previous notation, n_A denotes the total number of events that occurred prior to interim time t_1 (size of group A). The remaining number of events that are left to achieve is $K_R = K - n_A$.

Let $\tau(t_1, K_R)$ be the remaining time to reach K_R events after the interim time t_1. Then, the following relation holds: for any $t > 0$,

$$\mathbf{P}(\tau(t_1, K_R) \leq t) = \mathbf{P}(R_O(t_1, t, \{z_k\}) \geq K_R) \qquad [9.7]$$

As the distribution of $R_O(t_1, t, \{z_k\})$ can be evaluated for any time t, this relation allows us to also calculate the distribution of $\tau(t_1, K_R)$.

Consider the calculation of PoS (probability to complete study before a planned time $t_1 + T$). Denote it as $Q(t_1, T, \{z_k\})$. From [9.7], we get

$$Q(t_1, T, \{z_k\}) = \mathbf{P}(R_O(t_1, T, \{z_k\}) \geq K_R) \qquad [9.8]$$

If we use a normal approximation for the process $R_O(t_1, T, (z_k))$, then

$$Q(t_1, T, \{z_k\}) \approx \Phi\left(\frac{M(t_1, T) - K_R}{V(t_1, T)}\right) \qquad [9.9]$$

where $\Phi(x)$ is the CDF of a standard normal distribution.

9.4. Predicting event counts accounting for ongoing recruitment

Consider the situation where interim time the planned number of patients to be recruited has not been reached yet, which means that the recruitment is still ongoing. In this case, we also need to predict the future recruitment and how many events may occur for patients to be recruited in the future.

9.4.1. *Modeling and predicting patient recruitment*

Assume that patients arrive at clinical centers according to Poisson processes with some rates λ_i. To model the variation in the rates among different centers, we assume that λ_i are jointly independent gamma distributed random variables with parameters (α, β) (shape and rate) and pdf

$$f(x, \alpha, \beta) = \frac{e^{-\beta x}\beta^\alpha x^{\alpha-1}}{\Gamma(\alpha)}, \; x > 0, \qquad [9.10]$$

where $\Gamma(\alpha)$ is a gamma function.

This model is called a Poisson–gamma (PG) recruitment model and was developed in Anisimov and Fedorov (2007) and further extended in Anisimov (2008, 2011a, 2020).

Denote by $\Pi_a(t)$ a standard Poisson process with rate a. Then, a mixed Poisson process $\Pi_\lambda(t)$, where the rate λ is gamma-distributed with parameters (α, β), is a PG process (Bernardo and Smith 2004) with parameters (t, α, β):

$$\mathbf{P}(\Pi_\lambda(t) = k) = \frac{\Gamma(\alpha + k)}{k!\,\Gamma(\alpha)}\,\frac{t^k \beta^\alpha}{(\beta + t)^{\alpha+k}}\;, \; k = 0, 1, 2, .. \qquad [9.11]$$

Note that

$$\mathbf{E}[\Pi_\lambda(t)] = \mathbf{E}[\lambda]t; \ \mathbf{Var}[\Pi_\lambda(t)] = \mathbf{E}[\lambda]t + \mathbf{Var}[\lambda]t^2 \tag{9.12}$$

Consider predicting recruitment at some interim time t_1. Assume for the sake of simplicity that all centers are active and in every center i the following data are available: (v_i, k_i) – the duration of active recruitment (recruitment window) and the number of patients recruited.

In the paper by Anisimov and Fedorov (2007) (see also Anisimov (2011a)), a maximum likelihood technique was developed for estimating parameters (α, β) of a PG model, assuming that in all active centers the parameters of the rates are the same. In Anisimov (2011a), the Bayesian technique was also developed to predict future recruitment using the property that the posterior rate in a center i, $\tilde{\lambda}_i$, also has a gamma distribution with parameters $(\alpha + k_i, \beta + v_i)$.

Let I_{Active} be a set of active centers with posterior rates $\tilde{\lambda}_i$. Assume also that it can be some set I_{New} of new centers that are planned to be initiated after interim time t_1 at times $t_1 + u_i$, $i \in I_{New}$. Let λ_i be the rates in the new centers. These rates can be provided by clinical teams or evaluated using historical data from similar trials. Then, the predictive total number of patients $n(t_1, t_1 + t)$ to be recruited in the time interval $[t_1, t_1 + t]$ can be represented as

$$n(t_1, t_1 + t) = \sum_{i \in I_{Active}} \Pi_{\tilde{\lambda}_i}(t) + \sum_{i \in I_{New}} \Pi_{\lambda_i}([t - u_i]_+) \tag{9.13}$$

where $[x]_+ = \min(0, x)$. Here, we assume for the sake of simplicity that the centers will not be closed for recruitment until the required sample size will be reached.

For a rather large number of centers, the predictive bounds for $n(t_1, t_1 + t)$ can be evaluated using a normal approximation, as the mean and the variance of $n(t_1, t_1 + t)$ can be easily calculated using the property [9.12] and relations $\mathbf{E}[\tilde{\lambda}_i] = (\alpha + k_i)/(\beta + v_i)$; $\mathbf{Var}[\tilde{\lambda}_i] = (\alpha + k_i)/(\beta + v_i)^2$. In particular, the mean predicted time to reach a required remaining number of patients n_R can be numerically calculated as the point when the line $\mathbf{E}[n(t_1, t_1 + t)]$ hits level n_R.

Note that for a not so large number of centers, to predict $n(t_1, t_1 + t)$, we can use a PG approximation developed in Anisimov (2020) and Anisimov and Austin (2020).

9.4.2. Predicting event counts

Consider predicting event counts accounting for the ongoing recruitment.

Denote by κ_A the time it takes until event A occurs first (before dropout), and let $p_A(x) = \mathbf{P}(\kappa_A \leq x)$, $x > 0$, be its CDF.

For the cure model with dropout defined in section 9.2, in the previous notation,

$$p_A(x) = \mathbf{P}(\nu_A \leq x, \nu_A < \tau_L) = (1 - r) \int_0^x f_A(u) S_L(u) du \qquad [9.14]$$

In particular, for the exponential model, using notation $\mu = \mu_A + \mu_L$,

$$p_{A,E}(x) = (1 - r)\frac{\mu_A}{\mu}(1 - e^{-\mu x}) \qquad [9.15]$$

For the Weibull model, using parameterization $\bar{\theta} = (\alpha_A, g_A, \alpha_L, g_L)$,

$$p_{A,W}(x) = (1 - r)W_1(x, \bar{\theta}) \qquad [9.16]$$

where

$$W_1(x, \bar{\theta}) = \alpha_A g_A \int_0^x y^{\alpha_A - 1} \exp(-g_A y^{\alpha_A} - g_L y^{\alpha_L}) dy \qquad [9.17]$$

Consider one clinical center. Assume that patients arrive according to a mixed Poisson process with a possibly random rate λ. Assume also that the center is active only in a fixed time interval $[a, b]$. In Anisimov (2011b, 2020), the following result is proved.

LEMMA 9.2.– *The predicted number of events A in interval $[0, t]$ that occur in the newly recruited patients in this center has a mixed Poisson distribution with rate $\lambda q_A(t, a, b)$, where*

$$q_A(t, a, b) = \int_a^b p_A(t - u) du \qquad [9.18]$$

For the exponential model, the function $q_A(t, a, b)$ can be easy calculated. Consider the duration of the recruitment window in a center at time t:

$$d(t, a, b) = \begin{cases} 0, & t \leq a \\ t - a, & a < t \leq b \\ b - a, & t > b \end{cases} \qquad [9.19]$$

Then, using parameters (r, μ_A, μ_L),

$$q_{A,E}(t, a, b) = (1 - r)\frac{\mu_A}{\mu}\left(d(t, a, b) - \frac{1}{\mu}e^{-\mu(t-a)}(e^{\mu d(t,a,b)} - 1)\right) \qquad [9.20]$$

For the Weibull model,

$$q_{A,W}(t, a, b) = (1 - r)\int_a^{min(t,b)} W_1(t - u, \bar{\theta})du \qquad [9.21]$$

where $W_1(t, \bar{\theta})$ is defined in [9.17]. This function can be numerically calculated.

These results form the basis for creating predictions of the event counts in any active center and globally.

9.4.3. *Global forecasting event counts at interim stage*

Consider forecasting the total number of events at some interim time t_1.

Denote the times of initiation of new centers (if any) by $\{u_i\}$ and the times of closure for all centers by $\{b_i\}$. In general, it is assumed that centers will be closed for recruitment at the time when recruitment hits the recruitment target. Thus, in applications, we usually assume that $b_i \equiv \widehat{T}_{Pred}$, where $\widehat{T}_{Pred}$ is the predicted mean remaining time to reach the recruitment target.

THEOREM 9.1.– *The predictive total number of new events A, $k(t_1, t, A)$, which may occur in a future time interval $[t_1, t_1 + t]$, can be represented as a convolution of two independent random variables:*

$$k(t_1, t, A) = \Pi(\Sigma(t, A)) + R_O(t_1, t, \{z_k\}) \qquad [9.22]$$

where according to [9.13],

$$\Sigma(t, A) = \sum_{i \in I_{active}} \tilde{\lambda}_i q_A(t, 0, b_i) + \sum_{i \in I_{new}} \lambda_i q_A(t, u_i, b_i), \qquad [9.23]$$

and $R_O(t_1, t, \{z_k\})$ is the predictive number of events A in group O defined in [9.5], section 9.3.1.

Here, the function $q_A(t, a, b)$ is defined by [9.18] (for the exponential and Weibull models, we have the expressions [9.20] and [9.21], respectively), $\tilde{\lambda}_i$ are the posterior rates defined in section 9.4.1.

Correspondingly, the probability to complete trial in time is

$$\mathbf{P}\Big(k(t_1, T_R, A) \geq \nu_R(A)\Big) \tag{9.24}$$

where T_R is the planned remaining time to complete the trial and $\nu_R(A)$ is the remaining number of events left to achieve.

The proof follows from results of Lemmas 9.1, 9.2 and section 9.4.1.

Note that the mean and variance of the process $\Pi(\Sigma(t, A))$ can be calculated in terms of functions $q_A(\cdot)$ and parameters of the rates.

In real trials, the number of centers is typically rather large; to create predictive bounds for $k(t_1, t, A)$, we can use a normal approximation. This technique is realized in R package *EventPrediction*; see section 9.6.

9.5. Monte Carlo simulation

A Monte Carlo simulation was used to test each model's performance. We considered 1,000 patients assuming uniform distribution of center initiation over six months, and took the target number of events of 550. At a specified cutoff date, the model parameters were estimated using the maximum likelihood technique (see section 9.2.1). Using these estimators, predictions of the future occurrence of events were created. For the Weibull model, two different cases for the initial parameters were considered, $a_A < 1$ and $a_A > 1$ (see Figures 9.1 and 9.2, respectively).

In both cases, the model successfully predicts the trajectory of the number of events A, with the real trajectory falling within the 90% predicted bounds. Furthermore, the parameters estimated at the cutoff time using maximum likelihood are close to the initial parameters showing an appropriate estimation.

9.6. Software development

In order to expose the event and recruitment prediction models (as detailed in the previous sections) to a large number of key stakeholders, an R package (*EventPrediction*) has been developed, tested and deployed to a centralized R server. The *EventPrediction* package allows a user to easily pass the data required (i.e. subject event data, center level data and configuration) and return back key parameter estimates and predictions with bounds, for both events and recruitment.

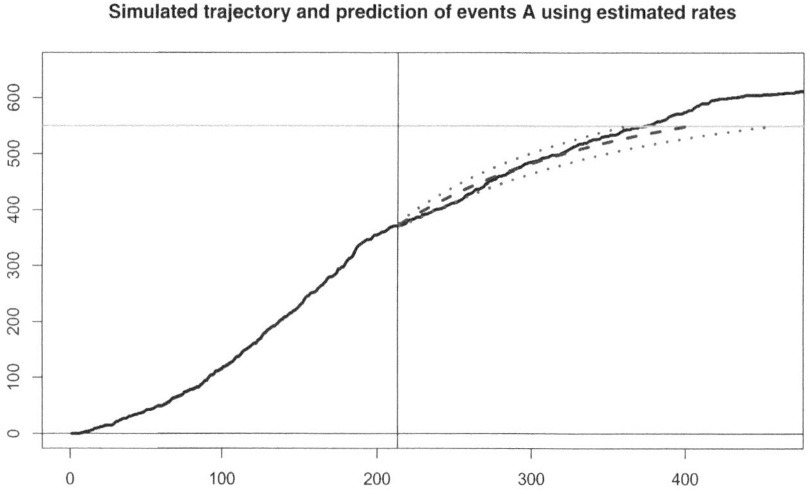

Simulated trajectory and prediction of events A using estimated rates

Figure 9.1. *Plot of the number of events against time (in days), following the timeline of a simulated trial. The simulated trajectory of events A is marked by the black solid line, the initial parameters were:* $a_A = 0.8$, $b_A = 182$, $a_L = 0.6$, $b_L = 2611$ *and* $r = 0.2$. *An interim analysis was taken at seven months, the estimated parameters were:* $a_A = 0.842$, $b_A = 145$, $a_L = 0.641$, $b_L = 2697$ *and* $r = 0.276$. *Predictions on future event counts were created using the estimated parameters; the mean trajectory is shown by the blue dashed line, and the 90% confidence bounds are shown by the red dotted lines*

9.6.1. *R package design*

R was chosen over other programming languages, and an R package was developed over standalone R scripts, for a number of reasons: R is easy to use and setup testing frameworks; R ships with easy-to-use code coverage tools; R has a comprehensive R archive network ("CRAN") set of packages that are easily accessible; R seamlessly integrates with GitLab (and other source control software); R allows for an object-oriented ("OO") approach (i.e. S3, S4 and R6); and also, primarily, it is simply straightforward to develop, test, document and centrally deploy an R package for key stakeholders to use.

R's S3 lightweight OO solution was a key design feature of the *EventPrediction* package, as using such an OO approach yields four main benefits: first, S3's simple to use OO benefit of polymorphism (aka in R as method dispatch); secondly, S3 gives the OO benefit of inheritance; thirdly, S3 is ubiquitously used by R contributors, easy to use and for others to comment; and fourthly, S3 is in accordance with the functional programming paradigm, when an object is passed into an S3 function it is not going to change (unlike full OO approaches like R6).

Simulated trajectory and prediction of events A using estimated rates

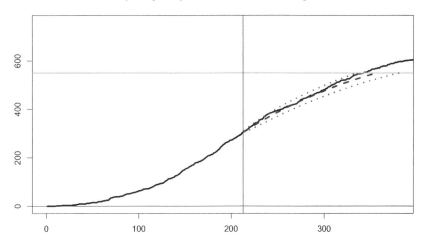

Figure 9.2. *Plot of the number of events against time (in days), following the timeline of a simulated trial. The simulated trajectory of events A is marked by the black solid line, the initial parameters were:* $a_A = 1.2$, $b_A = 213$, $a_L = 1.4$, $b_L = 3701$ *and* $r = 0.2$. *An interim analysis was taken at seven months, the estimated parameters were:* $a_A = 1.265$, $b_A = 175$, $a_L = 1.406$, $b_L = 3916$ *and* $r = 0.305$. *Predictions on future event counts were created using the estimated parameters; the mean trajectory is shown by the blue dashed line, and the 90% confidence bounds are shown by the red dotted lines*

9.6.1.1. *Good software engineering principles*

Another major benefit of developing an R package (and using R's OO approach) is to ensure adherence to good software engineering principles, with code that is at a minimum: reliable; easy to use; efficient; well tested, with tests traceable to requirements and/or design; well documented; and (importantly) easy to maintain. The *EventPrediction* conforms to each of these key programming elements, not only because these are simply good software engineering practices, but also as the biotechnology sector is highly regulated and there is a requirement to document a number of Software Development Life Cycle ("SDLC") tasks in accordance with departmental, company and regulatory policies.

9.6.1.2. *R package SDLC and platform architecture*

Before the design, development and testing of any code was initiated, two further key platform architectural design decisions were made: first, GitLab was used for source control, continuous integration, documentation, vignettes, readme files and also as part of the full deployment process; and secondly, R Studio Server Pro was used for the development and testing of code, a Docker Image with a physical R server on AWS.

9.6.1.3. *Further R package design: function layers*

With a large number of complex R scripts and source papers, another design choice (primarily, to make the code easier to use and easier to maintain) was grouping the code into four layers using R's S3 OO approach. The four programming layers are as follows:

Layer 1: highest level: main exposed application programming interface (API).

This level is exposed to the user and contains: S3 classes (functions) that allow the instantiation of the objects that contain the input data required and configuration; functions to predict events and recruitment; plotting and printing functionality; and key getter functions.

Layer 2: second level functions.

This level is not exposed to the user, is simply used to dispatch to the third level functions based on the S3 configuration objects instantiated in layer 1.

Layer 3: third level functions.

This level is not exposed to the user, contains the main set of controller code and does all of the hard work in the package.

Layer 4: lowest level functions.

This level is not exposed to the user and contains a large number of complex R scripts/algorithms that have been developed and tested using Monte Carlo simulation, as detailed in the previous section.

9.6.2. *R package input data required*

The following set of input data is required by the *EventPrediction* package to predict events and recruitment (if recruitment is ongoing), with each set of data instantiated using R's S3 approach (as detailed in the previous sections).

9.6.2.1. *Event data*

analysis_time_days	censor_flag	drop_out_flag	randomization_date
28	0	0	YYYY-MM-DD
33	0	0	YYYY-MM-DD
87	1	0	YYYY-MM-DD
42	0	0	YYYY-MM-DD
77	1	1	YYYY-MM-DD

This data is in accordance with how the key stakeholders produce their data; it is transformed into the values as described in the previous sections, such that:

– analysis_time_days is the number of days from randomization to either the event date T_A or censoring date (i.e. the dropout date T_L for subjects that have dropped out or the date used to censor at the cutoff if a subject has not dropped out);

– censor_flag == 0 represents group A, a subject experienced event A;

– censor_flag == 1 and drop_out_flag == 0 represent group O, a subject did not experience an event nor dropout;

– drop_out_flag == 1 represents group L, a subject dropped out before the interim time.

9.6.2.2. *Site recruitment data*

Study_center_id	Center_actual_enrol	Center_recruitment_window_days
xx001	0	140
xx002	1	224
xx003	2	238
xx004	1	221
xx005	0	201

– center_actual_enrol represents the number of subjects recruited at the unique center ID;

– center_recruitment_window_days represents the actual duration of recruitment at the unique center ID (not including any screening period).

9.6.2.3. *New sites*

A vector of days for new centers is to be initiated $\{u_i\}$, for example, c(3, 5, 5, 10, 10, 11, 12, 20).

9.6.2.4. *Configuration*

The following key pieces of information are accepted by the *EventPrediction* package (with appropriate defaults), which are used to select the appropriate algorithms and provide key modeling values:

– distributions_to_use: a list detailing the distributions to model the dropouts and events: for example, list(events = "Exponential", drop_outs = "Exponential");

– target_number_of_events: the target number of events for the analysis to be predicted;

– sample_size: the number of patients planned to recruit;

– confidence_level: the confidence probability for the upper and lower bounds.

9.7. R package and implementation in a clinical trial

9.7.1. *Introduction*

In order to help the key stakeholders with the operational planning of a clinical trial and test the quality of the prediction, the *EventPrediction* package was used in several historic studies. The following is one such case study in a historical oncology clinical trial, using the data at a given interim time when recruitment had not been completed. The task was to predict the future recruitment and event counts with bounds and compare the results with the real trajectory of the recruitment and the events that have already occurred in the past.

The event and center data was provided in accordance with the package APIs (as detailed in the previous section), along with a target number of events of 250 and a patient sample size of 405. At the interim cutoff time, the data for the study had the following recruitment and event status:

– 152 events (i.e. censor_flag == 1);

– 155 at risk (i.e. censor_flag == 1 and drop_out_flag == 0);

– 13 dropouts (i.e. drop_out_flag == 1);

– 85 patients left to recruit.

9.7.2. *Key predictions*

Given the above input and implementing the developed model, the *EventPrediction* package predicted:

Recruitment: predicted number of days until the target number of patients is reached with 90% bounds, (mean, lower bound, upper bound): 151, 120, 191

Events: predicted number of days until the target number of events is reached, with 90% bounds, (mean, lower bound, upper bound):
Exponential model: 227, 181, 322

Weibull model: 241, 188, 423

9.7.3. *Plots and parameter estimates*

Further, the *EventPrediction* package produced the following three key plots, along with key parameter estimates, for the key stakeholders to consume:

1) prediction of the remaining recruitment;

2) prediction of the remaining number of events using the exponential model;

3) prediction of the remaining number of events using the Weibull model.

Predicting remaining recruitment over time

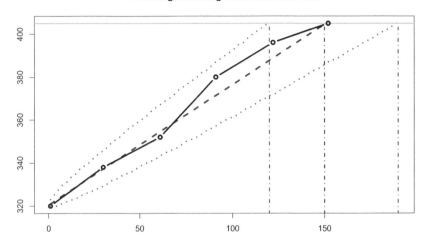

Figure 9.3. *Prediction of the remaining recruitment against time from cutoff (in days). Real trajectory of patient recruitment is shown by a black line. Mean prediction and 90% bounds are shown by the blue dashed and red dotted lines*

Interim re-forecasting the number of event counts over time

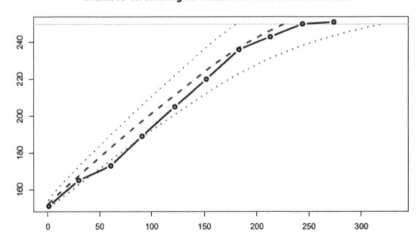

Figure 9.4. *Prediction of the remaining number of events against time from cutoff (in days). Real trajectory of events is shown by a black line. The exponential model, mean prediction and bounds are depicted by the blue dashed and red dotted lines*

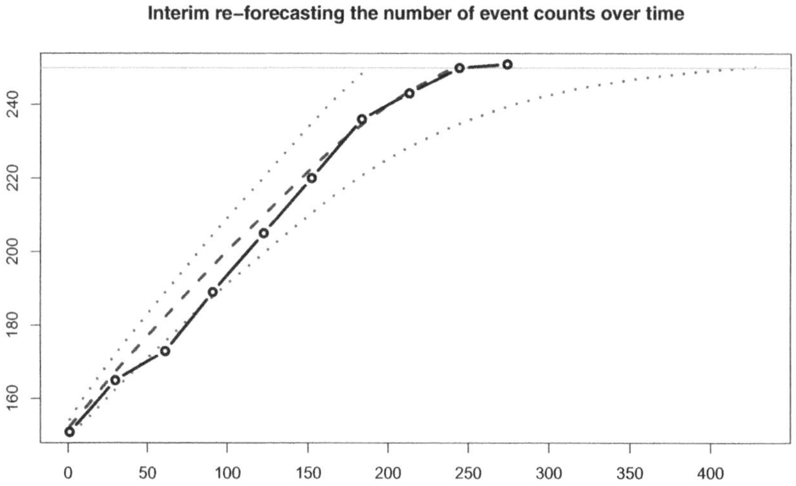

Interim re–forecasting the number of event counts over time

Figure 9.5. *Prediction of the remaining number of events against time from cutoff (in days). Real trajectory of events is shown by a black line. The Weibull model, mean prediction and bounds are depicted by the blue dashed and red dotted lines*

Figure 9.3 shows very good fit of the predictive area of recruitment, where the real trajectory of the historical recruitment falls into the predictive area.

As we can see from Figures 9.4 and 9.5, the predictions for both types of models, exponential and Weibull, are rather close, with the following estimated parameters for each:

Exponential model: $\mu_A = 0.0069$, $\mu_L = 0.00034$ and $r = 0.2566$.

Weibull model: $a_A = 1.1636$, $b_A = 126.9995$, $a_L = 0.3177$, $b_L = 2053795.7$ and $r = 0.2996$.

The actual number of days that the target number of patients reached in this trial was 152, and the actual number of days when the planned number of events occurred was 244. As shown in the figures, the predictions were indeed very close to the actual data.

9.8. Conclusion

We have developed a new analytic approach for the event count prediction when recruitment is complete and ongoing, allowing not only for the prediction of recruitment (using PG recruitment model), but also the prediction of the event counts with bounds using an exponential and a Weibull model accounting for dropout and the opportunity to be cured. Using these novel models and with access to real subject level and center level data, we are now able to address key business use cases for a number of key stakeholders in order to better forecast the operational design of clinical trials. Further, by centralizing an exposed R package *EventPrediction*, using good software engineering principles, each of our key stakeholders has access to the package and can obtain plots, key parameter estimates and predictions with bounds, without contacting the mathematical modelers nor the R package developer.

We have a large number of opportunities for future improvements to the mathematical modeling and *EventPrediction* package, including the major priorities: evaluate the predictions against real clinical trial operational data to ensure the existing and any future models are as accurate as we found in testing and incorporate new statistical distributions for both dropout and events.

9.9. References

Anisimov, V. (2008). Using mixed Poisson models in patient recruitment in multicentre clinical trials. *Proceedings of the World Congress on Engineering*, II, 1046–1049.

Anisimov, V. (2011a). Statistical modeling of clinical trials (recruitment and randomization). *Communications in Statistics – Theory and Methods*, 40, 19–20, 3684–3699.

Anisimov, V. (2011b). Predictive event modelling in multicentre clinical trials with waiting time to response. *Pharmaceutical Statistics*, 10(6), 517–522.

Anisimov, V. (2016a). Predictive hierarchic modelling of operational characteristics in clinical trials. *Communications in Statistics – Simulation and Computation*, 45(5), 1477–1488.

Anisimov, V. (2016b). Discussion on the paper "Real-time prediction of clinical trial enrollment and event counts: A review" by D.F. Heitjan et al. *Contemporary Clinical Trials*, 40, 7–10.

Anisimov, V. (2020). Modern analytic techniques for predictive modelling of clinical trial operations. *Quantitative Methods in Pharmaceutical Research and Development: Concepts and Applications*. Springer International Publications, 361–408.

Anisimov, V. and Austin, M. (2020). Centralized statistical monitoring of clinical trial enrollment performance. *Communications in Statistics – Case Studies and Data Analysis*, 6(4), 392–410.

Anisimov, V. and Fedorov, V. (2007). Modeling, prediction and adaptive adjustment of recruitment in multicentre trials. *Statistics in Medicine*, 26(27), 4958–4975.

Anisimov, V., Downing, D., Fedorov, V. (2007). Recruitment in multicentre trials: Prediction and adjustment. *mODa 8 – Advances in Model-Oriented Design and Analysis*, 1–8.

Bagiella, E. and Heitjan, D.F. (2001). Predicting analysis times in randomized clinical trials. *Statistics in Medicine*, 20, 2055–2063.

Barnard, K.D., Dent, L., Cook, A. (2010). A systematic review of models to predict recruitment to multicentre clinical trials. *BMC Medical Research Methodology*, 10, 63.

Bernardo, J.M. and Smith, A.F.M. (2004). *Bayesian Theory*. John Wiley & Sons, Hoboken, NJ.

Carter, R.E., Sonne, S.C., Brady, K.T. (2005). Practical considerations for estimating clinical trial accrual periods: Application to a multi-center effectiveness study. *BMC Medical Research Methodology*, 5, 11–15.

Chen, T.T. (2016). Predicting analysis times in randomized clinical trials with cancer immunotherapy. *BMC Medical Research Methodology*, 16(1), 1–10.

Gkioni, E., Riusd, R., Dodda, S., Gamblea, C. (2019). A systematic review describes models for recruitment prediction at the design stage of a clinical trial. *Journal of Clinical Epidemiology*, 115, 141–149.

Heitjan, D.F., Ge, Z., Ying, G.S. (2015). Real-time prediction of clinical trial enrollment and event counts: A review. *Contemporary Clinical Trials*, 45(Part A), 26–33.

Senn, S. (1997). *Statistical Issues in Drug Development*. Wiley, Chichester.

Senn, S. (1998). Some controversies in planning and analysis multi-center trials. *Statistics in Medicine*, 17, 1753–1756.

10

Structural Modeling: An Application to the Evaluation of Ecosystem Practices at the Plot Level

This chapter proposes the use of structural modeling for the evaluation of ecosystem-based practices (e.g. biological control of crop pests) on the basis of data collected at the scale of the agricultural plot. In the first part, we present the analytical approach used – structural modeling by partial least squares. In the second part, we present the field of study and the data considered in this work. In the third part, we present and discuss the results from the implementation of the partial least squares-path modeling (PLS-PM) approach. Finally, we conclude on the validation of this approach and the prospects for its possible extension.

10.1. Introduction

The biological control of crop pests and weeds is an example of ecosystem services (ES) – the benefits that ecosystems provide to humankind (Millennium Ecosystem Assessment 2005) – provided at the farm plot level. The amenities provided by ecosystem infrastructures and agro-ecological practices in terms of soil protection, water resource management and preservation of the habitat of agricultural auxiliaries constitute productive services that can be evaluated at the plot and farm levels. For example, the biological control of crop pests and weeds by naturally occurring beneficials (such as ladybirds that predate aphids) is one of the

Chapter written by Dominique DESBOIS.
This work is dedicated to the memory of Jean-Paul Benzécri (1932–2019), emeritus professor at Université Pierre et Marie Curie.
For a color version of all the figures in this chapter, see www.iste.co.uk/zafeiris/data2.zip.

productive services that can be mobilized at the plot level to reduce the dependence of agricultural production systems on pesticides. However, the relationships between crop management methods, levels of pest control by beneficials and crop yields are still insufficiently assessed (Franck et al. 2017). The structure of plot landscapes can also influence the level of pest abundance, so the relationship between plot landscape and yield remains to be more comprehensively inventoried (Jonsson et al. 2015). The objective of this work is therefore to analyze, via a partial least squares-path modeling (PLS-PM) approach, the relationships between: i) plot landscapes, ii) crop pests and weeds, iii) agronomic practices and iv) economic results.

The first part of this chapter presents the specificity of the PLS-PM approach; the second part presents the field of study and describes the data considered in this work; the third part presents the results of the implementation of the PLS-PM approach; finally, the last part presents the conclusions on the validity of this approach and the perspectives of its application.

10.2. Structural equation modeling using partial least squares

Structural equation modeling mainly allows the study, via a hypothetical model specified in the form of equations, of the causal links (relationships) between several variables in order to account for the theoretical functioning of the system studied (Hoyle 1995). In this structural equation modeling, the variables can be either directly derived from observations or measurements (referred to as "manifest" variables) or not directly observable (referred to as "latent" variables).

The PLS-PM approach is a variant of structural equation modeling that allows for the analysis of a complex system of relationships between the different variables under study, based on an a priori causal model (Path Modeling – PM) describing the relationships between the explanatory or "exogenous" variables and the explained or "endogenous" variables (Tenenhaus et al. 2005). The particularity of the PLS-PM approach lies in the fact that the estimation of the links of the structural model (path coefficients) is based on the partial least squares (PLS) estimation criterion, rather than the maximum likelihood (ML) criterion, classically used in structural equation modeling.

The properties of partial least squares (PLS) regression for estimating interdependent systems, established by Wold (1981), led Lohmöller (1989) to propose the PLS approach to structural equation modeling, PLS-path modeling (PLS-PM). Thus, the use of the PLS-PM approach does not require any assumptions on the distribution of variables (e.g. normality of the distribution) and is suitable for small sample sizes. Recent theoretical and algorithmic developments (Tenenhaus et al. 2005) have opened up the field of its application to multidisciplinary research, where many groups of variables are likely to interact to condition social phenomena or economic behavior. Indeed, such multidisciplinary research can often only be conducted for data sets where the conditions relating to the normality of the distribution, independence between observations or sample size are not met (Chin and Newsteed 1999, p. 314).

The specification of a PLS-PM model involves the following steps: i) specification of an initial hypothetical model describing the a priori relationships between the latent and manifest variables; ii) estimation of the model parameters via appropriate statistical software; iii) assessment of the goodness of fit of the structural model to the data (GoF) and iv) when the goodness of fit of the model is judged to be satisfactory, a final step is the interpretation of the results.

In the PLS-PM approach, the structural model is a set of conceptual constructs (or "latent variables") linked by hypothetical causal relationships (the "internal model") that can be estimated by means of measured or observed "manifest variables" reflecting or, respectively, forming the latent variables (external model). Figure 10.1 illustrates the concepts of structural modeling, specifying the internal and external models and describing the relationships between latent and manifest variables.

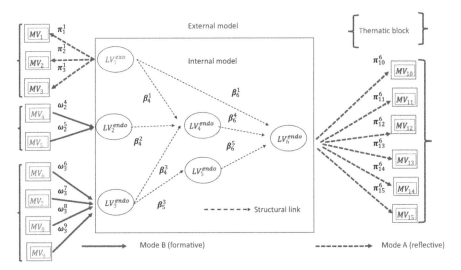

Figure 10.1. *Concepts of structural modeling*

Reading: The beta coefficients represent the "links" of the internal model; the manifest variables MV_h are associated with the exogenous LV_k^{exo} or endogenous

LV_k^{endo} latent variables according to a mode that can be either "reflective" (mode A: manifest variables "reflect" latent variables), or "formative" (mode B: manifest variables "form" latent variables).

10.2.1. *Specification of the internal model*

The structural relationships between latent "endogenous" (explained) and "exogenous" (explanatory) variables constitute the internal model and are formalized by the following linear equations:

$$LV_l^{endo} = \beta_l^0 + \sum_{k=1}^{K} \beta_l^k \, LV_k^{exo} + \varepsilon_l$$

where β_l^k, called the "structural link" (path coefficient), represents the sign and strength of the deterministic relationship between the endogenous latent variable LV_l^{endo} and the exogenous latent variables LV_k^{exo}. The part not explained by the deterministic model of LV_l is relegated to the residual ε_l. The structural links are estimated by a geometric projection (least squares) procedure whose only assumption is the independence between the deterministic part and the residual part, imposing that the covariance between each exogenous latent variable and the residual is zero $(cov(LV_k^{exo}, \varepsilon_l) = 0)$.

10.2.2. *Specification of the external model*

Latent variables are defined by the "manifest variables" (MVs), derived from measurements and/or observations whether direct or indirect, via two modes (see Figure 10.1): i) the "reflective" mode where latent variables are reflected through their effects or consequences on the observed indicators; the "formative" mode where latent variables are supposed to be formed or constituted by the measured variables.

In the A reflective mode, the X_k manifest variable reflects the LV_k latent variable with mean m and standard deviation 1, according to the following projective scheme (least squares regression):

$$X_h = \pi_h^0 + \pi_h^k LV_k + \varepsilon_h$$

where the π_h^k coefficient is the "outer weight" of the latent variable influencing the manifest variable. The residual ε_h has zero mean and is independent of the latent variable $(cov[LV_k, \varepsilon_h] = 0)$.

In the B formative mode, the measured variables "form" the latent variables, according to the following equation:

$$LV_k = \sum_{h=1}^{H} \omega_k^h X_h + \delta_k$$

where the ω_k^h coefficient is a "structural loading" contributing to the latent variable. The δ_k residual has zero mean and is independent of each of the manifest variables ($cov[X_h, \delta_k] = 0$).

The most commonly used mode is the A reflective mode. In estimating the model parameters, the PLS-PM approach aims to maximize the overall explained variance of the endogenous variables.

10.2.3. *Validation statistics for the external model*

The one-dimensionality of the block of manifest variables corresponding to each latent variable is a structural assumption of the external model that should be validated using the different criteria presented below.

i) Difference between the first two eigenvalues of the data block

The first criterion of one-dimensionality, the principal component analysis of the block of data corresponding to each of the latent variables (see Table 10.1) provides a first criterion of one-dimensionality adapted from the Kaiser rule: if the first eigenvalue of the correlation matrix is greater than 1 and the second eigenvalue is much smaller; this means that the vast majority of the manifest variables are positively correlated with the first principal component.

ii) Cronbach's alpha

The second criterion of one-dimensionality is Cronbach's alpha, the ratio of the sum of the co-variances over the variance of the sum of the H manifest variables of the data block corresponding to a latent variable, i.e.:

$$\alpha = \frac{\sum_{h=1}^{H} cov(X_h, X_{h'})}{var(\sum_{h=1}^{H} X_h)} \times \frac{H}{H-1}$$

Cronbach's α is widely used in reliability analyses with the following rule: if this ratio is greater than 0.7, then the block can be considered unidimensional.

iii) Dillon–Goldstein's rho

The last criterion used is Dillon–Goldstein's rho, the ratio of the variance of the latent variable to the variance of its block of manifest variables, estimable by

$$\hat{\rho} = \frac{[\sum_{h=1}^{H} corr(X_h, t_1)]^2}{[\sum_{h=1}^{H} corr(X_h, t_1)]^2 + \sum_{h=1}^{H}(1 - [corr(X_h, t_1)]^2)}$$

where t_1 is the first principal component of the thematic block of manifest variables.

If the estimate of Dillon–Goldstein's ρ is greater than 0.7, then the block is considered one-dimensional.

Dillon–Goldstein's ρ is considered a better criterion than Cronbach's α by Chin[2] because it is based on the structural factors of the internal model, rather than on the correlations between the manifest variables of the external model implicitly making the assumption that the manifest variables are a priori equivalent to each other in defining a latent variable (τ-equivalence assumption).

iv) Communality

The com_k "communality" of the kth thematic block indicates the extent to which the variability of the manifest variables of the kth block is restored by the scores of the kth latent variable. The "commonality" of the kth thematic block is equal to the weighted sum of the squares of the correlations between the manifest variables and the Y_k reduced centered latent variable, i.e.:

$$com_k = \frac{1}{H_k} \sum_{h=1}^{H_k} cor^2(X_h, Y_k)$$

10.2.4. *Overall validation of structural modeling*

i) The average redundancy index

In order to link the predictive performance of the external measurement model to the consistency of the internal model components, the redundancy index calculated for each endogenous thematic block measures the share of variability of the manifest variables related to the Y_h latent variables explaining the kth endogenous latent variable, Y_k^{endo}, i.e.:

$$Red_k = com_k \times R^2\left(Y_k^{endo}, Y_{h:Y_h \rightarrow Y_k^{endo}}\right)$$

It interprets like an index of the capacity to predict the observed values of the kth latent endogenous variable.

The average redundancy index, $\overline{Red}$, computed on the set of K^{endo} endogenous variables, i.e.:

$$\overline{Red} = \frac{1}{K^{endo}} \sum_{k=1}^{K^{endo}} Red_k$$

then gives a global index of the capacity to predict the observed values of the endogenous latent variables of the model.

ii) The goodness of fit

Proposed by Amato et al. (2004), the goodness of fit (GoF) of the model is defined by the squared root of the product of the average "communality" over the average R^2, i.e.:

$$GoF = \sqrt{\overline{com} \times \overline{R^2}} = \sqrt{\frac{\sum_{k=1}^{K} \sum_{h=1}^{H_k} corr^2(X_k^h, Y_k)}{\sum_{k=1}^{K} H_k} \times \frac{\sum_{k=1}^{K^*} R^2\left(Y_k^{endo}, Y_{h:Y_h \to Y_k^{endo}}\right)}{K^{endo}}}$$

where $\overline{com}$, the "average communality", is the weighted mean of the communalities of each of the thematic blocks, i.e.:

$$\overline{com} = \frac{1}{\sum_{k:H_k>1} H_k} \sum_{k:H_k>1} H_k com_k$$

Because for each block, the thematic communalities are the means of square of the correlation coefficients, the average communality is the mean of the set of the square of the correlation coefficient between the latent variables and their manifest variables.

iii) The bootstrap

As the PLS-PM approach is not based on distributional assumptions, the use of bootstrap-based validation procedures (Efron and Tibshirani 1993) becomes necessary in both an exploratory and confirmatory approach. Bootstrapped estimates are computed for external weights, factors, structural links, communality and redundancy indices and overall goodness of fit. The principle of the bootstrap procedure is to randomly draw B new samples (usually $B<100$) of N observations (the "seeds") into the initial sample of observations, in order to obtain an estimate of the quantile function φ, reciprocal of the cumulative distribution function. For example, the bootstrapped values of the structural links are estimated on a B bootstrap basis using a Monte-Carlo procedure, yielding empirical confidence intervals estimated at the $(1-\tau)$ level of the quantile function of the bootstrapped communalities $\hat{\varphi}_{link}^{B}$, reciprocal of the cumulative distribution function, i.e.:

$$[\hat{\varphi}_{link}^{B}(\tau/2) \, ; \hat{\varphi}_{link}^{B}(1-\tau/2)]$$

10.3. Material and method

10.3.1. *Agro-ecological context of the study*

In this study, we apply the PLS-PM approach to the agro-ecological context defined by the plots of experimental or agricultural fields observed in the research framework constituted by four study zones (ZE) (Figure 10.3). These studies are federated by the multidisciplinary project "Predictive Ecological Engineering for Landscape Ecosystem Services and Sustainability" (Peerless) and funded by the French National Research Agency (ANR).

$$LV_{l}^{endo} = \beta_{l}^{0} + \sum_{k=1}^{K} \beta_{l}^{k} \, LV_{k}^{exo} + \varepsilon_{l}$$

where β_{l}^{k}, called the "structural link" (path coefficient), represents the sign and strength of the deterministic relationship between the endogenous latent variable LV_{l}^{endo} and the exogenous latent variables LV_{k}^{exo}. The part not explained by the deterministic model of LV_{l} is relegated into the residual ε_{l}. The structural links are estimated by a geometric projection (least squares) procedure whose only assumption is the independence between the deterministic part and the residual part, imposing that the covariance between each exogenous latent variable and the residual is zero $(cov(LV_{k}^{exo}, \varepsilon_{l}) = 0)$.

The Peerless project aims to identify the alternate managing strategies enhancing the pest control practices based on the functional biodiversity in arboriculture and field crops to optimize the agricultural production systems, at the local landscape scales, in a double perspective of durability and economical viability of these productions (Franck et al. 2017). Peerless has been structured towards the three following objectives: i) the evaluation of agronomical and ecological factors of plant protection; ii) the identification of ecological mechanisms enhancing the bio-control of pests and iii) the landscape conception of viable plant productions. The Peerless project aggregates four study zones (see Figure 10.3) with field crops ("Anjou", "Brittany" and "Côte d'Or") and one study zone with arboriculture ("Low Valley of the Durance"). These study zones (ZE) represent a set of 158 plots surveyed during 2014 and 2015.

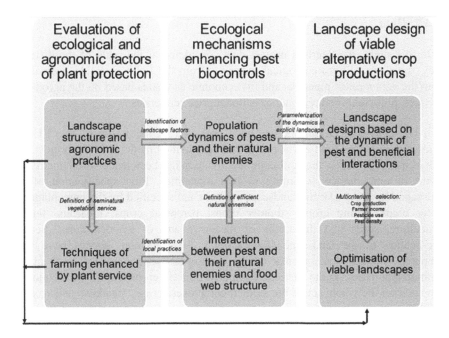

Figure 10.2. *Agro-ecological practices and infrastructure of the Peerless project*

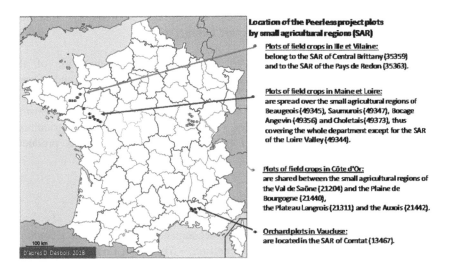

Figure 10.3. *Localization of the study zones in the Peerless project*

10.3.2. *Data*

In this study, the Peerless project data considered at the scale of the different study zones are: i) agro-ecological measures from the field; ii) field observations about the agronomical practices and iii) economic estimates based on the agronomic practices, plot yields and regional or national price references.

i) The agro-ecological data has been collected in the frame of the T1 task (landscape structure, field environment and agronomic practices) of the project. For each of the study zones, the landscape specification has been made within a circle of 1 km^2 of unit surface according to two modalities. First specification of the landscape (*Landscape1*): the landscape contexts are specified by the percentages in winter crops, spring crops, summer crops, perennial crops, fabaceus, fallow, horticulture, seeds and the ratios of meadows and of wooden areas. Second specification of the landscape (*Landscape2*): two Shannon indexes have been computed between distinct sites taking the lowest correspondence level of the common typologies: a) the first one computed on field crops and b) the second one computed on the whole set of the studied complexes (crops, meadows and wooden areas).

ii) The agronomic practices are documented by the indicators of cultural techniques, i.e.: the number of plows and soil works (deep and superficial); the number of fertilizations generally and particularly in nitrogen (N), as minerals as organics; the seedling and harvest dates; as well as the frequency treatment indicators (IFTs), as conventional as organic farming mode.

iii) The economic data have been produced in the framework of the "Optimization of viable landscapes" task (T6) of the Peerless project and merged with the agro-ecological data (Desbois 2018) using the price references issued from the French statistical office, those produced by the technical institutes (*Arvalis, Centre technique interprofessionnel des Fruits et Légumes*) and the agricultural offices (*FranceAgriMer, Chambres d'Agriculture*) to compute gross products, specific costs and gross margin.

10.3.3. *The structural model and the estimation*

Built from the concepts of the corporate accountancy, the simplified accounting relationship $Gross\_Margin = Gross\_Product - Specifics\_Costs$ defining the concept of gross margin as an algebraic sum of gross product and specific costs, offers a simple example of application not only to the farm holding, but also to the cropped plots of the concept of internal structural model.

Once specified, this internal model allows us to structure the set of measured or observed variables (the "manifest" variables – MVs) into several blocks corresponding to the conceptual artifacts, each block of manifest variables representing a latent variable. The particular composition into manifest variables of thematic blocks corresponding to different latent variables (*Landscape1, Landscape2, Pests, Weeds, SpecCost, GrossProd, Subsidies, Marginpua*) is given in Table 10.5.

In a context of agro-ecological application, the concept of "landscape" for the agricultural plot can be specified in a formative mode (B) by the occupation profiles of the soil (different crops, fabaceus, fallow, gardening, seeds, meadows and wooden areas) as it can be in reflective mode (A) in the various indices of diversity that can be built from its description ("field crops" or "every production" Shannon indices).

Applied to eco-systemic contexts resulting from the conjunction of infrastructures and practices, the specification of a structural model of agro-ecological interaction and economic impact (see Figure 10.5) allows us to analyze the interrelations between ecological infrastructures (landscape profiles at the plot level), agronomic practices (plowing, intermediary crops) and the induced results (growth of the product, reduction of the costs).

In this work, the initial structural model takes in the one proposed by Mezerette (2016), completing it with the business management variables of costs, subsidies, product and margin (see Figure 10.1) and extending its application to the Peerless arboreal sites. This initial structural model specifies the a priori relationships between the agro-ecological variables describing the landscape (*Landscape1, Landscape2*), the agronomical practices (*Practice*), as well as the occurrence of diseases or pests (*Pests*) and weeds (*Weeds*), with the economic variables of specific costs (*SpecCost*), of gross production (*GrossProd*), of subsidies (*Subsidies*) and of gross margin per unit area (*Marginpua*) at the plot level.

In the scheme of Figure 10.5, the ecological infrastructures (*Landscape1, Landscape2*) influence both the diseases or pests (*Pests*), the weeds (*Weeds*) and agronomical practices (*Practice*), in an a priori undetermined way ($\rightarrow$). The agronomical practices impact a priori the gross products (*GrossProd*) and the specific costs (*SpecCost*), either directly by strengthening them ($\rightarrow$) or indirectly by diminishing them ($\rightarrow$). The pests and the weeds are supposed to have a diminishing impact ($\rightarrow$) on the gross products and expanding impact ($\rightarrow$) on specific costs. The sum of these influences on the gross products and on the specific costs determines, with the subsidies (*Subsidies*), the impact in fine of the agro-ecological practices on the gross margin per hectare (*Marginpua*). In this scheme, the conceptual artifacts *Landscape1*, *Landscape2* and *Subsidies* appear as a priori exogenous (i.e. not determined by other phenomena) LVs, while the concepts *Practice, Pests, Weeds, SpecCost, GrossProd* and *Marginpua* are a priori endogenous (i.e. influenced by other phenomena) LVs.

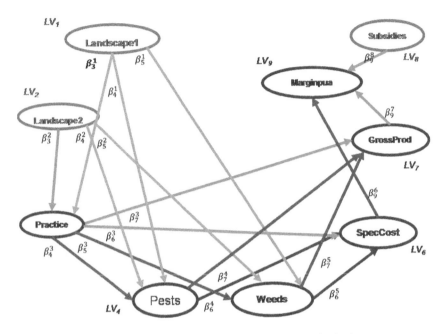

Figure 10.4. *Structural model of agro-ecological interaction and economic impact at the plot level*

Reading: in **green**, the exogenous LVs; in **burgundy**, the endogenous LVs; in **blue**, the structural links of strengthening; in **red**, the structural links of weakening; in **gray**, the structural links a priori undetermined.

10.4. Results and discussion

The initial structural model is estimated on the basis of a set of 158 plots surveyed in 2014 and 2015. The setting of the PLS-PM approach has been realized via the R statistical software, version 3.6.2 (see: https://www.r-project.org/), and specifically with the "pls-pm" package, version 0.4.9 (Sanchez et al. 2017). The estimation of structural links (path coefficients) of the model has been conducted using the reflective (A) mode for the set of latent variables.

Figure 10.6 displays the whole view of the external model. For example, for the latent variable *Pests*, the manifest variables reflecting this latent variable within the corresponding thematic block are: *S.avenae*, *M.dirhodum*, *Total.aphids*, *Lema.larvae* and *PctDamage.by.Lema*. The value of the structural factors is positive for the occurrences of pests (*Total.aphids*, *Lema.larvae*) and the index of their attacks (*PctDamage.by.Lema*). However, this value is negative for occurrences of the cereal ear aphid Sitobion (*S.avenae*), in contrast to the other pest occurrences of cereal and rose aphids (*M.dirhodum*) and cereal leaf beetles (*Lema*).

10.4.1. *Checking the block one-dimensionality*

The one-dimensionality statistics (Cronbach's alpha and Dillon–Goldstein's rho) computed on the basis of the initial structural model displayed (see Figure 10.6) show too low values for the thematic blocks *Subsidies*, *Landscape2* and *SpecCost* (see Table 10.1). In fact, for these blocks, we observe some negative correlations (loadings).

The blocks *Landscape2*, *Practice*, *Pests*, *Weeds* and *Marginpua* are considered as one-dimensional because they satisfy all the criterions. The blocks *Landscape1*, *SpecCost*, *GrossProd* and *Subsidies* show values lower than 0.7 for Cronbach's alpha; however the blocks *GrossProd* and *Subsidies* can be considered as unidimensional because they satisfy to the criterion of Dillon–Goldstein's rho.

10.4.2. *Fitting the external model and assessing the quality of the fit*

The goodness of fit (*GoF*) value of the initial model is 0.4285. This index can be improved by adjusting the external model: indeed, some negatively correlated links can be transformed into positive links by appropriate recoding of manifest variables (MVs). Thus, in the block *Subsidies*, the recoding of the *CouplAid_pha* (coupled aid per hectare) MV into the *DecouplAid_ha = TotalAid_pha – CouplAid_pha* variable makes it possible to obtain a positive correlation. Similarly, for the *Landscape1* thematic block, the *VegCrop_pct* (percentage of vegetable crop) MV is recoded into the *NonVegCrop_pct = 100 – VegCrop_pct* variable. For the block *Practice*, the *Fung_IFT* (index of the frequency of fungal treatments) MV is transformed into the *NonFung_IFT=Total_IFT – Fung_IFT* variable. For the block *SpecCost*, the *FungTCost_pha* (cost per hectare of fungal treatments) MV is transformed into the *NonFungTCost_pha =TotalCost_pha – FungTCost_pha* variable.

Blocks	Mode	Observed Var	Cronbach's Alpha	Dillon-Goldstein's Rho	Eigenvalue 1	Eigenvalue 2
Landscape1	A	9	0.398	0.073	2.04	1.67
Landscape2	A	10	0.473	0.642	1.84	1.45
Practice	A	18	0.943	0.950	9.45	3.20
Pests	A	5	0.807	0.874	3.03	0.96
Weeds	A	6	0.871	0.904	3.68	1.09
SpecCost	A	10	0.834	0.879	4.75	2.30
GrossProd	A	4	0.690	0.805	2.30	1.59
Subsidies	A	4	0.243	0.125	2.09	0.18
Marginpua	A	3	0.986	0.991	2.92	0.07

Table 10.1. *One-dimensionality statistics of thematic blocks of the initial model. For a color version of this table, see www.iste.co.uk/zafeiris/data2.zip*

Reading: the values in **blue** mean that the selected one-dimensionality criterion is satisfied.

After this recoding, the one-dimensionality statistics are enhanced (see Table 10.2): they are all greater than 0.7 (acceptance level of the one-dimensionality hypothesis), except for the blocks *Landscape1*, *GrossProd* and *Subsidies* with the values lower than 0.5 for the Cronbach's alpha, but near the acceptance level with Dillon–Goldstein's rho (>0,6) for *Landscape2*. The value of the goodness of fit for the amended model is enhanced in a marginal way, to 0.5078 (see Table 10.3).

Blocks	Mode	Observed Var	Cronbach's Alpha	Dillon-Goldstein's Rho	Eigenvalue 1	Eigenvalue 2
Landscape1	A	10	0	0.215	2.10	1,79
Landscape2	A	2	0.829	0.921	1.71	0.29
Practice	A	19	0.720	0.741	9.11	3.33
Pests	A	5	0.717	0.838	3.03	0.96
Weeds	A	6	0.871	0.904	3.68	1.09
SpecCost	A	10	0.541	0.611	3.02	2.50
GrossProd	A	4	0.592	0.790	2.30	1.59
Subsidies	A	4	0.664	0.804	2.08	1.31
Marginpua	A	3	0.986	0.991	2.92	0.07

Table 10.2. *One-dimensionality statistics for the thematic blocks of the amended model. For a color version of this table, see www.iste.co.uk/zafeiris/data2.zip*

Reading: the values in **blue** mean that the selected one-dimensionality criterion is satisfied.

Theme block	Manifest variables	Communality	Type	R^2	Average redundancy
Landscape1	9	0.178	Exogeneous	0.0000	0.0000
Landscape2	2	0.850	Exogeneous	0.0000	0.0000
Practice	18	0.517	Endogeneous	0.0921	0.0477
Pests	5	0.606	Endogeneous	0.1254	0.0759
Weeds	6	0.608	Endogeneous	0.2806	0.1707
SpecCost	10	0.462	Endogeneous	0.6764	0.3127
GrossProd	4	0.542	Endogeneous	0.6906	0.3746
Subsidies	4	0.362	Exogeneous	0.0000	0.0000
Marginpua	3	0.972	Endogeneous	0.6391	0.6215
Weighted Mean		0.499			
Endogenous block Mean		0.618		0.417	0.2579
Goodness of Fit				0.5078	

NOTE.– The goodness of fit is computed from the endogenous blocks.

Table 10.3. *Communalities, R^2 and redundancies*

10.4.3. *The structural model after revision*

Taking into account the correlations between blocks results in the following structural model (see Figure 10.4), where the relationships between latent variables are of expected sign except for the latent variable "Weeds" issued from the block *Weeds* displaying a negative relationship of somewhat low intensity, with the variable "Specific Costs" issued from the SpecCost block.

We note that the relationship between the latent variable *Practice* representing the agronomic practices and the latent variable *Pests* representing the occurrence of pest is positive, while it is negative with the latent variable *Weeds* representing the presence of weeds. It would be interesting to distinguish between the specific practices of the pest control from those specific of the weed control.

The direct and indirect effects are displayed in Figure 10.6 as a categorical diagram, occasionally piled when they are cumulative. With regard to the direct or indirect effects, we distinguish those which are important (greater than 0.4), from those which are moderate (greater than 0.2 and lower than 0.4) and those which are low (lower than 0.2 and greater than 0.1), even from those which are very low (lower than 0.1).

Among the effects that are important, we have: i) the negative effects of the agronomic practices on the weeds; ii) the negative effects of the pest and the weeds on the gross product and iii) the positive effects of the gross product on the gross margin. The most important indirect effects (greater than 0.4) are those which are negative of the pest on the gross margin.

Among the moderate direct effects, we distinguish: i) the negative one, the specific costs on the gross margin and ii) the positive one, the cover of the landscape (*Landscape1*) of the practices on the weeds, of practices on the pests and the specific costs and also of subsidies on the gross margin. The moderate indirect effects are the negative one of weeds on the gross margin.

Among the low direct effects, we note: i) the negative one of weeds on the specific cost and; ii) the positive one, by decreasing importance order, of landscape complexity (*Landscape2*) on the pests and of practices on the gross product. The lower indirect effects are: i) the negative one, the landscape cover on the gross product and the margin, and ii) the positive one, the landscape cover on the specific costs and of practices on the product.

Among the lower direct effects, we note: the positive ones of the landscape complexity on the specific costs and the practices and ii) the negative one of weeds on the specific costs. The very low indirect effects are: i) the positive one of landscape complexity, of the cover landscape on the pests and of practices of the gross margin, and ii) the negative ones of landscape complexity on the gross product and the gross margin.

Hence, the major effects are the ones positive of pests on the specific costs and of gross product on the gross margin. The minor effects that appear as manifest are i) the negative ones of practices on the weeds and the ones of pests and of the weeds on the gross product, and indirectly on the gross margin, and ii) the positive ones of practices on the specific costs.

The use of random resampling validates these initial findings, particularly with regard to the structural links in the internal model (see Table 10.4 and Figure 10.5).

Link	Estimate	Bootstrap Estimate	Standard-error	Q(0.025)	Q(0.975)
Landscape1 -> Practice	0.305	0.249	0.323	-0.521	0.639
Landscape1 -> Pests	0.115	0.203	0.251	-0.380	0.552
Landscape1 -> Weeds	0.398	0.431	0.215	-0.227	0.692
Landscape2 -> Practice	-0.005	-0.045	0.188	-0.365	0.297
Landscape2 -> Pests	0.176	0.175	0.120	-0.031	0.359
Landscape2 -> Weeds	0.017	0.017	0.122	-0.233	0.197
Practice -> Pests	0.222	0.182	0.180	-0.186	0.499
Practice -> Weeds	-0.487	-0.478	0.209	-0.748	0.097
Practice -> SpecCost	**0.229**	**0.247**	**0.159**	**0.016**	**0.451**
Practice -> GrossProd	0.103	0.071	0.131	-0.239	0.234
Pests -> SpecCost	**0.739**	**0.706**	**0.115**	**0.496**	**0.893**
Pests -> GrossProd	-0.504	-0.482	0.098	-0.651	-0.255
Weeds -> SpecCost	-0.096	-0.100	0.139	-0.400	0.156
Weeds -> GrossProd	-0.519	-0.506	0.118	-0.640	-0.329
SpecCost -> Marginpua	-0.216	-0.204	0.079	-0.341	-0.015
GrossProd -> Marginpua	**0.632**	**0.688**	**0.107**	**0.482**	**0.896**
Subsidies -> Marginpua	0.246	0.129	0.227	-0.390	0.447

Table 10.4. *Bootstrapped estimation of the structural links of the internal model. For a color version of this table, see www.iste.co.uk/zafeiris/data2.zip*

Reading: values in **blue** (respectively, in **red**) indicate that according to the bootstrap estimation, the value of the structural link is significantly positive, respectively, negative.

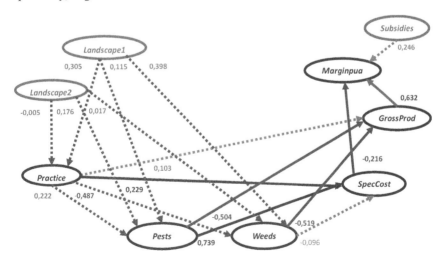

Figure 10.5. *Estimated internal scheme of the final structural model after revision*

Reading: blue (respectively, **red**) arrows indicate that the expected value of the structural link is positive, respectively, negative; values (e.g. 0.398) indicate the strength of the structural link connecting the latent variables (e.g. Landscape1-> Weeds); dotted structural links (····>) are not significant according to the bootstrapped estimation.

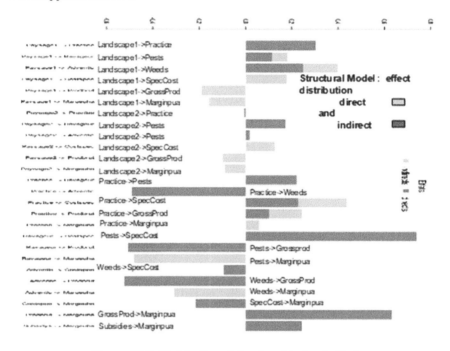

Figure 10.6. *Distribution of direct and indirect effects*

Reading: direct effects are in **dark blue** and indirect effects are in **light blue**; if direct and indirect effects co-exist, then the bars are stacked.

Thus, according to the estimation initiated with 99 random removals (bootstrap) and a confidence level ($\tau = 0.05$) at 95%, the only significantly non-zero links turn out to be:

i) on the one hand, the positive influence of practices on specific costs (*Practice ->SpecCost* ≈ 0.25), of pests on specific costs (*Pests->SpecCost* ≈ 0.71) and of product on gross margin (*GrossProd->Marginpua* ≈ 0.69);

ii) on the other hand, the negative influence of pests on production (*Pests->GrossProd* ≈ -0.50), weeds on production (*Weeds->GrossProd* ≈ -0.48) and specific costs on margin (*SpecCost->Marginpua* ≈ -0.20).

10.5. Conclusion

The objective of this work is to propose an introduction to an alternative structural modeling method adapted to the evaluation of ecosystem practices, in a context characterized by the complexity of the interrelationships between parcel landscapes, agronomic practices and economic results, as well as the small size of the available observation samples.

The partial least squares approach revealed statistically significant effects: i) negative on products for weeds and pests; ii) positive on specific costs for practices and pests and iii) of opposite sign on margin, negative for specific costs and positive for products.

However, while the effects of agronomic practices on weeds are of the expected sign, they are not for pests. The signs of the effects of landscapes on pests and weeds are also not as expected. However, these estimated values of these effects are not statistically significant.

Thus, it is necessary to estimate this structural model on a larger sample of observations that would allow the extension of this study to a larger spatial scale to include other plot landscapes and its continuation over several years, in order to isolate possible effects of inter-annual variation.

10.6. References

Amato, S., Esposito Vinzi, V., Tenenhaus, M. (2004). A global goodness-of-fit index for PLS structural equation modeling. Communication to PLS Club, HEC Paris.

Chin, W.W. (1998). The partial least squares approach for structural equation modeling. In *Modern Methods for Business Research*, Marcoulides, G.A. (ed.). Lawrence Erlbaum Associates, London.

Chin, W.W. and Newsted, P.R. (1999). Structural equation modeling analysis with small samples using partial least squares. In *Statistical Strategies for Small Sample Research*, Hoyle, R. (ed.). Sage Publication, London.

Desbois, D. (2018). Livrable PEERLESS D1-2 : constitution et validation de la base de données agroécologiques et économiques. ANR-12-AGRO-006 Project, 55.

Efron, B. and Tibshirani, R.J. (1993). *An Introduction to the Bootstrap*. Chapman & Hall, New York.

Franck, P., Bischoff, A., Bohan, D., Klein, E., Lavigne, C., Martinet, V., Memmah, M., Parisey, N., Petit, S., Plantegenest, M. et al. (2017). Le projet PEERLESS : viabilité d'une gestion écologique renforcée de la santé des plantes dans les paysages agricoles. *Ecologisation des systèmes de productions agricoles pour renforcer le contrôle biologique des bioagresseurs*, Inra, 5–6.

Hoyle, R.H. (ed.) (1995). *Structural Equation Modeling: Concepts, Issues, and Applications*. Sage, Thousand Oaks.

Jonsson, M., Straub, C.S., Didham, R.K., Buckley, H.L., Case, B.S., Hale, R.J., Gratton, C., Wratten, S.D. (2015). Experimental evidence that the effectiveness of conservation biological control depends on landscape complexity. *Journal of Applied Ecology*, 52, 1274–1282.

Lohmöller, J.-B. (1989). *Latent Variable Path Modeling with Partial Least Squares*. Physica-Verlag, Mathematics.

Mezerette, F. (2016). Quels effets de la gestion agricole et du paysage sur l'abondance de bioagresseurs et le rendement ? Ecologie fonctionnelle, comportementale et évolutive Master Memorandum, Rennes I University, 34.

Millennium Ecosystem Assessment (2005). *Ecosystems and Human Well-being: Synthesis*. Island Press, Washington, DC.

Tenenhaus, M., Esposito Vinzi, V., Chatelin, Y.M., Lauro, C. (2005). PLS path modelling. *Computational Statistics & Data Analysis*, 48, 159–205.

Wold, H. (1981). *The Fix-Point Approach to Interdependent Systems. Contributions to Economic Analysis 132*. North-Holland, Amsterdam.

11

Lean Management as an Improvement Factor in Health Services – The Case of Venizeleio General Hospital of Crete, Greece

In recent years, the issue of lean management has been of great concern to the health sector, as its previous applications in other sectors have demonstrated the significant benefits it can bring to the organizations that adopt it. This chapter examines the extent of the application of simple management in the health units of Greece and specifically in the Venizelio General Hospital of Heraklion, Crete, examining the views of the employees.

The sample for the research consisted of 83 employees of the Venizelio General Hospital of Heraklion, Crete, who were selected according to convenient sampling. The research method used was quantitative, and the research tool used was the questionnaire. The research data were analyzed according to the SPSS statistical package.

The results of the research showed that the Venizelio General Hospital of Heraklion, Crete, has adopted and applies the principles of lean management to a significant degree. It was also found that employees have knowledge of lean management issues, while understanding the benefits of its implementation. In addition, the hospital staff is positive about acquiring additional knowledge about lean management.

Chapter written by Eleni GENITSARIDI and George MATALLIOTAKIS.
For a color version of all the figures in this chapter, see www.iste.co.uk/zafeiris/data2.zip.

11.1. Introduction

In the 21st century, the health sector has faced a multitude of fiscal problems as the demand for health services increases, as does their cost (Toussaint and Berry 2013). The rapid increase in health expenditure, combined with the stagnation observed at the level of resources, has resulted in financial exhaustion and the inability of hospitals to meet the demand for health services. The above situation in turn leads to a reduction in the quality of health services (Blackmore et al. 2013).

The provision of immediate and quality health services to patients is considered a key concern of every health system, in order to ensure continuous improvement in efficiency and productivity levels of health services. The application of lean management, and more generally of the lean philosophy in the provision of health services, aims to restructure the existing health status, without additional financial aid or new investment approaches in the field of health (Tsasis and Bruce-Barrett 2008; Machado and Leitner 2010).

Lean management interventions in the health sector seek to change the procedures implemented by each hospital to ensure the provision of health services is characterized by a high level of safety, quality, efficiency and suitability (Trägardh and Lindberg 2004; Ballé and Rénier 2007). In no case does lean management coincide with the restriction of employees, but aims with the existing or less resources, to achieve as many and better results as possible (Poksinska 2010).

The present research aims to examine if and to what extent lean management is applied in the health units of the Greek state and specifically in the Venizelio General Hospital of Heraklion, Crete. The ultimate goal of the work is to demonstrate whether the employees of Venizelio understand the meaning and content of lean management and the ways in which they believe it contributes to improving the level of efficiency, effectiveness and cost of health organizations.

11.2. Theoretical framework

Lean management refers to the process that aims to achieve as much as possible, with the least possible effort, equipment, space and time, to ensure the maximum ability of customers to obtain the products they want (Womack and Jones 2003). The starting point of lean management is considered to be the elimination of unnecessary expenses so that the work performed has a positive impact on the value of the business and the satisfaction of customers' needs. The main axis of application of lean management is the identification of those actions that, if implemented, will add value to the business, as well as the identification of those actions that do not offer value (Institute for Healthcare Improvement 2005; Lavalle 2011).

According to the literature on lean management, it is based on a framework of five principles, as follows (Womack and Jones 2003): a) determination of value by end customers, b) mitigation of actions that do not have value, c) actions that contribute to value and must be carried out continuously so that the product reaches the customer smoothly, d) the product or service is produced for the customer and e) pursuit of perfection through continuous improvement. In addition to these five values, lean management is based on the subtraction of actions, which lead to the consumption of resources but without producing value, resulting in waste. In the context of lean management, eight types of waste should be avoided, which are: a) defects, b) overproduction, c) transport, d) waiting, e) stocks, f) traffic, g) overwork and h) non-use of cognitive capital (Graban 2011).

At the time lean management was first introduced, strategies aimed at developing value and reducing spending for each business began to emerge. One of the most popular tools used by lean management is "value stream mapping". The instrument graphically represents all the responsibilities that are present within the value stream that concern either a product or a service (Womack and Jones 2003). Also, one of the most well-known strategies of lean management concerns continuous and gradual improvement. This strategy refers to a set of actions that occur over a period of four to five days, aiming to make significant changes in the body (Lavalle 2011). A very common strategy of lean management is the "5S" method, which refers to five Japanese words beginning with the letter "S". Specifically, it is the word *seiri*, which refers to the sorting of those tools and accessories that are considered important for the working environment and, respectively, the removal of those that are not necessary. The second word is *sieton*, which refers to the identification and arrangement of tools and media so that they can be easily used. The third word is *seiso*, which refers to the existence of a clean working environment. The fourth word is *seiketsou*, which is associated with the creation and development of those processes that aim to ensure improvements in the above three steps. The fifth word is *shitsuke*, which is related to the acquisition of habits so that the realization of the four above mentioned steps takes place (Womack and Jones 2003). The 5S strategy can be applied in warehouses where there are tools, medicines or accessories, for example, a hospital unit (Lavalle 2011).

Visual inspection is another widely used tool, as it has been proven to be useful in the field of health. Essentially, all the tools, components, productive activities and performance indicators of each system are placed in common view so that all employees can understand the state of the system at a glance (Womack and Jones 2003; Lavalle 2011).

Many scientists point out that the application of lean management in the health sector is considered necessary and imperative as it allows health units to improve (Leggat et al. 2015), enabling them to become more flexible (Neufeld et al. 2013).

The application of lean management in the health sector aims to orient health units in a specific framework of changes, which must be made when clinical care is provided so that there is continuous improvement in the quality, productivity, efficiency, safety and suitability of patient–client services (Houchens and Kim 2013). Within this field, lean management offers a specific regulatory framework that determines which of the actions that an organization, a hospital, will perform, are "value-added" actions and which are "non-value-added" actions.

The 5S strategy has been proposed as the most appropriate strategy for lean management in the health sector, as it leads to the reduction of excessive spending, while improving the workplace in terms of organization and visual management. 5S in the case of hospitals refers to the following terms: sort, standardize, store, shine and sustain (Machado and Leitner 2010).

The systematic application of lean management has shown that, in a short period of time, hospitals have had much better patient flow and improved staff mobility (Tsasis and Bruce-Barrett 2008; Houchens and Kim 2013) and improved the level of systematic application of patient care (Houchens and Kim 2013) and the level of employee satisfaction (Graban 2011). Regional activities of hospitals are improving, such as administrative services, laboratory controls and logistics infrastructure (Edwards et al. 2012). There has also been a significant improvement in the flow of patients who were emergencies, especially in terms of their waiting time and the correct use of surgical instruments (Edwards et al. 2012). Through the application of lean management, the defects of the organism can be understood and eliminated (Adamson and Kwolek 2008). Any non-added value actions or actions that are considered redundant are eliminated. The consequence of all of the above is that procedures applied in the hospital are distinguished by efficiency and effectiveness, focusing on the benefit of the patient (Ben-Tovim et al. 2007).

Research has shown that the application of lean management in health facilities can reduce injuries, infections and even deaths. It is not a magic solution, but it helps to eliminate many mistakes in order to change the mentalities of the employees and to limit those mistakes that can be predicted (May 2007). Graban (2011) stressed that the application of lean management achieves quick and effective results in terms of hospital laboratories, disinfection, sterilization of hospitals, reduction of infections, waiting time and increasing hospital revenues.

In addition, through the implementation of lean management, there is an improvement in the financial performance of hospitals, as costs are reduced and, at the same time, patient satisfaction is improved in terms of both results and flexibility of health units. Lean management also improves the policies followed by health units at the level of healthcare, while increasing cost control. Quantitative assessment of the results of lean management can also lead to further improvement in the quality of services provided. Employees are more wary of waste and their productivity increases, as problematic situations in the workplace are resolved. At the same time, the stress of the employees is reduced, while they themselves become more flexible in the performance of their duties. Through their training and participation in lean management processes, they also make a decisive contribution to the provision of high quality health services (Plsek and Greenhalgh 2001).

Lean management helps to transmit an organizational culture to healthcare units, which leads to easier acceptance of the reforms that need to take place in healthcare. The organizational culture of lean management can have a decisive effect on employee performance, greater job satisfaction, commitment and commitment to patients (Ross-Baker 2014).

However, in order for lean management to be implemented in the health sector, a number of important obstacles must cease to exist. First of all, it is necessary to convince the human resources of the hospital unit of the importance of lean management and to proceed with its implementation. Many employees believe that lean management involves reductions and layoffs, with the result that, due to the above perception, they do not want to apply it because they believe that they or their colleagues may lose their jobs (Houchens and Kim 2013).

Apart from the issue of limited time and the accumulated practical experience of implementing lean management, the non-development of methods that suit the specifics of the industry, such as issues of complexity and value associated with them, also acts as a deterrent to its effective implementation in health organizations (Plsek and Greenhalgh 2001).

In addition, it is observed that most hospitals are organized in functional silos so that they can take advantage of the benefits of specialization, making it difficult to create coherent and uninterrupted patient flows and observe conflicts at the level of roles and ambiguity regarding the duties of employees (Perrow 1986). In addition to the above obstacles, it should be noted that hospital units depend on the coordination of institutions from different professions (Plsek and Wilson 2001). The complexity of the health sector explains, to some extent, why it is difficult to implement lean management in relation to other sectors.

In conclusion, an important obstacle to the correct and effective use of the application of lean management is the existing perception of the concept of its value. The hospital context can hardly determine the value in a strict context, as the nursing staff who focus on care understand the value differently, otherwise the medical staff who focuses on treatment and otherwise the administrative staff who focuses on the hospital performance and its value to the community (Young and McClean 2008).

11.3. Purpose of the research

The purpose of this research is to investigate the application of lean management in the case of the Greek health reality, with reference to the Venizelio General Hospital of Heraklion, Crete. The work seeks to demonstrate that the staff of the aforementioned health unit understand the meaning and content of lean management and how it believes that it can lead to the provision of effective and efficient health services.

11.4. Methodology

A quantitative method and specifically a questionnaire was used to conduct the research (Creswell 2016). The questionnaire of the present survey consists of 23 questions, of which the first 8 refer to the demographic data of the respondents (gender, age, marital status, education, field of work, etc.), while the rest concern the issue of lean management. The combination of different types of questions was chosen as it was considered that this would help to conduct the research more effectively, since the results would be better codified and quantified. More specifically, the questions in the research were dichotomous, Likert scale questions, multiple-choice questions and short-answer questions (Babbie 2013). The research sample consisted of 82 employees at the Venizeleio General Hospital of Heraklion, Crete, who were asked to fill in the questionnaire electronically, which was created on the Google Forms platform. The survey was conducted from May 12 to June 10, 2021. The results were analyzed according to the statistical package SPSS-27 (Sahlas and Mpersimis 2017).

11.5. Research results

The survey sample consists of 82 participants, of which 79.3% are women and 20.7% are men; 46% of the participants are aged from 36 to 45 years, while 76.3% are higher education graduates.

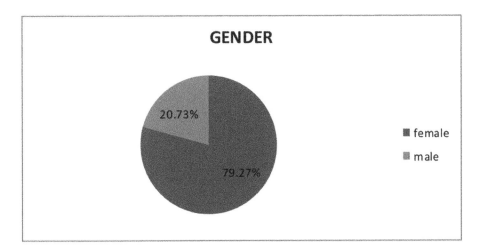

Figure 11.1. *Gender*

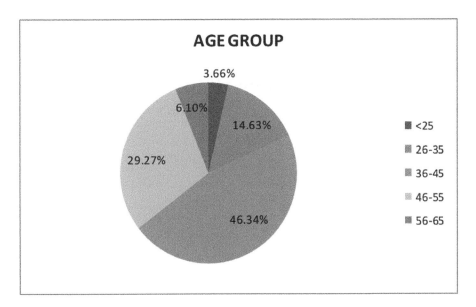

Figure 11.2. *Age group*

Of the participants, 82.9% are married, almost one in two work as nurses at Venizelio Hospital, while 50% have previous service, ranging from 16 to 27 years.

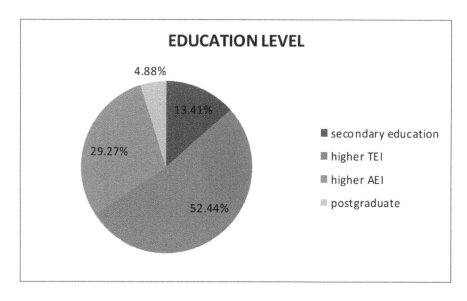

Figure 11.3. *Education level*

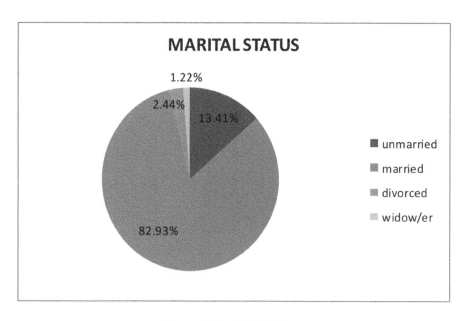

Figure 11.4. *Marital status*

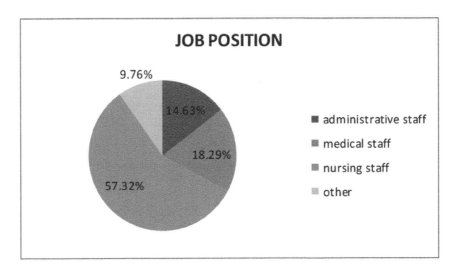

Figure 11.5. *Job position in the hospital unit*

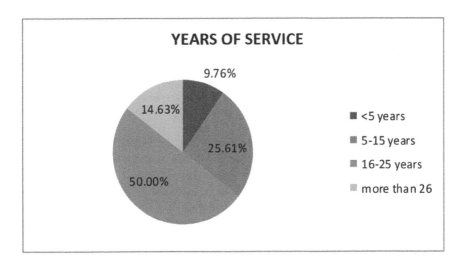

Figure 11.6. *Years of service*

It should be mentioned that in the minds of the research participants, lean management is understood in combination as a reduction of excessive costs, number of employees, constant control of the production process and a system of organization of the organization's management.

		Frequency	Percent	Valid percent	Cumulative percent
Valid	1	10	12.2	12.2	12.2
	2	3	3.7	3.7	15.9
	3	3	3.7	3.7	19.5
	4	7	8.5	8.5	28.0
	5	59	72.0	72.0	100.0
	Total	82	100.0	100.0	

Table 11.1. *How to define lean management*

Of the samples, 84.1% answered that the organization that works and systematically applies lean management techniques. It is therefore concluded that Venizelio has adopted and applied the principles of lean management, which is confirmed through its vision and mission[1].

		Frequency	Percent	Valid percent	Cumulative percent
Valid	Yes	69	84.1	84.1	84.1
	No	13	15.9	15.9	100.0
	Total	82	100.0	100.0	

Table 11.2. *Do you think that lean management is systematically applied to the health organization you work for?*

Another fact established by the research is that the health organization, in its effort to introduce some of the principles of lean management to employees, emphasizes the training for its human resources. Education is a key factor in promoting lean management in an organization, as found by Plsek and Greenhalgh (2001). This view is also endorsed by Poksinska (2010), who stated that training in lean management issues helps employees to understand the waste and proceed to reduce it in the context of the implementation of lean management.

The most common lean management technique in the health unit is that of "5S". The above technique is the most common technique of lean management (Womack and Jones 2003; Lavalle 2011), which shows that the health organization has specialized knowledge on the issue of lean management. Another common technique is progress monitoring meetings. Techniques that seem to be less developed are visual inspection and design to limit/avoid mistakes.

---

1 https://www.venizeleio.gr/.

	N	Minimum	Maximum	Mean	Std. deviation	Variance
ε13_1	82	1	2	1.93	.262	.069
ε13_2	82	1	2	1.26	.439	.193
ε13_3	82	1	2	1.11	.315	.099
ε13_4	82	1	2	1.10	.299	.089
ε13_5	82	1	2	1.28	.452	.204
ε13_6	82	1	2	1.67	.473	.224
ε13_7	82	1	2	1.44	.499	.249
ε13_8	82	1	2	1.57	.498	.248
ε13_9	82	1	2	1.90	.299	.089
ε13_10	82	1	2	1.09	.281	.079
Valid N (listwise)	82					

Table 11.3. *Indicate if each of the following lean management techniques applies to the organization you work for*

The most important reasons that led the organization to apply some lean management techniques, according to the respondents, were: to adapt to modern management techniques, to improve security and to reduce errors/mistakes. The reasons for the incentive to adopt lean management techniques are consistent with the results of previous research that concluded that lean management contributes to better management of the organization, improving its level of security and reducing mistakes (Golden 2006; Kim et al. 2006; Graban 2011; Houchens and Kim 2013; Hasle et al. 2016).

Based on the results of the survey, most respondents answered that lean management cannot be easily implemented due to the refusal of employees, due to fear of change, due to lack of knowledge of the principles and benefits of lean management and due to lack of proper training. The reasons presented as obstacles to the application of lean management of the present research are in line with the results of the study by Zidel (2006) and Hummer and Daccarett (2009) who reached the same conclusions. It is therefore observed that the obstacles that have been in place for more than 15 years in the implementation of lean management still exist in 2021.

	N	Minimum	Maximum	Mean	Std. deviation	Variance
ε14_1	82	1	5	4.21	1.003	1.006
ε14_2	82	1	5	4.37	1.000	1.000
ε14_3	82	1	5	3.24	1.117	1.248
ε14_4	82	1	5	4.21	.939	.882
ε14_5	82	1	5	4.00	.943	.889
ε14_6	82	1	5	2.79	.842	.710
ε14_7	82	1	5	3.70	.812	.659
ε14_8	82	1	5	4.22	1.031	1.062
ε14_9	82	1	5	4.26	1.184	1.403
ε14_10	82	1	5	4.41	1.133	1.283
ε14_11	82	1	5	4.49	1.057	1.117
ε14_12	82	1	5	3.20	.881	.776
Valid N (listwise)	82					

Table 11.4. *Reasons that led the health organization to implement lean management*

	N	Minimum	Maximum	Mean	Std. deviation	Variance
ε15_1	82	2	5	4.54	.789	.622
ε15_2	82	1	5	4.43	.861	.741
ε15_3	82	2	5	4.62	.641	.411
ε15_4	82	1	5	4.62	.696	.485
ε15_5	82	1	5	2.17	1.303	1.699
ε15_6	82	1	5	2.01	1.138	1.296
ε15_7	82	1	5	1.89	.994	.988
ε15_8	82	1	5	2.01	1.171	1.370
ε15_9	82	1	5	2.78	.802	.643
ε15_10	82	1	5	3.32	.887	.787
ε15_11	82	1	5	4.61	.766	.587
ε15_12	82	2	5	4.54	.905	.820
ε15_13	82	2	5	4.59	.785	.616
Valid N (listwise)	82					

Table 11.5. *Barriers to the implementation of lean management*

The research also distinguishes the main forms of excessive spending pointed out by the employees of the Venizelio Hospital in Heraklion. They mentioned defects as the most important waste, while unused knowledge was the least. According to Graban (2011), defects are the main cause of waste in a health organization, something that is confirmed in this case as well.

Concluding the discussion of the research results, the research presents the main benefits that the respondents considered to be obtained by a health organization from the application of lean management. As evidenced by the answers given, the most important benefits were the reduction of the cost of the services provided, the improvement in the level of care and safety of the patients (Locock 2003; Leggat et al. 2015) and the improvement in the level of patient satisfaction and staff. Benefits are less well-achieved, such as staff mobility and overcrowding. Respondents' views converge with the results of previous research by Thompson et al. (2003), Graban (2011), Houchens and Kim (2013) and Kraebber (2014), who had reached exactly the same conclusions in investigations conducted.

It is understood from the above that the Venizelio General Hospital of Heraklion, Crete, seeks the application of the principles of lean management in the context of the services it offers to patients, which shows that the health units in Greece have understood the importance and benefits for its operation, as well as for patients. It was also found that the participants have a basic knowledge framework for lean management, although there should be further training; something that they themselves point out. A very positive perspective for the implementation of lean management was the fact that the respondents knew the content of the concept of lean management and correctly identified the benefits that the organization derives from its implementation. The above mentioned positions of the employees can work encouragingly for the universal application of lean management in health units, as the correct knowledge of the content of the concept, both in theory and in practice, removes misconceptions and stereotypes in relation to it, which can work to discourage its implementation.

11.6. Conclusion

Lean management is a practice that, with appropriate adjustments, can be applied in the health sector and produce very positive results. This is especially the case in Greece where the health sector is plagued by a multitude of problems associated with misconceptions, limited resources, mismanagement, etc. The application of lean management could bring substantial solutions and lead to modernization of health facilities. The need to implement lean management in the Greek public health system also seems more urgent than ever if public health units want to compete on an equal footing with the rapidly growing private health sector, as well as the international health systems that systematically seem to apply lean management.

However, in order for lean management to be implemented properly, it is necessary for healthcare workers to be informed about the content of its implementation and to be properly trained. Only under the above conditions will they stop demonizing lean management and having misconceptions about it, as the perception still prevails that its implementation is associated with staff and resource cuts in health facilities.

Venizelio hospital, as can be seen from what is mentioned in its vision and mission, has understood that it is important to implement lean management in order to be functional and to provide the best and highest quality health services to their patients. The above perception seems to permeate the employees of the health unit who have understood the importance of its implementation. It is particularly encouraging that a regional hospital seeks to modernize and follow the international European trends of the time in the health sector, as the disposition of the Greek health system becomes more efficient and effective.

The results of the present research show that lean management can and should be applied in Greek health units as there is suitable ground and disposition in this direction. The Greek state, for its part, must "exploit" this disposition and develop policies in this direction, as well as incentives for the health units, in order to adopt it and implement it systematically.

Further research on the issue of lean management and the evaluation of the existing picture it presents in health units will significantly help in this direction as, in this way, it will be possible to overcome the obstacles that hinder its implementation and to develop the prospects so that it can be a reference point for the Greek health institutions.

11.7. References

Adamson, B. and Kwolek, S. (2008). Strategy, leadership and change: The North York General Hospital Transformation. *Journey, Healthcare Quarterly*, 11(3), 50–53.

Babbie, E. (2013). *Entry into Social Research*. Critique, Athens.

Ballé, M. and Rénier, A. (2007). Lean as a learning system in a hospital ward. *Leadership in Health Services*, 20, 33–41.

Ben-Tovim, D.I., Bassham, J.E., Bolch, D., Martin, M.A., Dougherty, M., Szwarcbord, M. (2007). Lean thinking across a hospital: Redesigning care at the Flinders Medical Centre. *Australian Health Review*, 31(1), 10–15.

Blackmore, C.C., Bishop, R., Luker, S., Williams, B.L. (2013). Applying lean methods to improve quality and safety in surgical sterile instrument processing. *Joint Commentary Journal of Quality of Patient Safety*, 39(3), 99–105

Creswell, J. (2016). *Research in Education*. Ion, Athens.

Edwards, K., Nielsen, A., Jacobsen, P. (2012). Implementing lean in surgery – Lessons and implications. *International Journal of Technology Management*, 57(1/2/3), 4–17.

Golden, B. (2006). Change: Transforming healthcare organizations. *Healthcare Quarterly*, 10, 10–19.

Graban, M. (2011). *Lean Hospitals: Improving Quality, Patient Safety, and Employee Satisfaction*, 2nd edition. CRC Press, New York.

Hasle, P., Nielsen, A., Edwards, K. (2016). Application of lean manufacturing in hospitals – The need to consider maturity, complexity, and the value concept. *Human Factors and Ergonomics in Manufacturing*, 26(4), 430–442.

Houchens, N. and Kim, C. (2013). *The Application of Lean in the Healthcare Sector: Theory and Practical Examples, in Lean Thinking for Healthcare*. Springer Science & Business Media, New York.

Hummer, J. and Daccarett, C. (2009). Improvement in prescription renewal handling by application of the Lean process. *Nursing Economy*, 27(3), 197–201.

Institute for Healthcare Improvement (2021). Going lean in health care. White Paper [Online]. Available at: http://www.ihi.org/IHI/Results/WhitePapers/GoingLeaninHealthCare.htm [Accessed 8 June 2021].

Kim, C., Spahlinger, D., Kin, J., Billi, J. (2006). Lean health care: What can hospitals learn from a world-class automaker? *Journal of Hospital Medicine*, 1(3), 191–199.

Kraebber, K. (2014). *Lean in Healthcare, in Management Engineering: A Guide to Best Practices for Industrial Engineering in Health Care*. CRC Press, New York.

Lavalle, D. (2011). *Improve Patient Safety with Lean Techniques, in Error Reduction in Health Care: A Systems Approach to Improving Patient Safety*. John Wiley & Sons, San Francisco.

Leggat, S.G., Bartram, T., Stanton, P., Bamber, G.J., Sohal, A.S. (2015). Have process redesign methods, such as Lean, been successful in changing care delivery in hospitals? A systematic review. *Public Money & Management*, 35(2), 161–168.

Locock, L. (2003). Healthcare redesign: Meaning, origins and application. *Quarterly Safety and Health Care*, 12, 53–58.

Machado, V. and Leitner, U. (2010). Lean tools and lean transformation process in health care. *International Journal of Management Science and Engineering Management*, 5(5), 383–392.

May, M.E. (2007). *The Elegant Solution: Toyota's Formula for Mastering Innovation*. Free Press, New York.

Neufeld, N.J., Hoyer, E.H., Cabahug, P., González-Fernández, M., Mehta, M., Walker, N.C., Mayer, R.S. (2013). A lean six sigma quality improvement project to increase discharge paperwork completeness for admission to a comprehensive integrated inpatient rehabilitation program. *American Journal of Medical Quality*, 28(4), 301–307.

Perrow, C. (1986). *Complex Organizations – A Critical Essay*. McGraw Hill, New York.

Plsek, P.E. and Greenhalgh, T. (2001). Complexity science – The challenge of complexity in health care. *British Medical Journal*, 323, 625–628.

Plsek, P.E. and Wilson, T. (2001). Complexity, leadership, and management in healthcare organisations. *British Medical Journal*, 323, 746–749.

Poksinska, B. (2010). The current state of Lean implementation in health care: Literature review. *Quality Management in Health Care*, 4(19), 319–329.

Ross-Baker, G. (2014). Improving healthcare using lean processes. *Healthcare Quarterly*, 17(2), 18–19.

Sahlas, A. and Mpersimis, S. (2017). *Applied Statistics Utilizing IBM SPSS Statistics 23: Focusing on Health Sciences*. Tziola Publications, Athens.

Thompson, D.N., Wolf, G.A., Spear, S.J. (2003). Driving improvement in patient care: Lessons from Toyota. *Journal of Nursing Administration*, 33(11), 585–595.

Toussaint, J. and Berry, L. (2013). The promise of lean in health care. *Mayo Clinic Proceedings*, 88(1), 74–82.

Trägardh, B. and Lindberg, K. (2004). Curing a meagre health care system by lean methods – Translating "chains of care" in the Swedish health care sector. *The International Journal of Health Planning and Management*, 19(4), 383–398.

Tsasis, P. and Bruce-Barrett, C. (2008). Organizational change through Lean Thinking. *Health Services Management Research*, 21(3), 192–198.

Womack, J.P. and Jones, D.T. (2003). *Lean Thinking. Banish Waste and Create Wealth in Your Corporation*. Free Press, New York.

Young, T.P. and McClean, S.I. (2008). A critical look at lean thinking in healthcare. *Quality and Safety in Health Care*, 17(5), 382–386.

Zidel, T.G. (2006). A lean toolbox – Using lean principles and techniques in healthcare. *JHQ*, 28(1), W1–7.

Motivation and Professional Satisfaction of Medical and Nursing Staff of Primary Health Care Structures (Urban and Regional Health Centers) of the Prefecture of Heraklion, Under the Responsibility of the 7th Ministry

The motivation and professional satisfaction of employees in their work environment is one of the most critical issues of modern administrations as it is inextricably linked to their efficiency and effectiveness and therefore to the viability of companies/organizations. These two determinants are critical, on the one hand, to the emotional and psychological state of the employees and, on the other hand, to the proper functioning of a company or an organization. The purpose of this chapter is to study the motivating factors that affect the job satisfaction of primary health care doctors and nurses.

This chapter begins by listing the basic theoretical approaches to job satisfaction and motivation and the key factors influencing these variables. It turns out that supervision, camaraderie and the nature of the work play a key role in contrast to the lower pay and operating conditions. In the scales of motivation, the highest average is presented by the characteristics of the work and colleagues, while the lowest percentage is displayed by the scale of successes. In between, the scale of colleagues and earnings is recorded. Important elements are that non-monetary incentives, such

Chapter written by Mihalis KYRIAKAKIS and George MATALLIOTAKIS.
For a color version of all the figures in this chapter, see www.iste.co.uk/zafeiris/data2.zip.

as job characteristics, supervision and camaraderie are key factors for both the variables job satisfaction and motivation.

12.1. Introduction

Motivation is a dynamic process that seeks to activate the skills and abilities of employees in order to maximize their performance. Job satisfaction includes the emotional reactions of the individual within their work environment, the values and behaviors they develop, the impact on their overall performance and their personal happiness. In this context, a rational strategy must make every effort to eliminate problems plaguing the workforce (Daskalakis 2010).

Nowadays, worldwide, health coverage systems, in addition to the problems they are called on to deal with over time (lack of funding, lack of logistical equipment, lack of recruitment of permanent specialized staff, etc.), are facing new challenges such as population aging, chronic diseases and poor working conditions. The pressure on the health sector is exacerbated by unexpected conditions such as the coronavirus pandemic, which has shrunk economies, suspended all productive activities, isolated population groups, closed schools, etc. Under these circumstances, the need to understand the psychology of employees and the conditions and problems they face becomes more relevant than ever (Hwu 1995).

12.2. Methodology and material

12.2.1. *Research tools for measuring motivation and professional satisfaction for this work*

The most reliable and widespread method of recording the views of employees regarding the main factors of motivation and job satisfaction is through the application of questionnaires. Questionnaires that are mainly used in descriptive and explanatory surveys can, through standardized questions, provide researchers with useful information about employee satisfaction as well as the factors that motivate them to optimize their performance.

In this study, the research tool used was essentially a combination of two questionnaires applied to similar surveys (Spector 1997). In more detail, the structured (weighted) questionnaire Job Satisfaction Survey (JSS) of the American professor of psychology Paul Spector was used, which examines job satisfaction on nine different scales – groups of questions, each of which includes four questions out of 36 in total. The motivation uses a 19-item questionnaire, based on the Maslow (1943) and Herzberg (1968) motivation theories.

12.2.2. *Purpose and objectives of the research*

The purpose of this chapter is the study of motivating factors that affect the job satisfaction of primary health care (urban and regional health centers) doctors and nurses of the Prefecture of Heraklion, under the responsibility of the 7th Health Department of Crete. The ultimate goal was, on the one hand, to try to identify and enhance the factors that positively motivate primary health care employees and, on the other hand, to identify the positive factors or eliminate the negative factors that affect their satisfaction in their work environment.

12.2.3. *Material and method*

The material of this study consisted of the doctors and nurses of the primary health care (health centers and local health units) of the Prefecture of Heraklion who, numbered until December 31, 2020, amounted to 338 (201 doctors and 137 nurses). The questionnaires were distributed to them personally by the researcher at their workplace after contacting the managers of the structures and observing all the health protection measures due to the coronavirus.

A/A	Structures
1	Health Centrer Heraklion (urban type)
2	Health Centrer St. Barbara
3	Health Centrer Arkalochori
4	Health Centrer Kastelli
5	Health Centrer Vianou
6	Health Centrer Xaraka
7	Health Centrer Moires
8	Local Health Unit 1st
9	Local Health Unit 2st
10	Local Health Unit 3st
11	Local Health Unit 4st
12	Local Health Unit 5st
13	Local Health Unit Maleviziou
14	Local Health Unit Xersonissos

Table 12.1. *Primary health care structures of the Prefecture of Heraklion under the responsibility of the 7th Ministry of Health of Crete (source: 7th Health District of Crete, available at: www.hc-crete.gr (2021))*

Of the 338 questionnaires personally distributed by the researcher, 208 were returned (61.5% response rate); 120 of the medical staff and 88 of the nursing staff responded.

12.2.4. *Statistical analysis*

Frequency and % frequency were used to describe the discrete variables, while mean, standard deviation, median and quadrants were used to describe the continuous variables. The regularity of the continuous variables was checked with the Kolmogorov–Smirnov relevance of the questions to Cronbach's alpha. Since the normality was observed to find differences between two groups in continuous variables, the t-test of independent samples was used, and when there was a deviation from the normality, the Mann–Whitney test was applied.

For comparisons of continuous variables in more than 2 groups, one-way ANOVA or the corresponding non-parametric Kruskal–Wallis test was applied. The correlation of two continuous variables was done with the Pearson coefficient r or the Spearman rs depending on the regularity, while in the categorical variables, the comparison was done with the Pearson x2 control. Bar charts and pie charts were used for the graphical representation of the quality variables, while scatter charts and case charts were used for the continuous variables.

Statistical analysis was done with the IBM SPSS Statistics 26.0 program, and the limit was set to $\alpha = 0.05$.

12.3. Results

In terms of demographic characteristics (age, gender, marital status, number of children), the distribution showed that women outnumber men. The predominant age group is that of 40–49 years, followed by the age group 50–59 years. The majority of the respondents were married, with the largest percentage having two children. In terms of marital status, 158 (75.6%) were married. Those married with two children are the majority (Table 12.1).

As for the professional characteristics in Figure 12.1, 60 people (30.1%) have a previous service of 20+ years, and the same high frequencies appear in both the medical and the nursing staff, respectively. Lower frequencies are also presented in previous service of 11–20 years.

		Staff						
		Medical		Nursing		Total		
		n	%	n	%	n	%	p
Sex	Male	51	43.6%	6	6.6%	57	27.4%	<0.001
	Female	66	56.4%	85	93.4%	151	72.6%	
Age group	20–29	6	5.1%	12	13.2%	18	8.6%	<0.001
	30–39	11	9.3%	26	28.6%	37	17.7%	
	40–49	46	39.0%	31	34.1%	77	36.8%	
	50–59	28	23.7%	17	18.7%	45	21.5%	
	60+	27	22.9%	5	5.5%	32	15.3%	
Marital status	Married	87	73.7%	71	78.0%	158	75.6%	0.496
	Unmarried	21	17.8%	16	17.6%	37	17.7%	
	Divorced/widower	10	8.5%	4	4.4%	14	6.7%	
Number of children	0	26	22.0%	19	21.8%	45	22.0%	0.975
	1	24	20.3%	15	17.2%	39	19.0%	
	2	52	44.1%	41	47.1%	93	45.4%	
	3	14	11.9%	11	12.6%	25	12.2%	
	4	2	1.7%	1	1.1%	3	1.5%	

Table 12.2. *Distribution of the demographic characteristics of the medical and nursing staff*

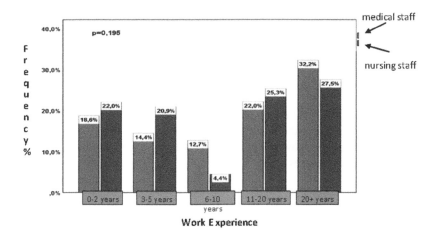

Figure 12.1. *Distribution of the previous service of the medical and nursing staff*

In the form of employment, 137 (66.5%) people dominate, either permanently or in the form of the private law of indefinite time. The permanent employment relationship concerns 50 (73.3%) doctors and 50 (55.6%) nurses.

		Staff						
		Medical		Nursing		Total		
		n	%	n	%	n	%	p
Employment relationship today	Permanent	80	69.0%	50	55.6%	130	63.1%	0.057
	Private law indefinite	5	4.3%	2	2.2%	7	3.4%	
	Of a certain time	31	26.7%	38	42.2%	69	33.5%	
Educational level	High school	0	0.0%	24	26.4%	24	11.5%	<0.001
	Higher/higher educational institutions	86	73.5%	53	58.2%	139	66.8%	
	Master	28	23.9%	13	14.3%	41	19.7%	
	PhD	3	2.6%	1	1.1%	4	1.9%	
Net monthly earnings	700–1,000 €	3	2.6%	44	48.4%	47	22.6%	<0.001
	1,000–1,500 €	36	30.8%	42	46.2%	78	37.5%	
	1,500–2,000 €	58	49.6%	5	5.5%	63	30.3%	
	>2,000 €	20	17.1%	0	0.0%	20	9.6%	

Table 12.3. *Professional characteristics of medical and nursing staff*

Table 12.4 presents a summary of the satisfaction and motivation scales. The maximum value is noted in the characteristics-task scale. On the satisfaction scale, most of the scales did not show satisfactory internal relevance with the exception of the supervision and colleagues scales.

		Average	Standard deviation	Median	KS	Cronbach α
Satisfaction	Payments	9.8	2.8	9.0	<0.001	0.559
	Promotion	10.7	4.5	10.0	0.001λ	0.632
	Supervision	17.9	4.3	19.0	<0.001	0.789
	Benefits	9.9	3.9	9.0	<0.001	0.470
	Additional fees	10.9	3.9	11.0	<0.001	0.524
	Operating conditions	7.6	4.1	8.0	<0.001	0.621
	Colleagues	17.0	4.4	18.0	<0.001	0.782
	Nature of work	16.6	3.7	17.0	<0.001	0.533
	Contact	11.9	3.0	12.0	<0.001	0.501
	Overall satisfaction	111.4	22.1	109.0	0.0	0.865
Motivation	Job characteristics	26.1	5.9	28.0	<0.001	0.892
	Earnings	15.2	3.4	16.0	<0.001	0.771
	Colleagues	20.4	3.6	20.0	<0.001	0.678
	Successes	13.2	1.9	14.0	<0.001	0.786
	Motivation	74.9	12.1	77.0	<0.001	0.913

Table 12.4. *Basic descriptions, regularity and internal relevance of the satisfaction and motivation scales*

The three largest average values of the satisfaction scales were supervision, colleagues and the nature of work. The lowest mean value on the scale was in the operating conditions scale. Motivation showed the highest average in job characteristics and the lowest average in the successes scale.

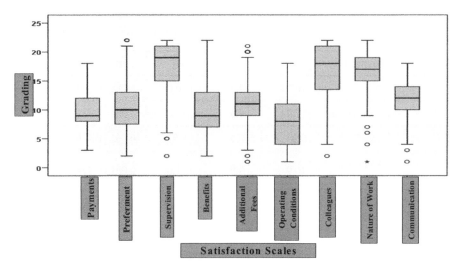

Figure 12.2. *Case chart of basic professional satisfaction groups*

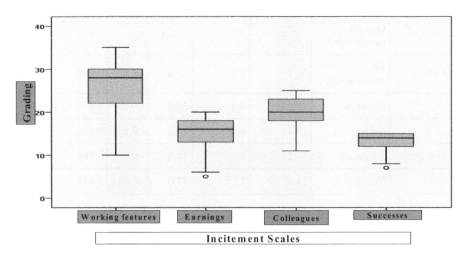

Figure 12.3. *Case chart of basic motivation groups*

Overall motivation was significantly correlated with the satisfaction-supervision scale, negatively with the satisfaction-functional conditions scale, with the satisfaction-colleagues scale and with the satisfaction-nature of work scale (Table 12.5).

			Motivation				
			Job characteristics	Earnings	Colleagues	Successes	Motivation
Job satisfaction	Payments	rs	-0.027	-0.013	0.011	-0.018	-0.014
		p	0.703	0.856	0.871	0.798	0.843
	Promotion	rs	-0.003	0.033	0.130	0.106	0.077
		p	0.962	0.638	0.065	0.133	0.275
	Supervision	rs	0.124	0.115	0.204	0.185	0.171
		p	0.080	0.106	0.004	0.009	0.016
	Benefits	rs	-0.188	-0.111	0.016	0.030	-0.130
		p	0.007	0.114	0.823	0.673	0.065
	Additional fees	rs	0.056	0.066	0.165	0.111	0.114
		p	0.432	0.350	0.019	0.116	0.106
	Operating conditions	rs	-0.325	-0.154	-0.026	0.041	-0.217
		p	0.000	0.029	0.717	0.560	0.002
	Colleagues	rs	0.254	0.244	0.337	0.323	0.334
		p	<0.001	<0.001	<0.001	<0.001	<0.001
	Nature of work	rs	0.093	0.021	0.314	0.351	0.174
		p	0.189	0.769	<0.001	<0.001	0.013
	Contact	rs	-0.044	0.017	0.088	0.130	0.009
		p	0.532	0.809	0.215	0.066	0.894
	Overall Satisfaction	rs	-0.023	0.023	0.202	0.225	0.074
		p	0.746	0.744	0.004	0.001	0.296

Table 12.5. *Correlation of key descriptive, regularity and internal relevance of satisfaction and motivation scales*

Overall satisfaction was statistically significantly correlated with the motivation-peers scale and with the motivation-success scale. When examining the other variables, another strong correlation was between the motivation-colleagues scale and satisfaction-nature of work scale as well as the motivation-colleagues and satisfaction-colleagues scales.

Table 12.6 records the differentiation between the sexes (men–women). There were no statistically significant differences between the sexes on the stimulus scales. On the satisfaction-promotion scale, men had a higher average than women. On the other hand, women showed a higher average on the satisfaction-peer scale than men.

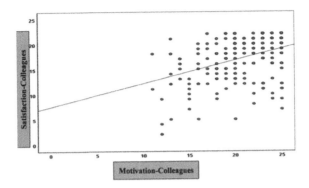

Figure 12.4. *Satisfaction-colleagues correlation, total satisfaction*

		Sex						
		Male			Female			
		Average	Standard deviation	Median	Average	Standard deviation	Median	p
Satisfaction	Payments	9.8	2.3	9.0	9.7	3.0	9.0	0.751
	Promotion	11.8	4.9	12.0	10.3	4.2	10.0	0.011
	Supervision	17.7	4.6	19.0	17.9	4.3	19.0	0.844
	Benefits	9.6	3.0	10.0	10.0	4.2	9.0	0.953
	Additional fees	10.4	3.9	11.0	11.1	4.0	11.0	0.512
	Operating conditions	6.9	3.4	7.0	7.9	4.3	8.0	0.236
	Colleagues	15.8	4.9	16.0	17.4	4.2	19.0	0.024
	Nature of work	15.9	4.3	16.0	16.9	3.4	17.0	0.243
	Communication	11.9	3.0	12.0	11.8	3.0	12.0	0.974
	Overall satisfaction	109.4	22.5	112.0	112.2	22.1	109.0	0.939
Motivation	Job characteristics	25.7	6.4	27.0	26.2	5.7	28.0	0.661
	Earnings	15.0	3.1	15.0	15.4	3.5	16.0	0.251
	Colleagues	19.6	4.0	20.0	20.7	3.4	21.0	0.070
	Successes	13.1	1.9	14.0	13.2	1.9	14.0	0.769
	Motivation	73.4	13.0	76.0	75.5	11.7	77.0	0.398

Table 12.6. *Differentiation of satisfaction and motivation scales between the sexes (men–women)*

Satisfaction scales did not show any statistically significant difference between medical and nursing staff. Of the motivation scales, only the motivation-earnings scale showed a statistically significant difference between physicians and nurses (Table 12.7).

| | | Staff | | | | | | |
| | | Medical | | | Nursing | | | |
		Average Standard	Standard deviation	Median	Average Standard	Standard deviation	Median	p
Satisfaction	Payments	9.9	2.9	9.0	9.6	2.7	9.0	0.467
	Promotion	11.0	4.6	11.0	10.2	4.2	10.0	0.226
	Supervision	18.0	4.6	20.0	17.8	4.0	18.0	0.576
	Benefits	10.0	3.7	10.0	9.7	4.1	9.0	0.390
	Additional fees	11.0	3.8	11.0	10.7	4.1	11.0	0.660
	Operating conditions	7.4	4.1	7.0	7.9	4.2	8.0	0.312
	Colleagues	17.1	4.3	18.0	16.9	4.7	18.0	0.862
	Nature of work	16.7	3.7	17.0	16.4	3.7	17.0	0.479
	Communication	12.1	2.9	12.0	11.6	3.2	12.0	0.258
	Overall satisfaction	112.2	22.7	110.0	110.5	21.4	106.0	0.152
Motivation	Job characteristics	26.0	6.4	27.5	26.2	5.2	28.0	0.868
	Payments	14.8	3.4	16.0	15.8	3.2	16.0	0.027
	Colleagues	20.3	3.7	20.5	20.5	3.4	20.0	0.792
	Successes	13.2	1.9	14.0	13.1	2.0	14.0	0.685
	Motivation	74.3	12.9	76.5	75.6	11.0	78.0	0.666

Table 12.7. *Differentiation of satisfaction and motivation scales between medical and nursing staff*

Age does not appear to affect any of the stimulus and satisfaction variables. Figure 12.5(a) shows the effect of age on overall satisfaction. Figure 12.5(b) shows the effect of age on overall motivation.

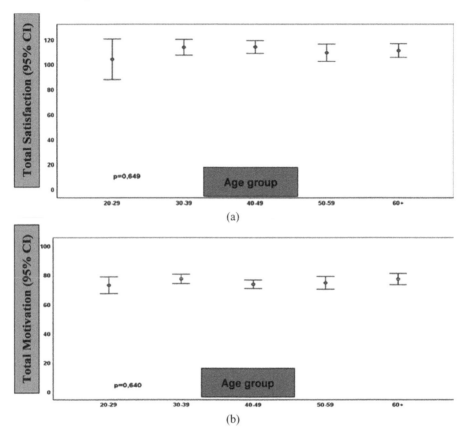

Figure 12.5. *Differentiation of scales of total satisfaction (a) and total motivation (b) by age group*

Pre-service seems to affect four of the satisfaction scales and one of the motivation scales. On the satisfaction-colleagues scale, the highest average was in the 3- to 5-year group and the lowest in the 6- to 10-year seniority group.

A similar picture was observed in people with previous service of 6–10 years and in people with previous service of 3–5 years in the satisfaction-nature of work scale.

Finally, on the motivation-success scale, the average in the previous 6–10 years service was the lowest compared to the other previous service groups.

	Work experience				
	0–2 years	3–5 years	6–10 years	11–20 years	20+ years
	Average (standard deviation) median	Average (standard deviation) median	Average (standard deviation) median	Average (standard deviation) median	Average (standard deviation) median
Payments	9.5 (3.3) 9.0	10.1 (2.4) 10.0	10 (3) 9.0	10 (2.9) 9.0	9.6 (2.6) 9.0
Promotion	10.7 (4.3) 11.0	10 (5.2) 9.5	10.7 (4.4) 10.0	10.8 (4.3) 10.0	11 (4.3) 10.0
Supervision	18.4 (4.6) 20.0	19.2 (3.8) 21.0	17.6 (4.1) 19.0	17.2 (4.9) 18.0	17.5 (4) 18.0
Benefits	11.3 (4.2) 11.0	10.8 (4.1) 11.0	8.7 (3.1) 8.0	9.2 (3.6) 9.0	9.3 (3.8) 9.0
Additional fees	12 (4.3) 11.0	11.2 (4.5) 11.0	9.9 (2.9) 10.0	10.7 (4) 11.0	10.4 (3.5) 10.0
Operating conditions	9.4 (4.5) 9.0	8.3 (4.5) 8.0	5.3 (3.4) 4.0	6.8 (3.3) 7.0	7.4 (4) 8.0
Colleagues	17.5 (4) 18.0	18.5 (4.2) 20.0	15.1 (4.3) 16.0	16.2 (4.9) 18.0	17 (4.3) 18.0
Nature of work	17.4 (3.1) 17.0	17.7 (3.5) 17.0	14.6 (4.2) 15.0	16.4 (3.2) 16.0	16.2 (4.1) 16.0
Communication	12.1 (3.2) 12.0	11.9 (2.7) 12.0	12 (3) 12.0	11.7 (3.2) 12.0	11.7 (3) 12.0
Overall satisfaction	115.7 (25.6) 113.0	116 (25.3) 112.0	103.7 (15.3) 105.0	109.1 (20.6) 109.0	110.1 (20.1) 107.0
Job characteristics	25.1 (5.5) 25.0	26.7 (4.6) 27	25.5 (6.9) 28.5	25.8 (6.9) 28.0	26.7 (5.7) 28.0
Earnings	14.7 (3.3) 15.0	16.4 (2.2) 16.0	14.7 (3.8) 16.0	14.9 (3.5) 16.0	15.4 (3.6) 16.0
Colleagues	19.6 (3.8) 20.0	21.1 (3.2) 22.0	18.5 (4.4) 19.5	20.5 (3.8) 21.0	20.9 (3) 21.0
Successes	12.7 (2.4) 13.0	13.7 (1.7) 14.0	11.9 (2.3) 12.0	13.1 (1.8) 13.0	13.6 (1.4) 14.0
Motivation	72.2 (12.1) 75.0	78 (8.5) 78.0	70.6 (13.4) 75.5	74.3 (14.1) 76.0	76.5 (11.2) 78.0

Table 12.8. *Differentiation of scales of total satisfaction and total by work experience*

Table 12.9 lists the differences in satisfaction and motivation scales between permanent/private law of indefinite time and fixed time. Only the satisfaction-payments scale showed a statistically significant difference with a higher average for permanent/private law of indefinite time.

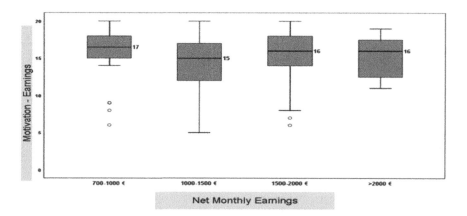

Figure 12.6. *Differentiation of motivation-earnings scale seems to differ significantly between the monthly earnings groups. The highest average was in the group 700–1,000 comparatively lower than the other groups*

		Employment relationship today					
		Permanent/private law indefinite			Of a certain time		
		Average	Typical deviation	Median	Average	Typical deviation	Median
Satisfaction	Payments	9.9	2.7	9.0	9.5	3.0	9.0
	Promotion	11.2	4.4	10.0	9.7	4.4	10.0
	Supervision	17.7	4.2	19.0	18.4	4.4	20.0
	Benefits	9.6	3.8	9.0	10.6	4.2	10.5
	Additional fees	10.7	3.7	11.0	11.4	4.3	11.0
	Operating conditions	7.2	3.8	7.0	8.5	4.5	9.0
	Colleagues	16.7	4.4	18.0	17.9	4.1	19.0
	Nature of work	16.4	3.5	16.0	17.4	3.3	17.0
	Communication	11.9	3.0	12.0	11.8	2.9	12.0
	Overall satisfaction	111.3	19.8	109.0	113.1	25.1	112.0
Motivation	Job characteristics	26.1	6.3	28.0	26.2	5.0	27.5
	Earnings	15.1	3.4	16.0	15.7	3.2	16.0
	Colleagues	20.5	3.6	21.0	20.2	3.6	20.0
	Successes	13.3	1.7	14.0	13.0	2.2	14.0
	Motivation	74.9	12.5	77.0	75.1	10.9	78.0

Table 12.9. *Differentiation of satisfaction and motivation scales in relation to work*

None of the satisfaction and motivation scales showed a statistically significant difference depending on the educational level of the medical staff (high school, higher education institution, Master/PhD) (Table 12.10).

		Educational level			
		High school	Higher education	Master/PhD	
		Average standard deviation, median	Average standard deviation, median	Average standard deviation, median	Average standard deviation, median
Satisfaction	Payments	9.3 (2.7)	9.8 (2.7)	9.9 (3.1)	0.525
		8.5	9.0	10.0	
	Promotion	10.7 (3.5)	10.8 (4.5)	10.5 (4.9)	0.830
		10.0	10.0	10.0	
	Supervision	17.8 (4.6)	17.9 (4.2)	17.7 (4.6)	0.987
		20.0	19.0	19.0	
	Benefits	9 (4.1)	10.2 (3.9)	9.4 (3.8)	0.176
		8.0	10.0	9.0	
	Additional fees	10.5 (4.2)	11 (4.1)	10.8 (3.5)	0.832
		10.5	11.0	11.0	
	Operating conditions	7.7 (4.8)	7.9 (4)	6.9 (4)	0.306
		8.0	8.0	7.0	
	Colleagues	18.4 (3.5)	16.9 (4.4)	16.5 (4.9)	0.305
		20.0	18.0	17.5	
	Nature of work	16.8 (3.1)	16.6 (3.7)	16.3 (4.1)	0.747
		17.0	17.0	16.0	
	Communication	10.8 (3.4)	11.9 (2.9)	12.3 (3)	0.150
		11.0	12.0	12.0	
	Overall satisfaction	110.9 (22.4)	112.5 (21.7)	108.6 (23.4)	0.703
		106.0	110.0	107.0	
Motivation	Job characteristics	27.1 (4)	25.7 (6)	26.7 (6.3)	0.487
		28.0	27.0	28.0	
	Earnings	16 (3.3)	15.2 (3.3)	14.9 (3.7)	0.413
		16.5	16.0	16.0	
	Colleagues	21.4 (3.2)	20.4 (3.5)	19.9 (3.8)	0.256
		21.0	21.0	20.0	
	Successes	13.3 (2.1)	13.3 (1.7)	12.7 (2.3)	0.460
		14.0	14.0	13.5	
	Motivation	77.8 (9.1) 79	74.6 (12.3) 76	74.2 (12.9) 77	0.565
		79.0	76.0	77.0	

Table 12.10. *Differentiation of satisfaction and motivation scales in relation to the educational level*

Urban health centers/local health units appeared to have higher averages and median satisfaction than rural health for most of the satisfaction variables. Regarding the scales of motivation, only the motivation-job characteristics showed a higher average health centers/local health units of rural areas and lower in urban units.

		Area						
		Urban			Rural			
		Average	Typical deviation	Median	Average	Typical deviation	Median	p
Satisfaction	Payments	10.3	3.0	10.0	9.4	2.6	9.0	0.021
	Promotion	10.6	4.8	11.0	10.8	4.2	10.0	0.888
	Supervision	18.7	4.0	20.0	17.4	4.5	19.0	0.015
	Benefits	11.2	3.8	11.0	9.0	3.7	8.0	<0.001
	Additional fees	11.5	4.2	11.0	10.5	3.8	11.0	0.125
	Operating conditions	8.8	3.5	9.0	6.9	4.3	6.0	<0.001
	Colleagues	17.4	4.2	18.0	16.7	4.6	18.0	0.262
	Nature of work	17.8	3.8	18.0	15.9	3.4	16.0	<0.001
	Communication	12.5	3.0	13.0	11.5	3.0	11.0	0.009
	Overall satisfaction	118.0	21.3	119.5	107.3	21.7	106.0	<0.001
Motivation	Job characteristics	25.5	5.1	26.0	26.4	6.3	28.5	0.042
	Earnings	14.8	3.3	15.0	15.5	3.4	16.0	0.064
	Colleagues	20.6	3.2	21.0	20.3	3.7	20.0	0.863
	Successes	13.3	1.7	14.0	13.1	2.0	14.0	0.661
	Motivation	74.2	10.0	75.0	75.3	13.2	79.0	0.079

Table 12.11. *Differentiation of satisfaction and motivation scales in relation to the area of health centers/local health units*

12.4. Discussion

Taking into account all the presented facts, it can be argued that the overall satisfaction of the respondents cannot be answered clearly, as it is influenced by factors that are related, such as the working environment, hygiene conditions, interpersonal relationships and levels of dissatisfaction (Dikaios et al. 1999). Based on the socio-cultural conditions, the economic and social situations and the health situations (e.g. pandemic crisis), the degree of professional satisfaction also differs.

The degree and the correlation between them affects the positive or negative feelings of satisfaction and pushes or motivates the employees to enhance their performance.

Pre-service does not show statistically significant differences in the two main variables. Based on the age distribution and marital status, it appears that neither age nor marital status affects the averages of the scores. Younger people are more likely to count on monetary benefits, which is probably due to increased family responsibilities as opposed to older employees.

Regarding the individual dimensions (parameters) of the research, the highest section of satisfaction terms were noted as "supervision", "colleagues", "nature of work", followed by "communication", "additional fees", "promotion", "benefits", "payments" and most recently "operating conditions".

Supervision, i.e. the way in which managers play an administrative role, the trust they show in their subordinates, the sympathy they show to other employees and their leadership capabilities in relation to equal treatment of all are considered to contribute decisively to the professional satisfaction of doctors and nurses.

The nature of the work is observed to cause relatively great satisfaction to doctors and nurses following supervision and fellowship in numerical data. The communication factor as well as the additional remuneration cause moderate levels of satisfaction. Similarly, the promotion factor moves to moderate levels, while the satisfaction of the respondents in relation to the material and mental benefits is at low levels.

Payments are low in respondents' preferences regarding job satisfaction. Functional conditions in the workplace have the lowest average indicating the high degree of dissatisfaction that doctors and nurses feel with their working conditions.

On the scales of motivation, the highest average had the "work characteristics" and the lowest on the scale "successes". The scale of colleagues and earnings is recorded in between. On the motivation-work scale, workers in provincial structures show slightly higher averages than their counterparts in urban areas. The "comradeship" factor is the second most important motivating factor. Collaborative relationships, teamwork, solidarity, appreciation from other employees, impartiality, supervision and pride are rated by respondents as critical motivating factors.

The "earnings" factor (salary benefits, pension-insurance program and leave program) is in third place in terms of the importance that doctors and nurses attach to as factors that motivate them to maximize their performance. This means that the role of non-monetary rewards plays a more important role in mobilizing health professionals in relation to financial incentives. Respondents place more value on opportunities for creative expression and interpersonal relationships than on rewards.

In the last place, in terms of motivation, are the "successes" that include interpersonal relationships, gaining respect and the importance of work. The lack of clarity of objectives by the management and the inability to define a clear work framework in which the work and performance of each employee will be recognized are inhibitory motivating factors.

Recording the correlations between stimulus and satisfaction scales in most of the pairs does not show any statistically significant correlation. The motivation-success scale and the job satisfaction-nature scale showed a moderate correlation. Regarding the relevance of the motivation and satisfaction scales, the satisfaction-payments and motivation-earnings scale, the satisfaction-colleagues and the motivation-colleagues scales are of special value.

The earnings factor, according to the respondents' answers, causes moderate motivation as they do not consider it to be as important as work characteristics and peer relationships. In terms of satisfaction, the monetary rewards are low as the respondents consider the salary benefits provided to them in relation to the project, the tasks they perform, to be insufficient.

The identifying colleagues record high interaction regarding motivation, as group and interpersonal relationships within the workplace, solidarity and teamwork are judged by respondents to be motivators to increase their performance. On the satisfaction-colleagues scale, the respondents ranked their relationships with their colleagues at a high level, a fact that is due to the collectivity, humanity and close relationships they have developed within the workplace that enhance feelings of job satisfaction.

12.5. Conclusion

The organization of primary health care as the first contact of the citizens in the health services must be functional, unified and coordinated with a clear orientation to the health coverage of all citizens regardless of a specific geographical area (Benos et al. 2015).

The main measures that can frame a rational mobilization plan for doctors and nurses are:

A) Measures to improve the working conditions of the primary health care structures:

– strengthening of medical equipment and building facilities;

– improving staff working conditions through stress management programs;

– more rational management of human resources with emphasis on identifying their skills and placing them in a position where they will perform better;

– strengthening interpersonal relationships of teamwork and participation through educational programs and actions.

B) Measures to define objectives and work framework:

– duty schedule, regular job rotation and clearly defined organization charts;

– better distribution of doctors and nurses through the utilization of their specialties and their particular skills.

C) Incentives for moral reward:

– rewarding the work of employees, recognition of the hard work of subordinates by superiors;

– internal awards or persuasion from superiors;

– flexible licensing program.

D) Incentives for self-realization:

– facilitating employees in order to participate in research or educational programs and seminars;

– encouragement of activities, assignment of special tasks in order to achieve specific goals;

– promoting participation through the creation of small and flexible working groups whose results will be directly implemented by the administrations (Benos et al. 2015).

12.6. References

Benos, A., Antoniadou, I., Koutis, A., Lionis, C., Myloneros, T., Panagiotopoulos, T. (2015). Basic principles, positions and proposals for the development of Primary Health Care in Greece [Online]. Available at: http://isx.gr/sites/default/files/Το%20πόρισμα%20της% 20Ομάδας%20εργασίας%20για%20την%20Π.Φ.Υ.pdf [Accessed 25 May 2021].

Daskalakis, D. (2010). *Industrial Sociology and Industrial Relations*. Ant. N. Sakkoulas Publications, Athens, Komotini.

Dikaios, K., Koutouzis, M., Polyzos, N., Sigalas, I., Chletsos, M. (1999). *Basic Principles of Health Services Management*. Hellenic Open University, Patra.

Herzberg, F. (1968), One more time: How do you motivate employees. *Harvard Business Review*, 46(1), 53–62.

Hwu, Y. (1995). The impact of chronic illness on patients. *Rehabilitation Nursing*, 20, 221–225.

Maslow, A.H. (1943). A theory of human motivation. *Psychological Review*, 50(4), 370–396.

Spector, P. (1997). *Job Satisfaction*. SAGE Publications, Thousand Oaks.

Developing a Bibliometric Quality Indicator for Journals Applied to the Field of Dentistry

In this work, we propose, via factor analysis, a new bibliometric indicator called the Integrated index, in order to provide a ranking of the Journal of Citation Reports alternative to that of the Journal Impact Factor. To this end, some metrics included in the JCR list are taken into account, such as the CiteScore, the SNIP and the Eigenfactor score. The Integrated index incorporates further information such as the quality of the citation sources. The performance of this new indicator is evaluated with respect to journals in the category Dentistry, Oral Surgery and Medicine.

13.1. Introduction

Although nowadays most evaluations of scientific output look to the Journal Impact Factor (JIF) as the gold standard, many authors, in the wake of Seglen (1997), have pointed out its limitations. For a critical review, readers may see Fleck (2013) or more recently Roberts (2017), both of whom hold that the JIF should be replaced as the reference by other metrics that afford more information about the quality of a journal, beyond simple citation analysis. Meanwhile, Malay (2013) warned that undue use of JIF could result in the self-citation of articles published in a given journal, reducing the citations of rival publications.

Chapter written by Pilar VALDERRAMA, Ana M. AGUILERA and Mariano J. VALDERRAMA.

The JIF – listing the journals of a certain category of the Journal of Citation Reports (JCR) developed by the Web of Science Clarivate Analytic (2020) – can be seen as a basic tool in disciplines such as the Health Sciences when it comes to the challenge of creating a research hierarchy. Recent studies that apply statistical techniques to estimate the JIF based on other indicators include those of Cheng et al. (2017), Lucena et al. (2017), Valderrama et al. (2018, 2020).

To bypass certain drawbacks of the JIF, bibliometric indicators such as the Eigenfactor score, the Article influence score and the Immediacy index (among others) have been developed. Sillet et al. (2012) worked with the Eigenfactor score in the field of Dentistry, meanwhile Ahmad et al. (2019) undertook a bibliometric assessment of the Journal of Dental Research, which came out in 1919 and is upheld for the high quality of its articles, covering a vast array of relevant topics.

The aim of this study is to define a new metric that sums up and compiles the information contained in various indicators, specifically: the JIF, JIF without self-citation, SNIP, CiteScore, total citations and the Eigenfactor score. Our prototype is applied to the JCR category Dentistry, Oral Surgery and Medicine. The methodology applies factor analysis, considering two factors of the model in such a way that over 90% of the total variability is explained. Its application gives rise to a novel journal ranking.

13.2. Methodology

When approaching a problem involving a large number of variables, it is common to use factor analysis, which makes it possible to represent a set of variables through a linear combination of underlying common and unobservable factors, plus a variable that synthesizes a specific part of the original variables. Thus, as many factors as the number of original variables can be obtained, ordered according to their variance in decreasing order and by choosing the first k, we arrive at an approximation of the original problem, with a percentage of explained variance as high as desired.

One inconvenience of factor analysis lies in the interpretation of the factors. They are often individually linked to the variables of the combination of origin, having higher coefficients in absolute terms. Normally, a clearer and more intuitive interpretation of the factors (hence, avoidance of excessive variance among the initial ones) calls for a rotation of the axes. Several procedures can be used to this end, the best known being VARIMAX (Jolliffe and Cadima 2016), which is used here.

After carrying out factor analysis, a graphic representation of the data is derived, on a system of coordinated axes that are precisely the factors. This creates a dispersion diagram known as a biplot – an extension in the multivariate realm of the two-variable dispersion diagram. A noteworthy study of biplot application for bibliometric data interpretation was carried out by Díaz-Faes et al. (2013).

This study considers six bibliometric variables extracted from the JCR, namely:

– JIF: quotient whose numerator is the number of citations received by the articles published in a given journal within a given year, during the two previous years, the denominator being the number of citable articles.

– JIF without self-citation: similar to the JIF but excluding any author self-citation.

– Eigenfactor score: in a five-year period, also eliminating self-citation but giving greater weight to the citations that appear in the higher-rated journals – that is, the ones most consulted and cited (West et al. 2010).

– SNIP: appraises the impact of contextual citations in terms of the total number of citations in a given field, weighing the number of citations received against the frequency of citation (Moed 2010).

– CiteScore: a metric, not an indicator, calculated by taking the average number of citations gathered in Scopus per year over the past three years, and dividing it by the number of i–tems published in that time period (Teixeira da Silva 2020). Its calculation, while similar to that of the JIF, manages to resolve some inherent problems, for example, it includes all types of publications in the denominator.

– Total citation: the bulk of citation received by a journal in a period of three years. Hence, for any specific year of choice, it represents the total citation of all the documents considered over the three previous years.

This study considered the 91 journals included in the category Dentistry, Oral Surgery and Medicine in the 2019 edition of the JCR (Clarivate Analytic 2020), although later the International Journal of Implant Dentistry was deleted because its SNIP and CiteScore were missing. Let us denote as $f_1, f_2, \ldots, f_6$ the factors obtained from the six bibliometric variables considered, with respective variances (eigenvalues) $\lambda_1, \lambda_2, \ldots, \lambda_6$, so that $V = \lambda_1 + \lambda_2 + \cdots + \lambda_6$ would be the total variance. The percentage of variance explained by each component is given by $w_i = \lambda_i/V$; hence, if we want to explain V up to a certain level, it is necessary to accumulate the first k factors so that $w_1 + w_2 + \cdots + w_k$ can reach that level. We then define the Integrated Index as the following weighted linear combination of the factor scores: $I_2 = w_1\xi_1 + w_2\xi_2 + \cdots + w_k\xi_k$, this being the tool to obtain the new journal ranking within the field. All statistical calculations were done using the program SPSS (version 26) under the license of the University of Granada.

Journal	JIF	Order JIF	I_2	Order I_2
Periodontology 2000	7.718	1	3.179	1
Journal of Clinical Periodontology	5.241	2	1.864	3
Journal of Dental Research	4.914	3	2.095	2
Dental Materials	4.495	4	1.631	4
Oral Oncology	3.979	5	1.147	6
International Endodontic Journal	3.801	6	0.898	10
Journal of Periodontology	3.742	7	0.989	8
Clinical Oral Implants Research	3.723	8	1.298	5
Clinical Implant Dentistry and Related Research	3.396	9	0.667	11
Journal of Dentistry	3.242	10	0.939	9
Journal of Endodontics	3.118	11	1.037	7
International Journal of Oral Science	3.047	12	0.390	15
Journal of Periodontal Research	2.926	13	0.388	16
Molecular Oral Microbiology	2.905	14	0.235	22
Clinical Oral Investigations	2.812	15	0.593	12
Journal of The American Dental Association	2.803	16	0.454	14
Journal of Prosthodontic Research	2.662	17	0.380	17
European Journal of Oral Implantology	2.619	18	0.152	28
Oral Diseases	2.613	19	0.207	23
Journal of Oral Pathology & Medicine	2.495	20	0.171	27
Journal of Prosthetic Dentistry	2.444	21	0.509	13
Journal of Evidence-Based Dental Practice	2.426	22	-0.165	47
Journal of Adhesive Dentistry	2.379	23	0.026	35
International Journal of Oral & Maxillofacial Implants	2.320	24	0.259	20
Journal Of Oral Rehabilitation	2.304	25	0.195	24
European Journal of Oral Sciences	2.220	26	0.009	38
Operative Dentistry	2.213	27	0.134	29
European Journal of Orthodontics	2.202	28	0.118	31
Journal of Prosthodontics-Implant Esthetic and Reconstructive Dent.	2.187	29	-0.148	44
Caries Research	2.186	30	0.176	25
Community Dentistry and Oral Epidemiology	2.135	31	0.122	30
International Journal of Implant Dentistry[1]	2.111	32		
International Journal of Oral and Maxillofacial Surgery	2.068	33	0.329	18
International Dental Journal	2.038	34	-0.098	40
International Journal of Paediatric Dentistry	1.993	35	0.021	36
American Journal of Orthodontics and Dentofacial Orthopedics	1.960	36	0.318	19
Archives of Oral Biology	1.931	37	0.075	33
Bmc Oral Health	1.911	38	0.018	37
Head & Face Medicine	1.882	39	-0.128	42
Journal of Periodontal and Implant Science	1.847	40	-0.234	54
Odontology	1.840	41	-0.152	45
Progress in Orthodontics	1.822	42	-0.059	39
Journal of Applied Oral Science	1.797	43	-0.120	41
Dentomaxillofacial Radiology	1.796	44	-0.155	46
Journal of Esthetic and Restorative Dentistry	1.786	45	-0.181	50
Journal of Cranio-Maxillofacial Surgery	1.766	46	0.171	26

Table 13.1. *Value and order of the JIF and the I_2 of journals in the category Dentistry, Oral Surgery and Medicine. (1) Journal not included in the analysis as CiteScore and SNIP are not available*

Journal	JIF	Order JIF	I_2	Order I_2
Journal of Public Health Dentistry	1.743	47	-0.221	52
International Journal of Computerized Dentistry	1.714	48	-0.453	73
Journal of Oral and Maxillofacial Surgery	1.642	49	0.240	21
Brazilian Oral Research	1.633	50	-0.139	43
Oral Surgery, Oral Medicine, Oral Pathology, Oral Radiology	1.601	51	0.081	32
Medicina Oral, Patologí–a Oral y Cirugí–a Bucal	1.596	52	-0.167	49
Pediatric Dentistry	1.594	53	-0.234	53
Acta Odontologica Scandinavica	1.573	54	-0.183	51
Oral and Maxillofacial Surgery Clinics of North America	1.554	55	-0.384	66
Angle Orthodontist	1.549	56	0.030	34
Dental Traumatology	1.530	57	-0.293	55
International Journal of Periodontics & Restorative Dentistry	1.513	58	-0.340	61
Journal of Advanced Prosthodontics	1.504	59	-0.350	63
European Journal of Paediatric Dentistry	1.500	60	-0.441	71
International Journal of Prosthodontics	1.490	61	-0.317	57
Quintessence International	1.460	62	-0.342	62
Orthodontics & Craniofacial Research	1.455	63	-0.449	72
Implant Dentistry	1.452	64	-0.324	58
Journal of Oral Implantology	1.424	65	-0.457	74
Australian Dental Journal	1.401	66	-0.166	48
Dental Materials Journal	1.359	67	-0.329	60
Cleft Palate-Craniofacial Journal	1.347	68	-0.326	59
Gerodontology	1.339	69	-0.392	67
Korean Journal of Orthodontics	1.326	70	-0.408	70
Journal of Dental Education	1.322	71	-0.476	75
British Dental Journal	1.306	72	-0.369	64
Journal of Orofacial Orthopedics-Fortschritte der Kieferorthopadie	1.286	73	-0.407	69
Journal of Oral & Facial Pain and Headache	1.260	74	-0.522	76
International Journal of Dental Hygiene	1.229	75	-0.402	68
Journal of Oral Science	1.200	76	-0.314	56
Journal of The Canadian Dental Association	1.200	76	-0.544	76
CRANIO-The Journal of Craniomandibular & Sleep Practice	1.173	78	-0.587	79
Journal of Stomatology Oral and Maxillofacial Surgery	1.152	79	-0.741	86
Australian Endodontic Journal	1.120	80	-0.625	80
British Journal of Oral & Maxillofacial Surgery	1.061	81	-0.379	65
European Journal of Dental Education	1.050	82	-0.574	78
Journal of Dental Sciences	1.034	83	-0.677	84
American Journal of Dentistry	0.957	84	-0.662	82
Oral Health & Preventive Dentistry	0.920	85	-0.690	85
Journal of Clinical Pediatric Dentistry	0.798	86	-0.632	81
Community Dental Health	0.679	87	-0.666	83
Oral Radiology	0.635	88	-0.892	87
Seminars in Orthodontics	0.625	89	-0.894	88
Implantologie	0.123	90	-1.189	90
Australasian Orthodontic Journal	0.113	91	-1.148	89

Table 13.2. *Value and order of the JIF and the I_2 of journals in the category Dentistry, Oral Surgery and Medicine*

The journals of the category appear in Tables 13.1 and 13.2, classified in descending order in view of their JIF. By performing factor analysis with VARIMAX rotation of the data listed in Tables 13.6 and 13.7 of the Appendix, the results shown in Table 13.3 were obtained. The first two components are seen to accumulate 93.81% of the total variance, for which reason we reduce our analysis to dimension 2.

Initial Eigenvalues			
Factor	Variance	% Variance	% Cumulative variance
	λ_i	$w_i = (\lambda_i/V)100$	
1	4.756	79.226	79.226
2	0.900	14.995	94.261
3	0.205	3.415	97.676
4	0.084	1.398	99.074
5	0.047	0.784	99.858
6	0.009	0.142	100.000
Eigenvalues after VARIMAX rotation			
Factor	Variance	% Variance	% Cumulative variance
1	3.527	58.785	58.785
2	2.129	35.476	94.261

Table 13.3. *Initial eigenvalues and those after VARIMAX rotation of the axes with their percentage of explained variance*

Metric	Factor 1	Factor 2
JIF	0.915	0.364
JIF no self-citation	0.926	0.324
SNIP	0.890	0.248
CiteScore	0.905	0.376
Total citation	0.379	0.899
Eigenfactor score	0.279	0.938

Table 13.4. *Correlation of the first and second factors*

Coefficient	Character	Value	Significance
Pearson	Quantitative	0.972	0.000
Spearman	Ordinal	0.944	0.000

Table 13.5. *Pearson's and Spearman's correlation coefficients and their significance*

Therefore, factor analysis gives two components whose coordinates appear in Table 13.4. In light of this result, it is deduced that the first component gathers the information related to the volume of citation through JIF, SNIP and CiteScore. The second reflects the quality characteristics of the citations, mainly materialized by means of the Eigenfactor score. The Integrated index (I_2) is expressed by:

$$I_2 = 0.58785\xi_1 + 0.35476\xi_2,$$

and its application to the journals of the category Dentistry, Oral Surgery and Medicine gives rise to the values and positions seen in the two right-hand columns of Table 13.1. In turn, the correlation between the values and the orders of the JIF and the I_2 are seen in Table 13.5.

The corresponding biplot can be found in Figure 13.1, where the points indicate the journals of greatest and least JIF in the listing. Criterion I_2 provokes some changes in the order of the journals with respect to the JIF, in certain cases very relevant ones, and the transfer among quartiles that is represented in Figure 13.2.

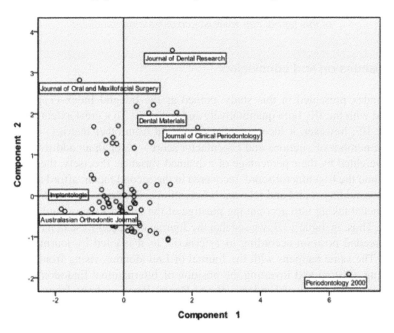

Figure 13.1. *Biplot of the two factors with the highest variance, and location (points) of the journals with the highest and lowest impact*

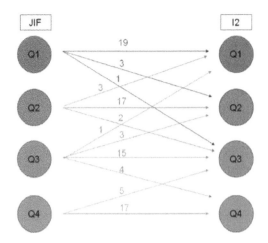

Figure 13.2. *Transfer of journals between quartiles when considering the Integrated Index* (I_2) *as opposed to the JIF. For a color version of this figure, see www.iste.co.uk/zafeiris/data2.zip*

13.3. Discussion and conclusion

The index presented in this study, coined as the Integral Index (I_2), is highly correlated with the JIF, both quantitatively and ordinally. To a great extent, its origins lie in the JIF; however, it incorporates information from other metrics – CiteScore, SNIP, the number of citations and Eigenfactor score – through an additive model of factors weighted by their percentage of explained variance. Precisely, the number of citations and the Eigenfactor score, recovered in the second factor, afford a privileged perspective, adding sound and relevant information about the journals. This indicator is constructed taking into account the prestige of the journals whose authors/articles are cited. Thus, in Table 13.3, we see that the Journal of Dental Research moves from third to second position according to I_2 criteria, as it is cited by journals of great prestige. The same happens with the Journal of Endodontics, rising from 11 to 7 in the ranking, ousting and inverting the position of International Endodontic Journal. In contrast, the Journal of Evidence-Based Dental Practice drops from number 22 to 49 because of its low Eigenfactor score, as does the International Journal of Computerized Dentistry, descending from position 48 to 75.

In the biplot, there are two journals that appear to have atypical value at first glance. One is Periodontology 2000, veering towards the right side of the table owing to its high value in the first factor, which includes the JIF and associated factors. This is logical in that the journal solely publishes review articles by invitation, from outstanding authors who are consequently often cited. Therefore, their impact factor is heightened; yet in the second factor, a negative value is seen due to the effect of an Eigenfactor score below the average. Second, the Journal of Dental Research attains a higher position for a different reason: both factors are positive, but especially the JIF. On the contrary, Implantologie and the Australasian Orthodontic Journal are found in the third quartile, where both coordinates are negative, justifying their last-place ranking according to the I_2, in accordance with their JIF.

In sum, the Integral Index or I_2, proposed here may very well substantiate the evaluation of journals from the quality standpoint, as it accounts for information provided by further metrics, most notably the Eigenfactor score, which lends weight to citations in view of the prestige of the source journals. The results of this study open a new bibliometric path that covers a broader array of indicators, and could be refined and applied, in the future, within numerous research fields.

13.4. Acknowledgments

This research was funded, in part, by projects PID2020-113961GB-I00 of the Spanish Ministry of Science and Innovation and A–FQM–66–UGR20 of Vice-Rectorate for Research and Transfer of the University of Granada (also supported by the FEDER program), IMAG–Maria de Maeztu grant CEX2020-001105-M / AEI / 10.13039/501100011033, project FQM-307 of the Government of Andalusia (Spain) and PhD grant (FPU18/01779) awarded to Christian Acal. The authors would also like to thank the University of Granada, Spain, under the project for young researchers PPJIB2020-01.

13.5. Appendix

Journal JIF order	JIF	JIF-WS	Citations	CiteScore	SNIP	Eigenfactor	Factor 1	Factor 2
1	7.718	7.600	10286	13.9	4.164	0.00638	6.570	-1.926
2	5.241	4.614	7453	7.4	2.527	0.01305	2.169	1.659
3	4.914	4.630	16306	9.0	2.120	0.01990	1.425	3.544
4	4.495	3.820	14178	8.0	2.194	0.01348	1.551	2.028
5	3.979	3.548	4496	6.0	1.445	0.01578	0.735	2.016
6	3.801	2.990	9650	6.2	1.825	0.00666	1.362	0.275
7	3.742	3.503	16952	5.2	1.287	0.01016	0.368	2.178
8	3.723	3.363	1204	7.5	1.724	0.01397	0.872	2.212
9	3.396	2.871	4315	5.4	1.487	0.00829	0.975	0.264
10	3.242	2.866	993	5.8	1.874	0.01133	0.812	1.301
11	3.118	2.556	6849	6.2	1.780	0.01231	0.233	2.537
12	3.047	2.969	6967	4.9	1.471	0.00202	1.299	-1.052
13	2.926	2.764	1283	5.1	1.167	0.00425	0.764	-0.173
14	2.905	2.774	1227	5.9	0.817	0.00171	0.954	-0.920
15	2.812	2.594	4463	4.4	1.479	0.01149	0.307	1.163
16	2.803	2.438	4741	4.3	1.631	0.00500	0.630	0.237
17	2.662	2.412	12491	4.7	1.961	0.00216	1.296	-1.078
18	2.619	2.060	585	4.1	1.464	0.00223	0.773	-0.853
19	2.613	2.291	1793	3.9	1.135	0.00509	0.295	0.097
20	2.495	2.290	9035	4.2	1.061	0.00385	0.300	-0.017
21	2.444	2.031	5827	4.4	1.480	0.00898	-0.161	1.702
22	2.426	2.093	3581	2.5	0.921	0.00106	0.244	-0.870
23	2.379	2.019	3850	3.6	1.231	0.00215	0.448	-0.670
24	2.320	2.071	4569	3.4	1.130	0.00840	-0.331	1.280
25	2.304	1.911	2848	3.8	1.449	0.00431	0.241	0.150
26	2.220	2.159	4324	3.3	1.090	0.00260	0.196	-0.301
27	2.213	1.941	4642	3.9	1.400	0.00380	0.342	-0.187
28	2.202	1.917	348	3.4	1.481	0.00339	0.290	-0.148
29	2.187	1.877	8467	1.8	1.081	0.00309	-0.104	-0.246
30	2.186	1.890	2216	4.5	1.515	0.00252	0.511	-0.350
31	2.135	1.936	2164	4.1	1.363	0.00292	0.321	-0.188
32	2.111	1.989	13348			0.00105		
33	2.068	1.838	7760	3.7	1.509	0.00948	-0.204	1.266
34	2.038	1.981	2829	2.7	1.227	0.00150	0.219	-0.639
35	1.993	1.710	831	3.6	1.582	0.00172	0.473	-0.725
36	1.960	1.613	557	3.4	1.716	0.00580	-0.314	1.418
37	1.931	1.809	863	3.4	0.962	0.00713	-0.494	1.032
38	1.911	1.708	743	2.7	1.461	0.00576	0.021	0.016
39	1.882	1.745	2179	3.1	1.325	0.00121	0.315	-0.883
40	1.847	1.736	2743	2.8	1.062	0.00100	0.117	-0.854
41	1.840	1.723	1350	3.4	1.165	0.00140	0.228	-0.805
42	1.822	1.722	6459	2.9	1.676	0.00140	0.483	-0.966
43	1.797	1.681	10286	2.9	1.273	0.00259	0.073	-0.459
44	1.796	1.510	7453	2.6	1.281	0.00253	-0.047	-0.360
45	1.786	1.571	16306	2.6	1.319	0.00175	0.106	-0.687

Table 13.6. *Journals included in the category Dentistry, Oral Surgery and Medicine, ordered by JIF, with their JIF values, JIF without self-citations (JIF-WS), total citations, CiteScore, eigenfactor score and values of the first two factors*

Journal JIF order	JIF	JIF-WS	Citations	CiteScore	SNIP	Eigenfactor	Factor 1	Factor 2
46	1.766	1.562	14178	3.3	1.302	0.01115	-0.525	1.351
47	1.743	1.663	1555	2.9	1.059	0.00154	-0.001	-0.622
48	1.714	1.500	504	1.9	0.702	0.00064	-0.331	-0.729
49	1.642	1.447	15209	2.8	1.147	0.01209	-1.291	2.816
50	1.633	1.596	1756	2.6	1.442	0.00260	0.090	-0.539
51	1.601	1.466	13462	3.1	1.136	0.00585	-0.877	1.680
52	1.596	1.537	2825	2.8	1.231	0.00287	-0.115	-0.280
53	1.594	1.329	2590	1.9	1.428	0.00201	-0.132	-0.442
54	1.573	1.483	3578	2.9	1.134	0.00282	-0.224	-0.144
55	1.554	1.478	1058	2.1	0.865	0.00180	-0.332	-0.531
56	1.549	1.385	6235	3.3	1.625	0.00389	-0.086	0.227
57	1.530	1.045	1925	3.1	1.141	0.00153	-0.187	-0.517
58	1.513	1.407	3638	2.2	0.804	0.00272	-0.574	-0.007
59	1.504	1.364	957	2.7	0.940	0.00159	-0.231	-0.603
60	1.500	0.924	896	2.2	1.053	0.00068	-0.322	-0.708
61	1.490	1.391	3675	2.4	0.884	0.00237	-0.491	-0.081
62	1.460	1.399	2660	2.3	0.921	0.00212	-0.420	-0.267
63	1.455	1.354	1032	1.7	0.893	0.00124	-0.409	-0.587
64	1.452	1.396	2340	2.7	0.837	0.00287	-0.435	-0.193
65	1.424	1.352	1798	2.0	0.667	0.00210	-0.601	-0.293
66	1.401	1.275	2804	3.1	1.439	0.00231	-0.045	-0.394
67	1.359	1.209	2816	2.6	0.979	0.00265	-0.458	-0.169
68	1.347	1.088	4762	2.0	1.074	0.00291	-0.644	0.149
69	1.339	1.240	1576	3.0	0.823	0.00132	-0.366	-0.500
70	1.326	1.140	532	2.5	1.067	0.00094	-0.242	-0.750
71	1.322	0.749	3124	2.1	0.885	0.00172	-0.716	-0.154
72	1.306	0.919	5453	1.2	1.115	0.00382	-0.876	0.413
73	1.286	1.202	842	2.2	1.120	0.00095	-0.261	-0.715
74	1.260	1.130	532	2.1	0.720	0.00161	-0.572	-0.524
75	1.229	1.146	923	2.7	1.042	0.00107	-0.281	-0.668
76	1.200	1.165	1460	1.8	1.562	0.00144	-0.128	-0.674
77	1.200	1.200	1195	2.0	0.730	0.00030	-0.551	-0.619
78	1.173	.096	861	1.5	0.764	0.00063	-0.638	-0.599
79	1.152	1.076	172	0.7	0.481	0.00049	-0.901	-0.595
80	1.120	1.080	389	1.6	0.672	0.00048	-0.668	-0.656
81	1.061	0.952	4631	2.0	0.916	0.00495	-0.950	0.506
82	1.050	0.839	934	1.9	0.874	0.00091	-0.639	-0.559
83	1.034	0.828	509	1.4	0.692	0.00058	-0.796	-0.588
84	0.957	0.872	1760	1.5	0.612	0.00102	-0.929	-0.326
85	0.920	0.883	822	1.6	0.571	0.00082	-0.886	-0.476
86	0.798	0.780	1033	1.7	0.857	0.00093	-0.771	-0.504
87	0.679	0.630	1246	1.7	0.871	0.00072	-0.842	-0.482
88	0.635	0.581	201	0.9	0.388	0.00026	-1.213	-0.505
89	0.625	0.597	634	0.6	0.432	0.00026	-1.250	-0.448
90	0.123	0.031	35	0.1	0.056	0.00003	-1.826	-0.326
91	0.113	0.094	8	0.1	0.190	0.00000	-1.721	-0.383

Table 13.7. *Journals included in the category Dentistry, Oral Surgery and Medicine, ordered by JIF, with their JIF values, JIF without self-citations (JIF-WS), total citations, CiteScore, eigenfactor score and values of the first two factors*

13.6. References

Ahmad, P., Alam, M.K., Jakubovics, N.S., Schwendicke, F., Asif, J.A. (2019). 100 years of the *Journal of Dental Research*: A bibliometric analysis. *Journal of Dental Research*, 98(13), 1425–1436.

Cheng, K.L., Dodson, T.H., Egbert, M.A., Susarla, S.M. (2017). Which factors affect citation rates in the oral and maxillofacial surgery literature? *Journal of Oral and Maxillofacial Surgery*, 75(7), 1313–1318.

Clarivate Analytics (2020). InCites Journal Citation Reports [Online]. Available at: https://jcr.clarivate.com/JCRHomePageAction.action.

Díaz-Faes, A.A., González-Albo, B., Galindo, M.P., Bordons, M. (2013). HJ-Biplot como herramienta de inspección de matrices de datos bibliométricos. *Revista Española de Documentación Científica*, 36(1), e001.

Fleck, C. (2013). The impact factor fetishism. *European Journal of Sociology*, 54(2), 327–356.

Jolliffe, I.A. and Cadima, J. (2016). Principal component analysis: A review and recent developments. *Philosophical Translations of the Royal Society A*, 374, 20150202.

Lucena, C., Souza, E.M., Voinea, G.C., Pulgar, R., Valderrama, M.J., De-Deus G. (2017). A quality assessment of randomized controlled trial reports in endodontics. *International Endodontic Journal*, 50(3), 237–250.

Malay, D.S. (2013). Impact factors and other measures of a journal's influence. *The Journal of Foot and Ankle Surgery*, 52(3), 285–287.

Moed, H.F. (2010). Measuring contextual citation impact of scientific journals. *Journal of Informetrics*, 4(3), 265–277.

Ortega, J.L. (2020). Proposal of composed altmetric indicators based on prevalence and impact dimensions. *Journal of Informetrics*, 14(4), 101071.

Roberts, R.J. (2017). An obituary for the impact factor. *Nature*, 546(7660), 600.

Seglen, P.O. (1997). Why the impact factor of journals should not be used for evaluating research. *British Medical Journal*, 314(7079), 498–502.

Sillet, A., Katsahian, S., Rangé, H., Czernichow, S., Bouchard, P. (2012). The Eigenfactor Score in highly specific medical fields: The dental model. *Journal of Dental Research*, 91(4), 329–333.

Teixeira da Silva, J.A. (2020). CiteScore: Advances, evolution, applications, and limitations. *Publishing Research Quarterly*, 36, 459–468.

Valderrama, P., Escabias, M., Jiménez-Contreras, E., Rodríguez-Archilla, A., Valderrama, M.J. (2018). Proposal of a stochastic model to determine the bibliometric variables influencing the quality of a journal: Application to the field of dentistry. *Scientometrics*, 115(2), 1087–1095.

Valderrama, P., Escabias, M., Valderrama, M.J., Jiménez-Contreras, E., Baca, P. (2020). Influential variables in the journal impact factor in dentistry journals. *Heliyon*, 6(3), e03575.

West, J.D., Bergstrom, T.C., Bergstrom, C.T. (2010). The Eigenfactor MetricsTM: A network approach to assessing scholarly journals. *College & Research Libraries*, 71(3), 236–244.

14

Statistical Process Monitoring Techniques for Covid-19

Control charts constitute a useful scientific tool for exploring and monitoring the variability present in a process and determining whether the results of their implementation are due to a deterministic action or if it is purely random. In the former case, appropriate mechanisms have to be employed for (permanently) eliminating the causes that led to this problem. As a result, control charts could be a key tool for ensuring quality and at the same time minimizing (deterministic) variation. Having the aforementioned in mind, in this work, we implement a reliable and accurate mechanism based on Statistical Process Monitoring techniques for studying the behavior of Coronavirus 2019 disease across countries that belong to the wider area of the Mediterranean.

14.1. Introduction

The global negative impact of Coronavirus 2019 (Covid-19) disease in vital sustainability points of social functionality, such as health and economics, is indisputable. State authorities and societies in general have found themselves confronted with new regularities while trying to understand and measure the behavior of this new disease. To this end, several researchers from various scientific fields, such as medicine and biosurveillance, have used a plethora of tools in order to achieve this.

Statistical process monitoring (SPM) constitutes a method of quality control which employs various powerful tools to monitor and control a process. Such tools should

Chapter written by Emmanouil-Nektarios KALLIGERIS and Andreas MAKRIDES.
For a color version of all the figures in this chapter, see www.iste.co.uk/zafeiris/data2.zip.

be able to illustrate the evolution over time of the behavior of quality characteristics, either measurable or countable, and at the same time detect anomalies. The latter are caused due to high variation which if it is misunderstood, could lead to: (1) difficulties regarding noise interpretation and (2) failure/late reaction in detecting the presence of a signal. The use of SPM is very common among various organizations which make use of control charts for capturing the behavior of processes or systems that evolve over time (Deming 2000; MacCarthy and Wasusri 2002; Benneyan 2003; Perla 2013; Ntotsis et al. 2020; Kalligeris et al. 2020).

Since Covid-19 constitutes an ongoing process, it could be approached via SPM so that the quality characteristics of the latter can be identified through appropriate graphical and statistical tools. Despite its potential value though, SPM is not part of standard public health practice (Benneyan 2003; Provost and Murray 2011; Bryk et al. 2015; Berwick 2016; Finnerty et al. 2019; Karagrigoriou et al. 2019; Perla 2020), mainly due to the fact that using such a method in rapidly changing data constitutes quite a challenging task. At the time of writing, there is not a rich amount of literature regarding the use of SPM in Covid-19. Inkelas et al. (2021) used control charts to provide timely and interpretable displays of Covid-19 data that inform local mitigation and containment strategies. Mahmood et al. (2021) used control charts to monitor variations in deaths in Pakistan due to the Covid-19 pandemic.

In most cases, control charts are used for the evaluation/monitoring of a process (signal) in order to identify whether it is out of control or not. However, in the case of an ongoing disease, it is of high importance to identify its evolution so that appropriate strategies need to be taken. To that end, Perla (2021) developed a four-epoch/phase (period of time) framework for the identification of crucial stages occurring throughout the pandemic. In this work, we apply the aforementioned framework to 10 Mediterranean countries, namely, Albania, Croatia, Cyprus, France, Greece, Israel, Italy, Portugal, Slovenia and Spain, with the goal of acquiring useful information regarding the behavior of Covid-19 in the wider Mediterranean basin.

The rest of the chapter is organized as follows. In section 14.2, the basic aspects of the framework used in this work are presented. In section 14.3, a real case study on Covid-19 cases regarding 10 countries of the Mediterranean basin is conducted based on the framework presented in section 14.2. Finally, we conclude with the main attributes found throughout the analysis.

14.2. Materials and methods

Classical tools in quality management include control charts which focus on the two main characteristics of a process, namely, the mean (target value) and the variance (variability). Failure to recognize and interpret either one may result in delays in taking proper (when a signal is present but not recognized) or unnecessary actions (when a false signal is recognized as a legitimate one). Such failures are quite common since most processes often vary due to chance, especially if we take into account what one observes in a process is the result of various effects. In the case where the process under study is closely related to community health, extra caution needs to be exercised.

Although typical processes have a standard central line (usually referred to as target line or target value) that is not the case when it comes to health processes like a disease or an epidemic, since the latter often grow as the number of cases reported as infected, increases. As a result, control charts need attention when monitoring data that grow according to a mathematical function, since the tools to be used should be based on the idea of learning under uncertainty. In biology, classical growth functions typically have an exponential form on which proper SPM tools have been developed for handling processes like the current Covid-19 pandemic. Perla (2021) proposed such a tool that adopts a hybrid control chart which takes under consideration the classical phases of a typical pandemic, namely, the stable (pre-growth phase), the growth period or epoch (based on an exponential growth), the exponential decline phase and the stabilization phase.

A visual representation of the progression of a process plays a key role in identifying the time points associated with the beginning and the end of each of the four phases (which constitute specific time periods within the visual display). A more detailed definition of each phase is as follows:

Phase 1 (pre-growth): the epidemic is low and stable and a rapid growth has not yet been detected.

Phase 2 (exponential growth): the pattern of the epidemic shifts from being low and stable to rapidly growing. During this phase, the growth rate from day to day is typically also increasing, resulting in an exponential or multiplicative growth.

Phase 3 (exponential decline): the epidemic is no longer growing exponentially or rapidly, and starts to plateau or decline.

Phase 4 (stability): the epidemic returns to a low and stable level.

The first and last phases are described by a C-chart while the decline phase is described by an I-chart. Note that the growth phase is investigated by an I-chart based on logarithmic (base 10) transformed data which are reverted to their original scale with the beginning of Phase 3. The research team that developed the aforementioned four-phase approach have identified four distinct opportunities for learning through its application:

– it is a useful method to engage subject matter experts, and furthermore enhance understanding about the effects of policy changes related to control and suppression of the epidemic;

– the charts can provide an early (pre-alert) signal that the rapid growth phase in the pandemic has commenced;

– the charts can also provide signals of the shift from the rapid growth phase to the plateau or downward trending phase, and subsequently, a return to a low and stable phase;

– this approach can prevent the public, subject matter experts and senior decision-makers from over-reacting to a single data point as if it were a signal of change in the course of the epidemic.

Control charts consist of a central line (CL) representing the sample mean of the data set and the upper and lower control limits (UCL and LCL) that play the role of the bounds of the data set. If two consecutive points are above or below the limits, there is strong evidence that something unusual may be happening and further inquiry is needed. If, in addition, eight consecutive points are above or below the CL, it is also a statistical sign that something unusual maybe happening and needs further attention and investigation. According to Shewhart criteria modified by Perla (2021), if two points are above the control limits, it is an indication that a new phase is beginning between Phases 2 and 3.

As for the construction of the control chart, it is necessary that at least eight observations satisfy the qualifications of an effective C-chart in Phases 1 and 4. Thus, the limits for the exponential growth period are derived from regression analysis while the limits for the exponential growth based on the median moving range of the residuals are derived as follows:

$$UCL = CL + 3.14\overline{MR}$$

$$LCL = CL - 3.14\overline{MR},$$

where $\overline{MR} = \sum_{i=2}^{n} \frac{|x_i - x_{i-1}|}{n-1}$.

Note that in the case where no exponential growth appears, a C-chart is employed for the whole observation period.

14.3. Behavior of Covid-19 disease in the Mediterranean region

In this section, the control charts of several Mediterranean countries – namely, Albania, Croatia, Cyprus, France, Greece, Israel, Italy, Portugal, Slovenia and Spain – are presented (Figures 14.1–14.5) and discussed, with the goal of both monitoring the progression of Covid-19 as well as identifying the periods where an outbreak occurred, between February 26, 2020 and July 6, 2021. The analyzed Covid-19 recorded cases are accessible via https://github.com/owid.

Note that in the analysis that follows, the countries considered have been divided into groups of two based on the similarity of their behavior with reference to the pandemic.

Cyprus–Greece

Cyprus and Greece exhibit two exponential growths of small magnitude, one in March 2020 and another one after the end of the 2020 summer period, while between these two periods, and under a strict lockdown policy by local authorities, there exists a clear stability phase. A sharper exponential growth phase took place, for both countries, in November 2020 which is then followed by an exponential decline. Despite the fact that both countries were placed under a second lockdown, another sharp exponential growth appeared during the winter of 2021. It has to be noted however that in Greece, the aforementioned sharp growth appears slightly smoother than the preceding one. Finally, both Cyprus and Greece came across a third sharp exponential growth after the end of June 2021 which seems even rougher for the case of Cyprus.

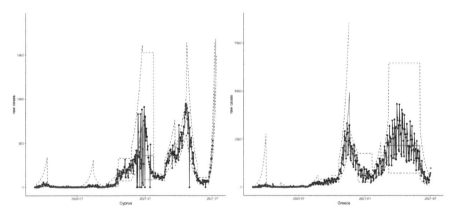

Figure 14.1. *Control charts of Covid-19 cases for Cyprus and Greece*

Croatia–Israel

Similar to the countries discussed above seems to be the case pattern for both Croatia and Israel. The only distinctive difference is that they do not seem to experience an exponential growth in July 2021. Note that for Israel, before the sharp exponential growth at the end of 2020, another phase of rapid growth occurs just a couple of weeks after the end of the second small exponential growth of August 2020.

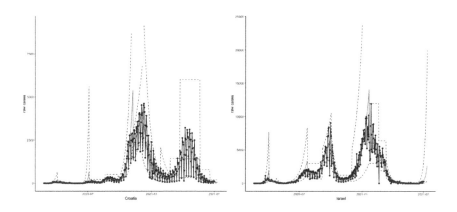

Figure 14.2. *Control charts of Covid-19 cases for Croatia and Israel*

Albania–Slovenia

Slovenia is one of the countries that did not show an exponential increase at the beginning of the pandemic with the daily cases around the CL. After a non-significant exponential increase on July 2020 and a stability period until the end of November 2020, a phase of sharp exponential growth follows and seems to be unique within the whole observation period, since there is no sign of an exponential growth after the end of the lockdown that preceded the summer period of 2021. In the case of Albania, the country experienced an increase regarding the recorded cases since the beginning of the pandemic, which, from November 2020, resulted in an exponential form. Finally, a second exponential growth wave occurred in the beginning of 2021 which started to exponentially decline as the summer period of 2021 approached.

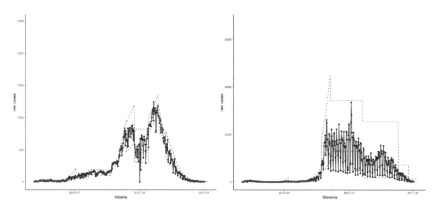

Figure 14.3. *Control charts of Covid-19 cases for Albania and Slovenia*

Portugal–Spain

A few days after the Covid-19 onset, Portugal and Spain exhibited a stability period after an increase in cases, a fact that is more evident in the case of Portugal. Although the second sharp exponential growth (after the beginning of 2021) seems to be more intense for Portugal, we have to take into account that Spain's population is quadruple that of Portugal's and as a result we need to pay close attention to the two exponential growths that occurred in Spain before and after the beginning of 2021. It is worth noting that after the lifting of restrictive measures, in view of the tourist season, both countries seem to be facing a new wave of exponential growth.

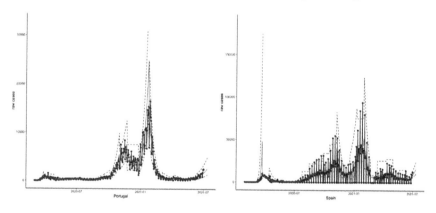

Figure 14.4. *Control charts of Covid-19 cases for Portugal and Spain*

France–Italy

After an exponential growth at the beginning of the pandemic, France faced another rough one by the end of the 2020 summer period where Covid-19 infections exceeded even 100,000 cases per day. Furthermore, although there was a period of stability until the beginning of June 2021, the number of cases remained high enough. For Italy, a country with a population almost equal to that of France, the pandemic behavior appears to be similar to the latter. However, in the last quarter, Italy exhibited once again an exponential growth with the Covid-19 cases exceeding 20,000 per day. The fact though that the infections in Italy seem to be in a continuous exponential decline, at least until July 6, 2021, is somewhat comforting.

Readers who would like to draw information regarding the exact numbers of Covid-19 cases can go through Tables 14.1 and 14.2 where the weekly new cases are provided, concerning the second week of March 2020 up to the third week of September 2021.

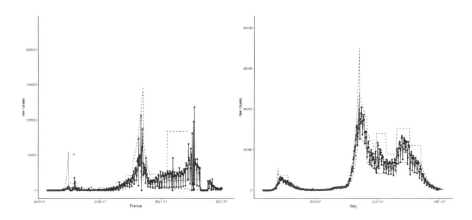

Figure 14.5. *Control charts of Covid-19 cases for France and Italy*

14.4. Conclusion

In this chapter, we studied the behavior of Covid-19 infected cases of 10 countries located in the wider Mediterranean region, that is, Albania, Croatia, Cyprus, France, Greece, Israel, Italy, Portugal, Slovenia and Spain. For the analysis, the four-epoch SPM framework Perla (2021) was used, acquiring useful information regarding the route of the disease as follows:

1) Although the enforcement of the first lockdown led to a phase of stability for all countries considered, that seems not to be the case for the following lockdown periods, since even though the former led to an exponential decline phase, it did not manage to achieve the stability brought by the first one.

2) The majority of countries under study experienced an exponential growth of recorded cases in March 2020 which was followed, after a nearly linear behavior during the summer season, by at least two periods of exponential growth, i.e. the one before the end of 2020 and another one before the summer season of 2021.

3) Most of the countries under study: (a) experienced significant case variation during the observation time and (b) showed two or more non-sequential daily rates that are above the UCL.

The control charts discussed in this study, once understood, could effectively help local authorities protect residents from extremely harmful events, and hence, their use may be proven beneficial to state authorities during the Covid-19 pandemic.

Week	Cyprus	Greece	Croatia	Israel	Albania	Slovenia	Portugal	Spain	France	Italy
1	26	258	26	191	42	57	149	5,891	1,867	13,024
2	58	302	96	903	38	244	908	15,178	6,831	25,922
3	95	471	390	3,058	116	189	2,759	39,823	14,657	38,673
4	210	652	521	4,308	103	316	5,256	54,603	24,525	36,616
5	206	469	415	3,117	141	293	4,999	46,019	7,929	30,808
6	201	338	428	2,746	92	226	5,204	33,424	10,669	27,415
7	110	100	271	2,053	117	144	3,621	31,843	90,457	23,654
8	50	282	184	1,401	164	105	3,707	14,179	11,992	20,560
9	54	114	76	711	77	64	2,554	12,226	8,776	15,490
10	34	79	49	290	68	37	1,670	8,012	3,121	10,866
11	18	92	94	183	56	18	1,950	8,366	7,617	8,203
12	17	90	25	113	84	11	1,519	4,007	3,299	6,072
13	21	52	16	166	80	3	1,579	3,794	3,135	4,423
14	12	36	2	567	139	5	1,877	3,707	4,797	3,337
15	20	80	1	884	109	6	2,148	2,082	3,514	2,283
16	20	132	2	1,252	232	11	2,211	2,231	7,306	2,129
17	5	129	20	1,676	422	11	2,179	2,561	3,476	2,065
18	7	94	130	2,595	404	25	2,432	2,403	3,629	1,333
19	8	122	411	4,908	466	53	2,404	2,519	2,667	1,716
20	7	180	495	7,588	503	92	2,217	2,819	3,106	1,301
21	18	264	571	9,991	607	142	2,615	3,363	3,823	1,408
22	17	204	581	11,376	636	115	2,169	6,347	3,763	1,328
23	16	183	578	11,911	629	118	1,615	12,166	4,991	1,602
24	67	342	437	10,943	706	134	1,489	15,264	6,388	1,744
25	118	722	383	9,993	819	98	1,235	23,126	8,157	1,931
26	96	1,203	422	10,234	928	76	1,264	23,798	10,104	2,596
27	82	1,530	1,007	9,795	978	136	1,409	36,102	17,572	3,349
28	100	1,597	1,604	10,152	1,106	204	1,495	43,241	22,525	4,698
29	66	1,470	1,961	12,001	953	229	1,996	53,232	30,245	8,344
30	24	1,409	1,879	16,589	823	238	2,383	59,703	44,997	8,963
31	18	1,534	1,823	23,905	1,054	307	3,075	65,630	49,683	10,068
32	41	1,948	1,403	31,537	1,088	537	4,085	70,981	58,630	9,837
33	106	2,245	1,387	37,974	971	706	4,642	79,100	71,981	10,745
34	125	2,195	1,253	41,148	852	812	4,829	76,798	85,624	11,714
35	134	2,435	1,462	39,842	1,019	1,049	5,547	73,451	76,986	14,647
36	182	2,516	2,531	21,338	1,133	1,430	7,327	71,180	94,758	23,862
37	595	2,854	4,219	12,067	1,543	2,467	11,974	75,448	126,907	43,204
38	935	4,607	7,316	6,931	2,055	4,847	16,247	104,907	174,998	76,849
39	897	7,294	12,712	4,671	2,065	9,808	22,121	131,208	256,339	130,329
40	1,170	12,593	15,466	4,539	2,260	13,033	25,011	142,628	322,408	188,799
41	1,362	16,324	16,116	4,164	3,390	10,155	36,573	140,521	384,177	225,769
42	1,187	18,216	16,959	4,979	3,701	9,776	37,977	129,759	262,353	242,062
43	1,465	17,414	18,566	5,314	4,931	10,025	44,704	98,139	188,570	238,464
44	1,775	12,913	22,869	6,617	4,594	10,143	36,340	71,478	106,591	201,347
45	1,829	11,898	23,789	8,918	5,057	10,036	27,224	58,547	77,520	160,736
46	2,126	9,716	24,491	11,168	5,560	10,424	28,227	46,326	74,211	136,493

Table 14.1. *Weekly cases for the countries under study concerning the period March 10, 2020 to September 20, 2021*

Week	Cyprus	Greece	Croatia	Israel	Albania	Slovenia	Portugal	Spain	France	Italy
47	2,904	7,837	24,866	15,578	5,449	10,706	25,600	59,884	84,971	113,180
48	2,215	6,058	18,370	19,980	3,814	9,818	25,282	67,365	95,871	109,473
49	2,404	4,334	9,968	29,911	3,147	9,978	20,452	57,715	105,073	100,676
50	4,317	4,643	7,950	40,888	3,184	9,806	30,874	73,314	93,338	101,022
51	3,566	4,584	5,939	49,777	4,042	11,065	46,080	122,095	105,420	113,195
52	1,935	4,366	6,249	58,065	4,257	13,855	61,273	187,063	126,507	117,091
53	1,512	3,196	4,433	53,979	3,922	9,844	74,497	236,229	128,190	97,335
54	908	4,110	3,854	46,026	5,329	8,737	86,920	259,075	143,142	85,270
55	872	5,490	3,466	47,284	6,243	8,777	83,208	229,423	142,918	86,219
56	868	7,080	2,976	43,741	7,297	8,105	44,898	198,871	143,139	83,315
57	754	8,182	2,333	33,765	7,739	5,694	22,173	114,045	155,758	85,637
58	763	7,452	2,174	25,663	7,075	6,156	13,546	77,087	128,733	82,009
59	1,135	10,707	2,726	28,822	7,320	5,234	8,917	58,525	140,949	96,907
60	2,095	13,027	3,157	25,685	6,208	5,314	6,040	-34,323	151,142	123,272
61	2,445	14,812	3,641	20,843	5,166	5,459	5,659	34,798	148,433	142,997
62	2,694	14,327	4,566	12,686	4,283	4,839	4,054	34,092	163,158	155,656
63	2,759	16,549	6,594	6,986	3,527	5,310	3,273	28,628	201,427	154,493
64	2,413	16,906	9,096	3,361	2,934	6,015	2,962	42,992	242,682	156,201
65	2,977	20,869	12,305	2,323	2,542	6,747	3,164	36,070	266,175	142,540
66	3,711	20,734	11,711	1,743	1,953	7,459	3,319	45,243	256,059	115,494
67	3,956	19,776	15,425	1,262	1,619	6,358	3,826	60,286	234,036	106,326
68	5,611	19,455	15,432	905	1,021	5,643	3,472	51,806	230,933	99,400
69	5,698	17,094	14,836	831	894	4,885	3,417	60,115	213,471	92,543
70	3,951	14,132	12,547	480	670	4,528	2,835	55,460	175,820	86,100
71	3,060	15,582	9,600	336	485	5,298	2,311	43,331	135,755	70,094
72	1,736	15,254	6,597	225	312	3,948	2,527	37,391	115,347	56,962
73	1,003	13,545	4,534	190	214	3,193	2,800	33,209	98,287	41,447
74	624	11,526	2,924	143	146	2,380	3,156	31,958	-275,150	30,867
75	414	10,448	2,014	112	107	1,962	3,698	29,899	63,438	23,149
76	404	7,371	1,427	68	60	1,833	3,941	29,133	49,410	16,425
77	388	5,235	998	116	77	1,411	4,801	35,619	32,960	13,329
78	453	3,409	611	300	31	794	7,369	23,842	19,878	9,142
79	987	2,575	490	1,021	21	485	8,557	25,021	14,809	5,945
80	2,519	3,870	572	1,825	20	251	12,127	43,766	14,001	4,475
81	5,248	9,836	611	3,008	42	181	16,469	89,036	16,539	5,571
82	6,717	16,758	582	4,285	59	425	19,665	134,472	26,509	8,366
83	7,062	18,690	772	7,230	132	405	22,784	190,726	46,988	16,182
84	6,317	18,829	1,026	10,478	194	423	22,374	180,207	109,029	28,341
85	4,505	18,988	1,119	16,933	246	467	18,197	166,615	146,286	35,984
86	4,174	19,038	1,202	24,681	649	706	16,323	141,088	155,446	40,282
87	3,312	22,371	1,558	37,570	1,549	852	15,962	111,312	164,348	43,198
88	2,631	21,985	2,217	48,938	2,836	1,319	16,330	85,085	178,197	43,365
89	2,180	22,891	2,899	57,665	4,290	1,970	16,219	70,822	156,897	44,441
90	1,854	21,152	3,492	65,156	5,866	2,799	15,473	52,946	130,602	45,633
91	1,681	18,058	4,647	51,244	6,166	3,477	12,100	45,946	119,480	41,834
92	1,163	15,206	5,809	66,457	6,029	4,550	8,816	29,706	80,612	36,588
93	385	15,660	7,708	55,876	6,011	6,435	6,982	22,085	63,022	32,214

Table 14.2. *Weekly cases for the countries under study concerning the period March 10, 2020 to September 20, 2021*

14.5. Acknowledgments

This work was carried out at the Lab of Statistics and Data Analysis of the University of the Aegean.

14.6. References

Benneyan, J.C., Lloyd, R.C., Plsek, P.E. (2003). Statistical process control as a tool for research and healthcare improvement. *Quality and Safety in Health Care*, 12(6), 458–464.

Berwick, D. (2016). Era 3 for medicine and health care. *JAMA*, 315(13), 1329–1330.

Bryk, A.S., Gomez, L.M., Grunow, A., LeMahieu, P.G. (2015). *Learning to Improve: How America's Schools Can Get Better at Getting Better*. Harvard Education Press, Cambridge, MA.

Deming, W.E. (2000). *The New Economics for Industry, Government, and Education*, 2nd edition. MIT Press, Cambridge, MA.

Finnerty, P., Provost, L., O'Donnell, E., Selk, S., Stephens, K., Kim, J., Berns, S. (2019). Using infant mortality data to improve maternal and child health programs: An application of statistical process control techniques for rare events. *Maternal and Child Health Journal*, 23(6), 739–745.

Inkelas, M., Blair, C., Furukawa, D., Manuel, V.G., Malenfant, J.H., Martin, E., Emeruwa, I., Kuo, T., Arangua, L., Robles, B. et al. (2021). Using control charts to understand community variation in COVID-19. *PLOS ONE*, 16, 1–11.

Kalligeris, E.N., Karagrigoriou, A., Parpoula, C. (2020). Periodic-type auto-regressive moving average modeling with covariates for time-series incidence data via changepoint detection. *Statistical Methods in Medical Research*, 29(6), 1639–1649.

Karagrigoriou, A., Makrides, A., Vonta, I. (2019). On a control chart for the Gini index with simulations. *Communications in Statistics – Simulation and Computation*, 48(4), 1121–1137.

MacCarthy, B.L. and Wasusri, T. (2002). A review of non-standard applications of statistical process control (SPC) charts. *The International Journal of Quality & Reliability Management*, 19(2), 295–320.

Mahmood, Y., Ishtiaq, S., Khoo, M.B.C., Teh, S.Y., Khan, H. (2021). Monitoring of three-phase variations in the mortality of COVID-19 pandemic using control charts: Where does Pakistan stand? *International Journal for Quality in Health Care*, 33(2), 1–8.

Ntotsis, K., Papamichail, M., Hatzopoulos, P., Karagrigoriou, A. (2020). On the modeling of pension expenditures in Europe. *Communications in Statistics: Case Studies, Data Analysis and Applications*, 6(1), 50–68.

Perla, R. (2020). Governors: Read this before reopening your state. U.S. News & World Report, 14 April.

Perla, R., Provost, L.P., Parry, G.J. (2013). Seven propositions of the science of improvement: Exploring foundations. *Quality Management in Health Care*, 22(3), 170–186.

Perla, R., Provost, S.M., Parry, G.J., Little, K., Provost, L.P. (2021). Understanding variation in reported covid-19 deaths with a novel Shewhart chart application. *International Journal for Quality in Health Care: Journal of the International Society for Quality in Health Care*, 33(1).

Provost, L.P. and Murray, S.K. (2011). *The Health Care Data Guide: Learning from Data for Improvement*. Jossey-Bass, San Francisco.

PART 3

Increase of Retirement Age and Health State of Population in Czechia

Population aging is very often regarded as a serious threat to the financial sustainability of welfare social systems, especially for the old-age pension system. Many states (including Czechia) intend to raise the retirement age above the standard usual threshold of 65 years. This threshold and its increase are usually determined by the economic or demographic point of view.

There arises a natural question if there will be enough appropriate working positions for persons of older age and if the health state of these persons will enable them to work after reaching 65 years.

This chapter presents a brief analysis of the health state of the population in Czechia in productive and post-productive ages, taking into account the increase in retirement age in the last decade and in the future.

15.1. Introduction

Population aging is one of the most important demographic phenomena of the recent decades of the previous century and of course of this century (e.g. Gavrilov and Heuveline 2003). Its reasons are well known: the long-standing decrease in mortality resulting in a prolongation of human life as well as the remarkable decrease in fertility during the previous century. Moreover, in some countries, the aging process is accelerated by a massive emigration of persons in productive and

Chapter written by Tomáš FIALA, Jitka LANGHAMROVÁ and Jana VRABCOVÁ.
For a color version of all the figures in this chapter, see www.iste.co.uk/zafeiris/data2.zip.

reproductive ages. This topic is very often discussed not only by demographers and economists, but also by the general public and media. All demographically advanced populations are facing or will face the aging process, which is, in many aspects, unprecedented and deepening dynamically.

The main economic consequences of population aging are commonly known. An increase in the proportion of persons in older age results in an increasing financial burden of the old-age pension system as well as the necessity of ensuring healthcare and social care from both a financial and personal perspective.

A natural and logical measure for eliminating the consequences of population aging for the financial sustainability of the old-age pension system is the increase in retirement age, even above the usual value of 65 years. At present, the retirement age threshold exceeds 65 years in only some European countries; in the future, the number of such countries will be higher (OECD 2019).

In Czechia, the retirement age threshold was relatively low in the second half of the 20th century – 60 years for males, 55 years for females with two children. After 1990, there emerged tendencies towards a gradual increase of the retirement age to the level usual in most developed countries (65 years) and of unifying the threshold for males and females. The retirement age in Czechia started to rise over time from 1996 by two months for males and by four months for females for each subsequent birth cohort (Law No. 155/1995 Coll. (Zákon 155/1995)). One of the latest amendments prolonged the increase of retirement age permanently without any upper limit and since 2019 the increase in retirement age for females has been accelerated to six months for each subsequent birth cohort to reach the threshold of males sooner (Law No. 220/2011 Coll. (Zákon 220/2011)).

The idea of such a permanent increase in retirement age, regardless of the development of life expectancy, has often been criticized. One of the themes dealt with in 2014 by the Expert Committee on Pension Reform of the Czech Republic was therefore the revision of the age limit for retirement in Czechia. The Expert Committee approved the recommendation that for the generations born before 1966, the retirement age should be in accordance with the previous legislation. The value of the retirement age (unique for males and females) for persons born in 1966 and later was recommended to be determined in such a way that people reaching senior age should receive an old-age pension on average for the last quarter of their lives (Expert Committee (Expert Committee on Pension Reform Czech Republic 2014)). But the final version of the law concerning old-age pensions passed by the Czech parliament aims to stop the increase of retirement age at the level of 65 years after 2030. The calculations of the retirement age, which would lead to receiving an old-age pension on average for the last quarter of an individual's life, would be regularly carried out every five years, but they would serve only as information for the government (Law No. 203/2017 Coll. (Zákon 203/2017)). The first such type of calculations based on the population projection of the Czech Republic for 2018–2100 (CZSO 2018) showed that the increase of the retirement age should continue. Nevertheless, the MLSA minister did not submit any proposal to increase the retirement age and so it will be proposed probably as late as 2024 after updated calculations are carried out.

The idea of retirement age increase seems to be very understandable and logical but there arises a natural question if there would be enough appropriate working opportunities for seniors over the age of 65 and if their state of health will be good enough for them to be able to work.

The goal of this chapter is a brief analysis of the development of the health state of the population in Czechia in productive and post-productive ages, taking into account the increase of retirement age at present times and in the future.

15.2. Data and methodological remarks

There are several indicators characterizing the state of health. We have used a self-perceived health indicator by sex and age groups published in the Ehlesis database (EHLEIS n/a).

Only three basic categories of state of health were differentiated:

– very good or good;

– fair;

– bad or very bad.

For simplicity, by the term "good" we mean a very good or good health state; the term "bad" will signify a bad or very bad health state.

Comparable data were available from the year 2008 and so the analysis has been performed for the period 2008–2060.

Available empirical values of sex- and age-specific prevalence rates were smoothed (for each sex and for each age interval) using a linear trend based on the period 2010–2019.

For the period 2020–2030, the values of prevalence rates were estimated by adjusted linear extrapolation of previous trends. From 2031 up to 2060, no change of prevalence rates have been assumed; their values in this period were assumed to be equal to those of 2030.

Population data as of January 1 by age and sex in 2008–2020 came from the Czech Statistical Office database. The source of the values for the period 2021–2061 was the Czech Statistical Office population projection, medium variant (CZSO 2018–2020).

Statutory retirement age until 2030 (linear increase up to 65 years of age) is determined by present legislation (Law No. 155/1995 Coll. (Zákon 155/1995)). From 2031, the value of the retirement age is assumed to be determined so that the person reaching senior age should receive an old-age pension on average for the last quarter of their lives (CZSO 2018).

15.3. Statutory retirement age

In Czechia, the statutory retirement age threshold was relatively low in the second half of the 20th century. For males, it was 60 years of age. The retirement age for females was 55 years and later was differentiated by their number of children from 53 years (five or more children) until 57 years (childless). Females with two children (which was the most frequent case) had an unchanged retirement age of 55 years (Fiala and Langhamrová 2015). Despite the constant level of the retirement age threshold, the value of the adjusted old-age dependency ratio was relatively stable in the 1970s, 1980s and early 1990s. The main reason for this was the fact that the numerous generations of seniors born before WWI were gradually dying, while at the same time, numerous cohorts born after WWII were reaching productive age. Moreover, life expectancy remained almost unchanged during this period (Arltová et al. 2013).

After 1990, there emerged tendencies that the retirement age in Czechia should increase to the level usual in most European and other economically developed countries (65 years), and that the threshold for males and females should be unified. According to the new legal arrangement of the pension system (Law No. 155/1995 Coll. (Zákon 155/1995)), the retirement age in Czechia started to rise over time from 1996 by two months for males and four months for females for each subsequent birth cohort. The period of this increase was prolonged several times. One of the latest amendments (Law No. 220/2011 Coll. (Zákon 220/2011)) prolonged the increase of retirement age permanently without any upper limit; for example, persons born in 2013 should retire at 73 years old, persons born in 2025 should retire at 75 years old, etc. At the same time, the increase in retirement age for females was accelerated to six months for each subsequent birth cohort to reach the threshold of males sooner.

The idea of such a permanent increase in retirement age, regardless of the development of life expectancy, has often been criticized by some politicians and experts. They argued that theoretically it could happen, if the increase in life expectancy slowed down or stopped, that in the future many people would not even reach retirement age or would receive a pension only for a relatively short time. One of the themes dealt with in 2014 by the Expert Committee on Pension Reform of the Czech Republic was thus the revision of the age limit for retirement in Czechia. The Expert Committee on Pension Reform approved the recommendation that the retirement age (which should be the same for both men and women) should continue to depend on the year of birth of the individual. For the generations born before 1966, the retirement age should be in accordance with the previous legislation, supposing an increase (in comparison with the preceding birth cohorts) for men by two months, for women by four months and, since 2019 by six months until they reach the level of men. Men born in 1965 should thus retire in 2030 at the age of 65, and women (born in the same year) with two children should retire at the age of 64 years 8 months.

The value of the retirement age for persons born in 1966 and later was recommended to be the same for males and females and determined in such a way that people reaching senior age should receive an old-age pension on average for the last quarter of their lives (CZSO 2018; see Figure 15.1).

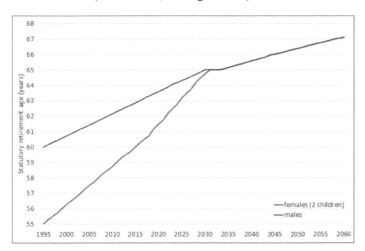

Figure 15.1. *Statutory retirement age in Czechia Source of data: until 2030: Zákon 155/1995 Sb. O důchodovém pojištění, aktuální znění, příloha. [Act no. 155/1995 of Coll., on pension insurance, as amended, an annex.] since 2031: CZSO (Czech Statistical Office). Příloha ke Zprávě o očekávaném vývoji úmrtnosti, plodnosti a migrace v České republice [An annex to the Report on the Expected Development of Mortality, Fertility and Migration in the Czech Republic] 2018. https://www.czso.cz/ documents/10180/94500304/zprava_priloha.xlsx/ba090895-3067-4243-a511-7d186a9d93e1?version=1.0*

The value x of the retirement age for persons born in the year g is determined by the equation

$$\frac{e_x^{(g)}}{x + e_x^{(g)}} = 0.25$$

where $e_x^{(g)}$ denotes the unisex life expectancy (or the mean of life expectancies of males and females) at the age x for the birth cohort of the year g. Linear interpolation method would be used for finding the solution.

Productive age (changing in time) means the age from 20 years until statutory retirement age in the year analyzed.

15.4. Development of the state of health of population

The proportion of persons in a good state of health is considerably increasing in almost all age groups, with the exception of the youngest and oldest persons. In the age group 16–24 years, the proportion of persons in a good state of health reaches about 95% for both males and females and only a slight increase in time is assumed. In other age groups, the increase of proportion of persons in a good state of health is more notable, especially for persons of the midlife age groups. On the other hand, the data for the oldest age group of 85 years and older show stagnation and the proportion of persons in a good state of health in this age group is assumed to be lower than 10% throughout the entire period analyzed. In many age groups, the proportion of persons in a good state of health is lower for females than for males, but the annual increase for females is usually higher than for males. If this trend continues, the proportion of females in a good health state will reach and exceed the level of males during the 2020s in most age groups (see Figure 15.2).

The proportion of persons in a fair state of health is decreasing over time for both males and females in all age groups up to 75 years of age. In the youngest age group (16–24 years), the annual decrease is relatively low, and the values for persons of the midlife age groups are considerably higher. The proportion of persons in a fair health state is in all age groups up to 65 years and since 2014 also in the age interval 65–74 years is higher for males than for females. But if the development trend of the 2010s decade continues, the proportion of persons in a fair health state in the age interval 35–54 years will be higher for females than for males in the 2020s.

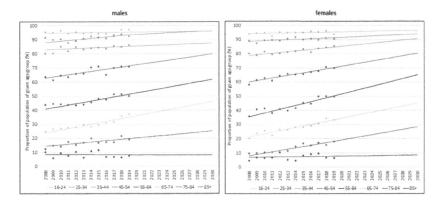

Figure 15.2. *Proportion of population in a good state of health Source of data: 2008–2019: EHLESIS database. http://www.eurohex.eu/IS/web/ app.php/Ehleis since 2020: authors' projection*

On the other hand, the proportion of persons in a fair health state at age 75 and older shows an increasing trend for both males and females. Because the proportion of persons in a good health state in these age groups is increasing or stagnating, the increase of persons in a fair health state indicates an improvement of the health state of older persons because the increase of persons in a fair health state results in a decrease of persons in a bad health state. At the beginning of the period analyzed, the proportion of persons in a fair health states was higher for males in these age groups but due to a higher annual increase for females the situation has been changing gradually and from the early 2020s the proportion for females will be higher than for males (see Figure 15.3).

As for persons in a bad state of health, their proportion is decreasing for males as well as for females in practically all age groups. Usually, the higher the age group, the higher the annual decrease of proportion of persons in a bad state of health. The relationship between males and females is ambiguous. In the youngest age group (16–24 years) as well as in the age group 55–64 years, the proportion of females in a bad state of health is lower than for males throughout the entire period analyzed. In other age groups, the situation is inverse. The annual decrease of proportion of persons in a bad state of health for persons up to 25 years and for persons at the age 55 years and older is higher for females, while for persons of the age 25–54 years, the annual decrease is higher for males. Because of this fact, it is projected that at the beginning of the 2030s, the proportion of persons in a bad state of health will be higher for females in the age interval 25–54 years, while in other age intervals, it will be higher for males (see Figure 15.4).

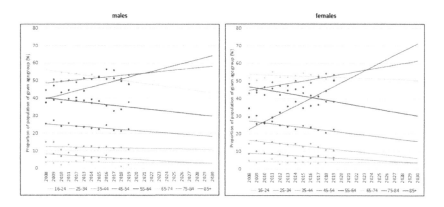

Figure 15.3. *Proportion of population in a fair state of health. Source of data: 2008–2019: EHLESIS database. http://www.eurohex.eu/IS/web/app. php/Ehleis since 2020: authors' projection*

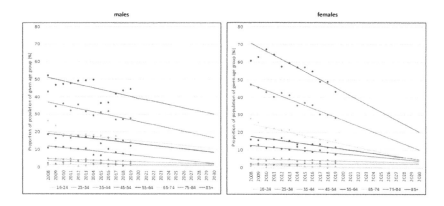

Figure 15.4. *Proportion of population in a bad state of health. Source of data: 2008–2019: EHLESIS database. http://www.eurohex.eu/IS/web/app. php/Ehleis since 2020: authors' projection*

15.5. Development of the state of health of population in productive and post-productive ages

The analysis presented in the previous section shows that the state of health should improve for both males and females in practically all age groups. At the same time, the aging of the population will continue and the statutory retirement age will increase and so the population in productive age as well as in post-productive age will get older. There arises a natural question if the continuing aging of the population of productive and post-productive ages will be sufficiently compensated by improving the state of health.

The decrease in proportion of persons in a fair and bad state of health in the 2010s fully compensates the impact of the population aging and the increase of retirement age on the state of health of the population in productive age. The proportion of persons in a fair as well as in a bad health state decreased for both males and females. If the trend of improving the state of health in all age groups continues in the 2020s, the improvement of the population in productive age will go on despite the population aging and the increasing retirement age.

On the other hand, if the health state improvement in particular age groups stops after 2031, the proportion of persons in a fair and in a bad health state will stagnate or even increase a little bit from 2031 due to continuing population aging and increase of the retirement age (see Figure 15.5).

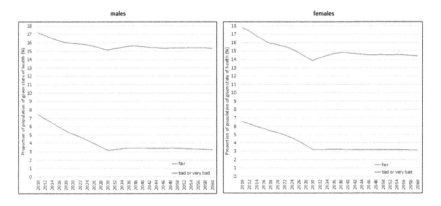

Figure 15.5. *State of health of population in productive age. Source: authors' calculations and graph*

The situation for the population of post-productive age in a bad state of health is similar. The proportion of persons in a bad state of health has a decreasing tendency until 2031; later on, it shows a slight increase for males as well as for females. The percentage of males in a bad state of health will be higher than for females. On the other hand, the trends of development of the proportion of persons in a fair state of health are quite different. In the case of males, the proportion of persons in a fair state of health will at first stagnate and later on slightly increase. In the case of females where the retirement age is increasing more rapidly than for males, the proportion of persons in a fair state of health grew in the 2010s and will also grow in the 2020s. Since 2031 when the increase of retirement age will considerably slow down, the proportion of persons in a fair state of health will stagnate or increase only a little bit. The development of the proportion of persons in a good state of health indicates that while in the period until 2030, we can expect an improvement of the state of health of persons in post-productive age, after 2031 (assuming no change in the state of health in individual age intervals), the proportion of persons in a good state of health will slightly decrease (see Figure 15.6).

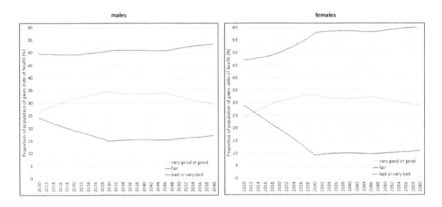

Figure 15.6. *State of health of population in post-productive age. Source: authors' calculations and graph*

15.6. Conclusion

In the period 2008–2019, the proportion of persons in a good state of health increased (except males in the age group 85+ where a slight decrease was observed). The proportion of persons in a fair state of health in age groups until 74 years decreased and age groups from 75 years increased. This increase indicates an improvement of the state of health of older persons. The proportion of persons with a bad state of health decreased in practically all age groups for males as well as for females. In some age groups, the state of health of females was worse than that of males but it was usually improving more rapidly.

If the improvement of the state of health in particular age groups continues until 2030 (following linear trends), the state of health of persons in productive age as well as in post-productive age will improve (despite the population aging and growing retirement age). If there a stagnation of the state of health development in individual age intervals were to occur after 2030, the population aging and growing retirement age would result in a slight worsening of the state of health of persons in productive and post-productive ages.

This analysis is very rough. In order to improve it, it would be necessary to have more particularly differentiated data of the state of health (say by 5 year age groups) and some more sophisticated scenarios of its future development.

15.7. Acknowledgment

This work was supported by the Czech Science Foundation No. GA ČR 19-03984S under the title "Economy of Successful Ageing".

15.8. References

Act no. 220/2011 of Coll. of 21 June 2011 amending Act no. 155/1995 of Coll, on pension insurance, as amended, and other laws.

Arltová, M., Langhamrová, J., Langhamrová, J. (2013). Development of life expectancy in the Czech Republic in years 1920–2010 with an outlook to 2050. *Prague Economic Papers*, 22(1), 125–143. ISSN 1210-0455.

CZSO (2018). Příloha ke Zprávě o očekávaném vývoji úmrtnosti, plodnosti a migrace v České republice [An annex to the Report on the Expected Development of Mortality, Fertility and Migration in the Czech Republic] [Online]. Available at: https://www.czso.cz/documents/10180/94500304/zprava_priloha.xlsx/ba090895-3067-4243-a511-7d186a9d93e1?version=1.0.

CZSO (2018–2022). Projekce obyvatelstva České republiky – 2018–2100. [Population projection of the Czech Republic 2018–2020.] Tab. 2. Střední varianta: Počet obyvatel podle věku (k 1. 1.) – muži. [Medium variant. Population as of 1st January – males.] Tab. 3. Střední varianta: Počet obyvatel podle věku (k 1. 1.) – ženy. [Medium variant. Population as of 1st January – females] [Online]. Available at: https://www.czso.cz/csu/czso/projekce-obyvatelstva-ceske-republiky-2018–2100.

EHLEIS (n/a). EHLEIS [Online]. Available at: http://www.eurohex.eu/IS/web/app.php/Ehleis.

Expert Committee on Pension Reform Czech Republic (2015). Final Report on Activities in 2014 [Online]. Available at: http://www.duchodova-komise.cz/wp-content/uploads/2015/02/Final-report-CoE-2014.pdf.

Fiala, T. and Langhamrová, J. (2015). Hranice důchodového věku zajišťující průměrnou dobu pobírání důchodu čtvrtiny života a modelové výpočty jeho hodnot [The threshold of retirement age guaranteeing the average time of receiving a pension for one quarter of life and model calculations of its values]. Fórum sociální politiky. Roč. 9, č. 5, s. 2–8. ISSN 1802-5854.

Gavrilov, L.A. and Heuveline, P. (2003). Aging of population. In *The Encyclopedia of Population*, Demeny, P. and McNicoll, G. (eds). Macmillan Reference USA, New York [Online]. Available at: http://onlinelibrary.wiley.com/doi/10.1111/j.1728-4457.2013. 00633.x/full.

OECD (2019). *Pensions at a Glance 2019: OECD and G20 Indicators*. OECD Publishing, Paris [Online]. Available at: https://doi.org/10.1787/b6d3dcfc-en.

Zákon 155/1995 Sb. O důchodovém pojištění, aktuální znění, příloha. [Act no. 155/1995 of Coll., on pension insurance, as amended, an annex.]

Zákon 203/2017 Sb. ze dne 8. června 2017, kterým se mění zákon č. 155/1995 Sb., o důchodovém pojištění, ve znění pozdějších předpisů, a některé další zákony. [Act no. 203/2017 of Coll. of 8 June 2017 amending Act no. 155/1995 of Coll, on pension insurance, as amended, and other laws.]

Zákon 220/2011 Sb. ze dne 21. června 2011, kterým se mění zákon č. 155/1995 Sb., o důchodovém pojištění, ve znění pozdějších předpisů, a některé další zákony.

A Generalized Mean Under a Non-Regular Framework and Extreme Value Index Estimation

The Hill estimator, one of the most popular *extreme value index* (EVI) estimators under a heavy right-tail framework, i.e. for a positive EVI, here denoted by ξ, is an average of the log-excesses. Consequently, it can be regarded as the logarithm of the geometric mean or mean of order $p = 0$ of an adequate set of systematic statistics. We can thus more generally consider any real p, the mean of order p (MO$_p$) of those same statistics and the associated MO$_p$ EVI-estimators, also called harmonic moment EVI-estimators. The normal asymptotic behavior of these estimators has been obtained for $p < 1/(2\xi)$, with consistency achieved for $p < 1/\xi$. The non-regular framework, i.e. the case $p \geq 1/(2\xi)$, will be now considered. Consistency is no longer achieved for $p > 1/\xi$, but an almost degenerate behavior appears for $p = 1/\xi$. The results are illustrated on the basis of large-scale simulation studies. An algorithm providing an almost degenerate MO$_p$ EVI-estimation is suggested.

16.1. Introduction

Given $X_1, \ldots, X_n$, a sample of size n of *independent, identically distributed* (IID), or possibly stationary weakly dependent *random variables* (RVs), with a *cumulative distribution function* (CDF) F, let us consider the notation $X_{1:n} \leq \cdots \leq X_{n:n}$ for the associated ascending *order statistics* (OSs). Let us further assume that there exist real constants $a_n > 0$ and $b_n \in \mathbb{R}$ such that the linearly normalized maximum, $(X_{n:n} - b_n)/a_n$, converges in distribution to a non-degenerate RV. Then, with $\lambda \in \mathbb{R}$, a location parameter, and $\delta > 0$, a scale parameter, the limit distribution

Chapter written by M. Ivette Gomes, Lígia Henriques-Rodrigues and Dinis Pestana.

is necessarily the general *extreme value* (EV) CDF (von Misès 1954; Jenkinson 1955), given by:

$$
\mathrm{EV}_\xi\left(\tfrac{x-\lambda}{\delta}\right) =
\begin{cases}
\exp\left(-\left(1 + \tfrac{\xi(x-\lambda)}{\delta}\right)^{-1/\xi}\right), & 1 + \tfrac{\xi(x-\lambda)}{\delta} > 0,\ \text{if}\ \xi \neq 0, \\
\exp(-\exp\left(-\tfrac{x-\lambda}{\delta}\right)),\ x \in \mathbb{R}, & \text{if}\ \xi = 0.
\end{cases}
$$

[16.1]

The CDF F is said to belong to the *max-domain of attraction* (MDA) of EV_ξ, in equation [16.1], the unique max-stable laws, under the aforementioned framework, and, as usual, the notation $F \in \mathcal{D}_\mathcal{M}(\mathrm{EV}_\xi)$ is used. The parameter ξ is the *extreme value index* (EVI), the primary parameter of extreme events.

The EVI measures the heaviness of the *right-tail* function $\overline{F}(x) := 1 - F(x)$, and the heavier the right-tail, the larger ξ is. Let us further use the notation $\mathcal{R}_a$ for the class of regularly varying functions at infinity, with an index of regular variation equal to $a \in \mathbb{R}$ (see Seneta (1976) and Bingham et al. (1987), among others, for details on regular variation theory). In this chapter, we work with Pareto-type underlying models, with a positive EVI, or equivalently, CDFs such that $\overline{F}(x) = x^{-1/\xi}L(x)$, $\xi > 0$, with $L \in \mathcal{R}_0$, a slowly varying function at infinity, i.e. a regularly varying function with an index of regular variation equal to zero. These heavy-tailed models are quite common in many areas of application, like bibliometrics, biostatistics, computer science, finance, insurance, statistical quality control and telecommunications, among others.

For Pareto-type models, the classical EVI-estimators are the Hill (H) EVI-estimators (Hill 1975), which are the averages of the log-excesses,

$$
V_{ik} := \ln X_{n-i+1:n} - \ln X_{n-k:n} = \ln \frac{X_{n-i+1:n}}{X_{n-k:n}} =: \ln U_{ik}, \quad 1 \leq i \leq k < n.
$$

[16.2]

We can thus write:

$$
\mathrm{H}(k) := \frac{1}{k}\sum_{i=1}^{k} V_{ik} = \sum_{i=1}^{k} \ln U_{ik}^{1/k} = \ln\left(\prod_{i=1}^{k} U_{ik}\right)^{1/k}, \quad 1 \leq k < n, \quad [16.3]
$$

i.e. the Hill estimator is the logarithm of the *geometric mean* (or *mean-of-order-0*) of the statistics U_{ik}, defined in equation [16.2]. More generally, first Brilhante et al. (2013), for $p \in \mathbb{R}_0^+$, and more recently Caeiro et al. (2016), for $p \in \mathbb{R}$, considered as basic statistics the *mean-of-order-p* (MO$_p$) of U_{ik}, i.e. the class of statistics:

$$
T_p(k) =
\begin{cases}
\left(\frac{1}{k}\sum_{i=1}^{k} U_{ik}^{p}\right)^{1/p}, & \text{if}\ p \neq 0, \\
\left(\prod_{i=1}^{k} U_{ik}\right)^{1/k}, & \text{if}\ p = 0,
\end{cases}
$$

and the class of functionals,

$$H_p(k) \equiv MO_p(k) := \begin{cases} \Big(1 - T_p^{-p}(k)\Big)/p, \text{ if } p \neq 0, \\ \ln T_0(k) = H(k), \text{ if } p = 0, \end{cases}$$ [16.4]

with $H_0(k) \equiv H(k)$, given in equation [16.3]. This class of MO_p functionals now depends on this *tuning* parameter $p \in \mathbb{R}$, which makes it highly flexible, and has been studied asymptotically and for finite samples in the aforementioned articles, and also, independently, in Paulauskas and Vaičiulis (2013) and Beran et al. (2014). Consistency was shown for $p < 1/\xi$, with an asymptotic normal behavior holding for $p < 1/(2\xi)$ (see also Paulauskas and Vaičiulis (2017), among others).

In section 16.2 of this chapter, apart from the introduction of a few technical details in the field of *extreme value theory* (EVT), we provide a few details on sum-stable laws and the asymptotic behavior of the MO_p EVI-estimators under regular and non-regular frameworks is put forward. In section 16.3, we provide a short illustration of the finite-sample behavior of the MO_p class of functionals under regular and non-regular frameworks. In section 16.4, a method for the adaptive choice of the tuning parameters k and p, essentially on the basis of sample path stability, is provided. The behavior of the new adaptive EVI-estimators is illustrated through an application to simulated random samples, and in section 16.5, some concluding remarks are presented.

16.2. Preliminary results in the area of EVT for heavy tails and asymptotic behavior of MO_p functionals

In the area of statistics of univariate extremes and whenever working with large values, i.e. with the right-tail of the model F underlying the data, a model F is often said to be *heavy-tailed* whenever the right-tail function $\overline{F} \in \mathcal{R}_{-1/\xi}, \xi > 0$. Then, $F \in \mathcal{D}_{\mathcal{M}}(EV_\xi)_{\xi>0} =: \mathcal{D}_{\mathcal{M}}^+$ and reciprocally, if $F \in \mathcal{D}_{\mathcal{M}}^+$, we necessarily have $\overline{F} \in \mathcal{R}_{-1/\xi}$ (Gnedenko 1943).

16.2.1. *A brief review of first- and second-order conditions*

If $F \in \mathcal{D}_{\mathcal{M}}^+$, and with the notation $F^{\leftarrow}(t) := \inf\{x : F(x) \geq t\}$ for the generalized inverse function of F, the reciprocal tail quantile function $U(t) := F^{\leftarrow}(1 - 1/t)$ is of regular variation with index ξ (de Haan 1984), i.e. we usually work with any of the first-order conditions:

$$F \in \mathcal{D}_{\mathcal{M}}^+ \iff \overline{F} \in \mathcal{R}_{-1/\xi} \iff U \in \mathcal{R}_\xi.$$ [16.5]

The *second-order parameter* ρ (≤ 0) rules the rate of convergence in the first-order condition, in equation [16.5], and can be defined as the non-positive parameter appearing in the limiting relation:

$$\lim_{t \to \infty} \frac{\ln U(tx) - \ln U(t) - \xi \ln x}{A(t)} = \psi_\rho(x) := \begin{cases} \frac{x^\rho - 1}{\rho}, & \text{if } \rho < 0, \\ \ln x, & \text{if } \rho = 0, \end{cases} \qquad [16.6]$$

which is assumed to hold for every $x > 0$, and where $|A| \in \mathcal{R}_\rho$ (Geluk and Haan 1987). This condition has been widely accepted as an appropriate condition to specify the right-tail of a Pareto-type distribution in a semi-parametric way and easily enables the derivation of the non-degenerate asymptotic bias of EVI-estimators, under a semi-parametric framework.

16.2.2. *Asymptotic behavior of the Hill EVI-estimators*

To have consistent Hill estimators, in all $\mathcal{D}_\mathcal{M}^+$, we need to work with intermediate values of k, i.e. a sequence of integers $k = k_n, 1 \leq k < n$, such that:

$$k = k_n \to \infty \quad \text{and} \quad k_n = o(n), \text{ as } n \to \infty. \qquad [16.7]$$

Under the aforementioned second-order framework, in equation [16.6], the asymptotic distributional representation

$$\mathrm{H}(k) - \xi \overset{d}{=} \frac{\xi}{\sqrt{k}} Z_k + \frac{A(n/k)}{1 - \rho} \left(1 + o_p(1)\right) \qquad [16.8]$$

holds (de Haan and Peng 1998), where, with $\{E_i\}$ being a sequence of IID standard exponential RVs, $Z_k = \sqrt{k} \left(\sum_{i=1}^{k} E_i/k - 1 \right)$ is asymptotically standard normal.

REMARK 16.1.– *For the Hill estimator, and whenever needed, we often consider the most common estimate of $k_{0|0} \equiv k_{0|H}(n) := \arg\min_k \mathrm{MSE}(\mathrm{H}_0(k))$ (Hall 1982), given by:*

$$\hat{k}_{0|0} = \min \left(n - 1, \left[\left((1 - \hat{\rho})^2 n^{-2\hat{\rho}} / \left(-2\,\hat{\rho}\,\hat{\beta}^2 \right) \right)^{1/(1-2\hat{\rho})} \right] + 1 \right), \qquad [16.9]$$

with $(\hat{\beta}, \hat{\rho})$ being the adequate estimates of the vector (β, ρ) of second-order parameters. References to the estimation of second-order parameters can be found in Caeiro et al. (2016), among others. However, the estimate $\hat{\xi}_0 := \mathrm{H}(\hat{k}_{0|0})$ usually has a high positive bias, and alternatives are often needed.

16.2.3. *Asymptotic behavior of MO$_p$ EVI-estimators under a regular framework*

More generally, for the distributional representation in equation [16.8], we refer to the main theorem in Brilhante et al. (2013) (see also Gomes and Caeiro (2014); Caeiro et al. (2016)):

THEOREM 16.1 (Brilhante et al. 2013, Gomes and Caeiro 2014, Caeiro et al. 2016).– *Under the validity of the first-order condition, in equation [16.5], and for intermediate sequences $k = k_n$, i.e. if equation [17.7] holds, the class of estimators $\mathrm{H}_p(k)$, in equation [16.4], is consistent for the estimation of ξ, provided that $p < 1/\xi$.*

Moreover, if we assume the validity of the second-order condition in equation [16.6], the asymptotic distributional representation

$$\mathrm{H}_p(k) - \xi \overset{d}{=} \frac{\sigma_p(\xi)\, Z_k^{(p)}}{\sqrt{k}} + b_p(\xi|\rho)\, A(n/k) + o_p(A(n/k))$$

holds for all $p < 1/(2\xi)$ and $\rho \leq 0$, with $Z_k^{(p)}$ being asymptotically standard normal.

REMARK 16.2.– *For details on the explicit expression of $\sigma_p(\xi)$ and $b_p(\xi, \rho)$, see any of the aforementioned articles.*

16.2.4. *A brief reference to additive stable laws*

Given the sequence $\{X_n\}_{\geq 1}$ of IID RVs, let us assume that, for each $n \in \mathbb{N}$, there exist normalizing constants $A_n > 0$, $B_n \in \mathbb{R}$, such that the linearly normalized sum converges in distribution to a non-degenerate RV, as $n \to \infty$. Then, such an RV is necessarily an additive or sum stable law, denoted by $S_{\alpha,\beta} = S_{\alpha,\beta}(\lambda, \delta)$, i.e. as $n \to \infty$,

$$\frac{\sum_{i=1}^n X_i - B_n}{A_n} \overset{d}{\longrightarrow} S_{\alpha,\beta}(\lambda, \delta). \qquad [16.10]$$

Among other books on the topic, see Gnedenko and Kolmogorov (1954). The scale parameter $\alpha \in (0, 2]$ is the so-called *characteristic exponent* (CE), also related to the tail weight of F and strongly linked to the EVI. The practical use of additive stable laws has been seriously hampered by the fact that the unique so far explicitly known additive stable probability density functions are the ones corresponding to $\alpha = 2$, the normal case, $(\alpha, \beta) = (1, 0)$, the Cauchy case and $(\alpha, \beta) = (1/2, 1)$, the Lévy case.

Regarding the common CDF F, the *generalized central limit theorem* (GCLT) (Samorodnitsky and Taqqu 1994) states that, as $n \to \infty$, the result in equation [16.10] holds if and only if

$$1 - F(x) + F(-x) \in \mathcal{R}_{-\alpha} \quad \text{and} \quad \frac{F(-x)}{1 - F(x) + F(-x)} \xrightarrow[x \to \infty]{} \frac{1 - \beta}{2}.$$

[16.11]

16.2.4.1. *The particular Pareto case*

Let us now consider a unit Pareto RV, Y, with CDF $F_1(y) = 1 - 1/y$, $y \geq 1$, and for $\xi > 0$, Y^ξ, an RV with CDF $F_\xi(y) = 1 - y^{-1/\xi}$, $y \geq 1$, with a right-tail function:

$$\overline{F}_\xi(y) = 1 - F_\xi(y) = y^{-1/\xi}, \quad y \geq 1.$$

On the basis of equation [16.11], since $\overline{F}_\xi \in \mathcal{R}_{-1/\xi}$ and $\beta = 1$, Y^ξ belongs to the additive domain of attraction of a stable law with $\beta = 1$ and a CE given by $\alpha(\xi) = \min\{2, 1/\xi\}$. Let us use the notation $S_\alpha = S_{\alpha,1}$. Then, and asymptotically,

$$\frac{1}{k} \sum_{i=1}^{k} Y_i^\xi = \begin{cases} \frac{1}{1-\xi} + \frac{\xi}{1-\xi}\sqrt{\frac{1}{k(1-2\xi)}}\, S_{2,0}(1 + o_\mathbb{P}(1)), & \text{if } \xi < \frac{1}{2}, \\ \frac{1}{1-\xi} + \sqrt{\frac{\ln k}{k}}\, S_{2,0}(1 + o_\mathbb{P}(1)), & \text{if } \xi = \frac{1}{2}, \\ \frac{1}{1-\xi} + k^{\xi-1}\left\{\frac{\xi\Gamma(2-1/\xi)|\cos(\pi/(2\xi))|}{1-\xi}\right\}^\xi S_{1/\xi}(1 + o_\mathbb{P}(1)), & \text{if } \frac{1}{2} < \xi < 1, \\ \ln k + 1 - \gamma - \ln(2/\pi) + \frac{\pi}{2} S_1(1 + o_\mathbb{P}(1)), & \text{if } \xi = 1, \\ k^{\xi-1}\left\{\Gamma(1 - 1/\xi)\cos(\pi/(2\xi))\right\}^\xi S_{1/\xi}(1 + o_\mathbb{P}(1)), & \text{if } \xi > 1. \end{cases}$$

[16.12]

16.2.5. *Asymptotic behavior of EVI-estimators under a non-regular framework*

We next state the main theorem in Gomes et al. (2020), a generalization of **Theorem 16.1** to non-regular cases.

THEOREM 16.2 (Gomes et al. 2020).– *Under the validity of the first-order condition, in equation [16.5], and for intermediate sequences $k = k_n$, i.e. if [16.7] holds, the class of functionals $H_p(k)$, in equation [16.4], is consistent for the estimation of ξ, provided that $p \leq 1/\xi$ and converges to $1/p$ $(< \xi)$ if $p > 1/\xi$.*

*In the region of values of p out of the scope of **Theorem 16.1**, i.e. $1/(2\xi) \leq p \leq 1/\xi$, if we assume the validity of the second-order condition in equation [16.6], the following asymptotic distributional representations hold:*

(ii) If $p = 1/(2\xi)$, with $S_{2,0} \equiv \mathcal{N}(0, 1)$, an asymptotically centered normal,

$$H_p(k) - \xi \stackrel{d}{=} \frac{S_{2,0}}{4p\sqrt{k/\ln k}} + \frac{A(n/k)}{1 - 2\rho} + o_p(A(n/k)).$$

(i) *If $1/(2\xi) < p < 1/\xi$, with $S_\alpha \equiv S_{\alpha,1}$ asymptotically stable with a CE $\alpha = 1/(p\xi)$, we obtain the validity of the asymptotic distributional representation,*

$$H_p(k) - \xi \stackrel{d}{=} \frac{\sigma_p^*(\xi)\,S_\alpha}{k^{1-p\xi}} + b_p(\xi|\rho)\,A(n/k) + o_p(A(n/k)).$$

(iii) *If $p = 1/\xi$, with S_1 asymptotically sum-stable with a CE, $\alpha = 1$, and with $\omega = 1 - \gamma - \ln(2/\pi)$, γ denoting Euler's constant,*

$$H_p(k) - \xi \stackrel{d}{=} -\frac{\xi}{\ln k} + \xi\left(\frac{w + \pi/2\,S_1}{\ln^2 k} - \frac{pA(n/k)}{\rho\ln k}\right)(1 + o_{\mathbb{P}}(1)).$$

We now further state the following:

THEOREM 16.3.– *Under the first-order condition in equation* [16.5]*, and for any $k = k_n \to \infty$, not necessarily intermediate,*

$$H_p(k) - \xi \stackrel{d}{=} -\frac{\xi}{\ln k}(1 + o_{\mathbb{P}}(1)), \quad \text{if} \quad p = 1/\xi, \qquad [16.13]$$

and

$$H_p(k) - 1/p \stackrel{d}{=} O_{\mathbb{P}}\left(1/k^{p\xi - 1}\right), \quad \text{if} \quad p > 1/\xi. \qquad [16.14]$$

PROOF.– For any $1 \leq k < n$, the distributional identity,

$$H_p(k) \stackrel{d}{=} \frac{1}{p}\left(1 - \left(\frac{1}{k}\sum_{i=1}^{k} Y_i^{\xi p}(1 + o_{\mathbb{P}}(1))\right)^{-1}\right) \qquad [16.15]$$

holds. As mentioned in Caeiro et al. (2016), the term $o_{\mathbb{P}}(1)$ above is uniform in i, $1 \leq i \leq k$. This comes from the results in Drees (1998) (see Theorem B.2.18 in de Haan and Ferreira (2006)), jointly with the fact that for uniform order statistics $U_{i:n}, 1 \leq i \leq n$, we have $1/U_{i:n}$, which can be uniformly bounded in probability by $C[i/(n+1)]^{-1}$ (for some constant C). [16.12], [16.13] and [16.14] follow.

16.3. Finite-sample behavior of MO_p functionals

The Monte Carlo simulations, already performed in Gomes et al. (2020, 2021), were extended to other models, like the $Burr_{\xi,\rho}$ models, with CDF $F(x) = 1 - \left(1 + x^{-\rho/\xi}\right)^{1/\rho}$, $x \geq 0$, with $\xi > 0$ and $\rho < 0$, the ones presented in this chapter. Multi-sample Monte Carlo simulations of size $5,000 \times 20$ (20 replicates of 5,000 runs each) were performed. The details on multi-sample simulation can be seen in Gomes and Oliveira (2001).

n	100	200	2000	5000
\multicolumn{5}{c}{BURR$_{\xi,\rho}$ parent, $\xi = 1$, $\rho = -0.1$}				
H_0	3.256 ± 0.0088	2.814 ± 0.0069	2.100 ± 0.0137	1.947 ± 0.0101
$H_{0.1}$	2.588 ± 0.0057	2.328 ± 0.0049	1.812 ± 0.0095	1.717 ± 0.0141
$H_{0.4}$	1.949 ± 0.0030	1.824 ± 0.0028	1.523 ± 0.0031	1.435 ± 0.0028
$H_{0.5}$	1.698 ± 0.0021	1.612 ± 0.0022	1.389 ± 0.0024	1.320 ± 0.0023
$H_{0.9}$	1.084 ± 0.0019	1.080 ± 0.0014	1.063 ± 0.0011	1.057 ± 0.0009
H_1	$\mathbf{1.000} \pm 0.0000$	$\mathbf{1.000} \pm 0.0000$	$\mathbf{1.000} \pm 0.0000$	$\mathbf{1.000} \pm 0.0000$
$H_{1.1}$	0.909 ± 0.0000	0.909 ± 0.0000	0.909 ± 0.0000	0.909 ± 0.0000
$H_{1.2}$	0.833 ± 0.0000	0.833 ± 0.0000	0.833 ± 0.0000	1.000 ± 0.0000
\multicolumn{5}{c}{BURR$_{\xi,\rho}$ parent, $\xi = 1$, $\rho = -0.5$}				
H_0	1.295 ± 0.0086	1.242 ± 0.0048	1.131 ± 0.0027	1.102 ± 0.0022
$H_{0.1}$	1.233 ± 0.0065	1.198 ± 0.0046	1.115 ± 0.0026	1.092 ± 0.0020
$H_{0.4}$	1.156 ± 0.0047	1.142 ± 0.0035	1.098 ± 0.0018	1.083 ± 0.0018
$H_{0.5}$	1.119 ± 0.0041	1.113 ± 0.0039	1.083 ± 0.0017	1.072 ± 0.0010
$H_{0.9}$	1.028 ± 0.0008	1.023 ± 0.0006	1.014 ± 0.0002	1.012 ± 0.002
H_1	$\mathbf{1.000} \pm 0.0000$	$\mathbf{1.000} \pm 0.0000$	$\mathbf{1.000} \pm 0.0000$	$\mathbf{1.000} \pm 0.0000$
$H_{1.1}$	0.909 ± 0.0000	0.909 ± 0.0000	0.909 ± 0.0000	0.909 ± 0.0000
$H_{1.2}$	0.833 ± 0.0000	0.833 ± 0.0000	0.833 ± 0.0000	1.000 ± 0.0000
\multicolumn{5}{c}{BURR$_{\xi,\rho}$ parent, $\xi = 1$, $\rho = -1$}				
H_0	1.138 ± 0.0042	1.110 ± 0.0033	1.050 ± 0.0010	1.037 ± 0.0009
$H_{0.1}$	1.111 ± 0.0027	1.093 ± 0.0030	1.045 ± 0.0010	1.033 ± 0.0006
$H_{0.4}$	1.092 ± 0.0026	1.080 ± 0.0020	1.046 ± 0.0007	1.035 ± 0.0007
$H_{0.5}$	1.075 ± 0.0024	1.065 ± 0.0018	1.042 ± 0.0008	1.034 ± 0.0006
$H_{0.9}$	1.018 ± 0.0005	1.015 ± 0.0001	1.010 ± 0.0001	1.008 ± 0.0001
H_1	$\mathbf{0.998} \pm 0.0001$	$\mathbf{0.999} \pm 0.0000$	$\mathbf{1.000} \pm 0.0000$	$\mathbf{1.000} \pm 0.0000$
$H_{1.1}$	0.908 ± 0.0001	0.909 ± 0.0000	0.909 ± 0.0000	0.909 ± 0.0000
$H_{1.2}$	0.833 ± 0.0000	0.833 ± 0.0000	0.833 ± 0.0000	1.000 ± 0.0000

Table 16.1. *Simulated mean values, at optimal levels, of* $\mathrm{H}_p(k)/\xi$, $p\xi = 0, 0.1, 0.4, 0.5, 0.9, 1, 1.1, 1.2$, *for BURR$_{\xi,\rho}$ underlying parents,* $\xi = 1$, $\rho = -0.1, -0.5, -1$, *together with 95% confidence intervals*

Apart from the simulated mean values, at optimal levels, in the sense of minimal *mean square error* (MSE), presented in Table 16.1, we also present an indicator of the *relative efficiency* (REFF) in Table 16.2, given by:

$$\mathrm{REFF}_{p|0} = \frac{\mathrm{RMSE}(\mathrm{H}_{00})}{\mathrm{RMSE}(\mathrm{H}_{p0})} := \sqrt{\frac{\mathrm{MSE}(\mathrm{H}_{00})}{\mathrm{MSE}(\mathrm{H}_{p0})}} =: \frac{\mathrm{RMSE}_{00}}{\mathrm{RMSE}_{p0}},$$

where H_{p0} is the $\mathrm{H}_p(k)$ EVI-estimator computed at the simulated value of $k_{0|p} := \arg\min_k \mathrm{MSE}(\mathrm{H}_p(k))$. For each model, the smallest bias, in Table 16.1, and the highest REFF, in Table 6.2, are written in **bold**.

n	100	200	2000	5000
	BURR$_{\xi,\rho}$ parent, $\xi = 1$, $\rho = -0.1$			
RMSE$_{00}$	2.592 ± 0.2304	2.133 ± 0.2287	1.326 ± 0.2224	1.134 ± 0.2197
$\mathrm{H}_{0.1}$	1.188 ± 0.0013	1.163 ± 0.0009	1.113 ± 0.0030	1.092 ± 0.0022
$\mathrm{H}_{0.2}$	1.475 ± 0.0027	1.408 ± 0.0016	1.291 ± 0.0042	1.249 ± 0.0037
$\mathrm{H}_{0.4}$	2.535 ± 0.0065	2.323 ± 0.0039	1.960 ± 0.0080	1.855 ± 0.0057
$\mathrm{H}_{0.5}$	3.467 ± 0.0097	3.133 ± 0.0062	2.555 ± 0.0112	2.390 ± 0.0077
$\mathrm{H}_{0.9}$	26.030 ± 0.1132	22.231 ± 0.0936	15.580 ± 0.0810	14.011 ± 0.0708
H_1	∞	∞	∞	∞
$\mathrm{H}_{1.1}$	28.514 ± 0.1025	23.464 ± 0.0777	14.588 ± 0.0757	12.469 ± 0.0453
$\mathrm{H}_{1.2}$	15.553 ± 0.0559	12.798 ± 0.0424	7.957 ± 0.0413	6.801 ± 0.0247
	BURR$_{\xi,\rho}$ parent, $\xi = 1$, $\rho = -0.5$			
RMSE$_{00}$	0.478 ± 0.1981	0.381 ± 0.1917	0.193 ± 0.1679	0.150 ± 0.1579
$\mathrm{H}_{0.1}$	1.074 ± 0.0011	1.059 ± 0.0008	1.034 ± 0.0008	1.029 ± 0.0006
$\mathrm{H}_{0.4}$	1.484 ± 0.0047	1.375 ± 0.0047	1.159 ± 0.0043	1.110 ± 0.0055
$\mathrm{H}_{0.5}$	1.761 ± 0.0058	1.603 ± 0.0063	1.260 ± 0.0051	1.175 ± 0.0073
$\mathrm{H}_{0.9}$	8.404 ± 0.0343	7.448 ± 0.0411	4.998 ± 0.0141	4.277 ± 0.0230
H_1	∞	∞	∞	∞
$\mathrm{H}_{1.1}$	5.253 ± 0.0225	4.196 ± 0.0231	2.128 ± 0.0090	1.654 ± 0.0083
$\mathrm{H}_{1.2}$	2.865 ± 0.0123	$2.289 \pm 0,0126$	1.160 ± 0.0049	0.9020 ± 0.0045
	BURR$_{\xi,\rho}$ parent, $\xi = 1$, $\rho = -1$			
RMSE$_{00}$	0.266 ± 0.1740	0.205 ± 0.1656	0.090 ± 0.1356	0.066 ± 0.1231
$\mathrm{H}_{0.1}$	1.047 ± 0.0013	1.038 ± 0.0011	1.023 ± 0.0009	1.020 ± 0.0009
$\mathrm{H}_{0.4}$	1.257 ± 0.0048	1.178 ± 0.0056	1.025 ± 0.0071	0.985 ± 0.0074
$\mathrm{H}_{0.5}$	1.415 ± 0.0063	1.288 ± 0.0068	1.018 ± 0.0081	0.943 ± 0.0090
$\mathrm{H}_{0.9}$	5.743 ± 0.0331	4.924 ± 0.0231	2.849 ± 0.0170	2.268 ± 0.0134
H_1	$\mathbf{88.50 \pm 0.782}$	$\mathbf{151.87 \pm 10.13}$	∞	∞
$\mathrm{H}_{1.1}$	2.894 ± 0.0140	2.2433 ± 0.0112	0.994 ± 0.0039	0.724 ± 0.0029
$\mathrm{H}_{1.2}$	1.590 ± 0.0077	1.228 ± 0.0062	0.542 ± 0.0021	0.395 ± 0.0016

Table 16.2. *Simulated RMSE of* H_{00}/ξ *(first row of any model) and REFF-indicators of* H_p, $p\xi = 0.1, 0.4, 0.5, 0.9, 1, 1.1, 1.2$, *for BURR$_{\xi,\rho}$ underlying parents, $\xi = 1$, $\rho = -0.1, -0.5, -1$, together with 95% confidence intervals*

A visualization of both tables is provided in Figure 16.1.

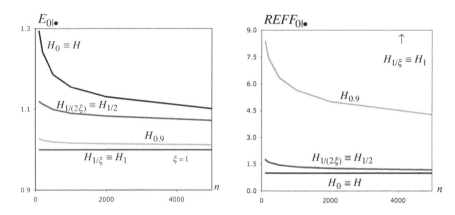

Figure 16.1. *Simulated optimal mean values (left) and REFF indicators (right), as a function of n for a $BURR_{\xi,\rho}$ parent with $\xi = 1$ and $\rho = -0.5$. For a color version of the figure, see www.iste.co.uk/zafeiris/data2.zip*

On the basis of the first replica of size 5,000, we finally present, in Figure 16.2, the simulated mean values and *root mean squared errors* (RMSEs), as a function of k, and also for a $BURR_{\xi,\rho}$ model with $\xi = -\rho = 1$.

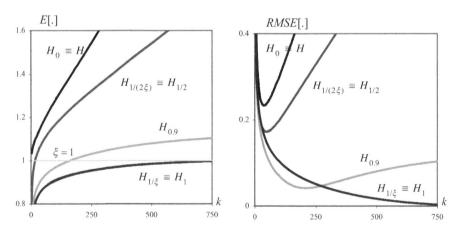

Figure 16.2. *Mean values (left) and RMSEs (right) as a function of k, for a $BURR_{\xi,\rho}$ model with $\xi = -\rho = 1$. For a color version of the figure, see www.iste.co.uk/zafeiris/data2.zip*

16.4. A non-regular adaptive choice of p and k

It seems sensible to take $k = n - 1$ and $p = 1/\xi$, but ξ is not known. And if $p\xi > 1$, $H_p(k)$ converges to $1/p < \xi$. Let us thus consider the following procedure:

Algorithm

– compute an initial EVI-estimate, $\widehat{\xi}_0 = H(\hat{k}_{0|0})$, with $\hat{k}_{0|0}$ given in equation [16.9];

– for p = $0.01(0.01) \cdots$, compute $p_{min} := \arg\min_{p}(H_p(n - 1) - \widehat{\xi}_0)^2$;

– consider the estimate $\hat{\xi} = 1/p_{min}$.

To illustrate the performance of the algorithm, sample sizes from n = 100 to n = 5000 were simulated from a set of underlying models that include the Burr$_{\xi,\rho}$ models with $\xi = \{0.5, 1\}$ and $\rho = \{-0.5, -1\}$, the Student-t_ν, with $\nu = 2$ degrees-of-freedom ($\xi = 1/\nu = 0.5$), the Cauchy model, $\xi = 1$, the Generalised Pareto model, GP$_\xi$, with $\xi = \{0.5, 1\}$ and the Fréchet model with $\xi = 0.5$. The results are summarized in Table 16.3.

n	100	200	1000	2000	5000
Burr$_{\xi,\rho}$ parent, $\xi = 0.5$, $\rho = -0.5$					
$|\hat{\xi} - \xi|$	0.0098	0.0074	0.0291	0.0051	0.0098
Burr$_{\xi,\rho}$ parent, $\xi = 0.5$, $\rho = -1$					
$|\hat{\xi} - \xi|$	0.0435	0.0348	0.0076	0.0098	0.0051
Burr$_{\xi,\rho}$ parent, $\xi = 1$, $\rho = -0.5$					
$|\hat{\xi} - \xi|$	0.1364	0.1111	0.0204	0.0989	0.0417
Burr$_{\xi,\rho}$ parent, $\xi = 1$, $\rho = -1$					
$|\hat{\xi} - \xi|$	0.0638	0.0204	0.01010	0.0291	0.0291
Student t_2 parent, $\xi = 0.5$					
$|\hat{\xi} - \xi|$	0.0076	0.0102	0.0025	0.0098	0.0051
Cauchy parent, $\xi = 1$, $\rho = -2$					
$|\hat{\xi} - \xi|$	0.0417	0.0638	0.0196	0.0101	0.0099
GP$_\xi$ parent, $\xi = 0.5$					
$|\hat{\xi} - \xi|$	0.0263	0.0128	0.0128	0.0025	0.0025
GP$_\xi$ parent, $\xi = 1$					
$|\hat{\xi} - \xi|$	0.0870	0.0870	0.0309	0.0000	0.0204
Fréchet$_\xi$ parent, $\xi = 0.5$					
$|\hat{\xi} - \xi|$	0.0025	0.0098	0.0122	0.0283	0.0902

Table 16.3. *Absolute bias of the adaptive MO$_p$ EVI-estimates provided by the Algorithm for several selected models*

The results obtained for the simulated samples show that the algorithm performs well for most of the models. However, the performance of the algorithm is strongly dependent on the initial EVI-estimate. If the bias of the initial EVI estimate is small, then the bias of the MO_p EVI-estimate will also be small. Other initial EVI-estimates, like the reduced bias EVI-estimates in Caeiro et al. (2005), could also be considered. The result for a simulation study of the algorithm compared to other adequate adaptive algorithms, is a topic outside the scope of this chapter.

16.5. Concluding remarks

It has been clear for a long time that the H EVI-estimators often lead to a high over-estimation of the EVI, even at optimal levels, in the sense of minimal MSE. The use of the extra tuning parameter $p \in \mathbb{R}$ and the MO_p methodology can thus provide a much more adequate EVI-estimation, with asymptotic normality achieved for $p \leq 1/(2\xi)$. But we can now go up to $p = 1/\xi$, then obtaining a sum-stable behavior, with an index of sum-stability $\alpha = 1/(p\xi)$. And for $p = 1/\xi$, we obtain, for $H_p(k) - \xi$, a deterministic dominant component, of the order of $1/\ln k$. The challenge is not to go beyond $p = 1/\xi$. But the algorithm discussed in section 16.4 is able to perform such a goal in a great variety of situations. Further note that for the adaptive choice of (p, k) a double-bootstrap algorithm, the type used in Brilhante et al. (2013), can be used, with some minor modifications. However, such an algorithm relies too much on the finite variance of the normal asymptotic RV associated with the asymptotic behavior of $H_p(k)$, and needs to be slightly modified as it is still under study. And the simple heuristic algorithm presented above seems to work adequately in a great variety of situations.

16.6. References

Beran, J., Schell, D., Stehlik, M. (2014). The harmonic moment tail index estimator: Asymptotic distribution and robustness. *Annals of the Institute of Statistical Mathematics*, 66, 193–220.

Bingham, N., Goldie, C.M., Teugels, J.L. (1987). *Regular Variation*. Cambridge University Press, Cambridge.

Brilhante, M.F., Gomes, M.I., Pestana, D.D. (2013). A simple generalization of the hill estimator. *Computational Statistics and Data Analysis*, 57(1), 518–535.

Caeiro, F., Gomes, M.I., Pestana, D.D. (2005). Direct reduction of bias of the classical Hill estimator. *Revstat Statistical Journal*, 3(2), 113–136.

Caeiro, F., Gomes, M.I., Beirlant, J., de Wet, T. (2016). Mean-of-order-*p* reduced-bias extreme value index estimation under a third-order framework. *Extremes*, 19(4), 561–589.

Drees, H. (1998). A general class of estimators of the extreme value index. *Journal of Statistical Planning and Inference*, 98, 95–112.

Geluk, J. and de Haan, L. (1987). *Regular Variation, Extensions and Tauberian Theorems*. CWI Tract 40, Center for Mathematics and Computer Science, Amsterdam.

Gnedenko, B.V. (1943). Sur la distribution limite du terme maximum d'une série aléatoire. *Annals of Mathematics*, 44, 6, 423–453.

Gnedenko, B.V. and Kolmogorov, A.N. (1954). *Limit Distributions for Sums of Independent Random Variables*. Addison-Wesley, Reading, MA.

Gomes, M.I. and Caeiro, F. (2014). Efficiency of partially reduced-bias mean-of-order-p versus minimum-variance reduced-bias extreme value index estimation. In *Proceedings of COMPSTAT 2014*, Gilli, M., González-Rodríguez, G., Nieto-Reyes, A. (eds). The International Statistical Institute/International Association for Statistical Computing, The Hague.

Gomes, M.I. and Oliveira, O. (2001). The bootstrap methodology in statistical extremes: Choice of the optimal sample fraction. *Extremes*, 4(4), 331–358.

Gomes, M.I., Henriques-Rodrigues, L., Pestana, D. (2020). Non-regular frameworks and the mean-of-order p extreme value index estimation [Online]. Available at: https://doi.org/10.13140/RG.2.2.28347.64804.

Gomes, M.I., Henriques-Rodrigues, L., Pestana, D. (2021). Estimação de um índice de valores extremos positivo através de médias generalizadas e em ambiente de não–regularidade. In *Estatística: Desafios Transversais às Ciências com Dados–Atas do XXIV Congresso da Sociedade Portuguesa de Estatística*, Milheiro, P., Pacheco, A., de Sousa, B., Alves, I.F., Pereira, I., Polidoro, M.J., Ramos, S. (eds). Edições SPE, Lisbon.

de Haan, L. (1984). Slow variation and characterization of domains of attraction. In *Statistical Extremes and Applications*, Tiago de Oliveira, J. (ed.). D. Reidel, Dordrecht.

de Haan, L. and Ferreira, A. (2006). *Extreme Value Theory: An Introduction*. Springer Science+Business Media, LLC, New York.

de Haan, L. and Peng, L. (1998). Comparison of extreme value index estimators. *Statistica Neerlandica*, 52, 60–70.

Hall, P. (1982). On some simple estimates of an exponent of regular variation. *Journal of the Royal Statistical Society*, 44, 37–42.

Hill, B.M. (1975). A simple general approach to inference about the tail of a distribution. *Annals of Statistics*, 3, 1163–1174.

Jenkinson, A.F. (1955). The frequency distribution of the annual maximum (or minimum) values of meteorological elements. *Quarterly Journal of the Royal Meteorological Society*, 81, 158–171.

von Misès, R. (1954). La distribution de la plus grande de n valeurs. *Selected Papers*, Vol II, American Mathematical Society, 271–294.

Paulauskas, V. and Vaičiulis, M. (2013). On the improvement of Hill and some others estimators. *Lithuanian Mathematical Journal*, 53, 336–355.

Paulauskas, V. and Vaičiulis, M. (2017). A class of new tail index estimators. *Annals of the Institute of Statistical Mathematics*, 69, 661–487.

Samorodnitsky, G. and Taqqu, M. (1994). *Stable Non-Gaussian Random Processes–Stochastic Models with Infinite Variance*. Chapman & Hall, Boca Raton, FL.

Seneta, E. (1976). *Regularly Varying Functions*. Springer-Verlag, Berlin.

Demography and Policies in V4 Countries

This chapter deals with the analysis of recent and currently-planned policies in relation to demographic development in the countries of the Visegrad Group (V4). V4 is an alliance of four Central European countries, including the Czech Republic, Hungary, Poland and Slovakia.

In addition to analyzing the current and recent situation, this chapter also deals with estimates of future fertility and mortality levels in these countries. It shows there are quite significant differences in the political laws in the natalist policy and in the pension system of individual countries and, at the same time, places them in the context of the future further aging of populations, which can be, based on projections, expected in all of the Visegrad countries.

17.1. Introduction

As the name suggests, the Visegrad Four regional group (abbreviated as V4) includes four Central European countries – the Czech Republic, Hungary, Poland and Slovakia. The group was established in 1991 based on a declaration signed by the V4 member countries, the aim of which is to cooperate on a common path to European integration. The task of the group is mainly the modernization of public administration, its information and educational systems. Following the accession of all V4 countries to the European Union in 2004, the group has focused on promoting cooperation and stability in the Central European countries (MVCR 2019).

Chapter written by Michaela KADLECOVÁ, Filip HON and Jitka LANGHAMROVÁ.
For a color version of all the figures in this chapter, see www.iste.co.uk/zafeiris/data2.zip.

This chapter describes the demographic situation in the Visegrad Four countries. The description also focuses on links between the policies of individual countries, such as family and natalist policy or the policy of pension systems. The first part of this chapter presents the demographic situation of individual countries, the second part describes fertility and its relationship with family and natalist policy, the third part focuses on the increasing life expectancy and its impact on pension systems and the last part presents a prediction of demographic development in the Visegrad Four countries. The aim is to find the link between individual policies and demographic development and discover how the population could develop in the future.

17.2. Demographic development in the V4 countries

The first part of this chapter focuses on the evaluation of current demographic development in the four monitored countries. The historical development was documented from 1990, i.e. one year before the establishment of the V4 regional group, until the year current data are available, i.e. 2019, or for some indicators until 2018.

All the monitored countries have undergone a transformation in terms of society and the political system since 1990, and these changes have also affected the demographic development of the population. Before 1989, the Czech Republic, Hungary, Poland and Slovakia were under the rule of the Communist political regime of the former Soviet Union. However, in 1989, there was a coup in all of these countries, after 1989, democracy began to form. Thanks to this, new economic and political issues began to be addressed very intensively. At that time, the Czech Republic and Slovakia were still one country – Czechoslovakia – which split into two countries on January 1, 1993 (Visegrad Group 2021). However, with new opportunities, such as business or traveling, the priorities of the population have also changed, affecting demographic reproduction.

The following figures will help to better visualize how the demographic behavior of individual populations changed and better compare the populations with each other. A figure of the development of the shares of biological generations as well as a table of age indices is used to evaluate the age of the population. Biological generations can be described as three groups of population according to reproduction. The first biological generation are children up to 15 years, the second of these generations are parents between 15 and 49 years and the third biological generation are grandparents from 50 years old.

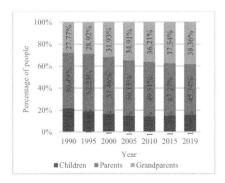

Figure 17.1. *Development of the shares of biological generations in the Czech Republic in the years 1990–2019 (data source: Eurostat, own processing)*

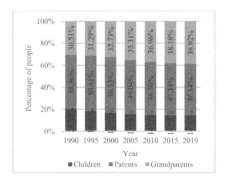

Figure 17.2. *Development of the shares of biological generations in Hungary in the years 1990–2019 (data source: Eurostat, own processing)*

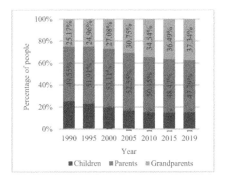

Figure 17.3. *Development of the shares of biological generations in Poland in the years 1990–2019 (data source: Eurostat, own processing)*

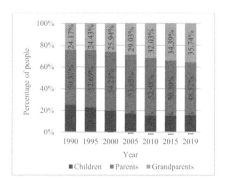

Figure 17.4. *Development of the shares of biological generations in Slovakia in the years 1990–2019 (data source: Eurostat, own processing)*

Based on Figures 17.1–17.4, which describe the development of biological generations in the V4 countries from 1990 to 2019, it is possible to evaluate the gradual increase in the share of the grandparent generation in the entire population, in all monitored countries. At the expense of this large gradual increase, the share of the parental and children components is declining. The result is a process called population aging. However, to confirm this phenomenon, it is appropriate to also point out other characteristics of the age of the population. This is, for example, the Sauvy age index, the development of which is shown in Table 17.1. The Sauvy age index can be defined as a proportion between grandparents and children described according to biological generations.

Sauvy age index	1990	1995	2000	2005	2010	2015	2019
Czechia	1.28	1.53	1.92	2.34	2.54	2.47	2.41
Hungary	1.49	1.71	1.93	2.26	2.51	2.64	2.67
Poland	1.00	1.08	1.37	1.84	2.26	2.43	2.43
Slovakia	0.95	1.07	1.31	1.70	2.07	2.25	2.27

Table 17.1. *Development of the Sauvy age index in 1990–2019 (data source: Eurostat, own processing)*

From Table 17.1, it is clear that in all the monitored countries, there has been a significant increase in the Sauvy age index since 1990. While in 1990 the index was around 1 or a maximum of 1.5, in 2019 there was not a single country where the Sauvy age index was below 2. The highest values in all years were in Hungary, while Slovakia had the lowest values of all the monitored countries. The number of seniors over the age of 50 per child is still gradually growing, which again confirms the aging trend of the population in all V4 countries.

The following parts of this chapter analyze fertility in more detail, in relation to family policy measures and subsequently the development of life expectancy and its impact on the pension systems of the monitored countries.

17.3. Development of fertility and family policy

Fertility has a very significant impact in assessing demographic development as it can ensure a sufficient influx of young people into the population, and thus certain economic prospects for the elderly population. Fertility, just like other demographic characteristics, is strongly influenced by the social and political situation in a given country. For this reason, it was also affected by the transformation of the political regimes of the V4 countries after 1989. The development of total fertility in the Visegrad Four is shown in Figure 17.5.

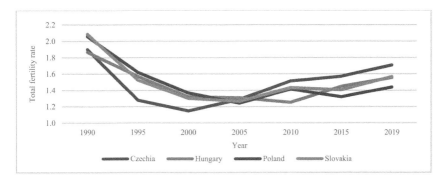

Figure 17.5. *Total fertility in the V4 countries in the years 1990–2018 (data source: Eurostat, own processing)*

Figure 17.5 confirms that the transformation of a socialist society into a democratic one has hit fertility very hard. With the advent of capitalism came many new opportunities – business, traveling, studies and more – which thrilled young people of reproductive age so much that they postponed starting a family, i.e. postponed fertility to an older age or gave it up altogether. In 1990, the total fertility rate was still the highest in the whole monitored period, in all the monitored countries. In Slovakia and Poland, it even reached the limit for maintaining simple reproduction, which is 2.1 children per woman (CZSO 2011). From this year, however, the total fertility rate began to decline rapidly, mostly in the Czech Republic, where in 2000 it fell to 1.15. In the last 10 to 15 years, however, there has been a gradual "rebirth" of total fertility in all the monitored countries, and its values are rising again. The Czech Republic underwent the largest transformation, from a very large drop in 2000 to the highest total fertility in the V4 countries – 1.71

children per woman in 2019. On the contrary, in 2019, very religious Poland had the lowest total fertility rate – 1.44 children per woman.

In the 1990s, we can see one more process in these countries that is called the second demographic transition. This period is typical for lower fertility and the changing position of family in society. So this can be one of the reasons why all fertility rates declined in that period of time.

Fertility rates are often also strongly influenced by a given country's family and natalist policy, which is discussed for each country in the remainder of the chapter. Family policy in all countries of the former socialist regime had the same aspects before 1989, such as relatively long paid maternity leave, wide availability of pre-school facilities and generous family benefits. After the transformation in 1989, all countries had to start building a new family policy of their own. However, there was one common trend of re-familialization, i.e. a shift from universalism to tested benefits, which means the transfer of state responsibility back to families. In any case, the orientations of national family policies have begun to diversify with regard to different cultural and historical customs, and different models of family policies have emerged (Mitchell 2010).

In the 1970s, there was a big population surge in what was then Czechoslovakia due to the introduction of a state pro-natalist policy, which was marked by newlywed loans, new housing for families or increased child allowances. Children born in the 1970s are often referred to as Husák's children (after Secretary General Gustav Husák, who led the policy). These pro-natalist measures lasted several years, until the state ran out of funds (Strašilová 2013). Unfortunately, this is one significant disadvantage of such policies. Pro-natalist measures should be implemented with great care and in a way that is sustainable for the future. Husák's children represented a one-off surge, however, which caused a strong fluctuation in the age structure of the population. If the pro-natalist policy had been more reasonable, not as many children would have been born immediately, but they would have been born at more even intervals over time.

Such strong pro-natalist measures from the 1970s have not been repeated so far. In the 1990s, the opposite situation in fertility actually occurred – its sharp decline. Children born in this period are called "Havel's children". These are children born during the transformation of Czech and Slovak society after 1989. Not only did the price of food and other staples increase, but in 1991 favorable newlywed loans were canceled, which, along with other factors, strongly influenced the decisions of many young people to postpone fertility indefinitely. This led to an increase in the average age of the mother at the birth of her first child and the associated increase in the distance between the generations (Strašilová 2013).

Starting in 2000, the total fertility of Czech women recovered, which can be attributed mainly to the deferred fertility from the 1990s as well as to family policy. In 2005, a national concept of family policy was approved, which aimed to provide more support for families with children, for example, by increasing certain benefits (e.g. parental allowance) or introducing a tax credit per child (MPSV 2005; Sobotka et al. 2008). At present, the family policy of the Czech Republic is still focused on a long maternity leave, which is 28 weeks (37 weeks for multiple births), as well as on a generous period of receiving parental allowance, until the child is four years old (MPSV 2021). Currently, the government plan of the Czech Republic is aiming at multiple motherhood, which could be helped, for example, by supporting housing for young families in the form of favorable housing loans or subsidies for cooperative housing, increasing the number of places in kindergartens or providing financial aid to women with children working part-time or having a flexible work schedule (Tománek 2019).

Hungary went the opposite way in the early 1990s. Instead of abolishing some benefits, its pro-natalist measures continued. In 1985, a second type of childcare allowance was introduced, which, as Kapitány (2008) assumed, increased total fertility in the period 1986–1995 by 8 to 10 percent. However, around 1992, despite the continuing surge of pro-natalist measures, total fertility began to decline due to stronger economic and social transformation. In 1994, there was an increase in fertility in third-born children, which is explained by the introduction of the allowance for mothers with three or more children. Nevertheless, this pro-natalist measure had only a short-term effect as the fertility of third-born children decreased again in the following years. In the second half of the 1990s, financial support for families decreased according to their income, which had a negative impact on middle-income families and especially on high-income families. On the other hand, benefits for low-income families were increased. As a result, the fertility of the most educated women dropped significantly. In general, and in view of rising unemployment, total aggregate fertility then declined (Spéder and Kamarás 2008).

Family policy in Poland in the 1990s can be characterized by gradual declining support for families. Child allowances were abolished, political leadership had not yet been firmly entrenched, unemployment was rising and gross domestic product was falling, making this period very uncertain for starting a family. Social benefits under family policy began to be targeted towards low-income families. Middle-income and high-income families were thus sidelined. For this reason, childlessness grew, which was perceived very negatively in such a religion-based society. However, after 2003, family policy was reformed and several new family support measures were introduced in the following years, such as an increase in family allowances or an extended maternity leave (Spéder and Kamarás 2008). The period of fertility re-growth between 2005 and 2009 was influenced by the country's good economic situation, i.e. growth in gross domestic product and declining unemployment (Kotowska et al. 2008).

The decline in total fertility in Slovakia in the 1990s, just like in other V4 countries, was caused mainly by the transformation of the political system and new economic and social influences, and Slovakia also made changes to family policy. Some benefits began to be derived from the subsistence level. Around 2005, total fertility began to rise again, which could be the result of some positive changes in policy supporting families with children (Spéder and Kamarás 2008). At present, family policy in Slovakia is characterized by the predominantly universal nature of individual measures, which means that entitlement to benefits arises together with life events and is not affected by the level of income (Gerbery 2016). The financial reform in 2004 introduced a tax credit for families with children (Vančurová et al. 2006). Slovak family policy is typical still for long-lasting maternity leave, which is longer than in the Czech Republic; it is 34 weeks (or 43 weeks in the case of multiple births) (Ústredný portál verejnej správy 2020). Parental allowance is provided until the child is three years old[1], which is still a very long time compared to other European countries.

17.4. Pension systems of the Visegrad Four countries

For a comprehensive assessment of the demographic situation in the V4 countries, it is necessary to assess life expectancy, which affects the number of older people in the population and thus the share of the grandparent generation in the population. Figure 17.6 shows the development of life expectancy for the population as a whole, i.e. regardless of gender, in the V4 countries in the period 1990–2018.

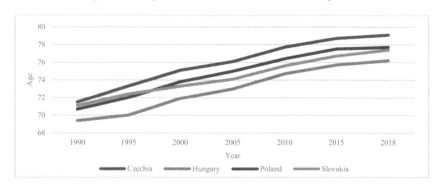

Figure 17.6. *Life expectancy at age 0 in the V4 countries in the years 1990–2018 (data: Eurostat, own processing)*

1 https://www.employment.gov.sk/sk/rodina-socialna-pomoc/podpora-rodinamdetmi/
penazna-pomoc/rodicovsky-prispevok/.

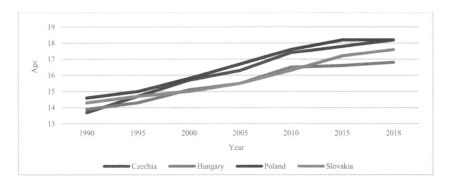

Figure 17.7. *Life expectancy at age 65 in the V4 countries in the years 1990–2018 (data source: Eurostat, own processing)*

Life expectancy is a demographic characteristic that increased in these countries over time, and its further increase can be expected in the future, although the actual projection of life expectancy is discussed later in the chapter. The Czech population had the highest life expectancy at age 0 in all monitored years, as shown in Figure 17.6. On the other hand, Hungary had the lowest life expectancy. Despite this difference between individual countries, it is clear that this average age at death is still rising and thus increasing the number of older people. This also confirms data from the first figures about the shares of biological generations where we can see how much the share of older people, or even grandparents, in the population is increasing.

On the other hand, Figure 17.7 shows life expectancy at age 65. The highest level is reported in Poland, and the lowest is reported in Slovakia and Hungary. It all means that the order of countries is changing with the age of population, and it is also important to look at life expectancy at older age, rather than just at age 0. This characteristic is very important for pension policy because it shows how many people and how long they could live on pensions.

Of course, rising life expectancy does not automatically mean that the population is aging. It is necessary to relate these data to other indicators, such as the shares of biological generations, the age index or the development of fertility. Since these indicators have already been analyzed in previous parts of this chapter, we can conclude that the populations of all V4 countries are aging. The aging of the population also has consequences. One of them is the financing of the pension system. Due to the growing number and share of people in the grandparent generation, it is necessary to take into account the growing old-age pension expenditures. Figure 17.8 shows what the pension liabilities in the individual countries looked like in the year 2015. Pension liabilities represent the funds that will be paid to retired people in the future (CZSO 2018).

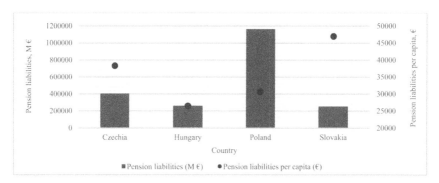

Figure 17.8. *Pension liabilities in the V4 countries in 2015 (data source: Eurostat, own processing)*

Pension liabilities are shown in Figure 17.8 as the total amount for the entire country as well as per capita on pensions. It is clear from the results that Hungary owes the least per capita, while Slovakia owes the most per capita. Pension liabilities are usually expressed as a percentage of gross domestic product, as shown in Table 17.2.

Country	Czechia	Hungary	Poland	Slovakia
% of GDP	239%	232%	270%	319%

Table 17.2. *Share of total pension liabilities on gross domestic product in the V4 countries in 2015 (data source: Eurostat, own processing)*

Slovakia is therefore the country with the highest burden of pension liabilities since they account for 319% of GDP. If the country's gross domestic product were to increase faster than its pension liabilities in the coming years, this share would decrease and the country could better settle its debt towards the population. Despite its high life expectancy and the second highest amount of pension liabilities per capita, the Czech Republic has a low share of pension liabilities on GDP. The reason may be the high gross domestic product, which reduces this share.

The pension systems of the individual countries were also formed after 1989 and differ from each other. The Czech pension system consists of two pillars, namely the first and third pillars. The first pillar is mandatory, and economically active persons pay their pension insurance into it. Every employee pays 6.5% of their salary, and every employer adds another 21.5%. The third pillar is voluntary. Every person can put money into their private pension fund and thus increase their old-age pension paid from the first pillar in the future. The motivation for participating in the third pillar is state aid and, in many cases, also a contribution from the employer (Kadlecová 2020). The Hungarian pension system also consists of two pillars, but – in this case – it is the first and second pillars. The first pillar is mandatory and has defined contributions. Every employee pays 9.5% of their salary, and every employer pays another 24% (Pension Funds Online 2020). The second pillar currently does not provide any ideal opportunities as, after 2010, Viktor Orbán's government almost bankrupted this pillar after the economic crises in order to save the first pillar. However, people are free to decide whether or not to participate in the second pillar (Léko 2011; Kučera and Tůma 2013). Poland's pension system has three pillars. The first pillar consists of mandatory, continuously paid pension insurance, the second pillar is financed from funds and has been mandatory since 1990 for persons who were 30 years of age or younger at that time. The third pillar consists of several pension schemes supported by the state through state contributions or tax credits. Payments into the first pillar represent 19.52% of the gross salary, one half of which is paid by the employee and the other half by the employer. In the case of participation in the second pillar, the contribution to the first pillar is reduced (Dvořáková 2014). The pension system in Slovakia is based on three pillars. The first pillar is almost the same as in the Czech Republic, only with the difference that pension insurance in Slovakia is separate from the state budget. The second pillar consists of old-age pension savings and has defined contributions, i.e. future benefits will depend on paid-in contributions. The third pillar is voluntary, except for people with a high-risk occupation, for whom it is mandatory but the contributions are paid by the employer (Takáč 2019).

17.5. Prediction of future development of V4 populations

We made our own projection of the population up to the year 2050 based on data from the Human Fertility Database and the Human Mortality Database and using the Functional Demographic Model with the settings recommended in the "R" program package called "demography" (Hyndman et al. 2019). The time series was always modeled from 1989 until the current last available year. We then compare the results with the EUROPOP 2019 projection calculated by Eurostat. The projection of demographic indicators of the population is very important for planning the future development of society and for setting the measures of family or natalist policy and the pension system of a given country.

The following figures compare the future development of total fertility in the Visegrad Four countries.

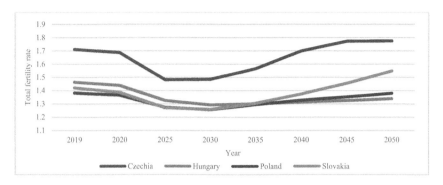

Figure 17.9. *Projection of total fertility in the V4 countries in the years 2019–2050 (data source: Eurostat, own processing)*

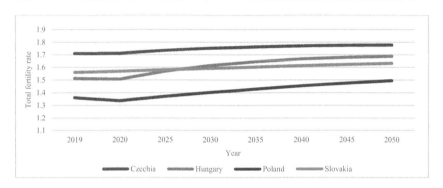

Figure 17.10. *EUROPOP projection of total fertility in the V4 countries in the years 2019–2050 (data source: Eurostat, own processing)*

Our projection slightly differs from the EUROPOP projection. However, both projections show a slight increase in total fertility by 2050, with the exception of Hungary and Poland where total fertility is expected to decline based on our projection. The EUROPOP projection assumes higher total fertility in all monitored countries. It is therefore possible that the current growth will continue, which is also helped by current family policy. As shown in previous chapters, family and natalist policies can have a very significant effect on fertility, so it is important to take into account that if there is a significant change in family policy in the future, there will also be a change in fertility. However, as has already been demonstrated, if all the monitored countries maintain or further improve their existing family policy with certain family-supporting measures, while maintaining their economic growth, it is very likely that fertility will continue to grow. Of course, it is important to keep in mind that changes in family policy must be implemented in a way that is long term or ideally lasting. On the other hand, short-term changes in the form of certain pro-natalist measures can cause a big fluctuation in the age structure of the population, as was the case with the so-called Husák's children in Czechoslovakia in the 1970s.

The result of our projection is first a decrease in total fertility in all the monitored countries but then a return to growth, which in Slovakia and the Czech Republic in 2050 should exceed the total fertility of 2019. The EUROPOP projection has a more optimistic outlook for future developments as it assumes greater growth in total fertility in all countries; based on this outlook, it is possible to expect an increase in the pre-productive component of the population in the future. However, it is also important to mention that it is not possible to expect an increase in fertility to the preservation level of simple reproduction, which is 2.1 children per woman. According to the EUROPOP projection, highest total fertility can be expected in the Czech Republic in 2050, when it will reach the value of 1.78 children per woman. For this reason, the number of children will increase slightly, but not enough to prevent the process of demographic aging of the population.

The second indicator, the future development of which is essential for political decision-making, includes life expectancy, the growth of which, in turn, increases the number of people of post-productive age.

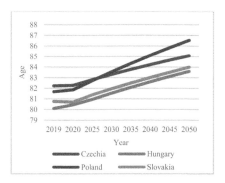

Figure 17.11. *Projection of life expectancy at the age of 0 in the V4 countries in the years 2019–2050, women (data source: Eurostat, own processing)*

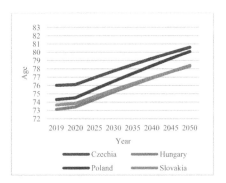

Figure 17.12. *Projection of life expectancy at the age of 0 in the V4 countries in the years 2019–2050, men (data source: Eurostat, own processing)*

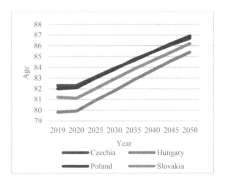

Figure 17.13. *EUROPOP projection of life expectancy at the age of 0 in the V4 countries in the years 2019–2050, women (data source: Eurostat, own processing)*

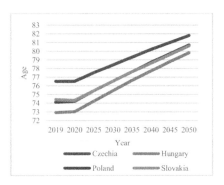

Figure 17.14. *EUROPOP projection of life expectancy at the age of 0 in the V4 countries in the years 2019–2050, men (data source: Eurostat, own processing)*

According to the figures of the future development of life expectancy, an increase in life expectancy for both genders can be expected in all the countries. The life expectancy of women is always higher than that of men due to men's higher mortality. It is therefore necessary to take these data into account when planning the future functioning of the pension system. Due to the increasing life expectancy, the number of people of retirement age will go up, and thus the number of people receiving old-age pension benefits. The financing of the old-age pension will thus become a very important issue in the future. Pension liabilities will also go up due to the increasing number of old-age pensioners. The financing of old-age pensions will thus become an increasing burden. It is therefore necessary to set up the individual pension systems accordingly. In this case, the third pillar of the pension system, which is voluntary and everyone is free to decide whether to put some money aside in order to increase their pension, seems interesting. However, state pensions from mandatory pension insurance are a key issue for all countries. The pay-as-you-go system may be a problem in the future, given that the number of people of working age who contribute to pension insurance will decrease, while the number of people of retirement age who are entitled to the money in the system will increase. Raising the retirement age is a solution that can disburden all the countries and their pension insurance systems. However, this should be done gradually and with regard not only to life expectancy but also to healthy life expectancy, i.e. life expectancy spent in health. The amount of pension insurance contributions and benefits also remains an issue. Pension insurance revenues and expenditures should be balanced and therefore revised. Nevertheless, any potential change should be made slowly and with caution. Every major modification of the system should be implemented gradually and in such a way that people could adapt to it.

17.6. Conclusion

Since 1989, there have been significant demographic changes in all V4 countries, which have been influenced mainly by the political and economic transformation of society. Each of the selected countries underwent similar yet slightly different development. For the whole V4 group, however, the growth of the share of the grandparent biological generation is typically at the expense of the children and parent generations. Just on the basis of initial indicators, including the Sauvy age index, we can see that the populations of these countries are aging.

A closer examination of fertility found that fertility in the 1990s fell sharply in all the countries. Although there was a renewed increase in fertility after the year 2000, total fertility never returned to that of the year 1990. The change in fertility was also strongly influenced by the transformation of family and natalist policy, which took place slightly differently in each country. For each of them, however, we can say that any major change in family policy also affected the overall fertility. The abolition of some contributions was followed by a reduction in fertility, and conversely any increased support for families with children in the form of some benefits led to an increase in total fertility, although it is of course rather difficult to quantify how much the change in fertility was a result of these measures. Fertility is also linked to the population's perception of parenthood as well as security and stability in society, which was a difficult task for the emerging democratic political parties in the 1990s. Unemployment rates or the country's economic situation also have an impact on fertility.

Life expectancy increased in all the countries in the past. However, its growth has an impact on the country's pension policy. Since 1989, all V4 countries have created their own pension systems. It is certainly positive for the future that every pension system has a third pillar, which is voluntary, so that everyone is free to decide whether to save money for old age in order to increase their old-age pension. Hungary is the only country out of the V4 members that does not have a third pillar, so it should learn from its neighbors and consider implementing it. For the sustainability of the pension system in each country, it is essential to make sure that there is enough money to pay old-age pensions, i.e. to meet the state's pension obligation towards its citizens. There are many ways to avoid pressure on the financing of pensions, such as raising the retirement age, increasing pension contributions or decreasing old-age pension benefits. However, it is important to consider the entire impact of these options. Increasing the retirement age could, for example, reduce quality of life, and lowering old-age pension benefits could increase old-age poverty. For this reason, it is even better to look for other solutions, such as promoting labor productivity, thereby increasing economic growth and gross domestic product and obtaining more funds for pension policy. It can be expected that in the future it will no longer be possible to rely on pension insurance contributions from the economically active population.

The projections of future fertility and life expectancy have shown that the population of the V4 countries will continue to age. The total fertility rate is likely to increase slightly by 2050, but not enough to ensure simple reproduction of the population. Life expectancy will continue to grow, with the inhabitants of the Czech Republic living to the highest age. For this reason, it is necessary to expect a further increase in the share of the grandparent generation in the populations of individual countries and thus to place greater emphasis on the creation of family and pension policy.

17.7. Acknowledgments

This work was supported by the Czech Science Foundation within the project no. GAČR 19-03984S under the title "Economy of Successful Ageing" and by the

Internal Grant Agency of Prague University of Economics and Business within the project no. F4/7/2020 under the title "Natalist policy in the Czech Republic".

17.8. References

CZSO (2011). Ukazatele plodnosti. Czech Statistical Office, Prague [Online]. Available at: https://www.czso.cz/documents/10180/20566735/400811a2.pdf/a9be1440-02df-45b7-a7a2-44fea8388f99?version=1.0.

CZSO (2018). Modelování penzijních závazků v ČR a jejich zachycení v tabulce 29. Czech Statistical Office, Prague [Online]. Available at: https://apl.czso.cz/nufile/Penzijni_zavazky_popis.pdf.

Dvořáková, E. (2014). The comparison of selected EU countries pensions systems. Masaryk University, Brno, Czech Republic [Online]. Available at: https://is.muni.cz/th/gfo77/Diplomova_prace_Dvorakova_Eva.pdf.

Gerbery, D. (2016) Slovak family policy in comparative perspective. Katedra sociológie Filozofickej fakulty UK v Bratislave Inštitút pre výskum práce a rodiny v Bratislave [Online]. Available at: https://www.researchgate.net/publication/307583727_Rodinna_politika_na_Slovensku_v_komparativnej_perspektive.

Hyndman, R., Booth, H., Tickle, L., Maindonald, J. (2019). Forecasting mortality, fertility, migration and population data [Online]. Available at: https://cran.r-project.org/web/packages/demography/demography.pdf.

Kadlecová, M. (2020). Ageing of European population from the point of view of pension entitlements. University of Economics, Prague, Czech Republic [Online]. Available at: https://vskp.vse.cz/english/79815.

Kapitány, B. (2008). Az 1985 és 1996 közötti családtámogatási rendszer termékenységre gyakorolt hatása. The "GYED-HATÁS" [The pronatalist effect of the Hungarian GYED system on fertility (1985–1996)]. Demográfia, LI(1), 51–78.

Kotowska, I., Jóźwiak, J., Matysiak, A., Baranowska, A. (2018). Poland: Fertility decline as a response to profound societal and labour market changes? Demographic Research, 19, 795–854 [Online]. Available at: http://www.demographic-research.org/Volumes/Vol19/22/.

Kučera, P. and Tůma, O. (2013). Znárodnění penzijních fondů? Jak dopadly za hranicemi. Economia, a.s.: Aktuálně.cz [Online]. Available at: https://zpravy.aktualne.cz/finance/znarodneni-penzijnich-fondu-jak-dopadly-za-hranicemi/r~i:article:767457/.

Léko, I. (2011). Jak vypadá maďarský penzijní systém. Mafra, a.s. Česká pozice – Informace pro svobodné lidi, ČTK Reuters [Online]. Available at: https://ceskapozice.lidovky.cz/tema/jak-vypada-madarsky-penzijni-system.A110118_063049_pozice_3046.

Mitchell, E. (2010). Finanční podpora rodin s dětmi v České republice v evropském kontextu. Sociologický ústav AV ČR, v.v.i. Prague, Czech Republic [Online]. Available at: https://www.soc.cas.cz/sites/default/files/publikace/m30-eva-mitchell_financni-podpora-rodin-s-detmi-web.pdf.

MPSV (2005). Národní koncepce rodinné politiky. Ministry of Labour and Social Affairs of the Czech Republic, Prague [Online]. Available at: https://www.mpsv.cz/documents/ 20142/372765/koncepce_rodina.pdf/e94cc331-74ad-b2cb-28fc-0b245438e95b.

MPSV (2021a). Nemocenské pojištění v roce 2021. Ministry of Labour and Social Affairs of the Czech Republic, Prague [Online]. Available at: https://www.mpsv.cz/web/cz/ nemocenske-pojisteni#dsnp.

MPSV (2021b). Rodičovský příspěvek. Ministry of Labour and Social Affairs of the Czech Republic, Prague [Online]. Available at: https://www.mpsv.cz/web/cz/-/rodicovsky-prispevek.

MVCR (2019). Visegradská čtyřka. Ministry of the Interior of the Czech Republic, Prague [Online]. Available at: https://www.mvcr.cz/clanek/mezinarodni-organizace-a-vs-visegradska-ctyrka.aspx.

Pension Funds Online (2020). Pension system in Hungary [Online]. Available at: https://www.pensionfundsonline.co.uk/content/country-profiles/hungary.

Sobotka, T., Šťastná, A., Zeman, K., Hamplová, D., Kantorová, V. (2008). Czech Republic: A rapid transformation of fertility and family behaviour after the collapse of state socialism. *Demographic Research*, 19, 403–454 [Online]. Available at: https://www.jstor.org/ stable/26349255.

Spéder, Z. and Kamarás, F. (2008). Hungary: Secular fertility decline with distinct period fluctuations. *Demographic Research*, 19, 559–664 [Online]. Available at: http://www.demographic-research. org/volumes/vol19/18/19-18.pdf.

Strašilová, G. (2013). Husákovy" versus „Havlovy děti". Statistika a my: Měsíčník Českého statistického úřadu. *Praha*, 3(11–12), s. 34–35 [Online]. Available at: http://www.statistikaamy.cz/2013/12/husakovy-versus-havlovy-deti/.

Takáč, D. (2019). 2. důchodový pilíř: Zkušenosti ze Slovenska. Investujeme.cz, Fincentrum & Swiss Life Select a.s. [Online]. Available at: https://www.investujeme.cz/clanky/ 2-duchodovy-pilir-zkusenosti-ze-slovenska/.

Tománek, T. (2019). Propopulační opatření mají v evropských zemích jen malou účinnost. ČTK Mafra, a.s. Česká pozice – Informace pro svobodné lidi, Reuters [Online]. Available at: https://ceskapozice.lidovky.cz/tema/propopulacni-opatreni-maji-v-evropskych-zemich-jen-malou-ucinnost.A190917_152656_pozice-tema_lube.

Ústredný portál verejnej správy (2020). Materská dovolenka. Slovakia [Online]. Available at: https://www.slovensko.sk/sk/zivotne-situacie/zivotna-situacia/_materska-dovolenka.

Vančurová, A., Kubátová, K., Hamerníková, B., Poláková, O., Klazar, S., Vítek, L., Pavel, J. (2006). Současná a připravovaná opatření rodinné politiky v zemích Střední Evropy. Prague: Ministry of Labour and Social Affairs of the Czech Republic [Online]. Available at: https://www.mpsv.cz/documents/20142/225508/studie_vancurova.pdf/7e5df0d8-7055-fde6-4a82-dc5abd95fe9b

Visegrad Group (2021). History of the Visegrad Group [Online]. Available at: https://www.visegradgroup.eu/about/history.

18

Decomposing Differences in Life Expectancy With and Without Disability: The Case of Czechia

The improvement in mortality is reflected in the fact that people have a longer life expectancy. At the same time, healthy life expectancy has been increasing. Nevertheless, the growth in life expectancy and healthy life expectancy is not exactly the same. What is the part of life that people live on average in good health without a disability? Are we adding years to life or life to years? The aim of this chapter is to compare life expectancy and life expectancy without disability in the case of Czechia. The next part of the evaluation of the mortality and the health level of the Czech population deals with decomposing differences in healthy life expectancies into the additive contribution of the mortality versus the effect of a disability, or the effect of change in health, of different age groups. The decomposition method was originally developed with regard to the Sullivan method that calculates healthy life expectancy and is an extension of the Arriaga method (1984) that decomposes differences in overall life expectancy. Together with prolonging a human life, measured by life expectancy, we observed the increase in healthy life indicators. The health status, and thus quality of life improved in Czechia during the period, both in men and women.

18.1. Introduction

Life expectancy is undoubtedly the most widely used indicator expressing the mortality of the population for a given period. Since this indicator is based on the stationary model of life tables and does not depend on the age structure of the

Chapter written by David MORÁVEK, Tomáš BĚLOCH and Jitka LANGHAMROVÁ.

current population, it is possible to compare the indicator over time and between territorial units. In connection with prolonging human life expectancy and improving the mortality of the population, there is a scope for monitoring the quality of human life from a health perspective. What part of life does a given population live on average in good health, i.e. without disability? Is the quality of life improving along with the prolongation of human life? Are we adding years to life or life to years?

Health expectancies divide life expectancy into years lived in a different health status. They are a natural extension of life expectancies and were developed in response to exploring which of the "aging scenarios" was true (Jagger and Robine 2011). In addition to mortality, this remaining number of years can be divided into years spent in good and bad health on the basis of data on ill-health at particular ages; these are then health expectancies (Jagger and Robine 2011). Healthy life expectancy was first introduced in 1964 by Sanders, and in 1971 with the calculation defined by Sullivan. Among the most common healthy life indicators expressing a health level of the population is the indicator of disability-free life expectancy (DFLE), which measures the equivalent number of years of life expected to be lived in full health (Mathers et al. 2001). It is an indicator that was formerly referred to as health-adjusted life expectancy (HALE) and is one of the most commonly used indicators for monitoring the health of the population and health policies. Nowadays, the indicator is most often referred to as healthy life years (HLY), which is used as a structural indicator at the level of the European Union. It may be an important indicator of the potential demand for health and long-term care services, especially for the older generations of the population (Vrabcová et al. 2017). As stated by Robine et al. (1999), healthy life indicators such as disability-free life expectancy, healthy life expectancy and active life expectancy provide information on the functional state and vitality of populations as well as on their quality of life, and are appropriate from the point of monitoring epidemiological conditions of today.

The growth in life expectancy has been omnipresent in recent years. In connection with the growth of life expectancy, it is also appropriate to examine how healthy life expectancy increases with regard to the growth of life expectancy. According to the theory of the compression of morbidity as defined by Fries (1980): "the lifetime burden of illness could be reduced if the onset of chronic illness could be postponed and if this postponement could be greater than increases in life expectancy." As Jagger (2000) noted, when levels of disability can be differentiated, the "*dynamic equilibrium*" theory appears to take precedence, where, although the number of years lived with disability increases, the number of years lived with less severe disability increases. The expansion of morbidity theory puts forward the pessimistic view that the gains in life expectancy are predominantly through the technological advances that have been made in extending the life of those with disease and disability (Jagger 2000). As stated by Kannisto (2000), it is considered useful to monitor changes in the compression of mortality because the indicators describe relevant aspects of the length of life and may acquire new significance as indicators of population heterogeneity.

Decomposing the difference in life expectancy into age groups is useful in estimating how the mortality of a given age group contributes to the overall difference in life expectancy (Preston et al. 2001). A general algorithm for the decomposition of differences between two values of aggregate demographic measure with respect to age and other dimensions is proposed by Andreev et al. (2002). In addition to the decomposition of difference in life expectancy at birth, application of the algorithm easily leads to the known formula for the age decomposition of differences between two life expectancies, and it also allows us to develop new formulae for differences between healthy life expectancies, where each age component is further split into effect of mortality and effect of health. As an extension of the algorithm by causes of death, Nusselder and Looman (2004) presented in 2004 the decomposition method based on the Sullivan method that decomposing differences in health expectancy is an extension of the decomposition method for life expectancy developed by Arriaga. The method is available to examine the contribution made by causes of death and disability to differences in healthy life expectancy among population groups or periods (Nusselder and Looman 2004) that allows us to evaluate the effect of the change in mortality and the effect of the change in disability on healthy life expectancies, by age groups and by cause of death. The decomposition tool is available for performing calculations as part of the EHEMU project (2007–2010). Moreover, Raalte and Nepomuceno (2020) describe the main developments in the general field of decomposition analysis: healthy life expectancy, which is decomposable using the step-wise and continuous change decomposition methods.

We used the decomposition method according to Andreev et al. (2002) in order to assess the impact of changes in mortality and health on the change in healthy life expectancy of men and women in Czechia between 2005 and 2016.

18.2. Methodology and data

As described by Jagger et al. (2007), the calculation of healthy life expectancy follows similar lines as in the case of calculating life expectancy. If we assume two states called disability-free (DF) and with disability (D), then the disability-free life expectancy at age x ($DFLE_x$) and the life expectancy with disability (DLE_x) are defined as:

$$DFLE_x = \frac{1}{\ell_x}\Sigma_{i=x}^{\omega} L_i(DF),$$

$$DLE_x = \frac{1}{\ell_x}\Sigma_{i=x}^{\omega} L_i(D),$$

where $L_i(DF)$ and $L_i(D)$ are the number of person-years lived from age x onwards in the state without disability (DF) and with disability (D).

Using the Sullivan method as an approximation of healthy life expectancy leads to the hypothesis that (Jagger et al. 2007):

$$L_i(D) = \pi_i L_i \; i = 0, \ldots, \omega,$$

where π_i is the prevalence of disability at age i.

Then, the disability-free life expectancy (DFLE) and life expectancy with disability (DLE) for ages $x = 0, \ldots, \omega$ can be written as (Jagger et al. 2007):

$$DFLE_x = \frac{1}{\ell_x}\Sigma_{i=x}^{\omega}(1 - \pi_i)L_i,$$

$$DLE_x = \frac{1}{\ell_x}\Sigma_{i=x}^{\omega} \pi_i L_i.$$

To describe the life expectancy of an individual based on the concept according to different health statuses, in addition to life expectancy, life expectancy without severe disability and disability-free life expectancy were calculated at selected ages for men and women in Czechia in 2005 and 2016. The periods 2005 and 2016 were chosen as the first and last years of data availability in order to compare the life expectancy in different health statuses over time. However, it is necessary to note here that there are certain limitations when comparing values for selected years. This is mainly due to the slightly different composition of the questions in the EU SILC questionnaire in the section on health. Despite these limitations in the data, we decided to perform calculations for these years.

The input data used were the life tables produced by the Czech Statistical Office (CZSO), as well as data from the project *The European Health and Life Expectancy Information System (EHLEIS)*, which includes survey data on the prevalence. The prevalence was obtained from the European Union Statistics on Income and Living Conditions (EU-SILC) on activity limitation (SILCAL), where the respondents are asked the question: *"For at least the last 6 months have you been limited in activities people usually do, because of a health problem? (If limited specify whether strongly limited or limited)"*. The possible answers to the question are: 1. *"Yes, strongly limited"*, 2. *"Yes, limited"* or 3. *"Not limited"*. Based on the data, we computed the disability-free life expectancy (DFLE) using the prevalence from the option *"Not limited"*. To exclude severe disability from the calculation of life expectancy, we used the prevalence from the option *"Yes, strongly limited"*, which was then subtracted from one (because the sum of the share of people with and without disabilities is equal to one). For this reason, the life expectancy without severe disability expresses the average expected years without severe disability that means for an individual: the disability is assumed to be in no or only a mild form.

In order to measure the impact of mortality on the difference in life expectancy, we performed a decomposition method that allows us to examine the contribution to the difference in life expectancy at birth in age groups and by sex. To calculate the age–sex decomposition, we followed the well-known method according to Arriaga (1984). In life-table terms of the number of survivors l_x and the life expectancy e_x, Ponnapalli (2005) describes the formula with regard to Arriaga's original proposal as the total effect (with our own notation as Δ_x):

$$\Delta_x = l_x^1(e_x^2 - e_x^1) - l_{x+n}^1(e_{x+n}^2 - e_{x+n}^1),$$

where l_x^1 and l_{x+n}^1 are the number of survivors at age x and $x+n$ for period 1, respectively, and e_x^1, e_{x+n}^1 and e_x^2, e_{x+n}^2 are life expectancies at age x and $x+n$ for period 1, respectively, for period 2.

For the open-ended age group, the contribution of the given age group to the overall difference in life expectancy at birth is calculated as (Ponnapalli 2005):

$$\Delta_x = l_x^1(e_x^2 - e_x^1).$$

Life tables for Czechia produced by the Czech Statistical Office (CZSO) from 2005 and 2019 were used as input data for the calculation of the age–sex decomposition in order to evaluate the effect of mortality on the change in life expectancy at birth. The decomposition is performed according to the age and period components, separately for men and women.

According to Andreev et al. (2002), decomposition of the difference between two health expectancies should include additional splitting of each age component into effects of mortality and health since the calculation of healthy life expectancy requires data on age-specific mortality rates and data on age-specific health weights. The calculation of decomposition on the effect of mortality λ_x and the effect of health γ_x at a given age, the respective age group, is defined according to the following formulas (Andreev et al. 2002):

$$\lambda_x = \frac{1}{4}(l_x^1 + l_x^2)({}_1P_x^2 - {}_1P_x^1)(\pi_x^1 + \pi_x^2) + \frac{1}{2}(h_{x+1}^1 l_x^2 + h_{x+1}^2 l_x^1)({}_1q_x^1 - {}_1q_x^2),$$

$$\gamma_x = \frac{1}{4}(l_x^1 + l_x^2)({}_1P_x^1 + {}_1P_x^2)(\pi_x^2 - \pi_x^1),$$

where l_x^i is the table number of survivors at age x in population i; P_x^i is the share of the table number of person-years lived at age x in population i (L_x^i) and the table number of survivors at age x in population i (l_x^i); π_x^i is the prevalence at age x in population i and h_x^i are the healthy life years at age x in population i.

The difference in life expectancy without severe disability and disability-free life expectancy between 2005 and 2016 is further broken down into the effect of mortality and the effect of health, by age groups. The decomposition is performed separately for men and women. Contributions in individual age groups then express what effect changes in mortality intensity have on the change in the values of a given indicator and what effect changes in the health status of persons have (Andreev et al. 2002).

18.3. Main results

Life expectancy, life expectancy without severe disability and disability-free life expectancy are shown for men and women in Czechia in Table 18.1. In the first period of 2005, men's life expectancy at birth was about four years higher than life expectancy without severe disability at that age. Far more significant is the difference between life expectancy and disability-free life expectancy at birth; for men, the difference was 14.4 years of age, and for women, it was 18.7 years of age. Thus, women have a longer life expectancy than men (72.9 vs. 79.3 in 2005); however, women live most of their lives with disabilities. The difference between women's life expectancy at birth and life expectancy without severe disability was equal to 5.5 years of age. At the age of 40 years, men will live about 34.5 years of age on average, 90% of them with no or mild disability and 65% of them with no mild and severe disability. While women have a much lower proportion of years of life with disability in remaining life expectancy at age 40 than men, in particular 87% for mild or no disability and a total of 59% without mild and severe disability. Similarly, at the age of 60, in which, however, the share of remaining life expectancy without mild and severe disability is almost less than half, 45% for women and 51% for men. Finally, at the age of 80, life expectancy without disability was about 40% of men's and 26% of women's remaining life expectancy.

Year	Sex	Age	Life Expectancy	Life Expectancy without Severe Disability	Disability-free Life Expectancy
2005	Men	0	72.9	68.9	58.5
		40	34.5	31.1	22.4
		60	17.8	15.4	9.1
		80	6.2	4.8	2.5
	Women	0	79.3	73.8	60.6
		40	40.2	35.1	24.0
		60	22.0	18.0	10.0
		80	7.5	5.3	2.0
2016	Men	0	76.0	72.7	62.9
		40	37.3	34.2	25.6
		60	19.7	17.4	11.0
		80	7.3	5.8	2.5
	Women	0	81.8	77.7	64.5
		40	42.6	38.7	26.9
		60	24.0	20.9	12.0
		80	8.7	6.4	2.0

Table 18.1. *Life expectancy, life expectancy without severe disability and disability-free life expectancy at selected ages for men and women, in Czechia, 2005 and 2016. Source: CZSO and EHLEIS data; author's processing*

In the second period, in 2016 (Table 18.1), life expectancy at birth increased compared to 2005, for men by 3.1 years of age and for women slightly less than for men, by 2.5 years of age. At the age of 40, life expectancy increased more significantly for men than for women (2.8 vs. 2.4), and conversely at the age of 60 (1.9 vs. 2.0). Finally, at the age of 80, life expectancy of both men and women increased by 1.1 years of age. Life expectancy without severe disability and disability-free life expectancy increased or did not change between 2005 and 2016 compared to life expectancy in the given ages, except for the age of 80, when life expectancy was higher than the other two indicators. Women's life expectancy without severe disability has increased more significantly compared to men's, in all selected ages. Conversely to that, for the disability-free life expectancy, there was a greater increase in men than in women aged 0 and 40 years of age, but at the age of 60, the increase was more significant in women, and at the age of 80, the indicator decreased (but less for women than men). In 2016, the difference between life expectancy and disability-free life expectancy at birth decreased compared to 2005; for men, the difference (13.1) was lower by 1.3 years of age, and for women by 1.4 years (17.3).

18.3.1. *Effect of mortality*

The result of the decomposition of the difference in life expectancy at birth is shown in Figure 18.1 for men and women in Czechia between 2005 and 2019. During the period, life expectancy at birth increased for men from 72.9 to 76.3 years of age, which represented an increase of 3.4 years of age. Over the same period, women's life expectancy at birth increased less than that of men's, namely by 2.8 years of age from 79.3 to 82.1 years of age. The difference in life expectancy at birth is decomposed in order to evaluate the mortality effect on the change in life expectancy at birth, of different age groups and sex.

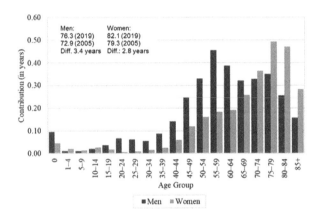

Figure 18.1. *Age–sex decomposition of difference in life expectancy at birth, men and women in Czechia 2005 and 2019. Source: CZSO data; author's calculations and processing*

Men's mortality improved the most between 2005 and 2019 in the 55–59 age group (Figure 18.1), which contributed to an increase in life expectancy at birth by 0.46 years of age. The second highest increase was recorded in men in the 60–64 age group (0.39) and the third in order of size in the 75–79 age group (0.35). Women's mortality also improved, but primarily in the older age groups compared to men. Namely, the highest contributions to the increase in women's life expectancy at birth were recorded in the age groups: 75–79 (0.49), 80–84 (0.47) and 70–74 (0.36). Contributions to the increase in life expectancy at birth between 2005 and 2019 were higher in men than in women at the age at birth and in the ages from 15 to 69. Contrary to that, women had higher contributions than men at the oldest ages from 70 years of age.

18.3.2. *Effects of mortality and health*

The decomposition of difference in life expectancy without severe disability at birth in 2005 and 2016 in Czechia is shown for men in Figure 18.2 and for women in Figure 18.3. The difference in life expectancy without severe disability was between 2005 and 2016 for men 3.8 and for women 3.9 years of age (see Table 18.1). In men, of the overall difference, the mortality effect was 2.7 and the health effect 1.1 years of age. The highest contribution to the change in the values of the indicator was recorded for men in the age groups: 55–59 (0.47), 70–74 (0.42) and 75–79 (0.34). The negative value of contributions was found in the 50–54 and 85+ age groups in the case of the health effect, while the other age groups had positive contributions of the mortality and health effects. The contribution of the effect of men's health was higher than the effect of mortality in the 15–24 and 30–44 age groups. In women, the value of the indicator improved more from the overall difference in life expectancy without severe disability due to the health effect by 2.0 years and due to the mortality effect by 1.9 years of age. The difference in individual effects was not as significant in women as in men. Contributions to the change in life expectancy values without severe disability in women were highest in the age groups: 75–79 (0.67), 70–74 (0.65) and 65–69 (0.43). The negative value of the contribution was found only in the 80–84 age group in the case of the health effect. In most age groups of women, namely the 15–39, 50–59 and 65–79, higher values of contributions due to the effect of health prevailed over the effect of mortality. When comparing the contributions of men, women have higher contributions, especially in older age groups, while men improved the value of the indicator due to better mortality and health status at younger and middle age.

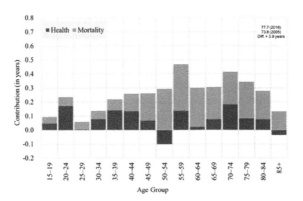

Figure 18.2. *Decomposition of difference in life expectancy without severe disability at birth in 2005 and 2016, men, Czechia. Source: CZSO and EHLEIS data; author's calculations and processing*

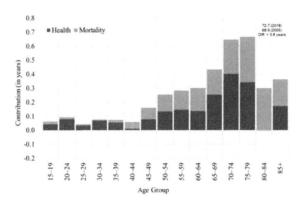

Figure 18.3. *Decomposition of difference in life expectancy without severe disability at birth in 2005 and 2016, women, Czechia. Source: CZSO and EHLEIS data; author's calculations and processing*

The results of decomposition of difference in disability-free life expectancy in 2005 and 2016 in Czechia are seen for men in Figure 18.4 and for women in Figure 18.5. The difference in disability-free life expectancy between 2005 and 2016 was 4.4 years of age for men and 3.9 years of age for women (Table 18.1). The contributions, due to the effect of health, outweigh the effect of mortality, both in men and women. Namely, for men, the health effect was 2.7 added years of age and the mortality effect was 1.7 added years of age. Disability-free life expectancy increased by 3.0 years for women due to improved health status and by another 0.9 years due to improved mortality. The highest contribution to the change in disability-free life expectancy of men was found in the age groups: 70–74 (0.63), 50–54 (0.51) and 75–79 (0.47). For women, the highest contributions were recorded in the age groups: 65–69 (0.71), 45–49 (0.55) and 70–74 (0.50). Contrary to that, men over the age of 85 and women in the 55–59 age group and over the age of 80 had negative values due to the effect of health. The contributions of age groups to the change in disability-free life expectancy due to the change in mortality were positive, in both men and women. The predominance of the effect of health over the effect of mortality is evident mainly in most of the age groups. Higher values of the health effect compared to the effect of mortality were recorded in men in the 15–24, 30–54 and 65–84 age groups. The health of women at a younger age, namely 15–34 years of age, improved more than the intensity of mortality at a given age, in the 40–54 and 60–79 age groups.

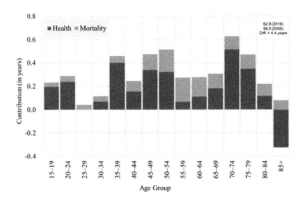

Figure 18.4. *Decomposition of difference in disability-free life expectancy at birth in 2005 and 2016, men, Czechia. Source: CZSO and EHLEIS data; author's calculations and processing*

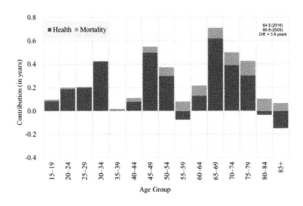

Figure 18.5. *Decomposition of difference in disability-free life expectancy at birth in 2005 and 2016, women, Czechia. Source: CZSO and EHLEIS data; author's calculations and processing*

18.4. Conclusion

Health indicators are considered important characteristics in terms of quality of life evaluation, as well as in connection with monitoring the health status of the population or measuring the impact of national or international health policies. Life expectancy is used to monitor the mortality of a given population, but it has its limitations because it is an average. In some cases, therefore, it may be more appropriate to monitor modal or median length of life, as they are considered more robust indicators. The increase in healthy life indicators, as discussed earlier, was more significant compared to the life expectancy over the period 2005 and 2016 in Czechia. In addition to that, with the exception of the age of 80, the increase prevailed among the selected indicators at ages 0, 40 and 60. Men's life expectancy increased faster than in women aged 0 and 40, and less so than in women aged 60 and 80. Women experienced a higher increase in life expectancy without severe disability compared to men, while in contrast, men showed a higher increase in disability-free life expectancy at the age of 0 and 40. With the decomposition method, the effect of mortality and the effect of health in terms of the difference in life expectancy and the other healthy life expectancy indicators were examined. The decomposition of the difference in life expectancy at birth showed an improvement in the mortality of middle-aged men, while for women, the mortality improved mainly in older age. We made further decomposition of the difference in life expectancy without severe disability and disability-free life expectancy at birth, which was divided into the effects of mortality and health, of different age groups. The effect of health or changes in health status on life expectancy without severe disability and with no disability has been shown to be far more significant in women compared to men. In men, the effect of health was more significant than the effect of mortality if disability was not considered. However, it should be noted that further research is needed in this field of study. A more detailed explanation could be provided by the decomposition analysis extended to the causes of death with regard to disability data (see Nusselder and Looman 2004), or between the sexes with regard to mortality and disability data (Andreev et al. 2002). As another example, Oyen et al. 2013 evaluated the female–male health survival paradox by estimating the contribution of women's mortality advantage versus women's disability disadvantage. As Nusselder and Looman (2004) mentioned, several studies have found differences in health expectancy among population groups and over time. Finally, we would like to mention certain limitations that apply in relation to the use of different types of data, namely an accidental error since the data on prevalence comes from a sample survey. We also pointed out possible limitations in the data when comparing the selected years 2005 and 2016, mainly due to the different composition of the questions of the EU SILC survey.

18.5. Acknowledgments

The chapter was supported by the Internal Grant Agency of the Prague University of Economics and Business No. 35/2020 "Decomposition analysis of mortality" and by the Czech Science Foundation No. GA CR 19-03984S under the title "Economy of Successful Ageing".

18.6. References

Andreev, E.M., Shkolnikov, V.M., Begun, A.Z. (2002). Algorithm for decomposition of differences between aggregate demographic measures and its application to life expectancies, healthy life expectancies, parity-progression ratios and total fertility rates. *Demographic Research*, 7, 499–522.

Fries, J.F. (1980). Aging, natural death, and the compression of morbidity. *The New England Journal of Medicine*, 303(3), 130–250.

Jagger, C. (2000). Compression or expansion of morbidity – What does the future hold? *Age and Ageing*, 29(2), 93–94.

Jagger, C. and Robine, J.M. (2011). Healthy life expectancy. *International Handbook of Adult Mortality*. Springer, Dordrecht.

Jagger, C., Cox, B., Le Roy, S., EHEMU Group (2007). Health expectancy calculation by the Sullivan method. EHEMU Technical Report, Montpellier.

Kannisto, V. (2000). Measuring the compression of mortality. *Demographic Research*, 3.

Mathers, C.D., Sadana, R., Salomon, J.A., Murray, C.J., Lopez, A.D. (2001). Healthy life expectancy in 191 countries, 1999. *The Lancet*, 357(9269), 1685–1691.

Nusselder, W.J. and Looman, C.W. (2004). Decomposition of differences in health expectancy by cause. *Demography*, 41(2), 315–334.

Ponnapalli, K.M. (2005). A comparison of different methods for decomposition of changes in expectation of life at birth and differentials in life expectancy at birth. *Demographic Research*, 12, 141–172.

Preston, S., Heuveline, P., Guillot, M. (2001). *Demography: Measuring and Modeling Population Processes*. Blackwell Publishing, Hoboken.

Robine, J.M., Romieu, I., Cambois, E. (1999). Health expectancy indicators. *Bulletin of the World Health Organization*, 77(2), 181.

Van Oyen, H., Nusselder, W., Jagger, C., Kolip, P., Cambois, E., Robine, J.M. (2013). Gender differences in healthy life years within the EU: An exploration of the "health–survival" paradox. *International Journal of Public Health*, 58(1), 143–155.

Van Raalte, A.A. and Nepomuceno, M.R. (2020). Decomposing gaps in healthy life expectancy. *International Handbook of Health Expectancies*. Springer, Cham.

Vrabcova, J., Daňková, Š., Faltysová, K. (2017). Healthy life years in the Czech Republic: Different data sources, different figures. *Demografie*, 59(4), 315–331.

Assessing the Predictive Ability of Subjective Survival Probabilities

Subjective survival probabilities vary based on socio-demographic and health factors, and reflect our own views of future survival. The objective of this study is to investigate whether subjective survival probabilities can predict actual mortality. To achieve this objective, we introduce the concept of "Force of subjective mortality" and use it to estimate subjective survival probabilities related to a prediction time interval of two years. We then use a longitudinal dataset from the 6th and 7th Waves of the Survey of Health, Ageing and Retirement in Europe. For the statistical analysis, we employ binary logistic regression and Cox regression models. Our results show that subjective survival probabilities contain supplementary information about our own survival, in addition to socio-demographic, health and lifestyle factors, which are known to predict mortality. Moreover, the incorporation of "Force of subjective mortality" in the analysis allows us to estimate subjective survival probabilities for different prediction intervals, and therefore facilitates the use of data from consecutive SHARE Waves.

19.1. Introduction

Subjective survival probabilities are numbers reflecting individuals' views on likely future survival and vary considerably based on the specific circumstances of respondents (Hamermesh 1985). Griffin et al. (2013) note that individuals consider their own experiences, health status, social influences, as well as information from media and health campaigns when forming survival expectations. Individuals who are less educated, have lower income and face financial strain tend to report lower subjective survival expectations (Mirowsky 1999; Rappange et al. 2016; Arpino

Chapter written by Apostolos PAPACHRISTOS and Georgia VERROPOULOU.

et al. 2018). Poor physical and functional health is associated with lower survival expectations (Hurd and McGarry 1995; Van Solinge and Henkens 2008; Rappange et al. 2016). In addition, behavioral risk factors such as obesity are also associated with lower survival expectations (Liu et al. 2007; Rarrange et al. 2016). One of the most interesting and challenging topics on subjective survival is the examination of the accuracy of subjective survival expectations.

19.1.1. *Actual mortality patterns*

According to the literature, there is a range of events that could change individuals' mortality risk profile. Higher socioeconomic status, better self-rated and functional health and higher life satisfaction are associated with lower actual mortality (Kaplan et al. 1988; Idler and Benyamini 1997; Backlund et al. 1999; Verropoulou 2014). Moreover, an increase in the number of comorbidities is linked to higher actual mortality (Scott et al. 1997; Lee et al. 2008). Factors depending on individuals' lifestyles such as obesity, being overweight or being underweight are associated with higher mortality (Takala et al. 1994). The transitions out of marriage through widowhood or divorce are also linked to higher actual mortality compared to being married for both males and females (Kaprio et al. 1987; Dupre et al. 2009).

19.1.2. *Objectives of the study*

The objective of this study is to investigate whether subjective survival probabilities can predict actual mortality. To achieve this objective, we introduce the concept of "Force of subjective mortality" and use this to estimate subjective survival probabilities related to a prediction time interval of two years. This will allow us to assess whether these transformed subjective survival probabilities are strong predictors of in-sample SHARE Wave 6 mortality.

19.2. Methods

19.2.1. *Data*

We used data from the 6th and 7th Waves of the Survey of Health, Ageing and Retirement in Europe (SHARE). SHARE (Börsch-Supan et al. 2013) is a cross-national and multidisciplinary panel database with information on health, socioeconomic status, and social and family networks. The data collection of the 6th wave was completed in November 2015 (Börsch-Supan 2017), and the sampling was carried out in 18 countries. The SHARE Wave 7 dataset became available in

April 2019 (Börsch-Supan 2019), and the data collection took place in 28 countries in 2017. More documentation and information on SHARE can be found at http://www.share-project.org.

The wave 6 sample covers 68,231 individuals; the wave 7 sample covers 76,520 individuals and the combined longitudinal sample covers 51,849 individuals. It is notable that 16,832 individuals who participated in wave 6 do not participate in wave 7. A supplementary analysis of the characteristics of these respondents, as well as the impact on our results is carried out in this study. The longitudinal sample consists of 51,245 individuals aged 50 or older. Due to SHARE rules, information about subjective survival probabilities was not collected for 1,764 individuals aged 50 or older (3.4%), for whom proxy interviews were conducted. Hence, the longitudinal sample used in this study reduces down to 49,505 individuals.

19.2.2. *Force of subjective mortality*

The main challenge that researchers face assessing the predictive power of subjective survival probabilities on mortality is the time interval of the prediction. For example, if the survival prediction refers to the next 10 years, researchers have to wait 10 years to confirm the accuracy of the prediction. In the "Expectations" module of the SHARE questionnaire, respondents were asked to state their survival expectations on a scale from 0 to 100 as follows:

What are the chances that you will live to be age [T] or more?

The target age T depends on the age of the respondent at the interview and is set as follows.

Age band	Target age
50–65	75
66–70	80
71–75	85
76–80	90
81–85	95
86–95	100
96–100	105
101+	110

Table 19.1. *Chronological age and target age*

The time horizon of subjective survival probabilities is the difference of target age and chronological age at the time of the interview.

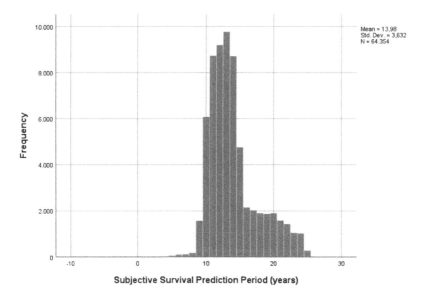

Figure 19.1. *Time horizon of subjective survival probabilities. For a color version of this figure, see www.iste.co.uk/zafeiris/data2.zip*

The "Force of mortality" represents the "rate of mortality" among people who have survived to that age. It describes the behavior of a mortality rate over an infinitely small duration of time. In mathematical terms, it is the conditional probability of a person surviving up to age x, given that they have survived up to that age (Dickson et al. 2009). The "Force of mortality" for a life aged "x" is defined as follows:

$$\mu_x = \frac{-\frac{d}{dx}S_0(x)}{S_0(x)}$$

where:

$S_0(x)$ is the survival probability of an individual surviving up to age "x";

$-\frac{d}{dx}S_0(x)$ is the conditional density of an individual surviving at age "x + dx", given that the individual survived up to age "x".

The probability of individual aged "x" to survive to age "x+t" can be calculated as follows:

$$S_x(t) = e^{-\int_x^{x+t} \mu_y \, dy} = e^{-\int_0^t \mu_{x+y} \, dy} \qquad [19.1]$$

where:

$S_x(t)$ is the survival probability of an individual aged "x" to survive to age "x+t";

μ_y is the "Force of mortality".

Assume that the "Force of mortality" is constant across all years of age, $\mu_x = \lambda$, then the survival probability is independent of the age "x" and becomes:

$$S_x(t) = e^{-\lambda t} \qquad [19.2]$$

The "Force of subjective mortality" – denoted as $\lambda^{subjective}$ – is a quality related to the subjective survival probability of a respondent aged "x", who reports the chance of their own survival for the next "t" years, which if it is assumed to be constant can be calculated as follows:

$$SSP_x^t = e^{-\lambda^{subjective} \, t} \qquad [19.3]$$

where:

SSP_x^t is a subjective survival probability of a respondent aged x, who reports the chance of their own survival for the next "t" years;

$\lambda^{subjective}$ is the "Force of subjective mortality" and it is assumed to be constant across all years of age.

Two special cases have to be dealt with, namely, SSP=0% and SSP=100%. These boundary values of SSPs are treated as missing values and they are estimated based on a statistical model. The "Force of subjective mortality" is estimated by equation [19.4]:

$$\lambda^{subjective} = -\frac{\ln(SSP_x^t)}{t} \qquad [19.4]$$

The distribution of "Force of subjective mortality" is concentrated on 4.6%, but there are large extreme values in the sample. Small subjective survival probabilities imply large values of "Force of subjective mortality" and vice versa.

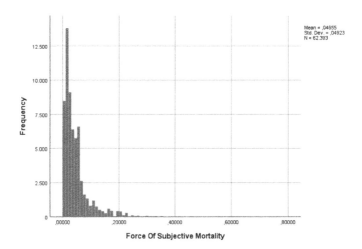

Figure 19.2. *Distribution of "Force of subjective mortality". For a color version of this figure, see www.iste.co.uk/zafeiris/data2.zip*

Percentile	SSPs as reported	SSP (two years)
5%	15.0%	74.6%
10%	30.0%	81.8%
15%	40.0%	85.8%
20%	50.0%	88.2%
25%	50.0%	89.1%
30%	50.0%	90.0%
35%	50.0%	91.1%
40%	55.3%	92.2%
45%	60.0%	93.1%
50%	66.0%	94.0%
55%	70.0%	94.7%
60%	70.0%	95.4%
65%	75.0%	96.0%
70%	80.0%	96.3%
75%	80.0%	96.8%
80%	80.0%	97.2%
85%	83.9%	97.9%
90%	90.0%	98.3%
95%	90.0%	98.7%
Mean	61.6%	91.6%
St. deviation	22.4%	7.9%

Table 19.2. *Distributions of SHARE Wave 6 SSPs as reported and SSPs (two years)*

The average SSP is reposted as 61.6%, whereas the average SSP, which corresponds to the next two years, is higher (91.6%), as expected.

19.2.3. Variables

The dependent variable is a binary variable indicating the death of a respondent, and is defined as follows:

$$In - sample\ mortality\ indicator =$$
$$\begin{cases} 1; if\ a\ respondent\ participated\ in\ Wave\ 6\ and\ then\ died \\ 0; otherwise \end{cases}$$

The explanatory variables are split into two groups. The first group includes variables describing the demographic characteristics and socioeconomic status of the respondents. More specifically, this group includes chronological age (in years), gender and the number of children of the respondent, as well as the country of residence as a control variable. Socioeconomic status is represented by the "equivalized" individual income in quartiles and educational attainment, considered in four levels, based on the ISCED-97 classification, primary (code 1), lower secondary (code 2), upper secondary (codes 3 and 4) and tertiary (codes 5 and 6). The equivalized income per individual was calculated using the reported household income and the OECD-modified equivalence scale. This scale, first proposed by Haagenars et al. (1994), assigns a value of 1 to the household head, 0.5 to each additional adult member and 0.3 to each child.

The second group includes variables describing the physical health, cognitive function, lifestyle and behavioral risk factors of the respondents. More specifically, this group of variables includes the number of limitations in activities of daily living (out of a list of six basic, everyday tasks) and self-rated health (ranging from 1=excellent to 5=poor). Furthermore, cognitive function includes the score of a numeracy test (1=bad to 5=good) and the score of orientation in time test (0=bad to 4=good). BI is included in four categories (underweight, normal weight, overweight and obese). Physical activity, smoking status and life satisfaction score are also included in the analysis.

19.2.4. Statistical modeling

In the analysis, we use binary logistic regression and Cox regression models. A binary-dependent variable indicates whether a respondent is alive or not at the time of Wave 7 data collection, while the time to death is used as an additional input in Cox regression models. The Cox model (Cox 1972, 1975) explores the relationship between survival and explanatory variables, by modeling the hazard rate (or force of mortality) and it has the general form:

$$h(t) = h_0(t) * \exp\left\{\sum_{i=1}^{p} b_i * x_i\right\}$$

where:

– "t" is the survival time. In this study, it is the time to death (in months) between SHARE Waves 6 and 7;

– "p" is the number of explanatory variables;

– $h_0(t)$ is the baseline hazard rate, and reflects the force of mortality for respondents if all explanatory variables take their reference values;

– the quantities e^{b_i} are called hazard ratios. If the hazard ratio for an explanatory variable is greater than 1, then this variable has a positive contribution on mortality. On the other hand, if the hazard ratio for an explanatory variable is less than 1, then this variable has a positive contribution on survival.

The models are used to estimate the impact of the explanatory variables, as well as subjective survival probabilities with a time horizon of two years on the actual mortality experience of SHARE Wave 6 respondents. We expect the value and sign of the regression coefficient to indicate whether subjective survival probabilities contain "supplementary survival information", in addition to variables known to predict mortality. Respondents who participated in W6, including W7 non-respondents, are treated as censored observations in the statistical models.

19.3. Results

19.3.1. Sample

The SHARE W6 in-sample crude mortality rate is 3%; this corresponds to SHARE W6 respondents aged 50 or older (see Table 19.3). Respondents who participated in W6 but died before W7 have a lower average subjective survival probability (87%), whereas those who survived have an average SSP of 92%.

Variables	Respondents who participated in W6, including W7 non-respondents	Respondents who participated in W6 but died before W7
SHARE W6 respondents, aged 50 or older	65,368	1,975 *(Crude mortality rate = 3%)*
SSP as reported (mean)	65%	47%
SSP two-years (mean)	92%	87%
Force of subjective mortality (mean)	5%	8%
Age (mean)	67.7	75.4
Males	96.7%	3.3%
Females	97.4%	2.6%
Number of children (mean)	2.12	2.10
Equivalized income		
1st Quartile (mean in €)	€ 4,691	€ 4,906
2nd Quartile (mean in €)	€ 12,937	€ 12,784
3rd Quartile (mean in €)	€ 25,477	€ 25,013
4th Quartile (mean in €)	€ 74,166	€ 65,648
Education level		
ISCED-97 codes 0 and 1 (primary)	95.7%	4.3%
ISCED-97 code 2 (Lower secondary)	96.5%	3.5%
ISCED-97 codes 3 and 4 (upper secondary)	97.6%	2.4%
ISCED-97 codes 5 and 6 (tertiary)	98.2%	1.8%
Self-rated health		
Excellent	98.9%	1.1%
Very good	98.4%	1.6%
Good	97.9%	2.1%
Fair	96.4%	3.6%
Poor	93.3%	6.7%
Number of ADLs (mean)	0.9	1.7
Cognitive function		
Numeracy test (mean)	1.03	1.04
Orientation in time (mean)	3.8	3.6
Lifestyle and Behavioral risk factors		

Variables	Respondents who participated in W6, including W7 non-respondents	Respondents who participated in W6 but died before W7
Do vigorous or moderate physical activities	97.8%	2.2%
Physically inactive	92.4%	7.6%
Smoked daily	97.1%	2.9%
Non-smoker	97.2%	2.8%
BMI		
Underwieght	93.5%	6.5%
Overweight	97.4%	2.6%
Obese	97.5%	2.5%
Normal	96.5%	3.5%
Life satisfaction (mean)	7.6	7.0

Table 19.3. *Sample characteristics*

Respondents who participated in W6 but died before W7 are on average older and have fewer children (2.1). On a relative basis, males have higher mortality than females. Respondents who participated in W6 but died before W7 have on average lower income, lower educational attainment, more ADLs (1.7), poor self-rated health (6.7%) and lower orientation in time score (3.6). In contrast, they have a marginally better average score of the numeracy test (1.04). Physical inactivity, smoking and lower life satisfaction indicate higher mortality. Respondents who participated in W6 but died before W7 include a higher proportion of underweight individuals (6.5%); underweight respondents tend to have relatively higher mortality compared to normal, overweight and obese.

19.3.2. *Multivariable analyses*

This section includes the results of the statistical models, as well as their interpretation. Table 19.4 presents the results of the models that include known mortality predictors, as well as subjective survival probabilities.

Predictor	Binary logistic	Cox proportional hazard
	OR (95% CI)	Hazard ratios (95% CI)
SSP (two-years)	0.191** (0.109–0.336)	0.215** (0.126–0.367)
Demographic Characteristics		
Chronological Age	1.054** (1.047–1.060)	1.052** (1.046–1.059)
Male (reference: Female)	1.504** (1.339–1.689)	1.485** (1.327–1.662)
Number of children	0.976 (0.939–1.015)	0.978 (0.941–1.016)
Socioeconomic status		
Education (reference: tertiary)		
Primary	1.105 (0.912–1.341)	1.112 (0.922–1.342)
Lower secondary	1.216* (1.005–1.471)	1.214* (1.008–1.461)
Upper secondary	1.168 (0.988–1.381)	1.172 (0.995–1.381)
Equivalized income (reference: Q4)		
Q1	1.794** (1.419–2.268)	1.760** (1.400–2.212)
Q2	1.575** (1.265–1.960)	1.547** (1.248–1.917)
Q3	1.383** (1.137–1.682)	1.379** (1.138–1.671)
Physical health and Cognitive function		
ADLs	1.064* (1.010–1.120)	1.057* (1.007–1.111)
Self-rated health (reference: poor)		
Excellent	0.487** (0.338–0.701)	0.488** (0.341–0.698)
Very good	0.628** (0.496–0.796)	0.629** (0.499–0.793)
Good	0.724** (0.605–0.867)	0.727** (0.611–0.866)
Fair	0.960 (0.820–1.124)	0.963 (0.828–1.121)
Orientation in time	0.903** (0.837–0.974)	0.912* (0.849–0.980)
Numeracy	0.920 (0.949–1.064)	1.003 (0.948–1.062)

Predictor	Binary logistic	Cox proportional hazard
	OR (95% CI)	Hazard ratios (95% CI)
Lifestyle and behavioral risk factors		
Physical activity (reference: physically Inactive)		
Physically Active	0.638** (0.552–0.738)	0.653** (0.567–0.751)
Ever smoked daily (reference: Yes)		
Never smoked daily	0.805** (0.717–0.904)	0.807** (0.721–0.903)
BMI (reference: Normal)		
Underweight	1.104 (0.740–1.647)	1.077 (0.738–1.571)
Overweight	0.673** (0.594–0.761)	0.680** (0.603–0.767)
Obese	0.683** (0.590–0.711)	0.692** (0.600–0.797)
Life satisfaction	0.900** (0.875–0.926)	0.904** (0.880–0.929)

**p<1%, *p<5%. Controlling for the country of residence. The binary-dependent variable indicates whether a respondent is alive or not at the time of Wave 7 data collection. Subjective survival probabilities with a time horizon of two years are included as predictors of in-sample mortality.*

Table 19.4. *Odds and hazard ratios of binary logistic and Cox proportional hazard models. Subjective survival probability model*

Older chronological age and male gender are predictors of mortality (OR = 1.054). A smaller number of children are associated with higher mortality (OR = 0.976). Low income and low educational attainment are strong predictors of mortality. Respondents whose income falls in the 1st quartile are 1.794 times more likely to die compared to those whose income falls in the 4th quartile. Respondents who attained lower secondary education are 1.216 times more likely to die compared to those who completed tertiary education. More ADLs, poor self-rated health and worse orientation in time are strong predictors of mortality. In contrast, numeracy is not significant. An additional limitation in daily activities increases the chances of death by 6.4%; respondents who have excellent self-rated health are 2.05 times less likely to die and better orientation in time by one scale decreases the chances of death by 9%.

Respondents who are physically active (OR = 0.638), as well as nonsmokers (OR = 0.805) have better chances of survival. Furthermore, respondents who are satisfied with their lives also have better chances of survival (OR = 0.9). Underweight people are 1.104 times more likely to die compared to people of normal weight. In contrast, overweight and obese people are 1.48 and 1.46 times, respectively, less likely to die compared to people of normal weight. In other words, in the SHARE W6 sample, only underweight respondents have lower chances of survival.

Higher subjective survival probability values are associated with lower mortality (OR = 0.191). For all variables, the values of hazard and odds ratios are similar.

19.4. Discussion

The objective of this study was to investigate whether subjective survival probabilities can predict actual mortality. To achieve that aim, data from 6th and 7th Waves of the SHARE study were used, including 43,505 respondents from 18 countries. We estimated the "Force of subjective mortality" and used this to estimate subjective survival probabilities related to a prediction time interval of two years. In the analysis, we used binary logistic regression and Cox regression models using a binary-dependent variable which indicates whether a respondent is alive or not at the time of the Wave 7 data collection.

According to our results, older chronological age and male gender are predictors of mortality. Furthermore, having less children and lower socioeconomic status are associated with higher mortality. Respondents who are physically active, non-smokers and those with better self-rated health and less ADLs tend to have lower mortality. Underweight people tend to have higher mortality, whereas overweight and obese people tend to have lower mortality.

Our results are broadly in line with the literature. Women live longer, but report worse health than men (Mathers et al. 2001; Austad 2006). The lifespan of parents increases with the number of children and higher SES (McArdle et al. 2006; Nandi et al. 2014). Poor self-rated health, more disability and chronic diseases are strong predictors of mortality, even after including other covariates known to predict mortality (Idler and Benyamini 1997; Verropoulou 2014). Poor cognitive function and smoking are linked to worse actual mortality (Kelman et al. 1994; Ezzati and Lopez 2003). Physical activity, better quality of life, better life satisfaction and higher social connectedness are associated with greater longevity, which is a factor-related lower mortality (Buono et al. 1998; Gregg et al. 2003; Netuveli et al. 2012).

According to the literature, obesity is a factor related to higher mortality (Solomon and Manson 1997), but our results indicate that only underweight people tend to have higher mortality. On this topic, Zheng and Dirlam (2016) note that the link between obesity and mortality weakens at older ages. Since we are analyzing the mortality experience of respondents aged 50 or older, obesity could explain the less important predictor of mortality for these individuals.

According to our results, higher subjective survival probability values are associated with lower mortality. Subjective survival probabilities vary based on individuals' experiences. Lower SES, poor physical and functional health and obesity are associated with lower survival expectations (Hurd and McGarry 1995; Mirowsky 1999; Liu et al. 2007; Rappange et al. 2016; Arpino et al. 2018). Furthermore, those with better education and cognitive skills are better at predicting their own survival (d'Uva et al. 2017). Our conclusion is that subjective survival probabilities contain supplementary information about our own survival, in addition to socio-demographic, health and lifestyle factors known to predict mortality.

19.5. Conclusion

This study shows that subjective survival probabilities contain supplementary information about our own survival, in addition to socio-demographic, health and lifestyle factors known to predict mortality. Moreover, the incorporation of "Force of subjective mortality" in the analysis allows us to estimate subjective survival probabilities for different prediction intervals and therefore facilitates the use of data from consecutive SHARE Waves. The next steps involve the estimation of the "Force of subjective mortality" using alternative assumptions, as well as the use of bigger longitudinal datasets from more SHARE Waves.

19.6. Acknowledgments

This work used data from SHARE Wave 6 (DOI: 10.6103/SHARE.w6.600) and SHARE Wave 7 (DOI: 10.6103/SHARE.w7.700); see Börsch-Supan et al. (2013) for methodological details. The SHARE data collection was primarily funded by the European Commission through FP5 (QLK6-CT-2001-00360), FP6 (SHARE-I3: RII-CT-2006-062193, COMPARE: CIT5-CT-2005-028857, SHARELIFE: CIT4-CT-2006-028812) and FP7 (SHARE-PREP: No. 211909, SHARE-LEAP: No. 227822, SHARE M4: No. 261982). Additional funding from the German Ministry of Education and Research, the Max Planck Society for the Advancement of Science, the U.S. National Institute on Aging (U01_AG09740-13S2, P01_AG005842, P01_AG08291, P30_AG12815, R21_AG025169, Y1-AG-4553-01, IAG_BSR06-11, OGHA_04-064, HHSN271201300071C) and various national funding sources is gratefully acknowledged (see: www.share-project.org).

19.7. References

Arpino, B., Bordone, V., Scherbov, S. (2018). Smoking, education and the ability to predict own survival probabilities. *Advances in Life Course Research*, 37, 23–30.

Austad, S.N. (2006). Why women live longer than men: Sex differences in longevity. *Gender Medicine*, 3(2), 79–92.

Backlund, E., Sorlie, P.D., Johnson, N.J. (1999). A comparison of the relationships of education and income with mortality: The National Longitudinal Mortality Study. *Social Science & Medicine*, 49(10), 1373–1384.

Börsch-Supan, A. (2017). Survey of health, ageing and retirement in Europe (SHARE) wave 6. Release version: 6.0.0. SHARE-ERIC. Data set. DOI: 10.6103/SHARE.w6.600.

Börsch-Supan, A. (2019). Survey of health, ageing and retirement in Europe (SHARE) wave 7. Release version: 7.0.0. SHARE-ERIC. Data set. DOI: 10.6103/SHARE.w7.700.

Börsch-Supan, A., Brandt, M., Hunkler, C., Kneip, T., Korbmacher, J., Malter, F., Schaan, B., Stuck, S., Zuber, S. (2013). Data resource profile: The survey of health, ageing and retirement in Europe (SHARE). *International Journal of Epidemiology*. DOI: 10.1093/ije/dyt088.

Buono, M.D., Urciuoli, O., LEO, D.D. (1998). Quality of life and longevity: A study of centenarians. *Age and Ageing*, 27(2), 207–216.

Cox, D. (1972). Regression models and life tables. *Journal of the Royal Statistical Society, Series B*, 34, 187–220.

Cox, D. (1975). Partial likelihood. *Biometrika*, 62, 269–276.

Dickson, D.C., Hardy, M.R., Waters, H.R. (2009). *Actuarial Mathematics for Life Contingent Risks*. Cambridge University Press, Cambridge.

Dupre, M.E., Beck, A.N., Meadows, S.O. (2009). Marital trajectories and mortality among US adults. *American Journal of Epidemiology*, 170(5), 546–555.

Ezzati, M. and Lopez, A.D. (2003). Estimates of global mortality attributable to smoking in 2000. *The Lancet*, 362(9387), 847–852.

Gregg, E.W., Cauley, J.A., Stone, K., Thompson, T.J., Bauer, D.C., Cummings, S.R., Ensrud, K.E., Study of Osteoporotic Fractures Research Group (2003). Relationship of changes in physical activity and mortality among older women. *Jama*, 289(18), 2379–2386.

Griffin, B., Loh, V., Hesketh, B. (2013). A mental model of factors associated with subjective life expectancy. *Social Science & Medicine*, 82, 79–86.

Hamermesh, D.S. (1985). Expectations, life expectancy, and economic behavior. *The Quarterly Journal of Economics*, 100(2), 389–408.

Hurd, M.D. and McGarry, K. (1995). Evaluation of the subjective probabilities of survival in the health and retirement study. *The Journal of Human Resources*, 30, S268–S292.

Idler, E.L. and Benyamini, Y. (1997). Self-rated health and mortality: A review of twenty-seven community studies. *Journal of Health and Social Behavior*, 21–37.

Kaplan, G.A., Salonen, J.T., Cohen, R.D., Brand, R.J., Leonard Syme, S., Puska, P. (1988). Social connections and mortality from all causes and from cardiovascular disease: Prospective evidence from eastern Finland. *American Journal of Epidemiology*, 128(2), 370–380.

Kaprio, J., Koskenvuo, M., Rita, H. (1987). Mortality after bereavement: A prospective study of 95,647 widowed persons. *American Journal of Public Health*, 77(3), 283–287.

Kelman, H.R., Thomas, C., Kennedy, G.J., Cheng, J. (1994). Cognitive impairment and mortality in older community residents. *American Journal of Public Health*, 84(8), 1255–1260.

Lee, S.J., Go, A.S., Lindquist, K., Bertenthal, D., Covinsky, K.E. (2008). Chronic conditions and mortality among the oldest old. *American Journal of Public Health,* 98(7), 1209–1214.

Liu, J.T., Tsou, M.W., Hammitt, J.K. (2007). Health information and subjective survival probability: Evidence from Taiwan. *Journal of Risk Research*, 10(2), 149–175.

Mathers, C.D., Sadana, R., Salomon, J.A., Murray, C.J., Lopez, A.D. (2001). Healthy life expectancy in 191 countries, 1999. *The Lancet*, 357(9269), 1685–1691.

McArdle, P.F., Pollin, T.I., O'Connell, J.R., Sorkin, J.D., Agarwala, R., Schäffer, A.A., Streeten, E.A., King, T.M., Shuldiner, A.R., Mitchell, B.D. (2006). Does having children extend life span? A genealogical study of parity and longevity in the Amish. *The Journals of Gerontology Series A: Biological Sciences and Medical Sciences*, 61(2), 190–195.

Mirowsky, J. (1999). Subjective life expectancy in the US: Correspondence to actuarial estimates by age, sex and race. *Social Science & Medicine*, 49(7), 967–979.

Nandi, A., Glymour, M.M., Subramanian, S.V. (2014). Association among socioeconomic status, health behaviors, and all-cause mortality in the United States. *Epidemiology*, 25(2), 170–177.

Netuveli, G., Pikhart, H., Bobak, M., Blane, D. (2012). Generic quality of life predicts all-cause mortality in the short term: Evidence from British Household Panel Survey. *Journal of Epidemiology and Community Health*, 66(10), 962–966.

Rappange, D.R., Brouwer, W.B., Exel, J. (2016). Rational expectations? An explorative study of subjective survival probabilities and lifestyle across Europe. *Health Expectations*, 19(1), 121–137.

Scott, W.K., Macera, C.A., Cornman, C.B., Sharpe, P.A. (1997). Functional health status as a predictor of mortality in men and women over 65. *Journal of Clinical Epidemiology*, 50(3), 291–296.

van Solinge, H. and Henkens, K. (2018). Subjective life expectancy and actual mortality: Results of a 10-year panel study among older workers. *European Journal of Ageing*, 15(2), 155–164.

Solomon, C.G. and Manson, J.E. (1997). Obesity and mortality: A review of the epidemiologic data. *The American Journal of Clinical Nutrition*, 66(4), 1044S–1050S.

Takala, J.K., Mattila, K.J., Ryynänen, O.P. (1994). Overweight, underweight and mortality among the aged. *Scandinavian Journal of Primary Health Care*, 12(4), 244–248.

d'Uva, T.B., O'Donnell, O., van Doorslaer, E. (2020). Who can predict their own demise? Heterogeneity in the accuracy and value of longevity expectations. *The Journal of the Economics of Ageing*, 17, 100135.

Verropoulou, G. (2014). Specific versus general self-reported health indicators predicting mortality among older adults in Europe: Disparities by gender employing SHARE longitudinal data. *International Journal of Public Health*, 59(4), 665–678.

Zheng, H. and Dirlam, J. (2016). The body mass index-mortality link across the life course: Two selection biases and their effects. *PLoS One*, 11(2), e0148178.

Exploring Excess Mortality During the Covid-19 Pandemic with Seasonal ARIMA Models

Excess deaths will be defined as the difference between the observed number of deaths in a specific period and the expected number of deaths in the same period. Excess death estimates can be calculated in several ways, and differ depending on the methodology used and the assumptions made about how many deaths are likely to occur. Often, a simple and easy to understand approach is chosen, in which excess deaths are calculated by comparing the current deaths with the average across previous years. A more complex and sophisticated approach is model-based (see, for example, the models of EuroMOMO or the Centers for Disease Control and Prevention – CDC). We suggest an alternative model. A seasonal autoregressive moving average model (SARIMA) is applied. Model identification and selection is based on autocorrelation and partial autocorrelation functions. After parameter estimation, the model is checked by testing whether the estimated model conforms to the specifications. Excess deaths for selected European countries are calculated as the difference between the observed count and one of two thresholds – either the expected value or the upper limit of a prediction interval. It turns out that these countries were affected very differently by excess mortality in 2020. The number of deaths each year depends both on death probabilities and on the size and the age structure of a population. Our proposed model seems to implicitly take these changes partly into account. Whether this kind of projection is superior to conventional regression models or not is a question of future research.

Chapter written by Karl-Heinz JÖCKEL and Peter PFLAUMER.

20.1. Introduction

The use of modern time series methods in demography is nowadays very common. The characteristics of demographic time series are determined in order to make forecasts. In this chapter, the daily and the weekly deaths in Germany, Sweden and Spain between 2016 and 2019 are analyzed. The aim of our work is to give an estimate of the future number of deaths in 2020 in those countries, with a special focus on uncertainty, and thereby to present alternative models and methods for estimating the excess mortality in 2020, the year of the Covid-19 pandemic. Suitable seasonal ARIMA (p, d, q) models are sought that allow the best possible fit to the available time series, in the sense that the properties of the resulting residual processes are compatible with those of white noise. All calculations and graphs have been produced with the statistics software R.

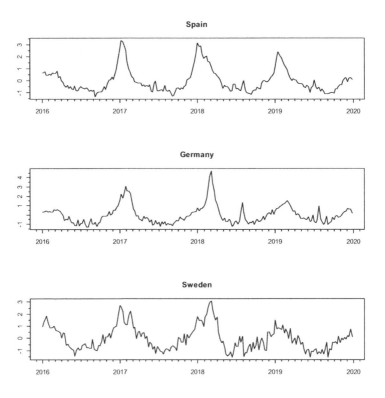

Figure 20.1. *Standardized deaths data 2016–2019: number of total deaths by week from European countries (source: Eurostat)*

In Figure 20.1, the deaths in each country in the chosen period of 208 weeks have been standardized (mean = 0 and standard deviation = 1) in order to present the time series of weekly death cases in one graph. The mortality pattern in the three countries is generally very similar. The time series show peak mortality each spring, with the peak mortality in spring 2018 particularly pronounced in Germany. The similarity of past mortality patterns allows the comparison of excess mortality.

20.2. Binomial mortality model and the empirical distribution of daily deaths in Germany

We consider n independent lives and suppose that q is the probability of dying within one year. Let the number of death cases per year D be a random variable. Then, D might follow a binomial distribution:

$$E(D) = n \cdot q$$

and

$$Var(D) = n \cdot q \cdot (1 - q)$$

This is a simple model of mortality. The model might be appropriate if the death cases in a population are independent. In order to study the hypothesis of a binomial model for deaths in Germany in different age groups, we measure the deviation of the empirical death distributions from the binomial distributions using the Lexis variation, which is defined as:

$$L = \frac{\sigma^2}{\sigma_B^2}$$

where σ is the observed standard deviation and σ_B is the standard deviation of a binomial distribution. Since the probabilities of death (D = deceased, P = population) are very small, a binomial distribution can be approximated by a Poisson distribution, where $\sigma_{Pois} = \sqrt{\mu}$ is the standard deviation of the Poisson distribution with the mean μ.

The statistician Wilhelm Lexis (1903) examined many demographic variables and found that the empirical variance usually always lies above the theoretical one (for details, see Bortkiewicz (1898), Edwards (1960), or Heyde and Seneta (1977)). The conclusion is that the distributions of these variables cannot be represented by a binomial distribution. The deviation from the binomial distribution is mainly explained by autocorrelations of the number of deaths and different death probabilities during the year. Table 20.1 shows Lexis L and other parameters of daily deaths in Germany between 2016 and 2019.

Age class	Mean	Sdv	Lexis L	Skewness	Kurtosis	Min	Q1	Median	Q3	Max
0–30	21.9	4.76	1.03	0.228	-0.068	8	18	22	25	37
30–70	530.2	44.8	3.78	0.804	1.954	415	500	527	555	758
70–100	2004.0	246.4	30.29	1.457	3.042	1,570	1,831	1960.5	2,115	3,151
0–100	2556.1	282.6	31.24	1.440	3.153	2,003	2,363	2,506	2681.75	3,932

Table 20.1. *Parameters of daily death cases in Germany in the years 2016–2019 (1,461 observations). Data: Statistisches Bundesamt (www.destatis.de): Sonderauswertung zu Sterbefallzahlen des Jahres 2020*

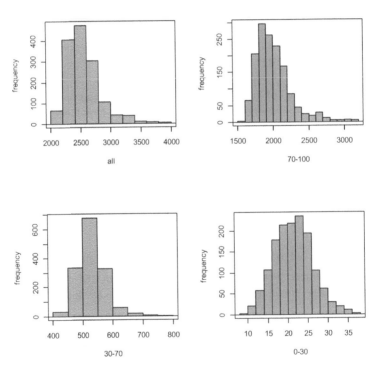

Figure 20.2. *Histograms of daily death cases in Germany 2016–2019. Data: Statistisches Bundesamt (www.destatis.de): Sonderauswertung zu Sterbefallzahlen des Jahres 2020*

It can be seen that only deaths in the age class 0–30 can be satisfactorily presented by a binomial mortality model. At older ages, the distributions are extremely skewed to the right, which means that the outliers of high case numbers are possible (see Figure 20.2).

20.3. Non-seasonal ARIMA model for weekly data in Germany

Our results in section 20.2 suggest that only models that take autocorrelations into account should be used for the total number of deaths. In order to avoid weekly seasonality, which is difficult to compare with different countries, we restrict our investigation to weekly deaths.

At first glance, a simple autoregressive model of order 1 AR(1) would be sufficient:

$$D_t = c + \alpha_1 \cdot D_{t-1} + \varepsilon_t \quad |\alpha_1| < 1$$

where ε_t is white noise with $Var(\varepsilon_t) = \sigma^2$, $Cov(\varepsilon_s, \varepsilon_t)$ for $s \neq t$.

The mean and the variance are: $\mu = \dfrac{c}{1 - \alpha_1}$ and $\sigma_D^2 = \dfrac{\sigma_\varepsilon^2}{1 - \alpha_1^2}$

The AR(1) model can also be transformed through continuing substitution to:

$$D_t = \mu + \varepsilon_t + \alpha_1 \varepsilon_{t-1} + \alpha_1^2 \varepsilon_{t-2} \alpha_1^3 \varepsilon_{t-3} \ldots$$

(moving average process of infinite order).

This mortality model makes sense. The mean mortality is disturbed by stochastic components. The mortality at time t depends both on the actual disturbance ε_t and on past disturbances $\varepsilon_{t-1}, \varepsilon_{t-2}, \varepsilon_{t-3} \ldots$. These influences are geometrically decreasing.

The AR(1) model belongs to a class of models which are known as ARIMA(p,d,q) models in time series analysis. The acronym ARIMA stands for auto-regressive integrated moving average, where:

– **p** is the number of autoregressive terms;

– **d** is the number of non-seasonal differences needed for stationarity;

– **q** is the number of moving average terms or disturbances ε_t.

Details of ARIMA modeling can be found in Hyndman and Athanasopoulos (2018) or Nau (2020). ARIMA is one of the most widely used forecasting methods for predicting univariate time series data.

Thus, our AR(1) model is an ARIMA(1,0,0) model, since we do not have to apply any differencing of the original series. ARIMA(1,1,0) and ARIMA(1,1,1), for example, are used by Jöckel and Pflaumer (1981) to analyze and forecast the sex ratio at birth in Germany.

Germany (original values)

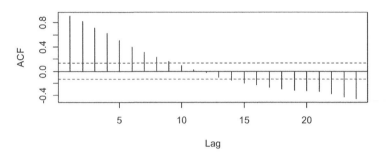

Germany (original values)

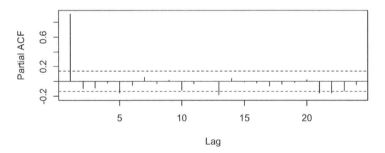

Figure 20.3. *Autocorrelation and partial autocorrelation functions of weekly deaths in Germany*

We use the autocorrelation function (ACF) and the partial autocorrelation function (PACF) in tandem to identify the stochastic process for German weekly deaths between 2016 and 2019 (see also section 20.6 for an analysis with daily data). We see that the weekly death cases can be more or less approximated by an autoregressive model of order 1 (AR(1)-model). The ACFs die out slowly and the PACFs truncate at lag 1 (see Figure 20.3).

After identifying the order of the model, we have to estimate the parameters. The statistics software R uses maximum likelihood estimation (MLE). This method determines the values of the parameters that maximize the likelihood of obtaining the observed data. R indicates the value of the log probability of the data, which is the logarithm of the probability that the observed data came from the estimated model.

The estimation of our model leads to the following estimates:

```
arima(x = Y, order = c(1, 0, 0))

Coefficients:
          ar1      mean
       0.9105  17945.5499
s.e.   0.0274    560.4328

sigma^2 estimated as 574060:   log likelihood = -1675.11,   aic =
3356.23
```

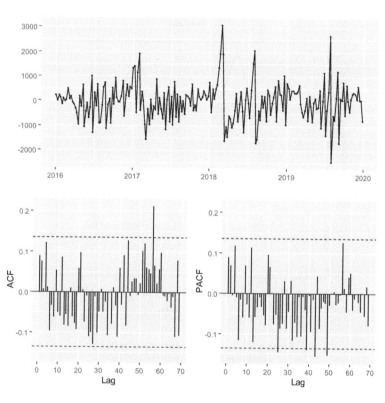

Figure 20.4. *Residual diagnostics for the ARIMA(1,0,0) model*

Residual diagnostics allows us to decide whether a model has been adequately specified.

A cluster of positive spikes around lag 52 (see Figure 20.4) indicates a partly insufficient specification of our model. The reason for the insufficient specification is a yearly periodicity in our data, which can be clearly seen in Figures 20.1 and 20.5, where the spectral density peaks at week 52.

Although the simple model leads to a good fit between 2016 and 2019 (see Figure 20.6), the point forecasts die out very quickly. They tend towards the mean of the stochastic process, which is 17,496. We can use the model only for short-term forecasts (one to two weeks). In general, the death figures of 2020 stay in the 95% and in the 99% prediction intervals. The mortality pattern is similar to that of previous years till the end of November. Hence, there is no obvious evidence of excess mortality in 2020 except in December.

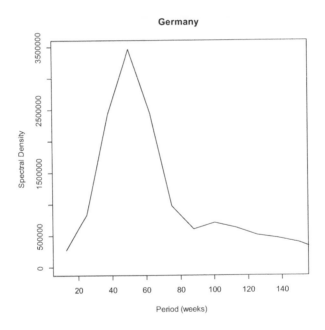

Figure 20.5. *Spectral density of weekly deaths in Germany 2016–2019*

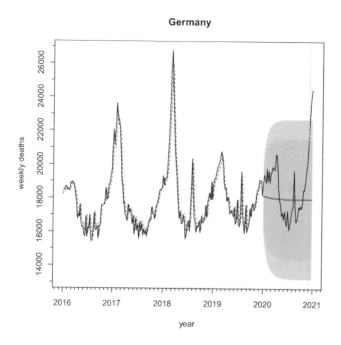

Figure 20.6. *Deaths 2016–2019 (actual and fitted) and point forecasts 2020 with 95%- and 99%-prediction intervals (black: actual; red: fitted; blue: forecast). For a color version of this figure, see www.iste.co.uk/zafeiris/data2.zip*

20.4. Seasonal ARIMA models of weekly deaths for Spain, Germany and Sweden

Because of the obvious periodicity of about 52 weeks in our data, we have to use a different model. A simple extension of ARIMA that enables the direct modeling of the seasonal component is called SARIMA (seasonal ARIMA model).

A shorthand notation of the model is:

$$\text{ARIMA}(p,d,q)(P,D,Q)[m]$$

The seasonal part of an ARIMA model (with m = span of the seasonality) is summarized by three additional numbers:

P = number of seasonal autoregressive (SAR) terms;

D = number of seasonal differences;

Q = number of seasonal moving average (SMA) terms.

With the backshift operator B, we can easily transform the shorthand notation to a difference equation:

e.g. ARIMA(1,0,0)(1,1,0)[52]

$$(1-\phi_1 B)(1-\Phi_1 B)(1-B^{52}) \cdot y_t = \varepsilon_t.$$

Backshift operator B:

$$B^d y_t = y_{t-d}$$

dth order difference: $(1-B)^d y_t$

$$d=1: (1-B) = y_t - y_{t-1};$$

$$d=2:$$
$$(1-B)^2 y_t = (1-2B+B^2) y_t = y_t - 2y_{t-1} + y_{t-2} = (y_t - y_{t-1}) - (y_{t-1} - y_{t-2})$$

Seasonal differencing: $(1-B^m) y_t$

$$y_t = (\phi_1 + \Phi_1) \cdot y_{t-1} - \phi_1 \cdot \Phi_1 \cdot y_{t-2} + y_{t-52} - (\phi_1 + \Phi_1) \cdot y_{t-53} + \phi_1 \cdot \Phi_1 \cdot y_{t-54} + \varepsilon_t$$

or

$$y_t = y_{t-52} + (\phi_1 + \Phi_1) \cdot (y_{t-1} - y_{t-53}) - \phi_1 \cdot \Phi_1 \cdot (y_{t-2} - y_{t-54}) + \varepsilon_t$$

Next, we discuss the process of fitting models to the 208 observations of the weekly deaths in Spain, Germany and Sweden. The procedure consists of four steps: model identification with the ACF, parameter estimation, residual checking, and model selection and forecasting.

Figure 20.7(a)–(c) shows the ACFs and PACFs up to lag 104 of weekly deaths in the three countries. The data of Spain, Germany and Sweden are without trend (see also Figure 20.1), but have pronounced seasonality, so we will first take a seasonal difference (m = 52). The seasonally differenced data are shown on the right of Figure 20.7(a)–(c).

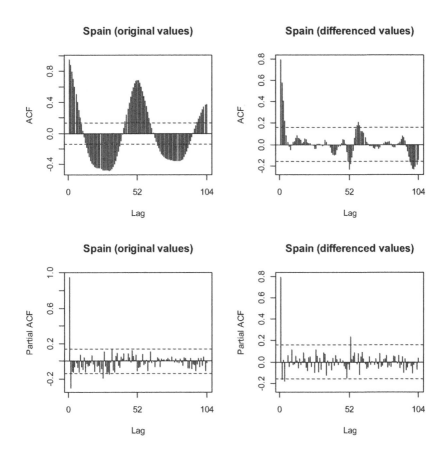

Figure 20.7(a). *ACFs and PACFs of weekly deaths in Spain (original values and differenced values with m = 52)*

Our goal is to find a suitable ARIMA model based on the ACF and PACF shown in Figure 20.7. The significant peak at lag 1 in the PACF indicates a non-seasonal AR(1) component, and the significant cluster of peaks at lag 52 in the PACFs indicates a seasonal MA(1) component. Since the time series is too short to clearly identify a seasonal autoregressive component, we also considered a seasonal AR(1) component. The non-significant spike in the PACF of Sweden proposed a seasonal model without both AR and MA components.

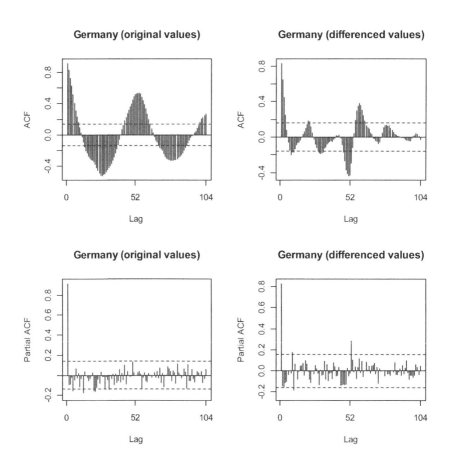

Figure 20.7(b). *ACFs and PACFs of weekly deaths in Germany (original values and differenced values with m = 52)*

The estimation results of the chosen three models for each country are shown in Table 20.2. We used the R package "forecast" for our analyses (Hyndman et al. 2020). In addition, the estimators of the non-seasonal ARIMA(1,0,0) were also listed. The consideration of the seasonal component leads to a sharp decline of the AICs. Of the seasonal models, the best is the ARIMA(1,0,0)(0,1,1) [52] model (i.e. it has the smallest AICc value), but the differences of the AICs are very small. Even the very simple ARIMA(1,0,0)(0,1,0) [52] would be a sufficient representation of the time series of weekly deaths. We limit further analysis to the ARIMA(1,0,0)(0,1,1) [52].

More complicated ARIMA models were also considered, specified, estimated and used for forecasting. However, we were always aware of the principle of parsimony, which means that, in a set of predictive models, the simplest possible models should be chosen. Akaike's information criterion (AIC) is also useful for determining the order of an ARIMA model. AIC is used to compare different possible models and determine which one fits the data best. The most suitable model according to AIC is the one that explains the greatest variation using the fewest possible independent variables. Good models are obtained by minimizing the AIC (see, for example, Hyndman and Athanasopoulos 2018). A predecessor of AIC is Theil's adjusted coefficient of determination.

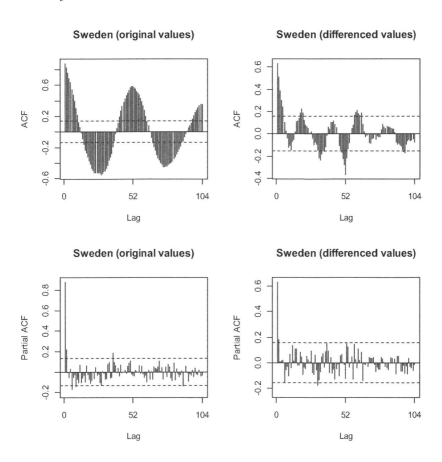

Figure 20.7(c). *ACFs and PACFs of weekly deaths in Sweden (original values and differenced values with m = 52)*

1. Spain

```
ARIMA(1,0,0)
Coefficients:
         ar1   intercept
      0.9511   8063.6136
s.e.  0.0198    395.7227
sigma^2 estimated as 92301:  log likelihood = -1485.33,  aic = 2976.65

ARIMA(1,0,0)(0,1,0)[52]
Coefficients:
         ar1
      0.8474
s.e.  0.0459
sigma^2 estimated as 135470:  log likelihood = -1143.68,  aic =
2291.35

ARIMA(1,0,0)(1,1,0)[52]
Coefficients:
         ar1      sar1
      0.8887   -0.4650
s.e.  0.0456    0.0807
sigma^2 estimated as 106303:  log likelihood = -1131.24,  aic =
2268.49

ARIMA(1,0,0)(0,1,1)[52]
Coefficients:
         ar1      sma1
      0.8633   -0.9976
s.e.  0.0440    0.2699
sigma^2 estimated as 65993:  log likelihood = -1123.46,  aic = 2252.93
```

2. Germany

```
ARIMA(1,0,0)
Coefficients:
         ar1    intercept
      0.9105   17945.5499
s.e.  0.0274     560.4328
sigma^2 estimated as 574060:  log likelihood = -1675.11,  aic =
3356.23

ARIMA(1,0,0)(0,1,0)[52]
Coefficients:
         ar1
      0.8357
s.e.  0.0433
sigma^2 estimated as 1034822:  log likelihood = -1302.23,  aic =
2608.47

ARIMA(1,0,0)(1,1,0)[52]
Coefficients:
         ar1      sar1
```

```
        0.8273   -0.4925
s.e.    0.0441    0.0718
sigma^2 estimated as 759211:  log likelihood = -1285.28,  aic =
2576.55

ARIMA(1,0,0)(0,1,1)[52]
Coefficients:
          ar1      sma1
        0.8118   -0.8353
s.e.    0.0461    0.4292
sigma^2 estimated as 591351:  log likelihood = -1282.58,  aic =
2571.17
```

3. Sweden

```
ARIMA(1,0,0)
Coefficients:
ar1    intercept
     0.8801   1704.5976
s.e.    0.0321     43.4568
sigma^2 estimated as 6037:  log likelihood = -1201.28,  aic = 2408.56



ARIMA(1,0,0)(0,1,0)[52]
Coefficients:
ar1
     0.6583
s.e.    0.0611
sigma^2 estimated as 10124:  log likelihood = -941,  aic = 1886.01

ARIMA(1,0,0)(1,1,0)[52]
Coefficients:
          ar1      sar1
        0.6422   -0.4986
s.e.    0.0623    0.0770
sigma^2 estimated as 7611:  log likelihood = -926.16,  aic = 1858.33

ARIMA(1,0,0)(0,1,1)[52]
Coefficients:
          ar1      sma1
        0.6200   -0.9998
s.e.    0.0633    0.2913
sigma^2 estimated as 4861:  log likelihood = -919.75,  aic = 1845.5
```

Table 20.2. *Estimation results*

The model residuals are shown in Figure 20.8(a)–(c). Residual diagnostics allow us to decide whether a model has been adequately specified.

There are a few significant spikes in the ACF, and the model fails the Ljung–Box test in Sweden. The model can still be used for forecasting, but the prediction intervals may not be accurate due to the correlated residuals (see also Hyndman et al. 2020).

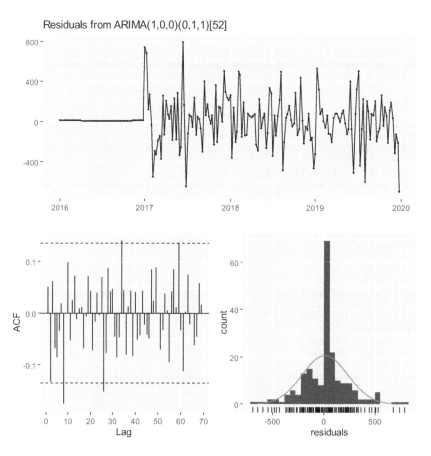

Figure 20.8(a). *Residual diagnostics of weekly deaths in Spain. For a color version of this figure, see www.iste.co.uk/zafeiris/data2.zip*

```
                    Ljung-Box test
data:   Residuals from ARIMA(1,0,0)(0,1,1)[52]
     Q* = 48.179, df = 40, p-value = 0.1757
        Model df: 2.    Total lags used: 42
```

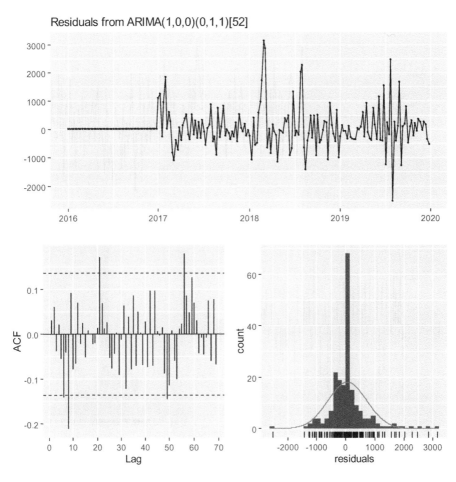

Figure 20.8(b). *Residual diagnostics of weekly deaths in Germany. For a color version of this figure, see www.iste.co.uk/zafeiris/data2.zip*

```
                    Ljung-Box test
data:   Residuals from ARIMA(1,0,0)(0,1,1)[52]
     Q* = 51.261, df = 40, p-value = 0.1093
     Model df: 2.    Total lags used: 42
```

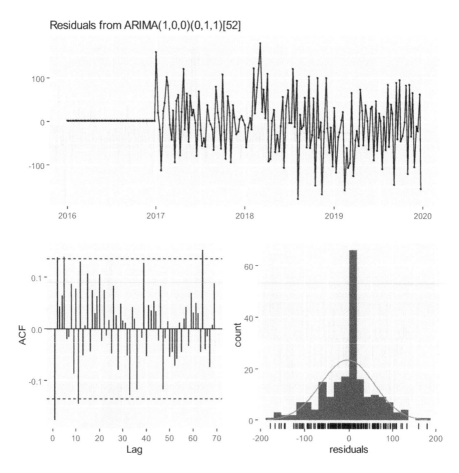

Figure 20.8(c). *Residual diagnostics of weekly deaths in Sweden. For a color version of this figure, see www.iste.co.uk/zafeiris/data2.zip*

```
                    Ljung-Box test
data:   Residuals from ARIMA(1,0,0)(0,1,1)[52]
     Q* = 58.572, df = 40, p-value = 0.02916
        Model df: 2.   Total lags used: 42
```

None of the models considered here passed all of the residual tests. However, according to Hyndman et al. (2020), we would usually be using the best model we could find, even if it did not pass all the tests. Forecasts from the ARIMA(1,0,0)(0,1,1) [52] model are shown in Figure 20.9(a)–(c).

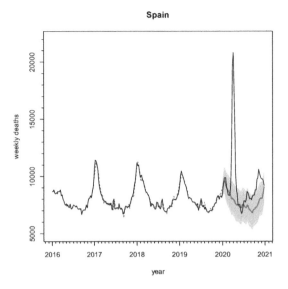

Figure 20.9(a). *Actual (black), fitted (red) and point forecast (blue)
data of weekly deaths in Spain with 99% prediction intervals. For
a color version of this figure, see www.iste.co.uk/zafeiris/data2.zip*

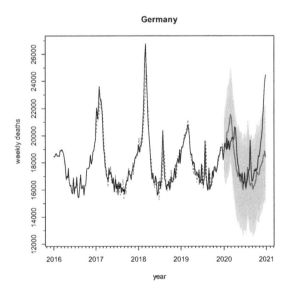

Figure 20.9(b). *Actual (black), fitted (red) and forecast (blue) data
of weekly deaths in Germany with 99% prediction intervals. For a
color version of this figure, see www.iste.co.uk/zafeiris/data2.zip*

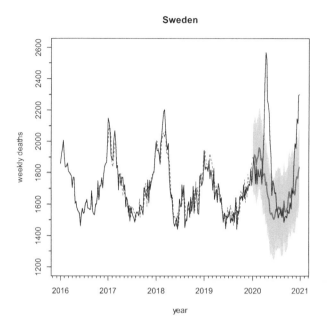

Figure 20.9(c). *Actual (black), fitted (red) and forecast (blue) data of weekly deaths in Sweden with 99% prediction intervals. For a color version of this figure, see www.iste.co.uk/zafeiris/data2.zip*

Both Spain and Sweden show deaths outside the upper limits of the 99% prediction intervals (Figure 20.9(a) and (c)). The seasonal ARIMA model recognizes excess mortality in spring 2020 well. After that immense increase, the deaths stay in the prediction intervals and the mortality pattern does not deviate from that of the previous years. However, towards the end of the year, the deaths are again above the upper limits of the prediction intervals. The increase of the weekly deaths is greater in Sweden than in Spain. In general, the death figures of 2020 in Germany stay in the 99% prediction intervals. The mortality pattern is similar to that of previous years. Hence, there is no obvious evidence of excess mortality till the end of the year. In December, the figures are increasing sharply (Figure 20.9(b)).

20.5. Measuring excess mortality, especially in Spain, Germany and Sweden

Excess deaths are defined as the difference between the observed numbers of deaths in a specific period and the expected numbers of deaths in the same period. Excess death estimates can be calculated in several ways and will be different, depending on the methodology and assumptions about how many deaths are likely to occur. Often, a simple and easy to understand approach is chosen, where excess deaths are calculated by comparing the current deaths with the average across previous years. A more complex and sophisticated approach is model-based (see, for example, the models of the research network EuroMOMO[1] or the U.S. Centers for Disease Control and Prevention – CDC[2]). Instead of a complex model, we chose a simple and easy to understand approach, where excess deaths from week to week in 2020 are compared with the point forecast as the threshold of our ARIMA(1,0,0)(0,1,1) [52]. An alternative calculation would not consider the point forecast but rather the upper limit of the prediction interval or any quantile of the prediction interval. For example, the U.S. CDC publishes two measures of excess mortality: one measure is based on the expected value of their model and the other on the upper limit of the prediction interval.

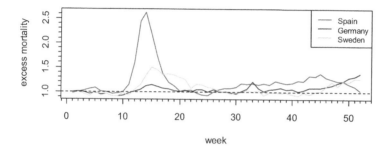

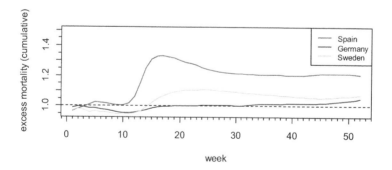

Figure 20.10. *Excess mortality in 2020. For a color version of this figure, see www.iste.co.uk/zafeiris/data2.zip*

---

1 www.euromomo.eu.

2 www.cdc.gov.

The upper part of Figure 20.10 shows the relative increase in deaths in 2020 by week compared to the point forecast in 2020. For example, the indicator for Spain rapidly increases from 1 to about 2.5 between the 10th and 20th weeks. This means that the number of deaths went up 2.5 times or 150%. The relative increases in Sweden and Germany are less pronounced. Gradually, the indicators sink, with fluctuations to a level which is slightly above one. For the lower part of Figure 20.10, we have to first calculate the cumulative weekly actual and forecast deaths by summing up the deaths in each week, from week 1 to week t of each year. At week 52, the total number of actual and forecast deaths in each year can be determined. Now, we can show the moving relative increase of the cumulative deaths in 2020 compared to the cumulative forecast deaths in 2020. Instead of focusing excess mortality on individual weeks, we can now more easily evaluate the long-term development. In Sweden, for example, until week 14, the cumulative mortality was lower than in the previous years. After that, the excess mortality rose to nearly 1.15 (15%) and then fell below 5%. At the end of 2020, excess mortality was 7.4%. In Spain, the cumulative excess mortality was higher (20.7%); in Germany, it was lower (4.6%).

20.6. Forecasting daily deaths in Germany

If data from official statistics are delayed, it is sometimes necessary to produce forecasts on a daily basis. We present an ARIMA model using daily deaths of Germany from 2016 to 2019. In the case of short-term forecasts, the annual fluctuations can be neglected, but, as will be seen, weekday effects will occur. We proceed again with our steps: identification, parameter estimation, residual checking and estimation of a new model (see Figures 20.11–20.15).

a) Identification

The ACF and PACF of the deaths in all age groups in Figure 20.11 indicate an ARIMA(1,0,0) model.

b. Estimation (all age groups)[3]

```
ARIMA(1,0,0) with non-zero mean

Coefficients:
          ar1          mean
       0.9229    2556.2500
s.e.   0.0100      36.4417

sigma^2 estimated as 11748:  log likelihood=-8918.86
AIC=17843.73    AICc=17843.74    BIC=17859.59
```

3 The estimation results of the other age classes can be found in the Appendix.

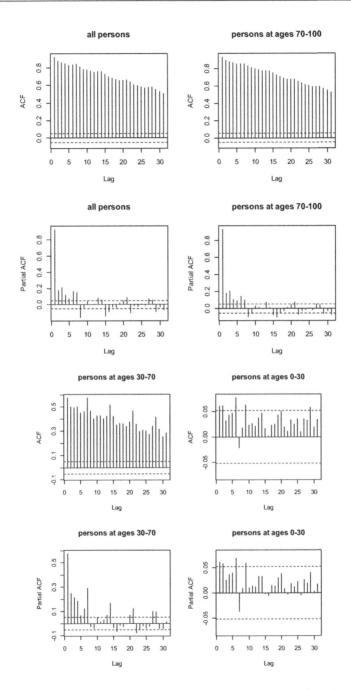

Figure 20.11. *Autocorrelation (ACF) and partial autocorrelation functions (PACF)*

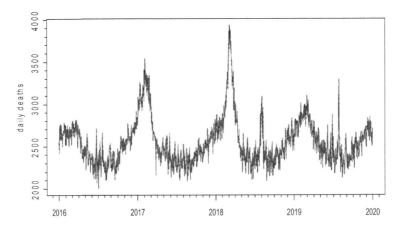

Figure 20.12. *Actual (black) and fitted (red) values with ARIMA(1,0,0). Data: Statistisches Bundesamt (www.destatis.de): Sonderauswertung zu Sterbefallzahlen des Jahres 2020. For a color version of this figure, see www.iste.co.uk/zafeiris/data2.zip*

c. Residual diagnostics

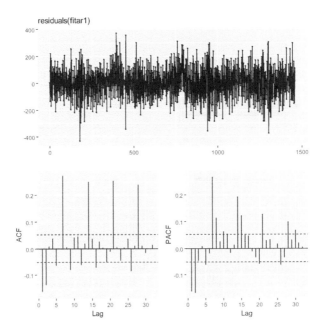

Figure 20.13. *Residual diagnostics for the ARIMA(1,0,0) model*

Spikes at lags 7,14, 21,… indicate the insufficient specification of our model. The reason is a weekly periodicity in our data. Deaths vary from day to day in the week (see Figure 20.14 and Table 20.3).

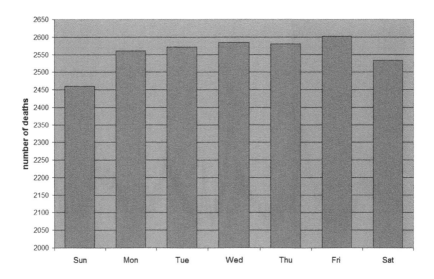

Figure 20.14. *Distribution of all deaths by weekday (mean) from 2016 to 2019*

Day	All ages	0–30 years	30–70 years	70–100 years
Sun	2460.3	22.0	498.4	1939.8
Mon	2561	21.7	544.5	1994.9
Tue	2572.2	21.9	537.7	2012.7
Wed	2584.1	22.2	537.4	2024.5
Thu	2580.8	21.7	535.7	2023.5
Fri	2602.4	22.2	539.3	2040.9
Sat	2532.9	21.7	518.3	1992.9

Table 20.3. *Mean number of death cases by weekday (2016–2019)*

In general, the death figures of 2020 stay in the 95% and in the 99% prediction intervals (see Figure 20.15). The mortality pattern is similar to that of previous years. Hence, there is no obvious evidence of excess mortality in 2020. But it is obvious that this model is not suitable for long-term forecasts, since the point forecasts die out very rapidly. Furthermore, residual checking leads us to a model that should consider weekday effects.

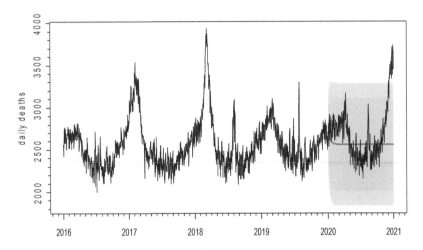

Figure 20.15. *Death numbers of all persons 2016–2021 with 95%- and 99%-prediction intervals (black: actual values 2016–2020; blue: point forecasts). For a color version of this figure, see www.iste.co.uk/zafeiris/data2.zip*

d. Re-estimation

We propose an ARIMA(1,0,0) with weekday dummies to consider weekly seasonality (see Figures 20.16 and 20.17):

```
Series: Y (all ages)          2016-2019
Regression with ARIMA(1,0,0) errors

             ar1        intercept    Mo       Tu       We
Coeffcients  0.9403     2460.2       100.7    111.8    124.0
s.e.         0.0088     41.3         6.2      8.0      8.8

             Th         Fr           Sa       Su
Coeffcients  120.7      142.3        72.7     0
s.e.         8.8        8.0          6.2
```

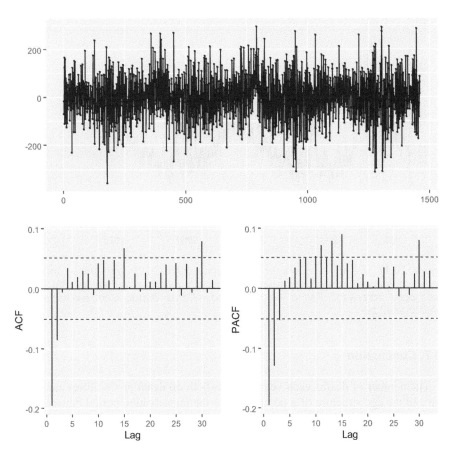

Figure 20.16. *Residual diagnostics for the ARIMA(1,0,0) model with weekly seasonality*

The weekly periodicity in the ACF and PACF has disappeared. Therefore, we recommend this ARIMA model with regressors for short-term daily forecasts. In practice, the fitting period should be continuously adjusted before making predictions.

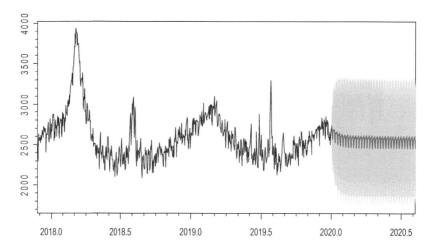

Figure 20.17. *Death numbers of all persons 2016–2021 with 95%- and 99%-prediction intervals considering weekly seasonality (black: actual values 2016–2020; blue: point forecast). For a color version of this figure, see www.iste.co.uk/ zafeiris/data2.zip*

20.7. Conclusion

The number of deaths each year depends both on death probabilities and on the size and the age structure of a population. In the investigation period between 2016 and 2019, the population sizes increased by 1.3% in Germany, by 1.9% in Spain and by 3.3% in Sweden. In the age class 80 years and older – responsible for more than 50% of deaths – the increases were 15% (Germany), 1.7% (Spain) and 0% (Sweden). The increase in Germany is due to the mini baby boom of 1936–1939. Therefore, an increase of excess mortality can be attributed solely to changes in the size and structure of a population. The correct way to eliminate these factors would require using a population model with age-specific mortality rates and population sizes in order to calculate standardized death numbers. For an example, see Kowall et al. (2021), who eliminated the effects for Germany, Spain and Sweden. They concluded that these effects are quite considerable for Germany and Sweden. Time series methods for forecasting the future are suitable, as long as demographic and social changes take place slowly, continuously and without breaks or sudden changes in direction, and the past, present and future differ only slightly. Our seasonal ARIMA model cannot eliminate these factors directly, but time series methods consider changes in the past. Future trends and cycles will depend on past trends and cycles. If there is no structural change, time series forecasts do not perform worse than more complex models. Therefore, our proposed model implicitly takes the changes in age structure and in population size at least partially into account.

20.8. Appendix

20.8.1. *Estimation results of the other age classes*

```
Age class 0-30

ARIMA(1,0,0) with non-zero mean

Coefficients:
         ar1       mean
      0.0611   21.9118
s.e.  0.0262    0.1322

sigma^2 estimated as 22.56:  log likelihood=-4348.28
AIC=8702.56   AICc=8702.58   BIC=8718.42
```

There exists a week autocorrelation. However, a useful approximation is white noise for the daily deaths in this young age class as shown by the parameters below.

```
Age class 0-30

ARIMA(0,0,0) with non-zero mean

Coefficients:
         mean
      21.9110
s.e.   0.1244

sigma^2 estimated as 22.62:  log likelihood=-4350.99
AIC=8705.99   AICc=8705.99   BIC=8716.56
```

Age class 30-70

```
ARIMA(1,0,0) with non-zero mean

Coefficients:
          ar1        mean
       0.5772   530.1676
s.e.   0.0213     2.2579

sigma^2 estimated as 1336:   log likelihood=-7329.96
AIC=14665.92    AICc=14665.94    BIC=14681.78
```

Age class 70-100

```
ARIMA(1,0,0) with non-zero mean

Coefficients:
          ar1        mean
       0.9337   2004.1844
s.e.   0.0093     34.2994

sigma^2 estimated as 7719:   log likelihood=-8612.11
AIC=17230.21    AICc=17230.23    BIC=17246.08
```

The autocorrelation increases with age.

20.8.2. *Time series decomposition*

If we assume an additive decomposition of a time series y_t, then we get

$$y_t = T_t + S_t + u_t$$

with T_t = Trend, S_t = Season, u_t = Remainder or irregular component at time t.

Performing classical time series decomposition (see, for example, Hyndman and Athanasopoulos 2018) yields the components illustrated in Figure 20.A1. The estimate of the trend is obtained by using a 365-day moving average.

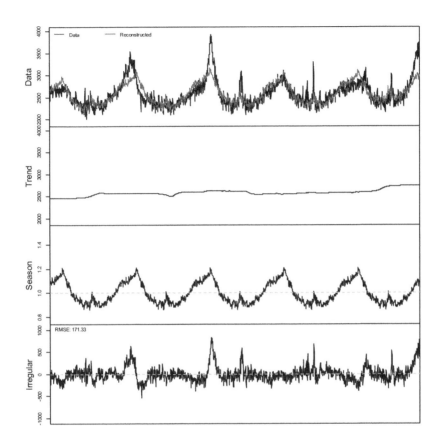

Figure 20.A1. *Time series components of the daily deaths in Germany 2016–2019 using a 365-day moving average (R: decomp(y, outplot=1) from package tsutils)*

Figure 20.A2 illustrates the seasonal distribution of the daily deaths between 2016 and 2020.

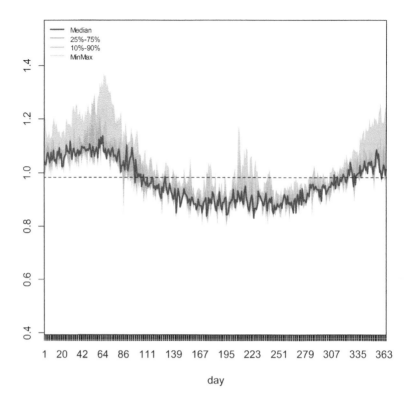

Figure 20.A2. *Seasonal distribution of daily deaths between 2016 and 2020 (R: seasplot(y, outplot=4) from package tsutils)*

20.9. References

Bortkiewicz, L.V. (1898). *Das Gesetz der kleinen Zahlen*. B.G. Teubner, Leipzig.

Edwards, A. (1960). Natural selection and the sex ratio. *Nature*, 188, 960–961.

Heyde, C.C., Seneta, A. (1977). *Statistical Theory Anticipated*, Springer-Verlag, New York.

Hyndman, R.J. and Athanasopoulos, G. (2018). *Forecasting, Principles and Practice*, 2nd edition. OTexts, Melbourne.

Hyndman, R., Athanasopoulos, G., Bergmeir, C., Caceres, G., Chhay, L., O'Hara-Wild. M., Petropoulos, F., Razbash, S., Wang, E., Yasmeen, F. et al. (2020). Forecast, forecasting functions for time series and linear models. R package version 8.13 [Online]. Available at: https://pkg.robjhyndman.com/forecast/.

James, W. (2000). The variation of the probability of a son within and across couples. *Human Reproduction*, 15(5), 1184-8.

Jöckel, K.-H. and Pflaumer, P. (1981). Demographische Anwendungen neuerer Zeitreihenverfahren. *Zeitschrift für Bevölkerungswissenschaft*, 7, 519–542.

Kowall, B., Standl, F., Oesterling, F., Brune, B., Brinkmann, M., Dudda, M., Pflaumer, P., Jöckel, K.H., Stang, A. (2021). Excess mortality due to Covid-19? A comparision of total mortality in 2016 to 2019 in Germany, Sweden and Spain. *PLoS ONE*, 16(8), e0255540 [Online]. Available at: https://doi.org/10.1371/journal.pone.0255540.

Lexis, W. (1903). *Abhandlungen zur Theorie der Bevölkerungs- und Moralstatistik.* G. Fischer, Jena.

Nau, R. (2020). Statistical forecasting, notes on regression and time series analysis, Fuqua School of Business, Duke University, Durham, NC [Online]. Available at: https://people.duke.edu/~rnau/411arim.htm.

R Core (2020). *R, A Language and Environment for Statistical Computing.* R Foundation for Statistical Computing, Vienna [Online]. Available at: https://www.R-project.org/.

The Impact of Cesarean Section on Neonatal Mortality in Rural–Urban Divisions in a Region of Brazil

Neonatal mortality represents, in the first seven days of life, about 70% of infant deaths and is mainly responsible for maintaining the levels of the infant mortality rate, both in Brazil and in the world, where these levels are below 18 deaths per 100,000 live births. One of the important factors associated with neonatal infant mortality is cesarean section, which in Brazil reaches levels around 57%, one of the highest in the world. This study aimed to investigate the impact of cesarean section on neonatal mortality in rural–urban divisions in the State of Paraíba, in northeastern Brazil, from 2009 to 2017. A set of maternal–infant variables was selected, commonly found in the microdata of the Ministry of Health's Mortality and Birth Information System: *gender and race/child color, mother's age, mother's level of education, number of children born alive, number of children born dead, type of pregnancy* and *type of childbirth*. After using the database linkage technique and the imputation of missing data of the variables, the multilevel logistic model was applied, which considered two levels: each neonatal death (level 1) and rural–urban municipal characterization (level 2). In light of the microdata of 5,149 neonatal deaths that occurred in Paraíba from 2009 to 2017, the highest proportions of neonatal deaths in children born via cesarean delivery were found in urban municipalities. The modeling results revealed that the chance of birth via cesarean section among children who died within 28 days increases as the mother's age and schooling increase and with the presence of multiple pregnancies, and the chance decreases as she increases the number of children born dead. The results reinforced the urgent need for more effective public and private policies to reduce the rate of

Chapter written by Carlos Santos and Neir Paes.

elective cesarean sections to acceptable levels (10–15%) mainly in urban municipalities for a consequent reduction in neonatal mortality levels.

21.1. Introduction

Infant mortality is considered one of the main targets of public health policies worldwide, whose main responsibility is neonatal mortality. In Brazil, the percentage of neonatal mortality has reached 70% of infant mortality, of which 25% occur in the first 24 hours postpartum (Gaiva et al. 2016).

It is important to study the maternal and child factors that influence neonatal mortality, as this information serves as a warning for the monitoring and surveillance of deaths, in addition to favoring the planning of health actions aimed at reducing mortality rates (Sampaio Neto 2018). Since post-neonatal mortality is under control, the focus of public managers is primarily directed towards neonatal mortality, in countries such as Brazil and, in particular, in regions such as the State of Paraíba, which has 223 municipalities, located in the northeast of the country.

This state had a population of 4.0 million inhabitants in 2018. Nearly three quarters of the population live in urban areas clustered along the Atlantic coast and had an HDI of 0.709 in 2017. This state is one of the least developed in Brazil, occupying the 20th position in development among the 27 states in the country. The public health sector – the SUS – provides universal access to health care, which is the sole provider of health care coverage for at least 75% of the population.

One of the important factors associated with neonatal mortality is childbirth (Gurol-Urganci et al. 2011; Huang et al. 2011; Almeida et al. 2014). The rate of cesarean sections is one of the highest in the world, with significant values in all regions of the country. The country ranks behind only the Dominican Republic (58.1%), according to a 2018 study. In the same year, the number of cesarean sections in relation to the total number of childbirths in Brazil reached 57%, well above the guidelines of the World Health Organization (WHO) which recommends a limit of 15% (WHO 1985; Lages 2012).

There are several reasons for the high percentage of cesarean sections. Among them, it is noteworthy that the highest proportion of cesarean section occurs in the most privileged social group in society, with a better socioeconomic and educational level, a paradox related to healthcare practices in the private sector (Domingues et al. 2014; Barros et al. 2015).

Many studies investigating the characteristics of mothers and children as factors that increase the risk of infant mortality disregard the intrinsic hierarchical structure in the data, i.e. they do not consider the existing correlation between individuals of the same group, which can produce incorrect inferences. Multilevel regression models allow for contemplating the effect of hierarchy, making it possible to explore the dimension of variability at each level (Goldstein 1995).

In the rural–urban context of the State of Paraíba, multilevel models are very useful tools, since these regions have peculiar characteristics among themselves, which reinforces the application of this modeling.

Studies that address neonatal mortality with the increasing number of cesarean sections are scarce in Brazil and absent in its regionalized spaces, particularly for regions with relatively low levels of development such as the State of Paraíba. Thus, this study aimed to investigate the impact of cesarean sections on neonatal mortality in rural–urban spaces in the State of Paraíba, in northeastern Brazil, from 2009 to 2017.

21.2. Materials and methods

This is a cross-sectional ecological study with all 5,149 records of neonatal deaths in the State of Paraíba, from 2009 to 2017. Information on variables present in the death certificate (DO) was used, available in the Mortality Information System (SIM) of the Ministry of Health (Brasil Ministério da Saúde 2019).

A set of maternal–infant variables was selected, considered to be associated with neonatal mortality and which influence the *type of childbirth*. The variable *residence municipality* of the mother was classified according to rurality and urbanization criteria as proposed by the Brazilian Institute of Geography and Statistics – IBGE (IBGE 2017), i.e. the municipalities were classified as: adjacent intermediate (22 municipalities), adjacent rural (166 municipalities) and urban (35 municipalities). Therefore, the new variable was renamed *municipal characterization*.

The methodological path for evaluating the quality of infant mortality records for the Paraíba region was considered according to the proposal of Paes et al. (2020). For this purpose, deterministic linkage procedures and data imputation for variables with ignored information were used, as well as techniques to assess the coverage of neonatal death records, before performing statistical modeling.

In order to identify the possible predictive variables of the multilevel binary logistic regression model, the relationship between the *type of childbirth* variable and the other variables was investigated using the chi-square test of independence since these are categorized variables, considering a significance level of 10% (Hosmer and Lemeshow 1989).

After selecting the variables which made up the multilevel modeling, two levels were taken into account: each neonatal death (level 1) and municipal characterization (level 2). The second level concerns the identification of the municipality according to the *municipal categorization*.

Considering the possible independent variables presented in the bivariate analysis, statistical modeling was performed using the multilevel binary logistic model. In the model, the *type of childbirth* variable was considered a dependent variable. Thus, the independent variables selected according to the bivariate analysis were: *race/color of the child, mother's age, mother's level of education, number of children born alive, number of children born dead* and *type of pregnancy*. In this study, the category of success considered for the event "neonatal death" was the category "being born via cesarean section".

21.2.1. *Multilevel logistic model*

When the response variable is categorical and the data have hierarchical structure, the appropriate model is the multilevel logistic regression. This model is very similar to the logistic regression model, including random effects and independent variables from the other levels (Bryk and Raudenbush 1992). The model for the case with two levels and binary response variable is:

$$logito(\pi_{ij}) = \mu + \sum_{p=1}^{P} \beta_p x_{pij} + \sum_{q=1}^{Q} \gamma_q w_{qi} + \sum_{p=1}^{P} \sum_{q=1}^{Q} \theta_{pq} x_{pij} w_{qj} + \sum_{p=1}^{P} \tau_{pi} x_{pij} + G_i \qquad [21.1]$$

where π_{ij} is the odds of success of the j individual in the i group. As it is usual in logistic regression notation, (1) it does not present the term e_{ij}. The interpretations of this model are analogous to those of the logistic regression model (Goldstein 1995).

Another question that arises is the intraclass correlation coefficient (ICC). With the scale factor equal to 1. Thus, we have:

$$\rho = \frac{\sigma_G^2}{\sigma_G^2 + 3.29}$$

With the aim of verifying how well the model fits into a database, using the likelihood function, the statistic called *deviance* was used, defined as:

$$deviance = -2\ln(ML)$$

where ML is the maximum likelihood. In general, models that have a lower *deviance* are better adjusted to the data under study (Santos 2017).

The steps proposed by Hox (2010) in the construction of the multilevel logistic regression model were followed. Therefore, initially, the null model was considered, i.e. the simplest multilevel model, without independent variables. Then, all independent variables at the lowest level were inserted into the model.

Multilevel modeling was performed using the free access statistical software R version 4.0.2 as a tool.

21.3. Results and discussion

The analysis of the quality of neonatal death data for the 5,149 neonatal deaths in Paraíba, from 2009 to 2017, revealed a coverage of about 81% in the period. However, for unregistered deaths, it was assumed that the response pattern in the categories of missing variables was the same as in the categories with responses.

After carrying out the imputation of missing data for some categories of variables, all of them were completed for multilevel modeling purposes. The modeling took into account two levels: each neonatal death (level 1) and the municipal characterization (level 2).

According to the results of the chi-square test of association of the *type of childbirth* variable with the other variables selected in the research, only the *sex* variable had no significant association with the level of 10% significance, which was removed from the modeling. Thus, for multilevel binary logistic modeling, the *type of childbirth* variable was considered a dependent variable and the independent variables selected according to the bivariate analysis were: *race/color of the child, mother's age, mother's level of education, number of children born alive, number of children born dead* and *type of pregnancy*.

Table 21.1 shows the statistics of the null model (only with the intercept). The global average of cesarean sections was γ_{00} = -0.2934, with a 5% significance level. When exponentializing the estimates of interception, the odds ratio was obtained, i.e. $e^{-0.29348}$ = 0.75. With this information, the unconditional probability of a neonatal death having been born via cesarean section was calculated. Thus, the probability was 0.43. The residue at the municipal characterization level had a zero mean and variance $\sigma_{\mu_{0j}}^2$ = 0.21637, which implied the ICC, ρ = 0.06171, indicating that approximately 6% of the variation of the *type of childbirth* variable can be explained by the municipal characterization. This result provides evidence that a multilevel model can make a difference in the model's estimates, compared to a non-multilevel model. Therefore, the use of multilevel models is necessary and guaranteed. According to Heck et al. (2014), an ICC of 0.05 is often considered a conventional threshold to indicate more substantial evidence of clustering. It was also found that the *deviance* value was 7060.5.

Model	Value	Standard error	p-value[*]
Intercept	-0.29348	0.08265	0.00038
ρ	0.06171	-	-
deviance	7060.5	-	-

[*] Significant if p <0.05.

Table 21.1. *Null model statistics: only with the intercept of neonatal deaths in the municipal characterizations of Paraíba, 2009–2017*

After adjusting the null model, the model selection stage started until one or several candidates for the final model were obtained. The fixed independent variables were inserted one by one until the estimates of the parameters were obtained and the significance of the parameters of these variables was verified.

The estimates of the model with all fixed independent variables were verified. When comparing it with the null model, there was an increase in the variation of the *type of childbirth* variable explained by the municipal characterization. It was also observed that the inclusion of the variables reduced the *deviance* value (6841.5). The parameters of the *race/color* and *number of children born alive* variables were not significant; therefore, these variables were removed and a new model was adjusted.

As it is an adjustment of a multilevel model, which takes into consideration the heterogeneity of the independent variables in the municipal characterizations, the non-significance of the variables *race/color* and *number of children born alive* suggests that the patterns of the proportions of the categories of these variables were similar in the three groups referring to municipal characterizations.

The removal of the *race/color* and *number of children born alive* variables allowed the generation of a model that would better fit the neonatal death data in Paraíba. According to Table 21.2, it was possible to verify that the estimate of the *deviance* had the lowest value, 6833.5. The global average of cesarean sections did not change in relation to the previous model, i.e. it was γ_{00} = -0.3068. As the exponential global average of cesarean sections (0.73581) allows us to obtain the unconditional probability of a neonatal death having been born via cesarean section, this value has remained at 0.42. The residue's value at the level of the municipal characterization also remained unchanged, having zero mean and variance $\sigma^2_{\mu_{0j}}$= 0.27853, which entailed an ICC of 0.07805, i.e. approximately 8% of the variation of the *type of childbirth* variable can be explained by the municipal characterization.

For the *mother's age* variable, the category of 20–29 years was referenced. It has been found that mothers who are between 30 and 39 years old increase the chance of birth by cesarean section by approximately 2.6 times among children who died within 28 days; for mothers aged 40 and over, this chance increases to approximately 3.3 times, while for mothers aged 10–19 years, the chance of birth by cesarean section among neonatal deaths compared to mothers aged 20–29 years increases by 77% (Table 21.2). Several studies have proven that high maternal age is considered to be one of the risk factors for a high proportion of cesarean sections (Gaiva et al. 2016; Araujo Filho et al. 2017; Madeiro et al. 2017). The population of the State of Paraíba, at least since the last decade, although with its own characteristics, has been following the world transformations in terms of demographic, nutritional and epidemiological transition, besides the phenomenon of decreased fertility that has contributed to the increase of cesarean-section rates. In addition, pregnancies of women with advanced maternal age are considered high risk for the mother and may cause complications for the fetus, motivating these mothers to opt for surgical delivery or have an indication for it (Eufrásio 2017). Studies indicate that advances in the available technologies related to childbirth, as well as changes in the behavior of the female population, which has been strongly inserted in the labor market, and also greater availability of information, scientific or otherwise, have also contributed to this increase (Zhou et al. 2015; Coelho et al. 2017).

With regard to the *mother's level of education* variable, the category "With no education" was considered as a reference. Thus, from the odds ratio values (Table 21.2), it was observed that as the mother's level of education increases, the chance of having a cesarean section among children who died within 28 days also increases. For mothers with primary education, the chance was 19% higher, for mothers with secondary education, the chance was twice as high and for those mothers with higher education, the chance was approximately three times higher, compared with mothers with no education. This result has not been occurring only in Paraíba. In Brazil, there are several studies that have signaled this trend of choosing this mode of delivery among women with higher levels of education in Brazil (Oliveira et al. 2015; Eufrásio 2017; Guimaraes et al. 2017). Studies for other countries also point in the same direction, as in Portugal (Oliveira 2013) and in Chile (Mendoza-Sassi et al. 2010). There is evidence that the mother's high level of education can be considered a factor that determines better living conditions, bringing the parturient to specialized health services; however, this circumstance does not minimize problems related to cesarean section, which place them in a paradoxical situation regarding the harmful consequences that this mode of childbirth may cause.

For the *number of children born dead* variable, the category "No" child born dead was used as a reference. It is observed that the odds ratio values showed inverse relationships with the type of childbirth variable (Table 21.2), i.e. as the number of children born dead increases, the chance of birth by cesarean section among neonatal deaths decreases. Among mothers who have already had a child born dead, the chance is reduced by approximately 18%; among those who had two children born dead, the chance was approximately 23% lower; and among mothers who already had three or more children born dead, the chance was approximately 45% lower compared to mothers who have never had children born dead. Maternal–fetal losses have been associated with a higher prevalence of infant deaths and future fetal losses, i.e. the history of previous fetal death may characterize the current pregnancy as high risk. Thus, conducting investigations of personal and obstetric antecedents is necessary as a way of improving care for pregnant women and reducing the risk of complications (Freitas and Araujo 2015; Lima et al. 2016).

Variables and categories	Estimates	Standard error	Odds Ratio	p-value[*]
Intercept	-0.3068	0.0859	0.7358	<0.0100
Mother's age (years)				
10–19	0.5722	0.0323	1.7721	<0.0100
20–29	-	-	1.0000	<0.0100
30–39	0.9873	0.0426	2.6839	<0.0100
40 and above	1.1804	0.0392	3.2557	<0.0100
Mother's level of education				
No education	-	-	1.0000	<0.0100
Primary school	0.1770	0.0228	1.1936	<0.0100
Secondary school	0.7164	0.0314	2.0471	<0.0100
Higher education	1.0590	0.0497	2.8834	<0.0100
Number of children born dead				
No	-	-	1.0000	<0.0100
One	-0.2027	0.0546	0.8165	<0.0100
Two	-0.2607	0.0334	0.7705	<0.0100
Three and above	-0.6110	0.0481	0.5428	<0.0100
Type of childbirth				
Single	-	-	1.0000	<0.0100
Twin	0.3125	0.0782	1.3669	<0.0100
Triplet and above	0.7787	0.0631	2.1786	<0.0100
ρ	0.07805	-	-	-
Deviance	6833.5	-	-	-

[*] Significant if p <0.05.

Table 21.2. Estimates of the parameters of the "most parsimonious model" with all significant fixed independent variables according to the multilevel binary logistic regression model adjusted for data on neonatal deaths in Paraíba, from 2009 to 2017

For the *type of childbirth* variable, the "single" pregnancy category was taken as a reference. It was observed that multiple pregnancy increases the chance of birth by cesarean section among children who died within 28 days (Table 21.2). Among mothers who had a twin pregnancy, the chance of birth by cesarean section among children who died within 28 days increases by approximately 36% compared to mothers who had a single pregnancy. Among mothers who had a triplet pregnancy or more, this chance increases by 2.18 times compared to mothers who had a single pregnancy. It is well known that there are more risks in multiple pregnancies for both the mother and the fetuses. The main complications include: premature birth, low birth weight, abnormal placentation, restricted intrauterine growth, premature rupture of the ovarian membranes, intrauterine fetal death, gestational diabetes, preeclampsia, increasing the chances of cesarean section, which are very prevalent among twins (Silva et al. 2019). According to Demitto et al. (2017), multiple pregnancy is considered an obstetric factor associated with neonatal death.

21.4. Conclusion

In light of the microdata of the 5,149 neonatal deaths in Paraíba, from 2009 to 2017, it was found that the variables *type of childbirth, mother's level of education and number of children born dead* and *type of pregnancy*, among the variables studied, stood out as differentiating factors from neonatal deaths in urban municipalities in relation to the adjacent rural and adjacent intermediate municipalities. Urban municipalities stood out with higher proportions of neonatal deaths of children born via cesarean section, and these proportions were higher than that of the State of Paraíba.

The results presented were interpreted, considering some limitations inherent to vital statistics, such as the often inadequate completion of death certificates, the addresses reported and the underreporting of deaths, which was in the order of 19%. However, there was the hypothesis that the high representativeness of registered deaths was sufficient to not compromise the results of the modeling since there was no evidence of selectivity for unregistered deaths.

Several factors contribute to the outcome of neonatal death; however, information available in the neonatal death certificates was used here and which are also relevant to explain the effect on the choice of the type of delivery and consequently on the occurrence of neonatal death. These "possible determinants" allowed us to identify inequalities and similarities between the municipal characterizations of Paraíba and in any region. Although some variables did not show statistical significance, the principle of parsimony is mandatory for statistical modeling, in the sense that the number of parameters is as small as possible.

The results strengthened the urgent need for more effective public and private policies to reduce the rate of elective cesarean sections to acceptable levels (10–15%), mainly in urban municipalities for a consequent reduction in neonatal mortality levels. In addition, it is necessary to strengthen existing public policies in order to reduce the rate of elective cesarean sections. It is essential to implement healthcare measures for mothers by health managers in addition to training health professionals, qualifying them to carry out prenatal care and monitoring, in addition to normal birth, and to intervene with cesarean sections in really necessary cases, guaranteeing good practices, the humanization of care, as well as the promotion of safe childbirth. Since the municipalities characterized as urban were the ones most affected by cesarean sections and whose relations were the most evident in relation to the variables studied here, they are the priority focuses of reproductive security policies.

21.5. References

Almeida, M., Gomes, C., Nascimento, L. (2014). Análise espacial da mortalidade neonatal no estado de São Paulo, 2006–2010. *Revista Paulista Pediatria*, 32(4), 374–380.

Araujo Filho, A. et al. (2017). Aspectos epidemiológicos da mortalidade neonatal em capital do nordeste do Brasil. *Revista Cuidarte*, 8(3), 1767–1776.

Barros, F. et al. (2015). Cesarean sections in Brazil: Will they ever stop increasing? *Revista Panamericana de Salud Pública*, 38(3), 217–225.

Brasil Ministério da Saúde (2017). Departamento de informática do SUS. Informações de saúde. Sistemas epidemiológicos. Disponível em: http://www2.datasus.gov.br/DATASUS/index.php?area=0203 [Accessed 16 April 2019].

Bryk, A. and Raudenbush, S. (1992). Advanced qualitative techniques in the social sciences 1. *Hierarchical Linear Models: Applications and Data Analysis Methods*. Sage Publications, Thousand Oaks.

Coelho, D. et al. (2017). Gravidez e maternidade tardia: sentimentos e vivências de mulheres em uma unidade de pré-natal de alto risco em barreiras, Bahia. *Hígia Revista de Ciências da Saúde do Oeste Baiano*, 2(1), 1–19.

Demitto, M. et al. (2017). Gestação de alto risco e fatores associados ao óbito neonatal [Online]. Available at: https://www.scielo.br/j/reeusp/a/WFBnKspHZrZvXs4Y4Fk7G6t/abstract/?lang=pt.

Domingues, R. et al. (2014). Processo de decisão pelo tipo de parto no Brasil: da preferência inicial das mulheres à via de parto final. *Cadernos de Saúde Pública, Rio de Janeiro*, 30, 101–116.

Eufrásio, L. (2017). Prevalência e fatores associados ao parto cesárea no contexto regional brasileiro em mulheres de idade reprodutiva [Online]. Available at: https://repositorio.ufrn.br/jspui/bitstream/123456789/23660/1/LaianeSantosEufrasio_TESE.pdf.

Freitas, P. and Araujo, R. (2015). Prematuridade e fatores associados em Santa Catarina, Brasil: análise após alteração do campo idade gestacional na declaração de nascidos vivos. *Revista Brasileira de Saúde Materno Infantil*, 15(3), 309–316.

Gaiva, M., Fujimori, E., Sato, A. (2016). Fatores de risco maternos e infantis associados à mortalidade neonatal. *Texto & Contexto – Enfermagem*, 25(4), 2–9.

Goldstein, H. (1995). *Multilevel Statistical Models*. Edward Arnold, London.

Guimaraes, R. et al. (2017). Fatores associados ao tipo de parto em hospitais públicos e privados no Brasil. *Revista Brasileira de Saúde Materno Infantil*, 17(3), 571–580.

Gurol-Urganci, I. et al. (2011). Risk of placenta previa in second birth after first birth cesarean section: A population-based study and meta-analysis. *BMC Pregnancy Childbirth*, 11, 95.

Heck, R., Thomas, S., Tabata, L. (2014). *Multilevel Modeling of Categorical Outcomes Using IBM SPSS*, 2nd edition. Routledge, New York.

Hosmer, D. and Lemeshow, S. (1989). *Applied Logistic Regression*. John Wiley & Sons, New York.

Hox, J. (2010). *Multilevel Analysis: Techniques and Applications*, 2nd edition. Routledge, London.

Huang, X. et al. (2011). Cesarean delivery for first pregnancy and neonatal morbidity and mortality in second pregnancy. *European Journal of Obstetrics & Gynecology and Reproductive Biology*, 158, 204–208.

IBGE (2017). *Classificação e caracterização dos espaços rurais e urbanos do Brasil: Uma primeira aproximação*. IBGE, Rio de Janeiro.

Lages, A. (2012). Parto por cesariana: Consequências a curto e longo prazo [Online]. Available at: https://docplayer.com.br/19217465-Parto-por-cesariana-consequencias-a-curto-e-longo-prazo.html.

Lima, J., Oliveira Júnior, G., Takano, O. (2016). Fatores associados à ocorrência de óbitos fetais em Cuiabá, Mato Grosso. *Revista Brasileira de Saúde Materno Infantil*, 16(3), 353–361.

Madeiro, A., Rufino, A., Santos, A. (2017). Partos cesáreos no Piauí: Tendência e fatores associados no período 2000–2011. *Epidemiologia e Serviços de Saúde*, 26, 81–90.

Mendoza-Sassi, R. et al. (2010). Risk factors for cesarean section by category of health service. *Revista de Saúde Pública*, 44(1), 80–89.

Oliveira, A. (2013). Fatores associados e indicações para a prática de cesariana: Um estudo caso-controlo. *Revista Portuguesa de Medicina Geral e Familiar*, 29(3), 151–159.

Oliveira, R. et al. (2015). The growing trend of moderate preterm births: An ecological study in one region of Brazil. *PLoS One*, 10(11), e0141852.

Paes, N., Santos, C., Coutinho, T. (2020). Quality of children's death records for regionalized spaces: A methodological route [Online]. Available at: https://www.scielo.br/j/rbepid/a/btTz7fnzTmDSKRTvdNdFMjC/?lang=en.

Sampaio Neto, A. (2018). Perfil da Mortalidade neonatal na cidade de Manaus. Trabalho de Conclusão de Curso. Graduação em Enfermagem. Universidade do Estado do Amazonas, Manaus.

Santos, B. (2017). Fatores associados ao diagnóstico de hipertensão arterial: Una aplicação de regressão logística multinível. 66 f. 2017. Trabalho de Conclusão de Curso (Bacharelado em Estatística) – Universidade de Brasília, Brasília.

Silva, F. et al. (2019). Complicações materno-fetais de gestações gemelares. *Cadernos da Medicina-UNIFESO*, 2(1).

WHO (1985). Appropriate technology for birth. *Lancet*, 326(8452), 436–437.

Zhou, Y. et al. (2015). Maternal obesity, caesarean delivery and caesarean delivery on maternal request: A cohort analysis from China. *Pediatric and Perinatal Epidemiology*, 29(3), 232–240.

Analysis of Alcohol Policy in Czechia: Estimation of Alcohol Policy Scale Compared to EU Countries

Czechia ranked fourth among OECD countries in pure alcohol consumption. Alcohol is one of the main causes of morbidity and mortality in Czechia – about 6% of total mortality is due to alcohol consumption. This is a serious health problem due to the high risk of cancer, alcohol morbidity and mortality, hospitalizations and treatment of alcohol dependence, and economic costs of alcohol consumption. This chapter summarizes the available information on alcohol policy and its restrictions in Czechia compared to EU-27 countries. A scale of Alcohol Policy for EU-27 states will be calculated. A literature review was conducted. Data sources included primarily the annual report on the state of drug affairs in Czechia in 2019 and WHO's Global status report on alcohol and health 2018. A new innovative Alcohol Policy Scale was enumerated. Latvia, Lithuania and Sweden have the highest score value (18 points) on the scale. Luxembourg has the lowest performance (10 points). The EU-27 region can be divided into nine groups. This chapter confirmed disparities, and also progressive harmonization of alcohol control policies in the EU. The findings of this chapter may be considered in future research by analyzing further aspects of alcohol policy regulations.

Chapter written by Kornélia SVAČINOVÁ, Markéta Majerová PECHHOLDOVÁ, and Jana VRABCOVÁ.

For a color version of all the figures in this chapter, see www.iste.co.uk/zafeiris/data2.zip.

22.1. Introduction

Czechia belongs to the countries with the highest level of excessive alcohol consumption in Europe. Per capita alcohol consumption is one of the highest in the world. Average consumption is 286 beers and 6.8 liters of pure alcohol per person per year (Karel 2018). The greatest health burden related to alcohol is seen in middle-aged and elderly people. Alcohol consumption in the Czech adult population remains a widespread phenomenon (Csémy et al. 2018; National Institute of Public Health: *Tobacco and alcohol consumption in the Czech Republic, 2018*).

The rate of alcohol consumption is currently declining among children and young people, but is still above average on a European scale: 16.8% of the population aged 15+ is in the category of hazardous alcohol consumption; 9.0% of young people aged 15+ belong to the high-risk category. In younger age groups (especially men under 45), alcohol-related accidents and injuries are one of the main causes of death.

In terms of government expenditure, less than 4% of total expenditure on addiction policy went to primary prevention. In 2017, health insurance expenditure for the treatment for alcohol use disorders was 1195 million CZK. There are 25,000 people per year undergoing treatment for alcohol dependence. About 800 people per year die under the influence of alcohol (mainly due to accidents and suicides). Price setting plays an important role in the consumption of alcohol in the population: a) beer in terms of volume is significantly cheaper than other non-alcoholic beverages and b) cheap and affordable alcohol has an impact on the high consumption by young adolescents. The legal regulation of addictive substances is not well formulated in the Czech environment (Mravčík et al. 2020). There is also a lack of motivation in national anti-drug strategies to provide changes in the law. The level of alcohol consumption can be regulated by the media by banning advertisements promoting alcoholic beverages and creating the impression that alcohol consumption is a natural and normal thing. Experts point out that alcohol is becoming increasingly affordable due to higher incomes than in the past. Positive results can be achieved by penalties for excessive alcohol consumption and the sale of alcohol to adolescents; an increase in the price of alcohol; a ban on advertising; repression. The Czech political scene is "inclined" to alcohol sale and producers have a strong position in the Czech market (Miovský 2019). An example should be the case of France, which has had a high alcohol consumption and high mortality from liver disease in the past. The unfavorable situation in France was alleviated by measures in the field of price regulation and health education (Csémy and Gabrielová 2019). In the US, by contrast, the reduction in total alcohol consumption in recent years is directly linked to the introduction of cannabis laws. Selected countries show up to a 15% reduction in alcohol sales per month (Csémy and Gabrielová 2019).

22.2. Literature review

a) Alcohol policy in Czechia

1989 was a very important year in the conditions of Czechia (change of political environment). Alcohol production and alcohol sale were entirely privatized and left to market forces. Newly acquired political and economic freedom introduced completely different topics to public debate. In general, the societal and political environment in the country gradually became much more liberal and unfortunately also more "alcohol friendly" with resulting impacts on alcohol consumption. Current alcohol law was replaced by legislation no. *37/1989 Coll.*, on protection against alcoholism and other drug addictions. After 1989, none of the proven alcohol treatment policy measures, such as high taxes, restrictions on the availability or the ban on advertisement have been applied. One reason for this may be the effective lobbying of the alcohol industries (Hnilicová et al. 2017).

Another legal regulation, the Act no. *379/2005 Coll.* on measures to protect against damage caused by tobacco products, alcohol and other addictive substances, seeks to reduce the availability and demand for tobacco products and alcohol. The law prohibits the consumption of alcoholic beverages in the workplace. In 1993, the government set the basis for the national drug policy, which has been continuously developed and updated. The National Drug Policy Strategy for the period 2010–2018 was approved by a government resolution on May 10, 2010. The first revision was approved by government resolution on December 15, 2014; the second revision was approved on January 25, 2016. In May 2019, the Czech government approved a new *"National Strategy for the Prevention and Reduction of Damages Associated with Addictive Behavior 2019–2027"* (National Strategy 2019–2027). Its main strategic goal is to prevent and reduce health, social and economic damage resulting from substance use, gambling and other addictive behavior; and the existence of legal and illegal markets for addictive substances, gambling and other products with addictive potential. In December 2019, the government approved the *Action Plan for the Implementation of the National Strategy for the Prevention and Reduction of Damages Associated with Addictive Behavior 2019–2027* (Action Plan 2019–2021), which is common to all areas (alcohol, tobacco, illegal drugs and psychoactive drugs, gambling and non-substance addiction). Since March 2020, excise duty rates on alcohol and tobacco products have been increased. From May 1, 2020, draft beer consumed in restaurants was reclassified to a reduced 10% VAT rate. The basic 21% VAT rate will continue to be applied to packaged beer and draft beer consumed outside the restaurant.

b) International framework

Attempts to address the harmful use of alcohol at international level have a much shorter and different history than for some other psychoactive substances with significant impact on human health. Alcohol remains the only psychoactive and dependence-producing substance with significant global impact on population health that is not controlled at the international level by legally binding regulatory frameworks (WHO 2018). In 2016, 80 responding countries (46%) reported having written national alcohol policies. An additional eight countries (5%) had subnational policies and 11 others (6%) had a total ban on alcohol. The presence of a written national alcohol policy has risen with national income levels: 34 high-income countries (67%), 23 upper-middle-income countries (43%), 18 lower-middle-income countries (42%) and four low-income countries (15%) reported having a written national policy on alcohol (WHO 2018). *"The Global strategy to reduce the harmful use of alcohol"* (WHO 2010) includes ten recommended target areas for policy interventions to reduce the harmful use of alcohol at country level: *leadership, awareness and commitment; health services' response; community action; drink-driving policies; availability of alcohol; marketing of alcoholic beverages; pricing policies; reducing the negative consequences of drinking; reducing the public health impact of illegally produced alcohol; monitoring and control.* Harmful use of alcohol is one of the key risk factors for the development of non-communicable diseases (NCDs) and mental health conditions (WHO 2018). *"The WHO mental health action plan 2013–2020"* acknowledges the role of alcohol use as a risk factor for mental health conditions and a high level of comorbidity of severe mental disorders with alcohol and other substance use disorders, and strengthens the synergies in implementation of the mental health action plan and the global strategy to reduce the harmful use of alcohol (WHO 2013).

22.3. Methods

The overall purpose of the UN Sustainable Development Goals is to evaluate and harmonize the alcohol control policies in the current EU member states. One of the main research questions in this chapter is to analyze the similarities and differences among alcohol control policies in EU-27 states with a focus on Czechia. This chapter reviews and discusses earlier studies that measured the strictness of alcohol policies (Karlsson and Österberg 2001; Brand et al. 2007). The aim of this chapter is to conduct a similar analysis for EU-27 countries by selecting quantified alcohol control measures. We will then create a unique scale for the Alcohol Policy Index to see the harmonization and diversity of alcohol policies in the EU.

Public policy (max. 3 points)

1. Written national policy on alcohol (Yes 1p. / Subnational ½ p./ No 0 p.)
2. National action plan (Yes 1p. /No 0 p.)
3. National government support for community action (Yes 1p. /No 0 p.)

Drink-driving policies (max. 3 points)

4. National maximum legal blood alcohol concentration (BAC) when driving a vehicle
   a. BAC 0.05% or less (3 p.)
   b. BAC 0.08% or less (2 p.)
   c. BAC limit at all (1 p.)

Personal control (max. 6 points)

5. National legal minimum age for off-premise sales of alcoholic beverages
   a. 20 for some alcoholic beverages (3 p.)
   b. 18 for some alcoholic beverages (2 p.)
   c. 17 for some alcoholic beverages (1 ½ p.)
   d. 16 for some alcoholic beverages (1 p.)
   e. Subnational (1/2 p.)
6. National legal minimum age for on-premise sales of alcoholic beverages
   a. 20 for some alcoholic beverages (3 p.)
   b. 18 for some alcoholic beverages (2 p.)
   c. 17 for some alcoholic beverages (1 ½ p.)
   d. 16 for some alcoholic beverages (1 p.)
   e. Subnational (1/2 p.)

Control of marketing (max. 3 points)

7. Legally binding regulations on alcohol advertising (Yes 1p. / No 0 p.)
8. Legally binding regulations on alcohol sponsorship (Yes 1p. / No 0 p.)
9. Legally required health warning labels on alcohol advertisement (Yes 1p. / No 0 p.)

Pricing policies (max. 3 points)

10. Excise tax on beer (Yes 1p. / No 0 p.)
11. Excise tax on wine (Yes 1p. / No 0 p.)
12. Excise tax on spirits (Yes 1p. / No 0 p.)

Monitoring (max. 1 point)

13. National monitoring system (Yes 1p. / No 0 p.)

Reducing the public health impact of illicit alcohol and informally produced alcohol (max. 1 point)

14. Estimates of unrecorded alcohol consumption (Yes 1p. / No 0 p.)

Table 22.1. *Alcohol policy framework and scoring used in the article (source: ECAS project[1]; Karlsson and Österberg (2001); authors' modification)*

Constructing a scale to measure alcohol control policies in EU countries is difficult and has many shortcomings and barriers. It may be too ambitious (actually impossible) to include all factors that are related to alcohol control policies. Practically we cannot obtain data reliable and comparable data for EU-27 countries

---

1 The European Comparative Alcohol Study.

(Karlsson and Österberg 2009). Therefore, we have to take into account some limitations: (1) alcohol control measures included in the scale and (2) time period for which data is collected and comparable (Moskalewicz 2016). Questions included in the scale are limited to measure formal alcohol policy (laws, national action plans and regulations) in EU countries. The information (source material) was obtained from the WHO's *Global status report on alcohol and health* with the respect that the latest report is available for 2018. Interviewing experts as information representatives from individual countries was not within the possibilities of this research and may be a proposal for future studies. The scale used in this chapter was constructed in a simple and clear way to avoid misinterpretations and ensure an appropriate comparability. Table 22.1 presents the questions and the scale used in this chapter (with a maximum of 20 points).

Two main research questions were formulated:

Research question 1: What is the position of Czechia compared to EU countries in alcohol control policy?

Research question 2: Which areas of the alcohol policy are already harmonized for EU-27 countries versus where are the disparities between regions?

22.4. Results

For the calculations in this chapter, selected alcohol policy areas (questions) and scoring described above were used. Maximum of achievable points was 20 points for 14 questions (selected individually according to available data and information). The main source of information was obtained from the WHO's *Global status report on alcohol and health 2018*. In the first step, a score for each of the 14 questions for 27 member states was allocated according to Table 22.1. The values vary between 0 and 3 points. No weights were used in this case. In the column "Total" in Table 22.2, the sum of all achieved points was calculated. Values were then sorted from the highest to the lowest in order to display the position of Czechia together with further EU member countries (Table 22.4). Average value, minimum and maximum points for individual questions are presented in Table 22.3. Correspondence in question 3, question 10 and question 12 for 27 states is visible (points = 1).

According to results, EU-27 countries may be divided into nine categories (Table 22.4). Latvia, Lithuania and Sweden have the best performance (18.0 points). Luxembourg has the lowest performance in terms of the alcohol control policy (score = 10.0 points). Czechia belongs to the fourth group (together with Greece, Italy, Netherlands, Romania and Slovenia with 15.0 points).

Country (EU-27)	1.	2.	3.	4.	5.	6.	7.	8.	9.	10.	11.	12.	13.	14.	Total
Austria	1	0	1	3	0,5	0,5	1	1	0	1	0	1	1	1	12
Belgium	0	0	1	3	1	1	1	0	0	1	1	1	1	1	12
Bulgaria	1	0	1	3	2	2	1	0	0	1	0	1	1	1	14
Croatia	1	0	1	3	2	2	1	0	0	1	0	1	1	1	14
Cyprus	1	1	1	3	1,5	1,5	1	0	0	1	0	1	1	1	14
Czechia	1	1	1	3	2	2	1	0	0	1	1	1	0	1	15
Denmark	0,5	0	1	3	1	2	1	1	0	1	1	1	1	1	14,5
Estonia	1	1	1	3	2	2	1	0	1	1	1	1	1	1	17
Finland	1	1	1	3	2	2	1	1	0	1	1	1	1	1	17
France	1	0	1	3	2	2	1	1	1	1	1	1	1	1	17
Germany	1	0	1	3	1	1	1	0	0	1	0	1	1	1	12
Greece	0	0	1	3	2	2	0	1	1	1	1	1	1	1	15
Hungary	0	0	1	3	2	2	1	0	0	1	0	1	1	1	13
Ireland	1	0	1	3	2	2	1	0	0	1	1	1	0	1	14
Italy	1	1	1	3	2	2	1	1	0	1	0	1	1	0	15
Latvia	1	1	1	3	2	2	1	1	1	1	1	1	1	1	18
Lithuania	1	1	1	3	2	2	1	1	1	1	1	1	1	1	18
Luxembourg	0	0	1	3	1	1	1	0	0	1	0	1	0	1	10
Malta	0	0	1	2	1,5	1,5	1	1	0	1	1	1	0	1	12
Netherlands	1	0	1	3	2	2	1	0	0	1	1	1	1	1	15
Poland	1	0	1	3	2	2	1	1	1	1	1	1	0	1	16
Portugal	1	1	1	3	2	2	1	1	1	1	0	1	1	1	17
Romania	0	0	1	3	2	2	1	1	1	1	1	1	0	1	15
Slovakia	1	1	1	3	2	2	1	0	0	1	1	1	1	1	16
Slovenia	1	0	1	3	2	2	1	0	1	1	0	1	1	1	15
Spain	1	1	1	3	2	2	1	1	0	1	0	1	1	1	16
Sweden	1	0	1	3	3	2	1	1	1	1	1	1	1	1	18
Total	20,5	10	27	80	48,5	48,5	26	14	10	27	16	27	21	26	401,5

Table 22.2. *Scoring of the EU-27 countries. For a color version of this table, see www.iste.co.uk/zafeiris/data2.zip*

Average	0,76	0,37	1	2,96	1,80	1,80	0,96	0,52	0,37	1	0,59	1	0,78	0,96
Min	0	0	1	2	0,5	0,5	0	0	0	1	0	1	0	0
Max	1	1	1	3	3	2	1	1	1	1	1	1	1	1

Table 22.3. *Average, minimum and maximum related to 14 questions. For a color version of this table, see www.iste.co.uk/zafeiris/data2.zip*

1.	Latvia, Lithuania, Sweden	(score: 18.0)
2.	Estonia, Finland, France, Portugal	(score: 17.0)
3.	Poland, Slovakia, Spain	(score: 16.0)
4.	Czechia, Greece, Italy, Netherlands, Romania, Slovenia	(score: 15.0)
5.	Denmark	(score: 14.5)
6.	Bulgaria, Croatia, Cyprus, Ireland	(score: 14.0)
7.	Hungary	(score: 13.0)
8.	Austria, Belgium, Germany, Malta	(score: 12.0)
9.	Luxembourg	(score: 10.0)

Table 22.4. *Ranking of the EU-27 countries (source: authors' calculation)*

In the next step, results are presented in Figures 22.1–22.9. The correspondence is confirmed for the majority of alcohol policy areas. The main disparities are clear in question 2 (national action plan), question 8 (legally binding regulations on alcohol sponsorship) and question 9 (legally required health warning labels on alcohol advertisement). According to the results, we believe that specifically these parts of alcohol control policies have to be strengthened and harmonized in EU regions.

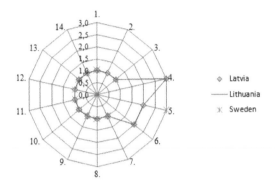

Figure 22.1. *Matches and differences in alcohol control policy framework (LV, LT, SE)*

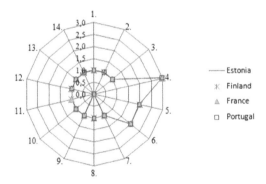

Figure 22.2. *Matches and differences in alcohol control policy framework (EE, FI, FR, PT)*

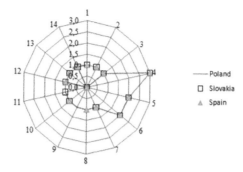

Figure 22.3. *Matches and differences in alcohol control policy framework (PL, SK, ES)*

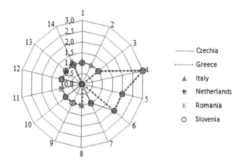

Figure 22.4. *Matches and differences in alcohol control policy framework (CZ, EL, IT, NL, RO, SI)*

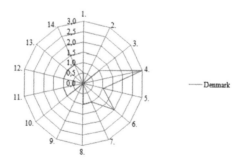

Figure 22.5. *Matches and differences in alcohol control policy framework (DK)*

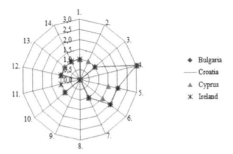

Figure 22.6. *Matches and differences in alcohol control policy framework (BG, HR, CY, IE)*

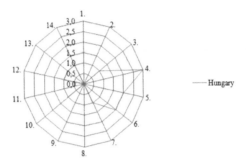

Figure 22.7. *Matches and differences in alcohol control policy framework (HU)*

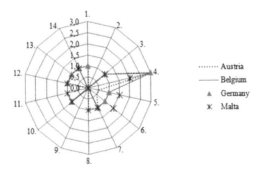

Figure 22.8. *Matches and differences in alcohol control policy framework (AT, BE, DE, MT)*

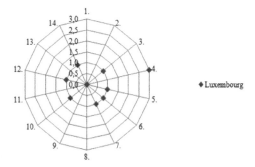

Figure 22.9. *Matches and differences in alcohol control policy framework (LU)*

22.5. Discussion

The Czech environment is "alcohol-friendly". Alcohol availability is high in the long term and well tolerated throughout society. There is a lack of regular systematic monitoring of the effects of alcohol consumption (IHIS; CZSO 2020). The role of politicians would be to effectively regulate indirect taxes, especially excise duty, which is also imposed on commodities such as alcohol. Examples are the Scandinavian countries (Sweden, Finland, Denmark, Norway and Iceland), where there is a higher excise duty on alcohol and the consumer has limited options for buying alcohol. There is also a lack of education in Czechia, which would acquaint the public with the fact that alcohol (despite its easy availability) is a drug and its negative effects do not lag behind marijuana, tobacco and other addictive substances, rather the opposite (Karel 2018). National Strategy 2019–2027[2] raises expectations in the field of decreasing alcohol consumption in the country. The main aims include strengthening prevention, raising awareness, increasing addictology services, regulation of markets, strengthening the governance and effective financing of drug policy (Mravčík 2019). These are very ambitious goals – hopefully the anti-alcohol campaigns and policies will be effective for this time (compared to ineffective past strategies) in the coming future (Dzúrová 2010). Interventions recommended by the WHO (2017) to reduce harmful use of alcohol are as follows: increasing excise taxes on alcoholic beverages, strengthening bans on exposure to alcohol advertising, enforcing restrictions on the physical availability of retailed alcohol (via reduced hours of sale), enforcing drink-driving laws, establishing minimum prices for alcohol where applicable, providing prevention, treatment and care for alcohol use disorders and comorbid conditions in health and social services, enforcing an appropriate minimum age for purchase or consumption of alcoholic

---

2 *National Strategy for Prevention and Reduction of Damage Related to Addiction Behavior 2019–2027.*

beverages, reducing density of retail outlets, and restricting or banning promotions of alcoholic beverages in connection with sponsorships and activities targeting young people.

22.6. Conclusion

The EU-27 region can be divided into nine groups. The innovative alcohol policy scale confirmed the most thoroughly sophisticated system of alcohol policy for three EU regions: Latvia, Lithuania and Sweden have the highest score value (18 points). Nordic countries have a strict alcohol control policy. Czechia has ranked in the upper quartile (score 15). This chapter confirmed disparities, and also a progressive harmonization of alcohol control policies in the EU. Generally, we should be very careful not to draw too far-reaching conclusions based solely on the results and evaluation of the scale or any other scale. Due to the large social and cultural differences between countries, the results are not fully comparable. The scores show a general trend in alcohol control policies in different countries, but do not allow us to make conclusions about the dynamics in alcohol regulations. The findings of this chapter may be considered in future research by analyzing further aspects of alcohol policy measures.

22.7. Acknowledgment

This work was supported by the Czech Science Foundation, grant no. GA ČR 19-23183Y, on a project titled "Alcohol burden in the Czech Republic: mortality, morbidity and social context".

22.8. References

Brand, D.A., Saisana, M., Rynn, L.A., Pennoni, F., Lowenfels, A.B. (2007). Comparative analysis of alcohol control policies in 30 countries. *PLoS Med.*, 4(4), e151 [Online]. Available at: https://doi.org/10.1371/journal.pmed.0040151.

Csémy, L. and Gabrielová, H. (2019). Cannabis and alcohol are shared by almost the same audience. Let's legalize marijuana, increase taxation on alcohol and reduce advertising, experts said. Medical Diary.

Csémy, L. et al. (2018). National Institute of Public Health: Tobacco and alcohol consumption in the Czech Republic.

CZSO (2020). Statistical Yearbook of the Czech Republic – 2020 [Online]. Available at: https://www.czso.cz/csu/czso/25-health-hjyc3o2su2.

Dzúrová, D., Spilková, J., Pikhart, H. (2010). Social inequalities in alcohol consumption in the Czech Republic: A multilevel analysis. *Health Place.* 16(3), 590–597. DOI: 10.1016/j.healthplace.2010.01.004.

Hnilicová, H., Nome, S., Dobiášová, K., Zvolský, M., Henriksen, R., Tulupova, E., Kmecová, Z. (2017). Comparison of alcohol consumption and alcohol policies in the Czech Republic and Norway. *Centr. Eur. J. Public Health*, 25(2), 145–151. DOI: 10.21101/cejph.a4918.

IHIS (2020). Institute of Health Information and Statistics of the Czech Republic. National Register of Therapy of Drug Users [Online]. Available at: https://www.uzis.cz/index.php?pg=registry-sber-dat--narodni-zdravotni-registry--narodni-registr-lecby-uzivatelu-drog#publikace.

Karel, K. (2018). Alcohol Policy in Czechia [Online]. Available at: https://nazorne.wordpress.com/2018/04/19/alkoholova-politika-v-cesku/.

Karlsson, T. and Österberg, E. (2001). A scale of formal alcohol control policy in 15 European countries. *Nordisk Alkohol Nark.*, 18(English Supplement).

Karlsson, T. and Österberg, E. (2009). Scaling alcohol control policies across Europe. *Drugs: Educ. Prev. Policy*, 14(6), 499–511. DOI: 10.1080/09687630701392032.

Kilian, C., Manthey, J., Moskalewicz, J., Sieroslawski, J., Rehm, J. (2019). How attitudes toward alcohol policies differ across European Countries: Evidence from the Standardized European Alcohol Survey (SEAS). *Int. J. Environ. Res. Public Health.* DOI: 10.3390/ijerph16224461.

Lindeman, M., Karlsson, T., Österberg, E. (2013). Public opinions, alcohol consumption and policy changes in Finland, 1993–2013. *Nord. Stud. Alcohol Drugs*, 30.

Miovský, M. (2019). Alcohol causes 9 types of cancer, we know for sure and the media is silent, there is no safe dose, says the addictologist. Reflex.

Moskalewicz, J., Room, R., Thom, B. (2016). Comparative monitoring of alcohol epidemiology across the EU. Baseline assessment and suggestions for future action. Synthesis report, RARHA. Reducing Alcohol Related Harm. ISBN: 978-83-88075-16-2.

Mravčík, V., Chomynová, P., Nechanská, B., Černíková, T. (2019). Alcohol use and its consequences in the Czech Republic. *Centr. Eur. J. Public Health*, 27, 15–28. DOI: 10.21101/cejph.a5728.

Mravčík, V., Chomynová, P., Grohmannová, K. et al. (2020). Annual report on the state of drug affairs in the Czech Republic in 2019. ISBN 978-80-7440-254-8.

WHO (2010). The Global strategy to reduce the harmful use of alcohol.

WHO (2013). The WHO mental health action plan 2013–2020.

WHO (2017). Policy in Action. A tool for measuring alcohol policy implementation.

WHO (2018). Global status report on alcohol and health 2018. ISBN: 978-92-4-156563-9.

WHO (2019). Status report on alcohol consumption, harm and policy responses in 30 European countries 2019.

Alcohol-Related Mortality and Its Cause-Elimination in Life Tables in Selected European Countries and USA: An International Comparison

Notable differences in the levels and patterns of alcohol-related harm persist within Europe. Cultural habits of alcohol consumption were identified as one of the reasons for this diversity. Traditionally, eastern Europeans tend to drink in a more harmful way than western Europeans. This has been reflected in higher levels of alcohol-related mortality in the East. However, times do change and the transition to free-market economies has changed the old habits, including the alcohol consumption structure and drinking attitudes. As a result, we are witnessing a unifying trend across Europe. The aim of this study was to compare alcohol-related consumption and its impact on health for a subset of European countries over time. Analyses are based on validated long-term data series from the Human Cause-of-Death Database (see: www.causesofdeath.org). All-cause and alcohol-related mortality age patterns were observed for six selected countries in three periods (1980, 2000 and 2016). In addition, potential gains in life expectancy were enumerated by the elimination of alcohol-related deaths from the life tables. In all selected countries, alcohol-related mortality shows a particular age pattern with a peak at adult ages.

Chapter written by Jana VRABCOVÁ, Markéta Majerová PECHHOLDOVÁ and Kornélia SVAČINOVÁ.

For a color version of all the figures in this chapter, see www.iste.co.uk/zafeiris/data2.zip.

Alcohol-related deaths occur earlier in the countries of the former socialist bloc. Alcohol-related mortality increases in the East, while it declines in the West. Potential gains are nowadays higher in the East, especially in Poland and Belarus. Despite converging consumption levels, East–West differences in alcohol-related harm persist. Reducing alcohol-related mortality to zero would result in an equivalent of several years of progress in life expectancy. Public health actions are thus particularly desirable in the former socialist countries.

23.1. Introduction

Alcohol is a psychoactive and dependence-producing substance, and its consumption is associated with morbidity and mortality. The use of alcohol affects the social, health and economic areas of society (Dhital 2001). The damaging use of alcohol ranks among the top five risk factors for disease, disability and death throughout the world (World Health Organization 2018). The WHO European region continues to have the highest level of alcohol consumption per capita globally. Given this high average drinking, the region has proportionately higher levels of the burden of disease attributable to alcohol use compared to others (World Health Organization 2019). More than 290,000 people died in the European region in 2016 due to alcohol-attributable diseases, and 7.6 million years of life were lost due to either premature mortality or disability (World Health Organization 2019). Alcohol-attributable deaths were largely due to cancer (29%), liver cirrhosis (20%), cardiovascular disease (19%) and injury (18%) (World Health Organization 2019).

There is evidence of both a positive and negative association between education and frequency of consumption. Hazardous consumption of alcohol is more likely in women with higher education, while men were the opposite – men with low education are more at risk (Bloomfield et al. 2005; Gmel et al. 2005; Grittner et al. 2013). It has been confirmed for both sexes that higher socio-economic status will be positively linked to the frequency of drinking (Gmel et al. 2005; Grittner et al. 2013). However, this relationship is stronger in higher-income countries; these results are strongly dependent on the choice of countries or regions.

As mentioned above, alcohol drinking patterns vary across countries. Heavy episodic drinking (60 grams or more per one occasion) is one of the most harmful ways of consuming alcohol and can indicate a problem with drinking. Furthermore, heavy episodic drinking, which is associated with higher mortality, is more common in less educated men than in higher educated men (Laatikainen et al. 2003; Gmel et al. 2005).

Alcohol is a strong contributor to the health gap between western, central and eastern Europe, with both average volumes of consumption and patterns of drinking contributing to the burden of disease and injury (Rehm et al. 2007). According to the EHIS Survey in 2014, countries such as Norway, Denmark, Germany, Luxembourg, Ireland and Finland were found to have a high proportion of people drinking at least every month and also a high proportion of heavy drinking episodes at least every month. Another group of countries consists of Italy, Portugal and Spain, with a relatively higher proportion of people who drink alcohol every day, but very low levels of heavy episodic drinking. Romania stands out as a country with a high proportion of heavy episodic drinking, but low alcohol consumption (frequency of consumption is typically at least every month). Looking at the EU-28, we have seen that every fifth person who consumes alcohol experiences at least one episode of heavy drinking every month.

This chapter aims to identify and quantify international differences in alcohol-related mortality with a focus on variations between regions (East vs. West) and across time. Alcohol-related harm will be expressed here as years of life gained after eliminating directly attributable alcohol-related conditions from the overall mortality, while keeping other causes of death constant. We also evaluate the relationship between alcohol consumption and the consequent health losses.

23.2. Data and methods

For this study, we used a unique data source – time series from the Human Cause-of-Death Database (see: www.causesofdeath.org), a new dataset providing the results of the reconstruction of coherent time series by cause of death in numerous countries. These are historical consolidated data which are internationally comparable and to which backward recalculation has been applied.

We use a selection of six countries representing these areas:

– Central European countries

   - Czechia (1980, 2000, 2016[1])

---

1 The brackets indicate the three years for which the dates for comparison were selected. These are always the years 1980, 2000 and 2016 or the nearest available one.

- Poland (1980, 2000, 2016)

– Eastern European countries (representing former USSR)

- Belarus (1980, 2000, 2016)

- Russia (1980, 2000, 2014)

– Western countries

- France (1980, 2000, 2015)

- USA (1980, 2000, 2018)

Central European countries are categorized as high-income countries; their per capita gross national income is lower than that in the other parts of the EU. The drinking style was traditionally characterized by the consumption of a comparably large proportion of spirits, with frequent episodes of heavy drinking (Shield et al. 2016). A considerable proportion of drinking occasions occur outside of meals. Eastern European countries have lower per capita gross national income than countries in the western parts of the WHO European region and are in the middle-income category. Their drinking style is characterized by heavy episodic drinking, with both a longer duration and a larger volume of alcohol consumed per occasion. Western countries are characterized as high-income countries. The drinking styles in these countries are characterized by the consumption of a large proportion of beer and wine as the preferred beverages, and by drinking both with and outside of meals in a relatively frequent style.

To identify the actual size and timing of change, we analyzed long-term cause-of-death data for a subset of European countries and the USA. An analysis of alcohol-specific causes of death and age patterns was performed. We enumerated cause-elimination in life tables, which explain how many years of life can be gained (hypothetical life expectancy gains) if death connected with alcohol is eliminated. Associated single-decrement life tables (ASDT) were used for the calculation (Preston et al. 2001).

Let k denote all causes of death other than j. If cause j is eliminated, then cause k is the only one operating in the cohort. Thus, the probability of surviving from age x_i to age x_{i+1} is

$$p_i^k = e^{-\int_{x_i}^{x_{i+1}} \mu^k(t)dt} = e^{-r_i^k \int_{x_i}^{x_{i+1}} \mu(t)dt} = (p_i)^{r_i^k},$$

where $\mu(t)$ is a force of the decrement from all causes combined and r_i^k is a share of deaths from cause k among all deaths at age i:

$$r_i^k = \frac{M_i^k}{M_i} = \frac{D_i^k}{D_i}.$$

If we know p_i^k, then it is possible to calculate life tables according to the standard procedure.

We assume that the distribution of deaths from cause k follows the quadratic function for five-year age groups:

$$a_i^k = \frac{-(1/24)d_{i-1}^k + (1/2)d_i^k + (1/24)d_{i+1}^k}{d_i^k},$$

for the age groups 0, 1–4 and 5–9, the following formula was used

$$a_i^k = n_i + r_i^k \frac{q_i}{q_i^k}(a_i - 1).$$

23.3. Alcohol consumption in European countries by the OECD

Figure 23.1 shows the trends in alcohol consumption (annual sales of pure alcohol in liters per person, 15+ years) for the available European countries and the USA from 1960 to 2018 according to the OECD data. The long-term trends in alcohol consumption vary substantially, showing increases, decreases and even reversals, but we observed an overall convergence – a decrease in variability: the range of alcohol consumption figures narrowed from 1.1 to 23.2 liters of alcohol per capita in the early 1970s (Turkey vs. France) to 1.4 to 12.6 liters in 2018 (Turkey vs. Latvia). The reason for this convergence is that alcohol consumption has particularly decreased in countries with previously extreme levels, such as France. In Figure 23.2, only the countries of interest in this study are highlighted.

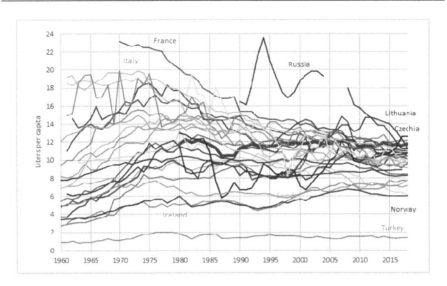

Figure 23.1. *Alcohol consumption (annual sales of pure alcohol in liters per person, 15+ years) in European countries and the USA during the period 1960–2018. Data source: OECD (2021), alcohol consumption (indicator). doi: 10.1787/e6895909-en (accessed on April 4, 2021)*

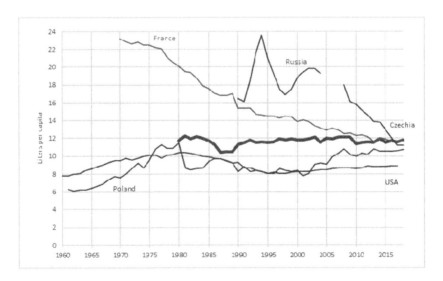

Figure 23.2. *Alcohol consumption (annual sales of pure alcohol in liters per person, 15+ years) in Czechia, Poland, Russia, France and the USA during the period 1960–2018. Data source: OECD (2021), alcohol consumption (indicator). doi: 10.1787/e6895909-en (accessed on April 4, 2021)*

Figures 23.4–23.5 show age-specific mortality rates for all causes combined and alcohol-related conditions separately (dotted lines). A logarithmic scale was used to better represent the curve at younger ages.

23.4. Czechia

Figure 23.3 shows the comparison of mortality rates by age for men and women and in selected years in Czechia. There was a decrease in the overall mortality rate from 1980 to 2000 and 2016. Alcohol-related mortality shows a particular age pattern, with a visible peak in middle and older adults. In 1980, however, we see a distortion in this age profile, which arose because of the recalculation of historical data. In the case of alcohol mortality curves in 2000 and 2016, the "A-shaped" profile is already slightly visible here. This is typical for alcohol connected mortality, as will be shown for other countries and periods.

In the international comparison, Czechia has long been characterized by high alcohol consumption. Beer and drinking alcohol are considered an important part of Czech culture, society and history, and the beer industry is seen as part of the national heritage (Dzúrová et al. 2010).

Trends in alcohol consumption and alcohol mortality have similar tendencies – little change is evident throughout the observation.

23.5. Poland

During the 1960s and 1970s, alcohol consumption in Poland was increasing. In 1980–1981, Solidarity blamed the Polish government for promoting alcohol to hide the deeper problems of society and to obtain more revenue. Faced with this pressure, the alcohol policy was tightened – production decreased, temporary prohibition and rationing. During the 1990s, there was a stagnation in alcohol consumption in Poland, but after 2000 it increased; there was also an increase in alcohol-related causes of death. Trends in alcohol consumption and alcohol mortality also have similar tendencies. For 2016, the "A-shaped" profile is very clearly visible in men.

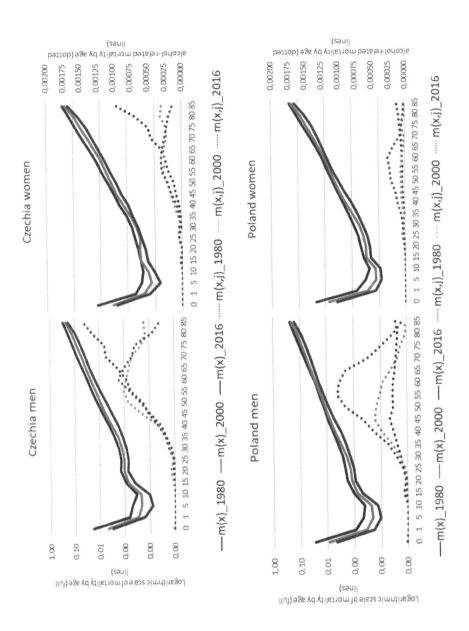

Figure 23.3. *Overall and alcohol mortality rate by age for men and women in Czechia and Poland in selected years. Data source: Human Cause-of-Death Database*

23.6. Belarus

Alcohol consumption in Belarus has been rising and falling since the 1990s. In recent years, we can still observe a slight decline. In Belarus, alcohol has a relatively high impact on the mortality burden from injury (60%). Since the 1990s, alcohol-related deaths have increased significantly. In contrast to the Czech Republic and Poland, Belarus has a shifted mode of an "A-shaped" profile to a younger age.

23.7. Russia

In 1990, shortly after an anti-alcohol campaign was initiated in 1985, the alcohol consumption level in the Russian Federation was relatively low, below the WHO European region average, slightly below the average of the Mediterranean countries and markedly below the average of the central–eastern EU countries (World Health Organization 2018). Since 2007, there has been a rapid decrease in alcohol consumption. Russia also has a mode of an "A" profile in men at younger ages, but in 2014 there was a visible shift to older age groups.

23.8. France

Since the 1970s, there has been a constant decline in alcohol consumption in France. Trends in alcohol consumption and alcohol mortality have a similar tendency to decline.

The "A" profile in men has its modal value in older ages than for eastern and central European countries.

23.9. USA

In the case of the USA, there is a decrease in the overall mortality rate from 1980 to 2000 and stagnation between the years 2000 and 2016. Trends in alcohol consumption and alcohol mortality are similar.

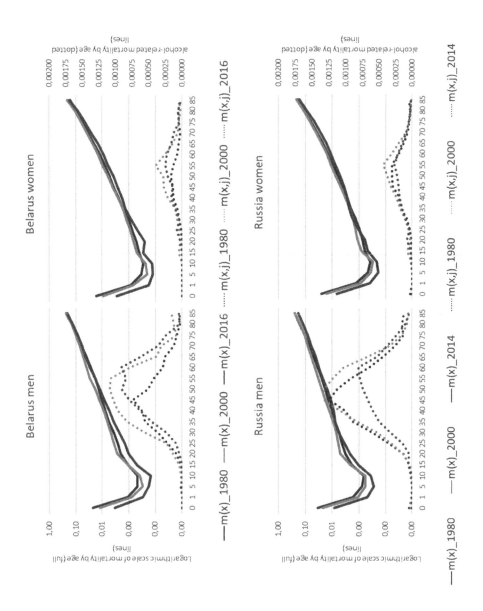

Figure 23.4. *Overall and alcohol mortality rate by age for men and women in Belarus and Russia in selected years. Data source: Human Cause-of-Death Database*

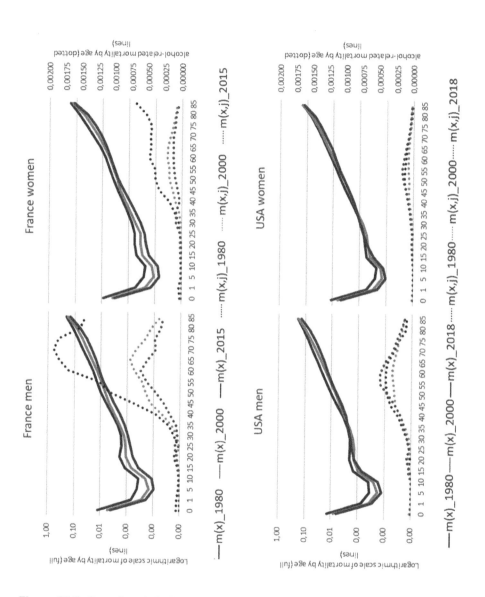

Figure 23.5. *Overall and alcohol mortality rate by age for men and women in France and the USA in selected years. Data source: Human Cause-of-Death Database*

Table 23.1 summarizes the results of the cause-elimination life table calculations, which show "how many years of life can be gained if alcohol is eliminated as the underlying cause of death". The tabulated values represent the difference between cause-eliminated life expectancy at birth (LEB) and the all-cause (master) LEB. These are the years of life by which it would be possible (almost immediately in the extreme case) to increase life expectancy because it is an avoidable cause of death. Higher values are observed for men in all countries. As time goes by, the potential gains of alcohol elimination increase. In France and Russia, the gains observed in 2016 are lower than those of 1980. Overall, the gains are much less than one year in men, with a maximum of 0.82 years observed in France in 1980, and even lower in women. The lowest gains among men are observed in the USA in all periods. In 2016, the levels are the highest in Belarus and Poland. The gains continue to be higher in the former socialist countries compared to France and the USA in both sexes. In Poland, alcohol-related harm has doubled since 2000 in both sexes, representing the worst tendency of all the countries observed.

Year	Czechia	Poland	Belarus	Russia	France	USA
Men						
1980	0.37	0.24	0.52	0.74	0.82	0.30
2000	0.48	0.36	0.72	0.68	0.49	0.28
2016 (or nearest available year)	0.50	0.70	0.60	0.54	0.43	0.37
Women						
1980	0.23	0.13	0.19	0.30	0.48	0.18
2000	0.27	0.13	0.31	0.36	0.25	0.14
2016 (or nearest available year)	0.28	0.25	0.28	0.32	0.21	0.20

Table 23.1. *Potential gains (in years of life) due to elimination of alcohol-related mortality. For a color version of this table, see www.iste.co.uk/zafeiris/data2.zip*

23.10. Conclusion

This chapter analyzed a unique data source, a dataset providing results of the reconstruction of coherent time series by cause of death. These are historical consolidated data which are internationally comparable and to which backward recalculation has been applied. Long-term cause-of-death data were analyzed for a subset of European countries and the USA, including visualization of alcohol-specific causes of death, age patterns and an enumeration of years of life to be gained after the elimination of alcohol-related deaths in life tables.

Among central European countries, the overall mortality decreased, alcohol-related mortality stagnated (in the case of Czechia) or increased (in the case of Poland), which was reflected in the values of potential LEB gains, which during the observed period increased from values of about 0.2 years of potentially added life at the beginning, to 0.5 or 0.7 years at the end of the observed period.

For the eastern European countries, the overall mortality stagnated or slightly decreased, and alcohol-related mortality first increased, then decreased. An "A-shaped" profile shifted to younger ages. The values of potential LEB gains during the observed period fluctuated between 0.2 and 0.5, or 0.7 years.

For the selected western European countries, the overall mortality decreased, alcohol-related mortality decreased (France) or stagnated (USA). Values of potential LEB gains during the observed period fluctuated between 0.14 and 0.8 years.

The potential LEB gains look small, but if we consider that the LEB, for example, increases in Czechia every year by an average of 0.2 years, then the elimination of alcohol-related deaths would suddenly move the Czech LEB one to three years forward (depending on the gender). In this light, alcohol-related mortality is no longer a negligible obstacle in further life expectancy improvement. Given that in the former socialist countries alcohol-related harm continues to increase, the issue deserves a political strategy and a public health action.

23.11. Acknowledgment

This work was supported by the Czech Science Foundation (grant no. GA ČR 19-23183Y) for a project titled "Alcohol burden in the Czech Republic: mortality, morbidity and social context".

23.12. References

Bloomfield, K., Allamani, A., Beck, F., Bergmark, K.H., Csemy, L., Eisenbach-Stangl, I., Elekes, Z., Gmel, G., Kerr-Corrêa, F., Knibbe, R. et al. (2005). Gender, culture and alcohol problems: A multi-national study. An EU concerted action. Project final report, Institute for Medical Informatics, Biometrics & Epidemiology, Charité Campus Benjamin Franklin, Berlin [Online]. Available at: https://www.researchgate.net/profile/Martha-Patricia-Mendoza/publication/309312782_Gender_Culture_and_Alcohol_Problems_a_multinational_study/links/580916cc08ae993dc0509f0f/Gender-Culture-and-Alcohol-Problems-a-multinational-study.pdf.

Dhital, R. (2001). Alcohol and young people in Nepal. *The Globe*, 4, 21–25.

Dzúrová, D., Spilková, J., Pikhart, H. (2010). Social inequalities in alcohol consumption in the Czech Republic: A multilevel analysis. *Health & Place*, 16, 590–597 [Online]. Available at: https://doi.org/10.1016/j.healthplace.2010.01.004.

Gmel, G., Kuntsche, S., Kuendig, H., Bloomfield, K., Kramer, S., Grittner, U. (2005). How do social roles and social stratification influence women's and men's alcohol consumption? A cross-cultural analysis. Institute for Medical Informatics, Biometrics & Epidemiology, Charité Universitätsmedizin Berlin [Online]. Available at: https://www.researchgate.net/ profile/Martha-Patricia-Mendoza/publication/309312782_Gender_Culture_and_Alcohol_ Problems_a_multinational_study/links/580916cc08ae993dc0509f0f/Gender-Culture-and-Alcohol-Problems-a-multinational-study.pdf#page=137.

Grittner, U., Kuntsche, S., Gmel, G., Bloomfield, K. (2013). Alcohol consumption and social inequality at the individual and country levels – Results from an international study. *European Journal of Public Health*, 23(2), 332–339 [Online]. Available at: https://doi.org/10.1093/eurpub/cks044.

Laatikainen, T., Manninen, L., Poikolainen, K., Vartiainen, E. (2003). Increased mortality related to heavy alcohol intake pattern. *Journal of Epidemiology and Community Health (1979–)*, 57(5), 379–384.

Preston, S.H., Heuveline, P., Guillot, M. (2001). *Demography. Measuring and Modeling Population Processes*. Blackwell Publishers, Oxford.

Rehm, J., Sulkowska, U., Mańczuk, M., Boffetta, P., Powles, J., Popova, S., Zatoński, W. (2007). Alcohol accounts for a high proportion of premature mortality in central and eastern Europe. *International Journal of Epidemiology*, 36(2), 458–467 [Online]. Available at: https://doi.org/10.1093/ije/dyl294.

Shield, K.D., Rylett, M., Rehm, J. (2016). Public health successes and missed opportunities: Trends in alcohol consumption and attributable mortality in the WHO European region, 1990–2014. World Health Organization [Online]. Available at: https://www.euro. who.int/__data/assets/pdf_file/0018/319122/Public-health-successes-and-missed-opportun ities-alcohol-mortality-19902014.pdf.

World Health Organization (2018). Global status report on alcohol and health 2018 [Online]. Available at: https://www.who.int/publications-detail-redirect/9789241565639.

World Health Organization (2019). Status report on alcohol consumption, harm and policy responses in 30 European countries 2019 [Online]. Available at: https://www.euro.who.int/__ data/assets/pdf_file/0019/411418/Alcohol-consumption-harm-policy-responses-30-European-countries-2019.pdf.

Labor Force Aging in the Czech Republic: The Role of Education and Economic Industry

The economic activity of both men and women workers seems to decrease with age. However, the issue is more complex since the rate of economic activity of older workers is very different in each industry; it also depends on the level of education. We assume that workers with a higher educational level will have a higher rate of economic activity than workers with a lower educational level.

This chapter deals with the analysis of economic activity of older workers by level of education in individual industries of the Czech economy. Our estimates are based on detailed data from both the Labour Force Survey and Statistics on Income and Living Conditions for the last few years.

We show that economic activity varies by educational level and is specific to each industry of the economy. As the Czech population is aging, the government is proposing to increase the statutory retirement age. We show that the setting of the retirement age should take place at the level of these analyzed factors, not uniformly.

24.1. Introduction

One of the government actions to mitigate the effects of an aging population in European countries is increasing the retirement age. In the Czech Republic, the retirement age is gradually increasing, which is currently capped at the age of

Chapter written by Martina SIMKOVA and Jaroslav SIXTA.
For a color version of all the figures in this chapter, see www.iste.co.uk/zafeiris/data2.zip.

65 years. The setting is uniform, regardless of any factors such as educational level, the health status of workers or the type of employment.

In this chapter, we illustrate that economic activity of older workers varies by educational level, which is specific for each industry of the economy. The aim of our analysis is the reflection on whether these factors should be considered by policymakers when setting the retirement age.

24.2. The setting of the statutory retirement age

Currently, the statutory retirement age varies by sex and number of children in the Czech Republic (see Figure 24.1). The retirement age is gradually being increased and unified at the age of 65 years, for people born after 1971, regardless of sex and number of children. This retirement age will be valid after 2036 (CSSA 2018).

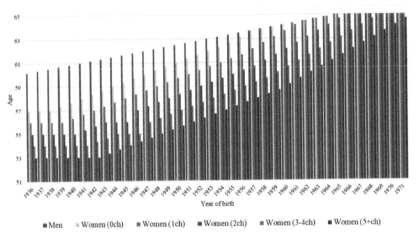

Figure 24.1. *The economic status of people over 60 years by sex and age (%)*

Many other European countries, such as Finland and Switzerland, also have this age set for regular retirement. Some European countries, for example Croatia or Germany, plan to increase it to 67 years in the next decade. Retirement age in Greece, Italy, Iceland or Norway is now at the level of 67 years (CSSA 2020). Recently, there was also such a plan in the Czech Republic but it was canceled by the following government. The question is whether this setting of the retirement age is effective in terms of various factors.

In this chapter, we deal only with the Czech Republic, and assess the effectiveness of setting the retirement age in terms of the current economic activity of people around retirement age. If we keep the dependency ratio constant, the retirement age would probably exceed 72 years in the Czech Republic (Šimková and Sixta 2013).

24.3. The economic status of elderly workers

According to the Labour Force Survey (LFS), the economic status of a person is employed, unemployed and economically non-active. We deal with workers who are above 60 years of age, because they are around the retirement age.

As shown in Figure 24.2, the proportion of employed people decreases with increasing age. In the age group of 60–64 years, 60.8% of men and 33.9% women were working (in 2019), whereas 18.8% men and 11.4% women were working in the age group of 65–69 years. Unemployment of people who are over 60 years of age is very low, below 1%. The rest of the population are economically non-active, mainly due to regular retirement, disability retirement or caring for another person. It is clear from Figure 24.2 that the proportion of working women aged 60–64 years is much lower than the proportion of working men in the same age group. However, this is due to the current setting of the retirement age, where men are currently entitled to a retirement pension at approximately 64 years and women at a lower age. For women, the retirement age also varies according to the number of children. For example, a woman with two children is entitled to a retirement pension at the age of about 62 years (see Figure 24.1). Even at a later age, after 65 years, the economic activity of women is lower than that of men.

We can also see some economic activity of people over 70 years of age. The law states that after reaching the retirement age, a person can work and receive a full old-age pension regardless of what work they do. In 2019, 5% of men and 2.7% of women were working in the age group of 70 years and above (see Figure 24.2).

However, this issue is more complex since the rate of economic activity of older workers is very different due to a large number of factors. Economic activity differs by educational attainment or health status and is different in each economic industry. We focus especially on sex and educational level of workers as we believe that these factors play an important role in this analyzed issue. Moreover, the health status of people plays an important role in discussions about retirement age, whereas life expectancy is increasing (Morávek and Langhamrová 2020).

We use the data from the LFS because they allow for detailed analyses of the economic activity by age and educational level in particular industries of the economy (CZSO 1993–2019).

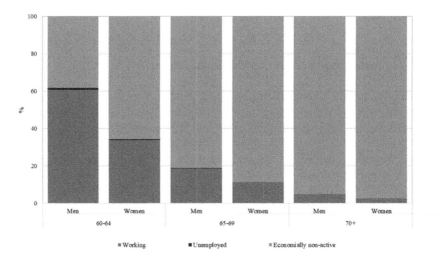

Figure 24.2. *The economic status of people over 60 years of age by sex and age (%)*

24.4. The structure of working people by factors

We consider looking at the issue at the level of the type of employment as very important. This is because many studies have confirmed that some professions, especially manual workers and those exposed to physical workload factors, have lower working life expectancy (Tang and MacLeod 2006; Feyrer 2007). It can be primarily explained by ill health-based exit routes. Given the availability of data from the LFS, we chose a view through economic industries that represent the diversity of economic activity. We look at the level of industries in the Czech Republic, as shown in Figure 24.3. The proportion of workers by age in a particular industry is always related to the total number of workers in each industry. In services (J–U) and agriculture (A), the proportion of older working people is generally higher, even those who are above 70 years of age. While in accommodation and food services (I) or manufacturing (B–E), the proportion of older working men and women is lower (Figure 24.3).

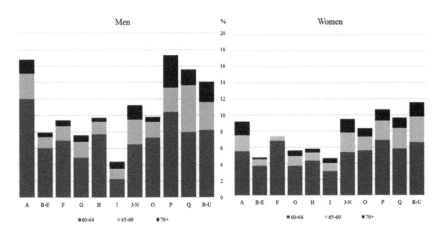

Figure 24.3. *The proportion of working people by sex and age in industries (%)*

NOTE ON FIGURE 24.3: A = agriculture, B–E = total manufacturing, F = construction, G = wholesale and retail trade, H = transportation and storage, I = accommodation and food services, J–N = information and communication, financial and insurance, real estate, scientific and administrative activities, O = public administration and defense, P = education, Q = health and social services, R–U = entertainment, arts and other services, and household activities

Another factor that plays a role in the issue of economic activity of elderly people is of course education. Figure 24.4 shows the economic status of men and women by their educational level in particular age groups. With increasing educational level of people, employment also grows, in all the assessed age groups. In the age group of 60–64 years, the proportion of men workers with a tertiary educational level is two times higher than the proportion of men workers with a primary educational level. In the age group of 65–69 years, the proportion of men workers with tertiary educational level is even 10 times higher than the proportion of men workers with primary educational level. Large differences in education are also evident for women workers. In the age group of 60–64 years, the proportion of women workers with a tertiary educational level is four times higher than the proportion of women workers with a primary educational level. In the age group of 65–69 years, the proportion of women workers with a tertiary educational level is even eight times higher than the proportion of women workers with a primary educational level (Figure 24.4).

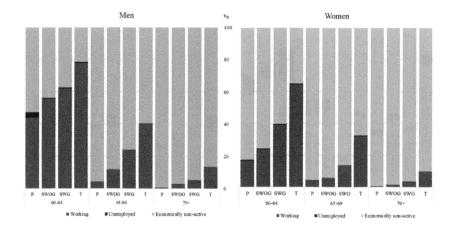

Figure 24.4. *The proportion of working women by age and industries (%)*

NOTE ON FIGURE 24.4.– A = agriculture, B–E = total manufacturing, F = construction, G = wholesale and retail trade, H = transportation and storage, I = accommodation and food services, J–N = information and communication, financial and insurance, real estate, scientific and administrative activities, O = public administration and defense, P = education, Q = health and social services, R–U = entertainment, arts and other services, and household activities

24.5. The change in the number of workers

Our analysis of the economic activity of people around retirement age continues with a comparison of the number of workers in particular age groups. We set the number of workers in the age group of 55–59 years as the reference age group. The purpose of these calculations is to show the different intensities of the decline in economic activity of workers after reaching 60 years of age, depending on their education level. There are no significant numbers, but a downward trend. The lower the value, the greater the decrease in the number of workers across the age groups. Figure 24.5 focuses on the age group of 60–64 years, in which both men and women are currently leaving to regular retirement. For example, in manufacturing (B–E), there are more men aged 60–64 years with primary education than those in other educational categories. In general, in services (J–U), the higher the educational level, the lower the decline in economic activity. There are obviously some fluctuations, but this is due to the data. To eliminate them, we will have to consider a longer time series, respectively average for more periods than only 2019.

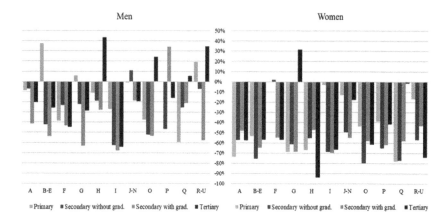

Figure 24.5. *The decrease in the number of workers aged 60–64 years compared to those aged 55–59 years (%)*

NOTE ON FIGURE 24.5.– A = agriculture, B–E = total manufacturing, F = construction, G = wholesale and retail trade, H = transportation and storage, I = accommodation and food services, J–N = information and communication, financial and insurance, real estate, scientific and administrative activities, O = public administration and defense, P = education, Q = health and social services, R–U = entertainment, arts and other services, and household activities.

Figure 24.6 compares the number of workers in the age group of 65–69 years with the reference age group of 55–59 years. Of course, here is a higher decrease in the number of workers than the previous age group in the whole economy, because we are over the threshold of the regular retirement age. However, there is a lower intensity of decline in some industries depending on the education level of workers. We can focus on public administration (O), education (P) or health and social services (Q), where we can see that the higher the number of workers with higher educational level, the longer they remain in the work process. They have a lower intensity of the decrease in the number of employees. This is true for both men and women who are aged 65–69 years.

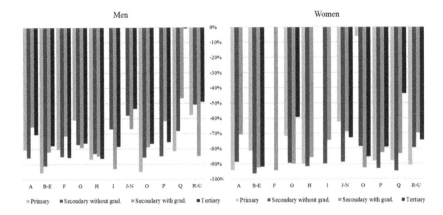

Figure 24.6. *The decrease in the number of workers aged 65–69 years compared to those aged 55–59 years (%)*

NOTE ON FIGURE 24.6.– A = agriculture, B–E = total manufacturing, F = construction, G = wholesale and retail trade, H = transportation and storage, I = accommodation and food services, J–N = information and communication, financial and insurance, real estate, scientific and administrative activities, O = public administration and defense, P = education, Q = health and social services, R–U = entertainment, arts and other services, and household activities.

The last assessed age group of workers, over 70 years, is presented in Figure 24.7. There are notable differences in economic activity according to the educational level of workers, especially in agriculture (A), trade (G) and education (P) or health and social services (Q).

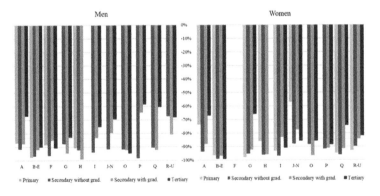

Figure 24.7. *The decrease in the number of workers aged 70 years and above compared with those aged 55–59 years (%)*

NOTE ON FIGURE 24.7.– A = agriculture, B–E = total manufacturing, F = construction, G = wholesale and retail trade, H = transportation and storage, I = accommodation and food services, J–N = information and communication, financial and insurance, real estate, scientific and administrative activities, O = public administration and defense, P = education, Q = health and social services, R–U = entertainment, arts and other services, and household activities.

Our conclusion is that the higher the educational level of workers, the longer they stay in work and the later leave to retirement. This is also confirmed by other studies (e.g. Tang and MacLeod (2006) or Schram et al. (2021)). Of course, we are aware of the limits of these calculations. It would be more appropriate to consider averages over longer periods or focus more on individual data. However, we believe that our conclusions would not change. In some industries, it is possible to increase the retirement age, even above the current 65 years. However, government initiatives may not achieve their goals if the plans to make the working life of older workers longer are not actively supported by employers (van Dalen et al. 2010). Moreover, Vickerstaff et al. (2003) declare that any significant change in retirement behavior will come mainly from changes in employer policies.

24.6. Conclusion

The aim of this chapter was to show that in some professions or industries, people are able to work longer and therefore the retirement age in these cases could be even higher than 65 years. We are persuaded that the role of education in such analysis is irreplaceable. We have to consider the industry of workers since it is obvious that due to physical constraints in some professions or industries, older workers cannot work. The process of setting the retirement age is a sensitive political issue. Unfortunately, in many cases, policymakers do not think about long-term stability. Future policymakers will have to find enough courage and persuade society that capping the retirement age at 65 years is likely to be unsustainable. The possible solution lies in the ex ante setting the share of humans' life spent in retirement as a broad social agreement. It is obvious that education and industry of economic activity can play an important supportive role.

24.7. Acknowledgment

This study was supported by the Institutional Support for Long Period and Conceptual Development of Research and Science at the Faculty of Informatics and Statistics, University of Economics, Prague and the project "Economy of Successful Ageing", no. 19-03984S.

24.8. References

CSSA (2018). Starobní důchod podrobně. Česká správa sociálního zabezpečení [Online]. Available at: https://www.cssz.cz/starobni-duchod-podrobne.

CSSA (2020). Důchodový věk ve státech EU, EHP a Švýcarsku. Česká správa sociálního zabezpečení [Online]. Available at: https://www.cssz.cz/duchodovy-vek-ve-statech-eu-ehp-a-svycarsku.

CZSO (2020). Trh práce v ČR – časové řady – 1993–2019. Český statistický úřad [Online]. Available at: https://www.czso.cz/csu/czso/trh-prace-v-cr-casove-rady-1993-2019.

van Dalen, H.P., Henkens, K., Schippers, J. (2010). How do employers cope with an ageing workforce? Views from employers and employees. *Demographic Research*, 22(32), 1015–1036.

Feyrer, J. (2007). Demographics and productivity. *Review of Economics and Statistics*, 89(1), 100–109.

Morávek, D. and Langhamrová, J. (2020). A decomposition analysis of differences in length of life in the Czech Republic. *Proceedings of the 6th Stochastic Modeling Techniques and Data Analysis International Conference with Demographics Workshop (SMTDA2020)*. Barcelona [Online]. Available at: http://www.smtda.net/images/!SMTDA2020-Proceedings-Final_compressed.pdf.

Schram, J., Solovieva, S., Leinonen, T., Viikari-Juntura, E., Burdorf, A., Robroek, S. (2021). The influence of occupational class and physical workload on working life expectancy among older employees. *Scandinavian Journal of Work Environment & Health*, 47(1), 5–14.

Simkova, M. and Sixta, J. (2013). The development of the standard of living of Czech pensioners. *Acta Oeconomica Pragensia*, 21(3), 14–31.

Tang, J. and Macleod, C. (2006). Labour force ageing and productivity performance in Canada. *The Canadian Journal of Economics*, 39(2), 582–603.

Vickerstaff, S., Cox, J., Keen, L. (2003). Employers and the management of retirement. *Social Policy & Administration*, 37, 271–287.

List of Authors

Rafik ABDESSELAM
Department of Economics
and Management
University of Lyon
Lumière Lyon 2
France

Ana M. AGUILERA
Statistic and Operations Research
University of Granada
Spain

Vladimir ANISIMOV
Data Science, Center for
Design & Analysis
Amgen
London
UK

Roberto ASCARI
Department of Economics,
Management and Statistics (DEMS)
University of Milano-Bicocca
Milan
Italy

Rosalind BAVERSTOCK
Data Science, Center for
Design & Analysis
Amgen
London
UK

Tomáš BĚLOCH
Department of Demography
Prague University of Economics
and Business
Czech Republic

Dominique DESBOIS
UMR Économie publique
INRAE-AgroParisTech
Université Paris-Saclay
France

Yiannis DIMOTIKALIS
Department of Management Science
and Technology
Hellenic Mediterranean University
Heraklion
Greece

Marko DIMITROV
Division of Mathematics and Physics
Mälardalen University
Västerås
Sweden

Tomáš FIALA
Department of Demography
Prague University of Economics
and Business
Czech Republic

Eleni GENITSARIDI
Health Units Management
Hellenic Open University
Patra
Czech Republic

Stephen GORMLEY
Data Science, Center for
Design & Analysis
Amgen
London
UK

Lígia HENRIQUES-RODRIGUES
Department of Mathematics
University of Évora
Portugal

Filip HON
Department of Demography
Prague University of Economics
and Business
Czech Republic

M. IVETTE GOMES
Department of Statistics and
Operational Research
University of Lisbon
Portugal

Lu JIN
Department of Informatics
University of Electro Communications
Tokyo
Japan

Karl-Heinz JÖCKEL
Institute of Medical Informatics,
Biometry and Epidemiology
University Hospital Essen
Germany

Michaela KADLECOVÁ
Department of Demography
Prague University of Economics
and Business
Czech Republic

Emmanouil-Nektarios KALLIGERIS
Department of Statistics and
Actuarial-Financial Mathematics
University of the Aegean
Karlovasi
Samos
Greece

Alex KARAGRIGORIOU
Department of Statistics and
Actuarial-Financial Mathematics
University of the Aegean
Samos
Greece

Christiana KARAGRIGORIOU-VONTA
Freelance translator and editor
Athens
Greece

Cynthia KINEZA
Data Science, Center for
Design & Analysis
Amgen
Thousand Oaks, CA
USA

Mihalis KYRIAKAKIS
Hellenic Open University
Patra
Greece

Jitka LANGHAMROVÁ
Department of Demography
Prague University of Economics
and Business
Czech Republic

Andreas MAKRIDES
Department of Statistics and
Actuarial-Financial Mathematics
University of the Aegean
Karlovasi
Samos
Greece

George MATALLIOTAKIS
Health Units Management
Hellenic Open University
Patra
Greece

Catherine MICHALOPOULOU
Department of Social Policy
Panteion University of Social
and Political Sciences
Athens
Greece

Sonia MIGLIORATI
Department of Economics,
Management and Statistics (DEMS)
University of Milano-Bicocca
Milan
Italy

David MORÁVEK
Department of Demography
Prague University of Economics
and Business
Czech Republic

Ying NI
Division of Mathematics and Physics
Mälardalen University
Västerås
Sweden

Neir PAES
Health and Decision Modelling
Postgraduate Course
Federal University of Paraíba
João Pessoa
Brazil

Apostolos PAPACHRISTOS
Department of Statistics and
Insurance Science
University of Piraeus
Greece

Dimitris PARSANOGLOU
Department of Social Policy
Panteion University of Social
and Political Sciences
Athens
Greece

Markéta Majerová PECHHOLDOVÁ
Department of Demography
Prague University of Economics
and Business
Czech Republic

Dinis PESTANA
Department of Statistics and
Operational Research
University of Lisbon
Portugal

Peter PFLAUMER
Department of Statistics
Technical University Dortmund
Germany

Carlos SANTOS
Department of Agrarian Sciences
Federal University of Campina
Grande
Pombal
Brazil

Martina SIMKOVA
Department of Demography
Prague University of Economics
and Business
Czech Republic

Jaroslav SIXTA
Department of Economics Statistics
Prague University of Economics
and Business
Czech Republic

Christos H. SKIADAS
ManLab
Technical University of Crete
Chania
Greece

Glykeria STAMATOPOULOU
Department of Social Policy
Panteion University of Social
and Political Sciences
Athens
Greece

Kornélia SVAČINOVÁ
Department of Demography
Prague University of Economics
and Business
Czech Republic

Maria SYMEONAKI
Department of Social Policy
Panteion University of Social
and Political Sciences
Athens
Greece

Kouki TAKADA
Department of Informatics
University of Electro Communications
Tokyo
Japan

Mariano J. VALDERRAMA
Statistic and Operations Research
University of Granada
Spain

Pilar VALDERRAMA
Department of Information and
Communication
University of Granada
Spain

Georgia VERROPOULOU
Department of Statistics and
Insurance Science
University of Piraeus
Greece

Jana VRABCOVÁ
Department of Demography
Prague University of Economics
and Business
Czech Republic

Aggeliki YFANTI
Social Anthropology
Panteion University of Social
and Political Sciences
Athens
Greece

Hidekazu YOSHIOKA
Graduate School of Natural Science
and Technology
Shimane University
Matsue
Japan

Yumi YOSHIOKA
Graduate School of Natural Science
and Technology
Shimane University
Matsue
Japan

Konstantinos N. ZAFEIRIS
Department of History and Ethnology
Democritus University of Thrace
Komotini
Greece

Index

A, B

adjacency matrix, 5–9, 11, 14, 18
aging population, 385
alcohol, 363–375
   policy, 349, 351–354, 356, 360
ARIMA, 307–309, 311–320, 323, 324, 326, 328, 329, 331
   seasonal models, 303, 304, 307, 311, 314, 322, 330
backward stochastic differential equations, 105, 108, 115
Bayesian inference, 29
bibliographic quality indicator, 199
binomial model, 77–79, 89
biological pests, 143

C, D

call option, 77, 81–89
cause-elimination in life tables, 366
cesarean, 337–346
chi-square test, 91, 95, 96, 101
cluster analysis, 67, 68, 70
cohort, 39, 40, 42, 45–49, 51, 52
compound distribution, 26
contingency table, 95
control chart, 211–218
Covid-19, 211–218

cure model, 124–127, 131
Czechia, 349–352, 354, 355, 359, 360
data variables
   qualitative and mixed, 9
death
   causes of, 365, 366, 369, 374
decomposition method, 271, 273, 275, 282
dentistry, 199, 201–203, 205, 206, 208, 209
dimension reduction, 3, 4, 12
disability-free life expectancy (DFLE), 272, 274–277, 280–282
distance, 39, 42–44, 46, 47, 52
dropout, 121–124, 131, 137, 138, 140, 141
dynamic risk measures, 105, 107, 111

E, F

economic activity, 377–382, 384, 385
ecosystem-based practices, 143
educational level, 377–385
employment, 55, 58, 60, 63
ESeC, 39, 91–101
EU-27 countries, 349, 352–355, 360
EU-LFS, 67–70, 72, 73
EUROGRADUATE pilot survey, 55–57
Europe, 363–368, 371, 374, 375

event-driven clinical trial, 121
extremes, 239
factor analysis, 199–201, 204, 205
flow discharge, 107, 114
forecasting, 304, 308, 310–312, 314, 315, 318, 320–324, 328–330

G, H, I

generalized mean, 237
gross margin, 152, 153, 158, 160
health
    state of, 227, 230–235
hierarchical clustering, 3, 4, 10
industry, 377–380, 385
integral index, 206, 207

J, L, M

job insecurity, 68, 74, 75
lean management, 163, 165–168, 172–175
life expectancy, 271–281
Markov system, 39, 42
medical and nursing staff, 179, 189
Mediterranean region, 214, 218
mobility
    indices, 40, 43, 44, 49, 51
    intergenerational, 39, 40
mortality, 303–305, 307, 310, 322–324, 328, 330, 363–365, 369–375
    force of, 288, 289, 292
    neonatal, 337–339, 346
multilevel logistic model, 337

N, O, P

natalist policy, 251, 252, 256, 261, 265
non-regular frameworks, 239
NUTS, 91–93, 95–101
optimal exercise region, 77–79, 87, 88
partial least squares (PLS), 143–145, 147, 149, 150, 154, 161

patient recruitment, 121–123, 129, 139
pension system, 251, 252, 255, 258–261, 265, 266
plot level, 143, 153, 154
Poisson-gamma recruitment model, 129
precarity, 67, 69–71, 74, 75
predicting event counts, 121, 123, 127, 129, 130
primary health care, 179, 181, 197
projection, 251, 259, 261–264, 266
proximity measure, 4–6, 8, 9, 11, 14, 18, 22
put option, 77, 78, 81–89

R, S

regionalized spaces, 339
retirement age, 225–230, 232–234
scale, 349, 350, 352, 353, 360
school-to-work transition, 56
second demographic transition, 256
self-rated health, 291, 293–297
SHARE, 285–287, 290, 292, 293, 297, 298
skills mismatch, 64
social class, 39–42, 44–46, 52
specific costs, 152, 153, 158, 160, 161
structural modeling, 143–145, 148, 152–155, 157, 159, 161
subjective survival probabilities, 285–289, 292, 294, 296–298
Sullivan method, 271, 273, 274

T, V, W

tempered stable subordinators, 105–107, 114, 116
time series analysis, 307
Venizelio General Hospital of Heraklion, Crete, 163, 164, 168, 169, 172, 175, 176
water quality dynamics, 105, 108, 115

Summary of Volume 1

Preface

Konstantinos N. ZAFEIRIS, Yiannis DIMOTIKALIS, Christos H. SKIADAS, Alex KARAGRIGORIOU and Christiana KARAGRIGORIOU-VONTA

Part 1

Chapter 1. Performance of Evaluation of Diagnosis of Various Thyroid Diseases Using Machine Learning Techniques

Burcu Bektas GÜNEŞ, Evren BURSUK and Rüya ŞAMLI

    1.1. Introduction
    1.2. Data understanding
    1.3. Modeling
    1.4. Findings
    1.5. Conclusion
    1.6. References

Chapter 2. Exploring Chronic Diseases' Spatial Patterns: Thyroid Cancer in Sicilian Volcanic Areas

Francesca BITONTI and Angelo MAZZA

    2.1. Introduction
    2.2. Epidemiological data and territory
    2.3. Methodology
        2.3.1. Spatial inhomogeneity and spatial dependence
        2.3.2. Standardized incidence ratio (SIR)
        2.3.3. Local Moran's I statistic
    2.4. Spatial distribution of TC in eastern Sicily
        2.4.1. SIR geographical variation

2.4.2. Estimate of the spatial attraction

2.5. Conclusion

2.6. References

Chapter 3. Analysis of Blockchain-based Databases in Web Applications

Orhun Ceng BOZO and Rüya ŞAMLI

3.1. Introduction

3.2. Background

    3.2.1. Blockchain

    3.2.2. Blockchain types

    3.2.3. Blockchain-based web applications

    3.2.4. Blockchain consensus algorithms

    3.2.5. Other consensus algorithms

3.3. Analysis stack

    3.3.1. Art Shop web application

    3.3.2. SQL-based application

    3.3.3. NoSQL-based application

    3.3.4. Blockchain-based application

3.4. Analysis

    3.4.1. Adding records

    3.4.2. Query

    3.4.3. Functionality

    3.4.4. Security

3.5. Conclusion

3.6. References

Chapter 4. Optimization and Asymptotic Analysis of Insurance Models

Ekaterina BULINSKAYA

4.1. Introduction

4.2. Discrete-time model with reinsurance and bank loans

    4.2.1. Model description

    4.2.2. Optimization problem

    4.2.3. Model stability

4.3. Continuous-time insurance model with dividends

    4.3.1. Model description

    4.3.2. Optimal barrier strategy

    4.3.3. Special form of claim distribution

    4.3.4. Numerical analysis

4.4. Conclusion and further research directions

4.5. References

Chapter 5. Statistical Analysis of Traffic Volume in the 25 de Abril Bridge

Frederico CAEIRO, Ayana MATEUS and Conceicao VEIGA de ALMEIDA

5.1. Introduction

5.2. Data

5.3. Methodology

    5.3.1. Main limit results

    5.3.2. Block maxima method

    5.3.3. Largest order statistics method

    5.3.4. Estimation of other tail parameters

5.4. Results and conclusion

5.5. Acknowledgements

5.6. References

Chapter 6. Predicting the Risk of Gestational Diabetes Mellitus through Nearest Neighbor Classification

Louisa TESTA, Mark A. CARUANA, Maria KONTORINAKI and Charles SAVONA-VENTURA

6.1. Introduction

6.2. Nearest neighbor methods

    6.2.1. Background of the NN methods

    6.2.2. The k-nearest neighbors method

    6.2.3. The fixed-radius NN method

    6.2.4. The kernel-NN method

    6.2.5. Algorithms of the three considered NN methods

    6.2.6. Parameter and distance metric selection

6.3. Experimental results

    6.3.1. Dataset description

    6.3.2. Variable selection and data splitting

    6.3.3. Results

    6.3.4. A discussion and comparison of results

6.4. Conclusion

6.5. References

Chapter 7. Political Trust in National Institutions: The Significance of Items' Level of Measurement in the Validation of Constructs

Anastasia CHARALAMPI, Eva TSOUPAROPOULOU, Joanna TSIGANOU and Catherine MICHALOPOULOU

7.1. Introduction
7.2. Methods
    7.2.1. Participants
    7.2.2. Instrument
    7.2.3. Statistical analyses
7.3. Results
    7.3.1. EFA results
    7.3.2. CFA results
    7.3.3. Scale construction and assessment
7.4. Conclusion
7.5. Funding
7.6. References

Chapter 8. The State of the Art in Flexible Regression Models for Univariate Bounded Responses

Agnese Maria DI BRISCO, Roberto ASCARI, Sonia MIGLIORATI and Andrea ONGARO

8.1. Introduction
8.2. Regression model for bounded responses
    8.2.1. Augmentation
    8.2.2. Main distributions on the bounded support
    8.2.3. Inference and fit
8.3. Case studies
    8.3.1. Stress data
    8.3.2. Reading data
8.4. References

Chapter 9. Simulation Studies for a Special Mixture Regression Model with Multivariate Responses on the Simplex

Agnese Maria DI BRISCO, Roberto ASCARI, Sonia MIGLIORATI and Andrea ONGARO

9.1. Introduction
9.2. Dirichlet and EFD distributions
9.3. Dirichlet and EFD regression models
    9.3.1. Inference and fit
9.4. Simulation studies
    9.4.1. Comments
9.5. References

Part 2

Chapter 10. Numerical Studies of Implied Volatility Expansions Under the Gatheral Model

Marko DIMITROV, Mohammed ALBUHAYRI, Ying NI and Anatoliy MALYARENKO

10.1. Introduction
10.2. Asymptotic expansions of implied volatility
10.3. Performance of the asymptotic expansions
10.4. Calibration using the asymptotic expansions
    10.4.1. A partial calibration procedure
    10.4.2. Calibration to synthetic and market data
10.5. Conclusion and future work
10.6. References

Chapter 11. Performance Persistence of Polish Mutual Funds: Mobility Measures

Dariusz FILIP

11.1. Introduction
11.2. Literature review
11.3. Dataset and empirical design
11.4. Empirical results
11.5. Monthly perspective
11.6. Quarterly perspective
11.7. Yearly perspective
11.8. Conclusion
11.9. References

Chapter 12. Invariant Description for a Batch Version of the UCB Strategy with Unknown Control Horizon

Sergey GARBAR

12.1. Introduction
12.2. UCB strategy
12.3. Batch version of the strategy
12.4. Invariant description with a unit control horizon
12.5. Simulation results
12.6. Conclusion
12.7. Affiliations
12.8. References

Chapter 13. A New Non-monotonic Link Function for Beta Regressions

Gloria GHENO

13.1. Introduction
13.2. Model
13.3. Estimation
13.4. Comparison
13.5. Conclusion
13.6. References

Chapter 14. A Method of Big Data Collection and Normalization for Electronic Engineering Applications

Naveenbalaji GOWTHAMAN and Viranjay M. SRIVASTAVA

14.1. Introduction
14.2. Machine learning (ML) in electronic engineering
   14.2.1. Data acquisition
   14.2.2. Accessing the data repositories
   14.2.3. Data storage and management
14.3. Electronic engineering applications – data science
14.4. Conclusion and future work
14.5. References

Chapter 15. Stochastic Runge–Kutta Solvers Based on Markov Jump Processes and Applications to Non-autonomous Systems of Differential Equations

Flavius GUIAŞ

15.1. Introduction
15.2. Description of the method
   15.2.1. The direct simulation method
   15.2.2. Picard iterations
   15.2.3. Runge–Kutta steps
15.3. Numerical examples
   15.3.1. The Lorenz system
   15.3.2. A combustion model
15.4. Conclusion
15.5. References

Chapter 16. Interpreting a Topological Measure of Complexity for Decision Boundaries

Alan HYLTON, Ian LIM, Michael MOY and Robert SHORT

16.1. Introduction
16.2. Persistent homology
16.3. Methodology
    16.3.1. Neural networks and binary classification
    16.3.2. Persistent homology of a decision boundary
    16.3.3. Procedure
16.4. Experiments and results
    16.4.1. Three-dimensional binary classification
    16.4.2. Data divided by a hyperplane
16.5. Conclusion and discussion
16.6. References

Chapter 17. The Minimum Renyi's Pseudodistance Estimators for Generalized Linear Models

María JAENADA and Leandro PARDO

17.1. Introduction
17.2. The minimum RP estimators for the GLM model: asymptotic distribution
17.3. Example: Poisson regression model
    17.3.1. Real data application
17.4. Conclusion
17.5. Acknowledgments
17.6. Appendix.
    17.6.1. Proof of Theorem 1
17.7. References

Chapter 18. Data Analysis based on Entropies and Measures of Divergence

Christos MESELIDIS, Alex KARAGRIGORIOU and Takis PAPAIOANNOU

18.1. Introduction
18.2. Divergence measures
18.3. Tests of fit based on Φ−divergence measures
18.4. Simulations
18.5. References

Part 3

Chapter 19. Geographically Weighted Regression for Official Land Prices and their Temporal Variation in Tokyo

Yuta KANNO and Takayuki SHIOHAMA

19.1. Introduction
19.2. Models and methodology
19.3. Data analysis
   19.3.1. Data
   19.3.2. Results
19.4. Conclusion
19.5. Acknowledgments
19.6. References

Chapter 20. Software Cost Estimation Using Machine Learning Algorithms

Sukran EBREN KARA and Rüya ŞAMLI

20.1. Introduction
20.2. Methodology
   20.2.1. Dataset
   20.2.2. Model
   20.2.3. Evaluating the performance of the model
20.3. Results and discussion
20.4. Conclusion
20.5. References

Chapter 21. Monte Carlo Accuracy Evaluation of Laser Cutting Machine

Samuel KOSOLAPOV

21.1. Introduction
21.2. Mathematical model of a pintograph
21.3. Monte Carlo simulator
21.4. Simulation results
21.5. Conclusion
21.6. Acknowledgments
21.7. References

Chapter 22. Using Parameters of Piecewise Approximation by Exponents for Epidemiological Time Series Data Analysis

Samuel KOSOLAPOV

22.1. Introduction
22.2. Deriving equations for moving exponent parameters
22.3. Validation of derived equations by using synthetic data
22.4. Using derived equations to analyze real-life Covid-19 data
22.5. Conclusion
22.6. References

Chapter 23. The Correlation Between Oxygen Consumption and Excretion of Carbon Dioxide in the Human Respiratory Cycle

Anatoly KOVALENKO, Konstantin LEBEDINSKII and Verangelina MOLOSHNEVA

23.1. Introduction
23.2. Respiratory function physiology: ventilation–perfusion ratio
23.3. The basic principle of operation of artificial lung ventilation devices: patient monitoring parameters
23.4. The algorithm for monitoring the carbon emissions and oxygen consumption
23.5. Results
23.6. Conclusion
23.7. References

Part 4

Chapter 24. Approximate Bayesian Inference Using the Mean-Field Distribution

Antonin DELLA NOCE and Paul-Henry COURNÈDE

24.1. Introduction
24.2. Inference problem in a symmetric population system
    24.2.1. Example of a symmetric system describing plant competition
    24.2.2. Inference problem of the Schneider system, in a more general setting
24.3. Properties of the mean-field distribution
24.4. Mean-field approximated inference
    24.4.1. Case of systems admitting a mean-field limit
24.5. Conclusion
24.6. References

Chapter 25. Pricing Financial Derivatives in the Hull–White Model Using Cubature Methods on Wiener Space

Hossein NOHROUZIAN, Anatoliy MALYARENKO and Ying NI

25.1. Introduction and outline

25.2. Cubature formulae on Wiener space

25.2.1. A simple example of classical Monte Carlo estimates

25.2.2. Modern Monte Carlo estimates via cubature method

25.2.3. An application in the Black–Scholes SDE

25.2.4. Trajectories of the cubature formula of degree 5 on Wiener space

25.2.5. Trajectories of price process given in equation [25.7]

25.2.6. An application on path-dependent derivatives

25.2.7. Trinomial tree (model) via cubature formulae of degree 5

25.3. Interest-rate models and Hull–White one-factor model

25.3.1. Equilibrium models

25.3.2. No-arbitrage models

25.3.3. Forward rate models

25.3.4. Hull–White one-factor model

25.3.5. Discretization of the Hull–White model via Euler scheme

25.3.6. Hull–White model for bond prices

25.4. The Hull–White model via cubature method

25.4.1. Simulating SDE [25.15] and ODE [25.24]

25.4.2. The Hull–White interest-rate tree via iterated cubature formulae: some examples

25.5. Discussion and future works

25.6. References

Chapter 26. Differences in the Structure of Infectious Morbidity of the Population during the First and Second Half of 2020 in St. Petersburg

Vasilii OREL, Olga NOSYREVA, Tatiana BULDAKOVA, Natalya GUREVA, Viktoria SMIRNOVA, Andrey KIM and Lubov SHARAFUTDINOVA

26.1. Introduction

26.2. Materials and methods

26.2.1. Characteristics of the territory of the district

26.2.2. Demographic characteristics of the area

26.2.3. Characteristics of the district medical service

26.2.4. The procedure for collecting primary information on cases of diseases of the population with a new coronavirus infection

26.3. Results of the analysis of the incidence of acute respiratory viral infectious diseases, new coronavirus infection Covid-19 and community-acquired pneumonia

26.4. Conclusion

26.5. References

Chapter 27. High Speed and Secured Network Connectivity for Higher Education Institutions Using Software Defined Networks

Lincoln S. PETER and Viranjay M. SRIVASTAVA

27.1. Introduction

27.2. Existing model review

27.3. Selection of a suitable model

27.4. Conclusion and future recommendations

27.5. References

Chapter 28. Reliability of a Double Redundant System Under the Full Repair Scenario

Vladimir RYKOV and Nika IVANOVA

28.1. Introduction

28.2. Problem statement, assumptions and notations

28.3. Reliability function

28.4. Time-dependent system state probabilities

28.4.1. General representation of t.d.s.p.s

28.4.2. T.d.s.p.s in a separate regeneration period

28.5. Steady-state probabilities

28.6. Conclusion

28.7. References

Chapter 29. Predicting Changes in Depression Levels Following the European Economic Downturn of 2008

Eleni SERAFETINIDOU and Georgia VERROPOULOU

29.1. Introduction

29.1.1. Aims of the study

29.2. Data and methods

29.2.1. Sample

29.2.2. Measures

29.3. Results

29.3.1. Descriptive findings

29.3.2. Non-respondents compared to respondents at baseline (wave 2)

29.3.3. Descriptive findings for respondents – analysis by gender

29.3.4. Findings regarding decreasing depression levels – analysis for the total sample and by gender

29.3.5. Findings regarding increasing depression levels – analysis for the total sample and by gender

29.4. Discussion
29.5. Conclusion
29.6. Acknowledgments
29.7. References

Other titles from

in

Innovation, Entrepreneurship and Management

2022

BOUCHÉ Geneviève
Productive Economy, Contributory Economy: Governance Tools for the Third Millennium (Innovation and Technology Set – Volume 15)

HELLER David
Valuation of the Liability Structure by Real Options (Modern Finance, Management Innovation and Economic Growth Set – Volume 5)

MATHIEU Valérie
A Customer-oriented Manager for B2B Services: Principles and Implementation

NOËL Florent, SCHMIDT Géraldine
Employability and Industrial Mutations: Between Individual Trajectories and Organizational Strategic Planning (Technological Changes and Human Resources Set – Volume 4)

SALOFF-COSTE Michel
Innovation Ecosystems: The Future of Civilizations and the Civilization of the Future (Innovation and Technology Set – Volume 14)

VAYRE Emilie
Digitalization of Work: New Spaces and New Working Times (Technological Changes and Human Resources Set – Volume 5)

2021

ARCADE Jacques
Strategic Engineering (Innovation and Technology Set – Volume 11)

BÉRANGER Jérôme, RIZOULIÈRES Roland
The Digital Revolution in Health (Health and Innovation Set – Volume 2)

BOBILLIER CHAUMON Marc-Eric
Digital Transformations in the Challenge of Activity and Work: Understanding and Supporting Technological Changes (Technological Changes and Human Resources Set – Volume 3)

BUCLET Nicolas
Territorial Ecology and Socio-ecological Transition (Smart Innovation Set – Volume 34)

DIMOTIKALIS Yannis, KARAGRIGORIOU Alex, PARPOULA Christina, SKIADIS Christos H
Applied Modeling Techniques and Data Analysis 1: Computational Data Analysis Methods and Tools (Big Data, Artificial Intelligence and Data Analysis Set - Volume 7)
Applied Modeling Techniques and Data Analysis 2: Financial, Demographic, Stochastic and Statistical Models and Methods (Big Data, Artificial Intelligence and Data Analysis Set – Volume 8)

DISPAS Christophe, KAYANAKIS Georges, SERVEL Nicolas, STRIUKOVA Ludmila
Innovation and Financial Markets (Innovation between Risk and Reward Set – Volume 7)

ENJOLRAS Manon
Innovation and Export: The Joint Challenge of the Small Company (Smart Innovation Set – Volume 37)

FLEURY Sylvain, RICHIR Simon
*Immersive Technologies to Accelerate Innovation: How Virtual and
Augmented Reality Enables the Co-Creation of Concepts
(Smart Innovation Set – Volume 38)*

GIORGINI Pierre
The Contributory Revolution (Innovation and Technology Set – Volume 13)

GOGLIN Christian
*Emotions and Values in Equity Crowdfunding Investment Choices 2:
Modeling and Empirical Study*

GRENIER Corinne, OIRY Ewan
*Altering Frontiers: Organizational Innovations in Healthcare (Health and
Innovation Set – Volume 1)*

GUERRIER Claudine
*Security and Its Challenges in the 21st Century (Innovation and Technology
Set – Volume 12)*

HELLER David
*Performance of Valuation Methods in Financial Transactions (Modern
Finance, Management Innovation and Economic Growth Set – Volume 4)*

LEHMANN Paul-Jacques
Liberalism and Capitalism Today

SOULÉ Bastien, HALLÉ Julie, VIGNAL Bénédicte, BOUTROY Éric,
NIER Olivier
*Innovation in Sport: Innovation Trajectories and Process Optimization
(Smart Innovation Set – Volume 35)*

UZUNIDIS Dimitri, KASMI Fedoua, ADATTO Laurent
*Innovation Economics, Engineering and Management Handbook 1:
Main Themes
Innovation Economics, Engineering and Management Handbook 2:
Special Themes*

VALLIER Estelle
*Innovation in Clusters: Science–Industry Relationships in the Face of
Forced Advancement (Smart Innovation Set – Volume 36)*

2020

ACH Yves-Alain, RMADI-SAÏD Sandra
Financial Information and Brand Value: Reflections, Challenges and Limitations

ANDREOSSO-O'CALLAGHAN Bernadette, DZEVER Sam, JAUSSAUD Jacques, TAYLOR Robert
Sustainable Development and Energy Transition in Europe and Asia
(Innovation and Technology Set – Volume 9)

BEN SLIMANE Sonia, M'HENNI Hatem
Entrepreneurship and Development: Realities and Future Prospects
(Smart Innovation Set – Volume 30)

CHOUTEAU Marianne, FOREST Joëlle, NGUYEN Céline
Innovation for Society: The P.S.I. Approach
(Smart Innovation Set – Volume 28)

CORON Clotilde
Quantifying Human Resources: Uses and Analysis
(Technological Changes and Human Resources Set – Volume 2)

CORON Clotilde, GILBERT Patrick
Technological Change
(Technological Changes and Human Resources Set – Volume 1)

CERDIN Jean-Luc, PERETTI Jean-Marie
The Success of Apprenticeships: Views of Stakeholders on Training and Learning (Human Resources Management Set – Volume 3)

DELCHET-COCHET Karen
Circular Economy: From Waste Reduction to Value Creation
(Economic Growth Set – Volume 2)

DIDAY Edwin, GUAN Rong, SAPORTA Gilbert, WANG Huiwen
Advances in Data Science
(Big Data, Artificial Intelligence and Data Analysis Set – Volume 4)

DOS SANTOS PAULINO Victor
Innovation Trends in the Space Industry
(Smart Innovation Set – Volume 25)

GASMI Nacer
Corporate Innovation Strategies: Corporate Social Responsibility and
Shared Value Creation
(Smart Innovation Set – Volume 33)

GOGLIN Christian
Emotions and Values in Equity Crowdfunding Investment Choices 1:
Transdisciplinary Theoretical Approach

GUILHON Bernard
Venture Capital and the Financing of Innovation
(Innovation Between Risk and Reward Set – Volume 6)

LATOUCHE Pascal
Open Innovation: Human Set-up
(Innovation and Technology Set – Volume 10)

LIMA Marcos
Entrepreneurship and Innovation Education: Frameworks and Tools
(Smart Innovation Set – Volume 32)

MACHADO Carolina, DAVIM J. Paulo
Sustainable Management for Managers and Engineers

MAKRIDES Andreas, KARAGRIGORIOU Alex, SKIADAS Christos H.
Data Analysis and Applications 3: Computational, Classification, Financial,
Statistical and Stochastic Methods
(Big Data, Artificial Intelligence and Data Analysis Set – Volume 5)
Data Analysis and Applications 4: Financial Data Analysis and Methods
(Big Data, Artificial Intelligence and Data Analysis Set – Volume 6)

MASSOTTE Pierre, CORSI Patrick
Complex Decision-Making in Economy and Finance

MEUNIER François-Xavier
Dual Innovation Systems: Concepts, Tools and Methods
(Smart Innovation Set – Volume 31)

MICHAUD Thomas
Science Fiction and Innovation Design (Innovation in Engineering and Technology Set – Volume 6)

MONINO Jean-Louis
Data Control: Major Challenge for the Digital Society (Smart Innovation Set – Volume 29)

MORLAT Clément
Sustainable Productive System: Eco-development versus Sustainable Development (Smart Innovation Set – Volume 26)

SAULAIS Pierre, ERMINE Jean-Louis
Knowledge Management in Innovative Companies 2: Understanding and Deploying a KM Plan within a Learning Organization (Smart Innovation Set – Volume 27)

2019

AMENDOLA Mario, GAFFARD Jean-Luc
Disorder and Public Concern Around Globalization

BARBAROUX Pierre
Disruptive Technology and Defence Innovation Ecosystems (Innovation in Engineering and Technology Set – Volume 5)

DOU Henri, JUILLET Alain, CLERC Philippe
Strategic Intelligence for the Future 1: A New Strategic and Operational Approach
Strategic Intelligence for the Future 2: A New Information Function Approach

FRIKHA Azza
Measurement in Marketing: Operationalization of Latent Constructs

FRIMOUSSE Soufyane
Innovation and Agility in the Digital Age (Human Resources Management Set – Volume 2)

GAY Claudine, SZOSTAK Bérangère L.
Innovation and Creativity in SMEs: Challenges, Evolutions and Prospects
(Smart Innovation Set – Volume 21)

GORIA Stéphane, HUMBERT Pierre, ROUSSEL Benoît
Information, Knowledge and Agile Creativity
(Smart Innovation Set – Volume 22)

HELLER David
Investment Decision-making Using Optional Models
(Economic Growth Set – Volume 2)

HELLER David, DE CHADIRAC Sylvain, HALAOUI Lana, JOUVET Camille
The Emergence of Start-ups
(Economic Growth Set – Volume 1)

HÉRAUD Jean-Alain, KERR Fiona, BURGER-HELMCHEN Thierry
Creative Management of Complex Systems
(Smart Innovation Set – Volume 19)

LATOUCHE Pascal
Open Innovation: Corporate Incubator
(Innovation and Technology Set – Volume 7)

LEHMANN Paul-Jacques
The Future of the Euro Currency

LEIGNEL Jean-Louis, MÉNAGER Emmanuel, YABLONSKY Serge
Sustainable Enterprise Performance: A Comprehensive Evaluation Method

LIÈVRE Pascal, AUBRY Monique, GAREL Gilles
Management of Extreme Situations: From Polar Expeditions to Exploration-Oriented Organizations

MILLOT Michel
Embarrassment of Product Choices 2: Towards a Society of Well-being

N'GOALA Gilles, PEZ-PÉRARD Virginie, PRIM-ALLAZ Isabelle
Augmented Customer Strategy: CRM in the Digital Age

NIKOLOVA Blagovesta
The RRI Challenge: Responsibilization in a State of Tension with Market Regulation
(Innovation and Responsibility Set – Volume 3)

PELLEGRIN-BOUCHER Estelle, ROY Pierre
Innovation in the Cultural and Creative Industries
(Innovation and Technology Set – Volume 8)

PRIOLON Joël
Financial Markets for Commodities

QUINIOU Matthieu
Blockchain: The Advent of Disintermediation

RAVIX Joël-Thomas, DESCHAMPS Marc
Innovation and Industrial Policies
(Innovation between Risk and Reward Set – Volume 5)

ROGER Alain, VINOT Didier
Skills Management: New Applications, New Questions
(Human Resources Management Set – Volume 1)

SAULAIS Pierre, ERMINE Jean-Louis
Knowledge Management in Innovative Companies 1: Understanding and Deploying a KM Plan within a Learning Organization
(Smart Innovation Set – Volume 23)

SERVAJEAN-HILST Romaric
Co-innovation Dynamics: The Management of Client-Supplier Interactions for Open Innovation
(Smart Innovation Set – Volume 20)

SKIADAS Christos H., BOZEMAN James R.
Data Analysis and Applications 1: Clustering and Regression, Modeling-estimating, Forecasting and Data Mining
(Big Data, Artificial Intelligence and Data Analysis Set – Volume 2)
Data Analysis and Applications 2: Utilization of Results in Europe and Other Topics
(Big Data, Artificial Intelligence and Data Analysis Set – Volume 3)

UZUNIDIS Dimitri
Systemic Innovation: Entrepreneurial Strategies and Market Dynamics

VIGEZZI Michel
World Industrialization: Shared Inventions, Competitive Innovations and Social Dynamics
(Smart Innovation Set – Volume 24)

2018

BURKHARDT Kirsten
Private Equity Firms: Their Role in the Formation of Strategic Alliances

CALLENS Stéphane
Creative Globalization
(Smart Innovation Set – Volume 16)

CASADELLA Vanessa
Innovation Systems in Emerging Economies: MINT – Mexico, Indonesia, Nigeria, Turkey
(Smart Innovation Set – Volume 18)

CHOUTEAU Marianne, FOREST Joëlle, NGUYEN Céline
Science, Technology and Innovation Culture
(Innovation in Engineering and Technology Set – Volume 3)

CORLOSQUET-HABART Marine, JANSSEN Jacques
Big Data for Insurance Companies
(Big Data, Artificial Intelligence and Data Analysis Set – Volume 1)

CROS Françoise
Innovation and Society
(Smart Innovation Set – Volume 15)

DEBREF Romain
Environmental Innovation and Ecodesign: Certainties and Controversies
(Smart Innovation Set – Volume 17)

DOMINGUEZ Noémie
SME Internationalization Strategies: Innovation to Conquer New Markets

ERMINE Jean-Louis
Knowledge Management: The Creative Loop
(Innovation and Technology Set – Volume 5)

GILBERT Patrick, BOBADILLA Natalia, GASTALDI Lise,
LE BOULAIRE Martine, LELEBINA Olga
Innovation, Research and Development Management

IBRAHIMI Mohammed
Mergers & Acquisitions: Theory, Strategy, Finance

LEMAÎTRE Denis
Training Engineers for Innovation

LÉVY Aldo, BEN BOUHENI Faten, AMMI Chantal
Financial Management: USGAAP and IFRS Standards
(Innovation and Technology Set – Volume 6)

MILLOT Michel
Embarrassment of Product Choices 1: How to Consume Differently

PANSERA Mario, OWEN Richard
Innovation and Development: The Politics at the Bottom of the Pyramid
(Innovation and Responsibility Set – Volume 2)

RICHEZ Yves
Corporate Talent Detection and Development

SACHETTI Philippe, ZUPPINGER Thibaud
New Technologies and Branding
(Innovation and Technology Set – Volume 4)

SAMIER Henri
Intuition, Creativity, Innovation

TEMPLE Ludovic, COMPAORÉ SAWADOGO Eveline M.F.W.
Innovation Processes in Agro-Ecological Transitions in Developing Countries
(Innovation in Engineering and Technology Set – Volume 2)

UZUNIDIS Dimitri
Collective Innovation Processes: Principles and Practices
(Innovation in Engineering and Technology Set – Volume 4)

VAN HOOREBEKE Delphine
The Management of Living Beings or Emo-management

2017

AÏT-EL-HADJ Smaïl
The Ongoing Technological System
(Smart Innovation Set – Volume 11)

BAUDRY Marc, DUMONT Béatrice
Patents: Prompting or Restricting Innovation?
(Smart Innovation Set – Volume 12)

BÉRARD Céline, TEYSSIER Christine
Risk Management: Lever for SME Development and Stakeholder
Value Creation

CHALENÇON Ludivine
Location Strategies and Value Creation of International
Mergers and Acquisitions

CHAUVEL Danièle, BORZILLO Stefano
The Innovative Company: An Ill-defined Object
(Innovation between Risk and Reward Set – Volume 1)

CORSI Patrick
Going Past Limits To Growth

D'ANDRIA Aude, GABARRET Inés
Building 21st Century Entrepreneurship
(Innovation and Technology Set – Volume 2)

DAIDJ Nabyla
Cooperation, Coopetition and Innovation
(Innovation and Technology Set – Volume 3)

FERNEZ-WALCH Sandrine
The Multiple Facets of Innovation Project Management
(Innovation between Risk and Reward Set – Volume 4)

FOREST Joëlle
Creative Rationality and Innovation
(Smart Innovation Set – Volume 14)

GUILHON Bernard
Innovation and Production Ecosystems
(Innovation between Risk and Reward Set – Volume 2)

HAMMOUDI Abdelhakim, DAIDJ Nabyla
Game Theory Approach to Managerial Strategies and Value Creation
(Diverse and Global Perspectives on Value Creation Set – Volume 3)

LALLEMENT Rémi
Intellectual Property and Innovation Protection: New Practices
and New Policy Issues
(Innovation between Risk and Reward Set – Volume 3)

LAPERCHE Blandine
Enterprise Knowledge Capital
(Smart Innovation Set – Volume 13)

LEBERT Didier, EL YOUNSI Hafida
International Specialization Dynamics
(Smart Innovation Set – Volume 9)

MAESSCHALCK Marc
Reflexive Governance for Research and Innovative Knowledge
(Responsible Research and Innovation Set – Volume 6)

MASSOTTE Pierre
Ethics in Social Networking and Business 1: Theory, Practice
and Current Recommendations
Ethics in Social Networking and Business 2: The Future and
Changing Paradigms

MASSOTTE Pierre, CORSI Patrick
Smart Decisions in Complex Systems

MEDINA Mercedes, HERRERO Mónica, URGELLÉS Alicia
Current and Emerging Issues in the Audiovisual Industry
(Diverse and Global Perspectives on Value Creation Set – Volume 1)

MICHAUD Thomas
Innovation, Between Science and Science Fiction
(Smart Innovation Set – Volume 10)

PELLÉ Sophie
Business, Innovation and Responsibility
(Responsible Research and Innovation Set – Volume 7)

SAVIGNAC Emmanuelle
The Gamification of Work: The Use of Games in the Workplace

SUGAHARA Satoshi, DAIDJ Nabyla, USHIO Sumitaka
Value Creation in Management Accounting and Strategic Management:
An Integrated Approach
(Diverse and Global Perspectives on Value Creation Set –Volume 2)

UZUNIDIS Dimitri, SAULAIS Pierre
Innovation Engines: Entrepreneurs and Enterprises in a Turbulent World
(Innovation in Engineering and Technology Set – Volume 1)

2016

BARBAROUX Pierre, ATTOUR Amel, SCHENK Eric
Knowledge Management and Innovation
(Smart Innovation Set – Volume 6)

BEN BOUHENI Faten, AMMI Chantal, LEVY Aldo
Banking Governance, Performance And Risk-Taking: Conventional Banks
Vs Islamic Banks

BOUTILLIER Sophie, CARRÉ Denis, LEVRATTO Nadine
Entrepreneurial Ecosystems (Smart Innovation Set – Volume 2)

BOUTILLIER Sophie, UZUNIDIS Dimitri
The Entrepreneur (Smart Innovation Set – Volume 8)

BOUVARD Patricia, SUZANNE Hervé
Collective Intelligence Development in Business

GALLAUD Delphine, LAPERCHE Blandine
Circular Economy, Industrial Ecology and Short Supply Chains
(Smart Innovation Set – Volume 4)

GUERRIER Claudine
Security and Privacy in the Digital Era
(Innovation and Technology Set – Volume 1)

MEGHOUAR Hicham
Corporate Takeover Targets

MONINO Jean-Louis, SEDKAOUI Soraya
Big Data, Open Data and Data Development
(Smart Innovation Set – Volume 3)

MOREL Laure, LE ROUX Serge
Fab Labs: Innovative User
(Smart Innovation Set – Volume 5)

PICARD Fabienne, TANGUY Corinne
Innovations and Techno-ecological Transition
(Smart Innovation Set – Volume 7)

2015

CASADELLA Vanessa, LIU Zeting, DIMITRI Uzunidis
Innovation Capabilities and Economic Development in Open Economies
(Smart Innovation Set – Volume 1)

CORSI Patrick, MORIN Dominique
Sequencing Apple's DNA

CORSI Patrick, NEAU Erwan
Innovation Capability Maturity Model

FAIVRE-TAVIGNOT Bénédicte
Social Business and Base of the Pyramid

GODÉ Cécile
Team Coordination in Extreme Environments

MAILLARD Pierre
Competitive Quality and Innovation

MASSOTTE Pierre, CORSI Patrick
Operationalizing Sustainability

MASSOTTE Pierre, CORSI Patrick
Sustainability Calling

2014

DUBÉ Jean, LEGROS Diègo
Spatial Econometrics Using Microdata

LESCA Humbert, LESCA Nicolas
Strategic Decisions and Weak Signals

2013

HABART-CORLOSQUET Marine, JANSSEN Jacques, MANCA Raimondo
VaR Methodology for Non-Gaussian Finance

2012

DAL PONT Jean-Pierre
Process Engineering and Industrial Management

MAILLARD Pierre
Competitive Quality Strategies

POMEROL Jean-Charles
Decision-Making and Action

SZYLAR Christian
UCITS Handbook

2011

LESCA Nicolas
Environmental Scanning and Sustainable Development

LESCA Nicolas, LESCA Humbert
Weak Signals for Strategic Intelligence: Anticipation Tool for Managers

MERCIER-LAURENT Eunika
Innovation Ecosystems

2010

SZYLAR Christian
Risk Management under UCITS III/IV

2009

COHEN Corine
Business Intelligence

ZANINETTI Jean-Marc
Sustainable Development in the USA

2008

CORSI Patrick, DULIEU Mike
The Marketing of Technology Intensive Products and Services

DZEVER Sam, JAUSSAUD Jacques, ANDREOSSO Bernadette
Evolving Corporate Structures and Cultures in Asia: Impact of Globalization

2007

AMMI Chantal
Global Consumer Behavior

2006

BOUGHZALA Imed, ERMINE Jean-Louis
Trends in Enterprise Knowledge Management

CORSI Patrick *et al.*
Innovation Engineering: the Power of Intangible Networks

Printed and bound by CPI Group (UK) Ltd, Croydon, CR0 4YY

27/10/2024

14580319-0002